HARD WIRED

LIFE, DEATH AND TRIATHLON

BY MULTIPLE WORLD CHAMPION EMMA CARNEY

EMMA CARNEY WITH *JANE E. HUNT*

First published 2020 by Ryan Publishing
PO Box 7680, Melbourne, 3004
Victoria, Australia
Ph: 61 3 9505 6820
Email: books@ryanpub.com
Website: www.ryanpub.com

RYAN
PUBLISHING

 A catalogue record for this
book is available from the
National Library of Australia

Title: *Hard Wired: Life, Death and Triathlon*
by Multiple World Champion Emma Carney

ISBN: 9781876498634 : Paperback

Internal and cover design by Luke Harris, Working Type Studio, Victoria, Australia. www.workingtype.com.au

For my wonderful son Jack, so you know.

CONTENTS

Preface

As a child, books intrigued me. It amazed me that you could simply read lines of words on a page and be taken away to the place that the author is describing. Because of this intrigue, I thought it would be a great thing to write a book, but it seemed all the good ideas had been used up.

As I grew older, I realised one story that hadn't been taken yet was my life. No one had written on that, and I had some really good expectations on the ending ...

Throughout my career, I diligently kept training diaries as most elite athletes do. I have a detailed record of every training session, personal training data, times, results: everything and anything that needed to be monitored.

What I also recorded, and what is not quite as common, were journals of my life as it unfolded. I detailed daily the training, personal commitments, lifestyle and intricacies of my experiences as an elite athlete. I recorded the good times and the disappointments, the lessons and the battles. These journals were the main source for this book.

The only time I stopped writing was through my Olympic Appeal. At that time, I could not put pen to paper. I have also never spoken publicly about it. I just didn't have the strength to do either.

My Olympic appeal couldn't be ignored though. It needed to be included in my autobiography. My Father was the key individual involved in the Olympic Appeals process, so he needed to provide his detailed account (much of it written at the time). Dad was always one for ensuring that the truth prevails.

I also needed someone to write about the Olympic Appeals, not as I saw it, or Dad saw it, but rather as a chronological order of the facts. I needed a historian, and someone who knew the Sport of Triathlon. The most appropriate person to do this was Assistant Professor Jane E. Hunt from Bond University. As the author of *Multisport Dreaming: The Foundations of Triathlon in Australia*, there is no one more qualified to provide my autobiography with this factual account.

At first, I wasn't sure if I could write a book about my life. So, initially I asked Dr Jane E. Hunt to write it as a biography. She did background research and drafted the book up to and including the Olympic Selection chapter, for which she interrogated all my Dad's papers on the Olympic Selection Appeals.

In the long run, Jane convinced me that I should tell my story in my own words, and I agreed. I finally did what I had always thought about doing. I re-wrote the draft chapters from my perspective and finished the book off. Jane smoothed it altogether when I finished.

I feel very fortunate for my life, I feel very fortunate I have been able to represent Australia at the highest level in Sport, and while my life may not have followed an expected path, it gives me a lot of pride.

This is my story so far …

Prologue — One Good Bra

I didn't know where I was, I didn't know where the Australian team hotel was, and I didn't know what was wrong with me. It was around 2 p.m., 8 July 2004. I was standing weakly on the side of the road somewhere in Edmonton, Canada. It had just started to rain lightly, and I couldn't work out why my heart was racing in my chest.

For the first time ever, I didn't really want to be left alone. I felt vulnerable.

The Triathlon Australia (TA) Team was in Edmonton for an International Triathlon Union (ITU) race to be held that weekend (prior to 2020, World Triathlon was known as the International Triathlon Union). Today was Thursday, so we had just completed one of our pre-race group training sessions, an easy swim session. Whatever was happening to me had started in the pool. I managed to finish the set swim program, but not because I felt good training, only because I was too stubborn to stop.

Over the past six years I had suffered flushes of weakness while racing. What had started as a minor issue experienced in the swim discipline of triathlons from late 1996, unexplained feelings of fatigue and dizziness, had become far more of a problem and far more severe in 2002 and 2003. Recently, the problem had become serious and, at times, frightening. I was the dominant and most prolific triathlete in ITU triathlon until these problems arose and, despite them, I was still competitive internationally. Yet somehow, I had lost my edge. I was always sure I could recapture it, if I could just manage the feelings of weakness and fatigue. I wasn't someone who gave up without a damn good reason.

I never did work out what was wrong. Until now. For the first time in my life, the weak feeling was followed by a very conscious awareness of my heart pounding in my chest. I thought maybe I was in a panic. That was initially. Now I was worried: surely you cannot panic for this long. I had been out of the pool almost an hour and boarded the bus back to the team hotel for lunch. The TA Team Manager told me that all I needed was a rest, ignoring my insistence that my heart was racing in my chest. The feeling made me uneasy.

As we sat in the traffic, my chest tightened further, with the back of the bus seat rolling my shoulders forward, forcing me to slump. My heart was banging away, seemingly pulling everything tighter still, and restricting my lungs. I couldn't breathe properly. As we approached a set of traffic lights, I lunged out of the bus to stretch my chest open and see if I could breathe freely in the fresh air. I was trying to work out whether it helped when the lights changed from red to green, and everyone on board yelled at me to climb back into the bus.

I didn't move. I was in a daze.

As the bus started to move away, I heard the Team Physio yell, 'I'll get out, you can't just leave her,' before jumping out onto the kerb.

He approached me, looking irritated, as the bus disappeared. By this time, I had found a park bench. It was raining lightly when we left the pool, but now it was increasing in intensity. So was my breathing. I was thankful someone got out, because I knew I was in trouble. Despite being the most independent member of the Australian team, I didn't want to be left alone.

The Team Physio started complaining, half at me, half at everyone else. 'What are we doing now Emma? I don't even know where we are staying. I don't have a phone. I don't know how to contact anyone.'

I felt desperate. The thought crossed my mind that I might possibly die. I needed to sit down, because standing was taking too much energy. Hardly able to breathe I felt extremely lightheaded. Better than sit, I lay down on the footpath. Still unaware of the severity of my situation, he snapped, 'What are you doing now?!'

Looking up from the footpath I decided I needed him to panic. I couldn't afford to panic, because simply breathing was becoming difficult. I said urgently, 'Shut up for a sec. There is something wrong with my heart, I think I'm going to die. You need to get help.'

That did it. Suddenly, he sprinted away. I didn't know whether he was abandoning me or seeking help. Fortunately, he dropped his bag, so I assumed he was going to return. I hoped so. I honestly thought this was it. I had always proudly said to friends that I would rather die than lose a race, but I didn't imagine that I might die while not even racing.

Trying to resist unconsciousness, I lay there. Strangely, it was peaceful when I shut my eyes. So peaceful in fact, it frightened me. I had never experienced this sort of peace, and wondered whether I was drifting off, never to return. I willed myself to remain awake.

Meanwhile, the Team Physio apparently ran around knocking on the doors of nearby houses, trying to find someone to phone for help. He finally returned with a cab. I looked at him, completely disheartened.

'No!' I called out, 'I need an AMBULANCE!!'

The cab driver took one look at me and dialled the emergency number for Canada. I still remember the phone number was 911 and I remember thinking lucky for the cab driver. Being Australian, I would have dialled Triple Zero and got nowhere.

Thankfully it only took about two minutes for the ambulance to arrive. I obsessively told the paramedics I had a very low resting heart rate (about five or six times) as they moved me onto the stretcher. They told me to relax.

Inside the ambulance, they cut my T-Shirt, and then started to cut my bra. In a life and death situation, amazingly, cutting my bra horrified me. As an athlete travelling overseas, I generally had all my training gear, and one good bra. I happened to have my good bra on, and cutting it seemed such a waste.

'Stop! It's my one good bra!' I yelled. But the paramedic with the scissors told me they had to. 'This day is going from bad to worse,' I remember thinking.

Someone asked how long my heart had been racing and I replied that I got out of the pool just after 1 p.m. It was now after 2.15 p.m. I had been in Ventricular Tachycardia (VT, racing heart) for over an hour.

One of the paramedics was sticking defibrillator pads to me and the other said, 'Can you feel this?' I asked them what they were doing, and they said they were flicking my feet. I couldn't feel a thing.

The paramedic putting the pads on me then said, 'Your body is shutting down, we are going to have to give you a shock.'

I remember thinking, 'What's a shock?' Then I heard someone flick a switch and everyone stepped back. Suddenly I understood.

'STOP!!' I yelled grabbed at the pads. Before I could do anything, I was being defibrillated: a bolt of electricity smashed through my chest.

This is not a normal experience, and to this day my cardiologist in Melbourne (Professor Harper) still can't believe I was put through this while fully conscious. The Physio told me they had no choice. I am still undecided, but bloody hell it hurt. It was like being hit by a truck, with no splatter. I felt myself being thrown in the air and land back on the stretcher. Once landed I ripped at the pads, just in case there was another shock coming.

'Can everyone calm down? What the hell!! Get these pads off me!!' I went berserk. 'Get me out of here!' There might have been some four-letter words.

The paramedics apologised and told me they had no choice. 'Why the hell couldn't you put me to sleep?' I yelled. They told me I had been in VT for too long. My heart rate was 248 beats per minute (bpm). Normally a human heart could sustain this elevated heart rate for less than a quarter of the time before going into Ventricular Fibrillation (VF), which results in sudden death.

'What?' I asked.

'You just had a near cardiac arrest.'

Amongst the panic, my screaming and the chaos of defibrillation, my heart suddenly felt calm in my chest. It was now doing what a heart does, back into its normal rhythm. The ambulance made its way to the University of Alberta Hospital, surprisingly less than a kilometre away. I lay in the back of the ambulance for this short trip with my arms crossed, thinking I could stop any more defibrillations if someone decided to try that again.

In emergency, I was given a hospital gown, and rigged up to a cardiac machine. Pads were stuck all over my chest to monitor my heart, but some were defibrillator pads — much to my horror. I was told sometimes after a VT there can be more heart episodes. I kept my arms crossed, very adamant every time someone entered my cubicle that they were not to going to defibrillate me again.

The Physio stayed until I was checked into a bed. I have no idea how he found the rest of the team, because he had no phone and didn't seem to know where we were staying. I must have been in emergency for a while before anyone from TA turned up. It seemed to be early evening when Team Management arrived.

We had a short conversation, and I asked for my stuff to be moved out of my hotel room, because from what the doctors were saying it appeared that I would be stuck in hospital for a while. I knew the Triathlon Australia Team was heading off to France that Sunday evening, so I was going to be left behind.

The Team Manager told me he didn't like hospitals as they made him nervous, then announced that he needed to go and have dinner. That was the last I saw of any of the team staff. They never returned to check on me, or to see how I was. I did receive one call though, just to let me know my all my racing gear and luggage had been moved out of my hotel room.

I spent just over two weeks in hospital: four days in ICU (Intensive Care Unit) and another ten days under close watch in the cardiac ward. When I was discharged, I had a dodgy heart, a black eye, two cracked teeth and five stitches in my eyebrow. Apparently, I wasn't a 'normal' cardiac patient and was a little too active following the various heart procedures I underwent.

Once discharged, I spent two weeks in Canada to ensure my heart remained stable enough for the long-haul flight home to Australia.

Finally, I was declared safe to fly. I had never been so happy to board a Qantas flight home.

Safe to fly maybe, but my life had changed forever.

1. Igniting the Dream

My life wasn't always that hectic I didn't think.

It was always fairly dramatic though, mainly due to my lack of patience. My attitude was always 'bash and crash' and get stuck into things and then beg for forgiveness later when things went pear shaped.

I also always loved sport and the outdoors, and I thought everyone did in Australia. For almost as long as I can remember I wanted to race and win for Australia. But I was actually born in England. So initially, the Australian dream of mine wasn't on the cards.

Fortunately, my Dad, David, decided when he was eleven years old that he was going to live in Australia. He apparently saw a movie called 'Under the Southern Cross' (made in 1954), with his Grandad. Dad was literally blown away with the landscape in the movie. He was captivated. Afterwards, he asked his Grandad where the images were from and 'Grandpappie' told Dad, 'That's Australia, if you ever get the chance you must live there.'

From that day on, Dad planned to live in Australia.

Mum didn't have any plans to move away from England. Mum's name is Sheila (born Sheila Joan White) so I think unknowingly she was destined to end up in Australia. After all, for those who don't know, 'Sheila' is Australian slang for a female.

Born in the north of England, near Newcastle, Mum was the third of four children. She had two older brothers and a younger sister. Her father, Henry White, was a small man in stature, but a big man on principles and an absolute perfectionist. So much so, he was awarded an MBE from the Queen for his work as a senior Architect at the Greater London Council. He designed many buildings from the 1950s to 1970s. Joan White, or Grandma White, was also small in stature and always pleasant. She never got angry, absolutely never swore and did everything for her family.

Dad's family was quite different. Dad (David Robert Carney) was the second of two boys to Nora and Jack Carney. Jack Carney was well over six feet. He was the saving grace that prevented me from being short, given Mum's side of the family. Grandad Carney flew Whitney bombers in the war, the oldest and slowest bombers in the Royal Air Force. His aircraft was so slow that when the Germans tried to blow him out of the sky, he could see the missiles whizz past. In WWII Grandad went up one night with his squadron and was the only plane that returned. He never flew again and never spoke about it.

Grandma Carney (Nora) was an absolute legend. She met Grandad during the war at a dance. He was stationed at the local Air Force base in Wolverhampton. She rather liked the look of him in his crisp uniform with Sergeant's stripes, asked her sister to hold her engagement ring, and got to know Grandad. That summed Grandma up. She was spontaneous and always prepared to try things. I think a lot of my bad habits came from Grandma: blaze ahead and beg for forgiveness if things go wrong, rather than ask for permission prior to starting out. Working as a nurse during the war Grandma was on duty when the young soldiers returned from Dunkirk and was really affected by what she saw, young men blown apart. The head nurse told her to go outside and have a cigarette to calm her nerves. When she told me that story, I understood why she smoked. After Dunkirk she left nursing, but as it was a reserve occupation, she could only change to another reserve occupation. She then worked in an ordnance factory and was able to return the favour, with interest, for all the damaged young men and boys she had been trying to save.

Grandad Carney also smoked. They both also drank a lot. They were the type of poms you see in those working-class movies; hard-working, always broke and generally down the pub in the evening on a Friday night. Grandma's maiden name was Stephenson, and she claimed to be related to George Stephenson who built the first passenger railway in the world. It ran from Stockton to Darlington in England. Her details were very sketchy, and everyone seemed too broke to me to be related to such a world changing inventor. To back her claim, Grandma said her Grandad drank two inheritances away. That bit sounded about right.

Grandma was deaf in one ear; she could never hear a thing. She often put her glasses on so she could hear better. That was her type of logic. Her mum was also deaf in one ear and so is my Dad. They all grew up yelling at each other so they could hear what was said.

Grandma Carney was my only grandparent who swore, so I got along well with her.

Dad was born in Wolverhampton. It was rough industrial town. Apparently in those days, most people tried to get out of Wolverhampton. This was true for Grandad Carney as well; he was born in London. Grandma and Grandad managed to move their little family back to London when Dad was eight years old. Dad has vivid memories of sitting in the back of the removal truck with his brother and his Mum extremely happy to be moving up in the world.

Mum and Dad met at school when they were both fifteen-years old. I was always amazed by this. When I was fifteen, most of the boys in the class annoyed the hell out of me. By the time Mum and Dad met at school, their families were living a couple of streets away from each other. Mum's street was very nice, and Dad's street was 'average'. Apparently, Mum was living in the civilised end while Dad's family was down the 'crappy' end, or as Dad calls it, 'down the oak' (whatever that means in London slang).

My parents finished school in the same year, Mum gaining O-Levels and Dad A-Levels (the English equivalent of Year 12). Dad's school Principal told him he was a failure and he should give up. He took that advice on and earnt his A Levels in half the time it normally takes. Dad always lifted when he was told he couldn't do something. He studied to become a chartered accountant once he finished school and joined Price Waterhouse after he graduated.

Mum and Dad married on Easter weekend 1967. They were both twenty-one years old. They were living at a place called Bourne End in Buckinghamshire, west of London and not far from Windsor, when they started a family a few years later. My sister Jane was born 9 March 1970. Apparently, Jane was a really nice, pleasant baby who would feed and sleep. I arrived on 29 July 1971, sixteen months later, and screamed the house down. I apparently arrived quickly. Mum always said I was 'impatient from the beginning'. Clare arrived on 6 February 1974, after we moved to Yorkshire in the North of England. Dad had received a job offer there that was too good to refuse. Just after Clare was born, we moved back south again. We lived near Hatfield House, Hertfordshire. Supposedly, Elizabeth I was sitting under an oak tree in the grounds of Hatfield House when she was told she had become Queen of England. The oak tree was still there. Most of my sketchy memories of England are of Hatfield. I remember a very English lifestyle, a large back garden, a large red front door, spending all summer outside playing and all winter trying to stay warm.

Growing up, I was very close to my sister Jane. While she was older than me, I grew to always be a similar height. I did everything Jane did and would not accept otherwise. I remember when Jane started going to pre-school in Yorkshire, I tagged along and just assumed I was going too. When we reached the pre-school, the teacher told me I could not attend as I was still wearing nappies. I remember standing there, shocked, watching Jane walk off. According to Mum I went home and took my nappy off, never to wear one during the day again. By the next week I was at pre-school with Jane at the tender age of eighteen months, the youngest of the group. Jane always looked after me. I took her lead with what we did every day. We generally dressed the same, had the same toys (mine were the broken ones), and had the same experiences. If I was ever in trouble Jane was always there for me.

Clare was just a little bit younger. She was always with Mum. Lucky for Clare, I would have probably damaged her anyway, because I was a bit hard on my playthings.

I remember the day we left England to emigrate to Australia. We stayed in a hotel at Heathrow airport. I can picture the thick 1970s shag carpet and the dominant orange colour of the room furnishings. The hotel room was crowded, crammed full of people. Most were crying, and all looked familiar, but I had never seen them all at once before. I remember asking Jane why everyone was upset. She was also crying, Jane always cried if others were upset. Mum was crying, Jane was crying, most in the room were crying. I remember looking for a reason why. Then I found it. In the middle of the room my Dad stood with the biggest smile on his face, looking genuinely happy. It dawned on me that we were doing something, and Dad couldn't wait. Suddenly I felt excited too, as always led by Dad's positivity. I had no idea that all our relatives on both sides of the family were there to say farewell, but I decided if Dad was happy, I was too.

Unknown to me at the time, Dad had taken up an accounting role at a firm in Melbourne, Australia. We flew out of England on 17 February 1975. In my memory, the flight stopped two or three times, and each time we stepped off the plane. I had never felt so tired and so hot. We were supposed to stop in Darwin, but Cyclone Tracy had just wiped the place off the map. When we landed in Melbourne, we were met with a scorching hot summer day.

For the first six months, we lived in an apartment hotel in Flemington, just off the Tullamarine Freeway. It seemed fine to me, but I know it was a big change for Mum and Dad. We were very fortunate the apartment hotel was run by a lady called Marie Owen who helped us adapt to Australian ways. She became our 'Aussie Grandma'.

Mum and Dad were so English, it is funny to recall. Each morning, Dad would head off to work, and as it was a sunny day, Mum would open all the windows 'to enjoy the sunshine'. Obviously by 2 p.m. in the middle of summer, Mum, Clare, Jane and I were flat out baking in our apartment wondering how the hell people survived in Australia. Fortunately, after about a week of this, Marie Owen dropped in for a visit and told Mum to never open the windows on a hot day and keep the curtains pulled to keep the place cool. Mum thought that was such a waste of a 'nice sunny day'. Marie Owen helped with other things too. Dad secured a work car after a few weeks. It was the old school Holden with the plastic bench seats. Jane, Clare and I would sit in the back and cry and Mum and Dad couldn't work out why. Our 'Aussie Grandma' told them to put towels on the seats to avoid burning our bums on the plastic that was scorching hot from the summer sun.

The first time Dad's English ways actually embarrassed me, we were out some-where, and he ordered a sausage roll. The bloke got one out of the pie warmer and put sauce on it. Dad said, 'No thank you. Can I have it cold with no sauce?' Who the hell eats cold sausage rolls? I told Dad this was wrong, and he needed to stop eating like that.

Eating ice cream was also different in Australia. In England, I could take my time and enjoy the treat. In the Australian summer I couldn't keep up with the melting, and every ice cream treat for me ended in a disaster with wasted ice cream on the floor. It was quite devastating.

But ice cream was a rare treat. For as long as I can remember, Mum took a lot of care as to what we all ate. Every meal was homemade. I thought every Mum did this, going out of their way to make sure their family only ate fresh, organic home-made meals. As I grew up, I began to realise others ate things like store bought bread, drank 'fizzy' drinks rather than fresh water, and were allowed lollies each day. Dad always liked growing veggies so with Mum and Dad's combined efforts, our nutrition was world class. Jane, Clare and I learnt the importance of healthy eating and real food from a very young age.

While we flew to Australia, all our furniture and household things were put on a boat and shipped over. Mum and Dad even shipped our Volkswagen Combi. Five months after we arrived, the boat load of family possessions finally reached Melbourne. Reunited with the Combi, Mum and Dad decided to explore more of Australia.

I'm not entirely sure whether Mum or Dad realised how big Australia is. I remember driving for days and nights up the east coast. Adamant that they would reach the top of Australia, they swapped drivers while going along to save time.

Jane, Clare and I slept in the back as they drove through the night. We never made it to the top. The Combi blew its engine in Cairns at around the 3,000 km mark. Mum and Dad were so naïve. Dad recalls standing on the beach in Port Douglas, where acre blocks of beachfront land were $10,000 and asking Mum, 'Who would ever want to build here?' The blocks are now worth millions. Not discouraged by the size of Australia, Mum and Dad also drove us around Tasmania, to Adelaide (to see what a pie floater was), and did other regular trips.

In the early years in Australia, Dad was paranoid about being returned to England, so we all became Australian citizens as soon as possible. We attended a ceremony on 17 November 1978, which I remember well. I did not know what we were doing, but we all were given a gum tree to plant. Mine died of course. I have always been terrible at gardening. Now we were Australian, Dad could relax. None of us ever had to leave Australia.

By then, Mum and Dad had bought a house in Glen Waverley. Around a thirty-minute drive east of Melbourne, we lived a very typical Australian suburban lifestyle. We weren't actually living as Australian as Mum and Dad thought, because we didn't have a lamb roast every Sunday like the rest of the street.

Before we moved to Glen Waverley, Jane, who was five, started at a school in Flemington. I was three years old and supposed to go to pre-school. I quit pre-school after about two weeks because they made me take an afternoon sleep. I didn't do sleep, so refused to return. I hated that place. After we moved, Jane attended Mimosa, the local primary school, and I attended a Montessori Pre-School. Clare was only one, so she was still hanging out with Mum.

I was happier with the Montessori Pre-School, but I missed Jane. I distinctly remember following Jane around and copying everything she did. I must have driven her crazy. We wore similar clothes too; we both had an ABBA T-shirt and socks set. Hers were yellow, mine white and they were emblazoned with the faces of our ABBA heroes. It was strange that we loved ABBA so much, because music in the house affected Dad's ability to hear anything with his one good ear. Somehow ABBA and the Beatles got through, with some Carpenters music if Clare needed to fall asleep.

One weekend Dad asked me if I wanted to see ABBA, and of course I said yes. I am not sure where everyone else in the family was at the time. I was sceptical as to how we would do actually see ABBA, because I knew they were from overseas. Dad and I drove into Melbourne and saw the end of a packed-out ABBA concert, at the Sidney Myer Music Bowl. We didn't have tickets, so Dad put me up on his shoulders at the back of the crowd. He couldn't see them, so I was the only one in the family to actually see ABBA live. It was the best outing in my ABBA T-shirt and socks ever. Jane was so jealous.

I used to wait anxiously for Jane to return home from school. As soon as we picked her up, we would go to our bedroom, and Jane would teach me everything she learnt that day. I would sit on a stool and listen, while she used a play blackboard to show me her day's work. By the time I started at Mimosa Primary School the following year, I was ahead of my class. Jane had actually taught me Prep! As a consequence, I was put into a composite Prep and Year 1 class and did the Year 1 work. This carried on until I started Year 3. Mum and Dad continuously asked the school to allow me to skip a year and the school refused, saying I was 'socially immature'.

Neither of my parents wanted us to be held back in our schooling, so they looked for options. We actually passed the answer every day as Mum drove me to the Montessori pre-school along High Street Road, Glen Waverley. I remember noticing what looked to me like a really impressive place. Being English born, I thought maybe the Queen lived there because the vast grounds looked manicured, and the buildings were set back with a big gold lion on the wall. When asked, Mum explained that it was a school. I was impressed.

The school was Wesley College, Glen Waverley campus. Originally a boy's school, the college began to enrol girls in 1978. Wesley suddenly needed girls as a priority. Mum and Dad must have enquired. It seems that with three girls, we were a great family for the new vision of co-education at Wesley.

In the late 1970s, Dad also moved jobs to be head of finance at the sporting goods company, adidas. Sitting in Dad's office I first realised that you could play sport as a career. I must have been about seven or eight years old. Renowned Australian football legend Ted Whitten was working at adidas at the time — well, he was there, he did not seem to do much work. He sat in a room with pictures of himself playing football covering the walls. I remember meeting him with Dad, and I couldn't understand why he would have so many pictures of himself. When I asked Dad about it, he explained that in Australia it is a great honour to be a sportsperson, especially if you were the best. I also remember seeing other greats including Rob De Castella (Deeks) come in to pick his adidas training and racing gear up. Then I saw him win marathons on TV. I noticed that everyone loved 'Deeks'. These sporting heroes intrigued me.

I did not realise at the time, but Mum and Dad must have been pretty alternative.

Mum was always creative, and Dad always loved the outdoors. It only dawned on me shortly after Dad started his new role at adidas, when they decided to build a larger home and bought three and a half acres of bush in Eltham, North East of Melbourne. It was south Eltham to be precise, off the famous Mount Pleasant Road, near the old artist colony, Montsalvat. There was no house, nothing. There wasn't even a driveway. I'm not sure who had the idea, but it was decided the family would build a mudbrick house; the subsoil was perfect in Eltham and many homes in the neighbourhood were built using the same method. Nor do I know what led to the decision, because in reality Dad was not the most reliable handyman. I remember standing on the block with Jane, looking around at the rugged Australian bush. 'They have finally gone mad,' Jane muttered to me.

At almost the same time, Wesley contacted Mum and Dad to offer places at the school for Jane and me. Wanting to get me out of a primary school that was slowing my progress they accepted. Jane and I commenced our Wesley education in 1980; me in Term 3 of Year 3 and Jane in Term 3 of Year 5. Clare was offered a place starting Year 2 in Term 1, 1981.

Leaving the local primary school to attend Wesley was harder for Jane than me. As it was a Term 3 commencement at Wesley Jane really struggled with the upheaval of a new school and leaving her friends behind. Jane and I shared a bedroom and she would cry every night. She was always so sensitive.

'Emma aren't you sad to leave your friends?' she would regularly ask me.

'Nope!' I'd reply.

I honestly didn't care. As soon as I walked out of that local primary school, I had forgotten everyone's names anyway. I could not wait to start a new school. I loved new stuff, and right now I was getting a real school uniform, a new school bag and even had a new sports outfit. For the life of me I could not see any negatives with starting at Wesley.

My first day at Wesley, I remember sitting in the office of the Head of Glen Waverley campus, Tony Conabere, with Mum, Dad and Jane. Everyone could see Jane was upset, so I was asked if I wanted to go to class. Mum and Dad said that I jumped up, grabbed my bag, took Mr Conabere's hand and walked out without even saying goodbye to anyone. That afternoon I did not want to go home either. Apparently, Mum and Dad took until recess to get Jane to even consider joining her class.

What I particularly loved about Wesley was I now had dedicated Physical Education (PE) lessons. Real lessons where we ran around and played games!

We actually put a uniform on for PE, so I felt like it was serious. And I took it very seriously, perhaps a little too much so. As well as PE we also had sport, with training before or after school and often competitions on the weekend. I could choose the sport I wanted to play, and I could represent the school. It was a compulsory part of the Wesley College education.

I was really pleased with this new access to organised sport. Despite my begging, Dad so far had not allowed me to join any athletics clubs or sporting programs. Before I started at Wesley, I noticed kids at my primary school with patches sewn onto their tracksuit tops. When I asked them about the patches, they told me they did Little Athletics and spent Saturday morning at a running track. I kept asking Dad if I could do Little Athletics and he never let me. He said too many kids never progress to become a senior athlete if they train too hard too young. I needed to just wait until I was older.

Now I was at Wesley, I had an athletics sports day, cross country house sport day, swimming sports day as well as PE and School Sport. I took up everything, and only ever played to win. Wesley gave me my first real introduction to my lifelong love of sport.

Sometime between the 1980 and 1981 school years, Mum and Dad started to pursue the mudbrick house idea seriously. Mum and Dad suddenly had three lots of school fees, a new block of land and also needed to build a house. Mum helped the family finances by selling her handmade pottery at a well-known art and craft market in the Melbourne bayside suburb of St Kilda. She did this every Sunday. I remember Mum and Dad always seemed to be flat broke, but we never missed out on things. Dad would just laugh and say he was heading to 'financial ruin'. I think he still is.

It was decided that we should do as much of the building work as possible. Dad attended a mudbrick making course and both Mum and Dad pored over drawings with renowned mudbrick architect Robert Marshall. The decision to use all recycled timber and anything really, led to many weekend visits to local wrecking yards. The recycled timber quest was so full on, Mum and Dad bought two old bridges for the timbers for the main house frame, and when the Town Hall at Seymour (an hour's drive north of Melbourne) was demolished, they bought the Jarrah staircase, pulled it apart and redesigned it to fit into our house. Every weekend Jane, Clare and I de-nailed timber for our Jarrah wooden floors, cleaned second-hand house bricks for the retaining wall (mud cannot sit against mud) and collected and sourced every single piece of our house.

On top of all this, we also had to make the mudbricks: 3,500 to be precise. For this we needed the house excavation to take place. Topsoil was no good for mudbricks; it was too crumbly. We needed the Eltham subsoil or clay, as it was perfect apparently. We had to remove any rocks larger than Dad's fist, as that would weaken the brick. We needed to then make a consistency that was neither too sloppy nor too dry to shovel into the brick moulds. We did this by stomping in the mud to churn it up. Great fun the first time, but two summers later, the novelty had well and truly worn off. We also added straw to strengthen the bricks. And that was it. I was ten at the time, and I actually think all this manual labour set me up for my famously strong core as an athlete over ten years later. We shoveled so much mud over two summers, I had to become strong.

We toiled on the house through the two extremely hot summers leading into the terrible 'Ash Wednesday' 1982 bushfires around Melbourne. We learnt a lot about drought and the harsh Australian environment. The night of Ash Wednesday was long and frightening. No one slept. The air was thick with smoke and I will never forget the endless screaming of the fire engine sirens. Fortunately, Eltham was one of the really vulnerable areas around Melbourne to escape the fires.

Making the house, we all seemed to have a light dusting of Eltham mud all the time. In Year 4, I remember my teacher once told me I had some mud on my ear.

'Yes, we broke our mudbrick record on the weekend — 129 mudbricks in an afternoon!' I told her, slightly embarrassed.

Most of the roads in Eltham then were dirt roads, so the cars were covered in dust too. I think we were the only Wesley family to continuously drive down the pristine driveway with the rear window covered in dust and mud.

Dad's driving didn't help. Dad was always pushing boundaries. He viewed a speed limit on a road as the minimum speed you should travel on that road at that particular time. As a result, he was always driving fast. The dirt roads didn't slow him down either. Dirt roads seemed to spur him on, because quite often belting along the notorious hills of Eltham in the dusty corrugations of the road, we would take off. Dad enjoyed this the most; driving in the air. To be fair to Dad, everyone did this in Eltham in those days. In this period, we did not return one company car in complete condition. The combined speed, thrashing of the road corrugations and dust would lift panels and break bumpers off. I loved it. Jane wasn't really impressed; she was always trying to do her homework in the back and Dad's driving messed up her writing.

For the actual building of the house, Mum and Dad engaged a builder. In our household Dad had a reputation for his terrible handyman skills, so much so that changing a lightbulb made us all cringe. The building process was slowed by the recycled timber work, because second-hand timber doesn't fall into place like the pristine, new stuff does. By then we lived nearer to our land in Eltham, renting a house so Mum and Dad could juggle the increasing building costs and the Wesley school fees. Mum spent most Sundays on St Kilda esplanade still, selling her pottery and making a pretty good contribution financially.

I was in Year 5 at Wesley when we finally moved into our brand-new mudbrick house. It was a monumental achievement for my family. Even Dad, the renowned awful handyman, could now do more than change a light bulb and Mum, I think, finally felt like Australia was home. I loved living in Eltham, but Jane hated the travel. Clare seemed ok with it all, she did not complain much about anything yet.

Having three-and-a-half acres of land meant there was quite a bit of maintenance. Eltham had strong fire prevention laws, which required clearing the undergrowth and keeping the grass down. At one point we had a crazy idea of getting a goat. Apparently, goats eat everything. Our goat must have been a dud. Dear old Mary-Lou hated weeds and grass. Instead she ate only the veggie patch, mum's flowers and the house itself. She seemed to love mud and straw, which was what we had just spent two years moulding into bricks for the house. It was the world's worst 'quick fix' land clearing attempt ever.

Dad also developed a very novel way of removing ants nests. The bull ants were pretty ferocious, and a nest generally meant one of us would get bitten. Dad decided one day to pour petrol down the ants nests and throw a match in. It worked a treat. You could hear muffled explosions from the house when Dad was working on the ants nearby. Fortunately, Dad only did this in winter, when the threat of bushfires had subsided.

As my sisters and I grew up, it was obvious we had a Dad who bent the rules. He basically saw rules as a guide, not the absolute. Mum never objected or commented, so it was just a thing in the Carney household to push things to the limit. I'm not sure whether Mum and Dad sought the same in my education, but Wesley College is known for its emphasis on character over discipline. It was an environment where the individual student could grow and develop while also exposed to a high performing culture. As students we all had a grey area. At Wesley the school rules were quietly seen as a guide; the College would allow us to bend them a little. If we pushed them too far, as I did at times, there were consequences and discipline.

That was how I was wired. I could not choose my parents and grandparents. Moving to Australia was Dad's dream. Building a mudbrick house in the bush was Mum and Dad's unconventional choice. But the combination of my family roots, home life, and schooling suited, or possibly contributed, to how I was wired. It all allowed me to develop the mindset, free thinking attitude and subconscious refusal to accept the norm that came out when I pursued my own dreams. Those dreams were only just beginning to take shape as I stomped on the mud at Eltham, and they had a lot to do with the new opportunities presented to me at Wesley.

2. My Dear Alma Mater

Wesley College is a school that will always make you stand out from the crowd, literally. The school colours are purple and gold. Every school day and every time you represent the school in sport you are dressed in a strong purple colour with gold (yellow) highlights. You cannot hide in a crowd wearing this colour combination.

It never bothered me though. I enjoyed my school days and I got myself involved in most things, except drama. I hated drama. I was also useless at music. I was actually so bad the woodwind teacher asked me politely to stop when I tried to play the oboe. I was slightly disappointed, because it made the dog howl if I bothered to practice.

At Wesley we could compete with the boys at Maths, Sciences, English, the Arts and also Sport. The school was originally purpose built for boys and they just included girls into the Wesley way. I was educated without any preconceived ideas that girls required different treatment or instruction. We were the same as the boys, and we could play sport as hard as the boys too.

In Year 4 at Wesley I met the first person outside of Dad, whom I felt took me seriously as an athlete. Jenny Cassidy (Jen) says she saw something in me that was very 'coachable' and noticed that I was very focussed on results and outcomes for my age. This was in the sport of softball. In Year 4, I played in the 'firsts' team. Jen could always rely on me to execute a play when she yelled from the sidelines; it might be a slog, a bunt, a double play, whatever. I just took the instruction from her. To add to my softball ability, my left-handedness made it harder for the pitchers on the other team. I could throw, catch, field, and only ever played to win. Today though, I take pleasure in reminding Jen that she is such a good softball coach, I became a world class triathlete.

I was also exposed for the first time to competitive running in the form of winter season cross country in Year 4. I started with cross country as a simple house sport, which most school age children were expected to do. The teachers explained to us this was a running race where we had to follow a marked course.

We ran about two kilometres, which, as the school was set on a large amount of land, followed the perimeter of the four main school ovals, into the 'bushland' at the back and finished in front of the school. The entire Year 4 level ran together, boys and girls mixed. I came second. I absolutely loved it. What I loved the most was that it was all up to me as to how I placed in the race. I didn't rely on anyone else. Relying on others was becoming a bit of a problem for me in both PE and Sport at Wesley.

Despite playing softball and netball well enough to make the Wesley first teams in Year 4, it was quite obvious I was not a good 'team' player. I was increasingly frustrated in PE classes and also sports practice because some of my teammates didn't play to win. I was alleged to have thrown the ball 'at' my teammates, not 'to' them on a number of occasions. With an accurate left-handed throw, those who copped the other end of my frustration were obviously upset. Wesley imposed on me a week's ban from PE for being a little too aggressive one particular lesson. I remember being reprimanded by a College PE teacher who explained, 'It's not all about winning Emma.' I literally had no idea what they were talking about. I couldn't for the life of me understand why anyone would ever play sport or PE without the intention to win. I'm not sure my punishment worked either. I never accepted Wesley didn't want us to win at things, and I still don't. Simply participating never crossed my mind.

The following year, Brisbane hosted the 1982 Commonwealth Games and Robert De Castella had his famous victory in the marathon. 'Deeks' looked gone in the closing stages, well and truly beaten into second. But he amazingly found something and ran down the leader, Juma Ikangaa from Tanzania, to storm into the stadium and take the gold medal. Dad and I stood in the living room glued to the television watching the famous finish unfold. As a result, I was terribly late for school and found myself in trouble again. As it turned out the whole of Australia was late to school and work that day. Deeks had everyone glued to their TVs that morning. That gutsy race was the first time I watched and learnt how enthralling a race can be. I wanted to be a part of the sport, if it was like that.

The same year, when I started Year 5, I moved out of the 'Preparatory' school and into the 'Middle School', or as we all saw it, the 'big school'. Suddenly when we were involved in co-curricular activities, we were interacting with older students. In sport, I loved this, because I could train with the faster boys. Wesley, being an open-minded educational institution, did not place limits on me and allowed me to train to my ability, not restricting me because of my young age.

That year I decided to take up cross country as a School Sport, encouraged by the introduction in house sport the previous year. Wesley had recently employed a female coach for the Cross Country Team, Adrienne Beames. I was not aware of this at the time, but Adrienne was a controversial character, claimed to have been the first woman in the world to break three hours for the marathon. Although it wasn't verified, she reportedly ran the marathon distance in 2.46.30 in 1971. This record, along with many more Adrienne was reported to have broken remain as footnotes, not ratified in the International Amateur Athletic Federation (IAAF) official world records. Regardless of this, I found Adrienne to be someone who loved her running and run coaching. She was always very encouraging and made time for me at races and spoke to me as if she really believed I was a good runner. I found it very beneficial to receive this consistent support outside my own family.

Dad still wouldn't let me join Little Athletics, so I looked forward to my first season of competitive running with Wesley. My now consistent routine involved training on Tuesdays and Thursdays after school with the Wesley Squad, and weekly Saturday morning competitions. Wesley students participate in their chosen Associated Public Schools sport competition (APS Sport) every Saturday. APS Sport was established by eleven private boys' schools (Wesley was one of the few schools to have turned to co-education). I was the first girl ever to run APS cross country. I must have taken the organisation by surprise, because most girls played netball in the winter season of sport. There was no girls' race, so I ran in the boys' race. I had absolutely no idea at the time, but it became apparent that if a girl beats a boy, that boy will be horrified, and that boys' father will be mortified. I vividly remember one Saturday morning coming third overall. That meant there were only two boys and two dads who were ok with the race outcome. Being a competitor, I could sense the fear and ran as fast as I could to try to make as many boys as I could cry. Perhaps a little callous, but I figured if I did not beat them, they would beat me, and I was not remotely interested in that. I was only ten. I only raced cross country with the boys for one season. The APS group of schools must have realised they needed a girls' competition, so one was promptly added.

Following my first cross country season in Year 5 I decided I would select athletics for the spring season of School Sport. I loved athletics even more. To this day, I still love the smell of cut grass, because at school freshly cut grass generally meant the groundsmen were preparing to mark out the track on the main oval. I used to go and watch them at lunchtime, wondering how the hell they got the lines so straight. Most Saturdays during the APS athletics season, I raced the

800 m and 1500 m events. I was also thrown into the 4 x 400 m relay as a reliable runner and sometimes the 400 m as well.

During my school years I never lost an 800 m or 1500 m APS track event. And, with the commencement of a girl's cross country competition, I never lost a cross country race. Once Jane and Clare started running too, Wesley usually came first, second and third every Saturday throughout the winter season. I became a student the school could rely on to win, which was good fun, because the APS competition had quite a deep-rooted competitive element between the schools.

In Year 6, I again asked Dad if I could join Little Athletics, and again the answer was no. I kind of knew he would say no, so I had something up my sleeve. I told Dad there was a Victorian All Schools Track and Field Championships every year and asked whether I could enter the 800 m and 1500 m events. Dad again said no but agreed that I could the following year. He was adamant I did not overtrain. It was well known that burnout often prevented juniors from progressing to successful senior careers in athletics.

Dad was fast becoming a leader in the sporting goods industry, and in 1984 (when I was in Year 7 at Wesley) became head of finance at Nike Australia. Nike at this stage was a small sporting goods company that was showing the potential to become as big as the sporting goods giants like adidas and Puma but was struggling in Australia.

Dad's role at Nike exposed me further to the world of elite athletes and confirmed in my mind I was going to become one. Nike was the first sporting goods company who didn't just set out to sell athletics wear, they sold 'dreams and aspirations.' They also didn't use models to advertise, they used high profile athletes to develop some authenticity around their products. To support this vision and approach, Nike produced endless videos (VHS in those days) of inspirational elite athletes achieving excellence in their chosen field. Completely enthralled, I sat in the Nike Australia head office showroom after school most days and watched every single video Nike ever produced. The sales managers used to be in the showroom selling the Nike range to clients and customers, and I was usually in the corner watching the videos. Sometimes someone would ask who I was, and they were told, 'Oh, that's Emma, David's daughter. She wants to become a professional athlete.' I am not sure anyone really thought I would though, but little did they know the thought processes going on in my head.

Along with promotional videos, Nike also provided me with access to the self-proclaimed athletics bible *Track and Field News*. This provided me with all the IAAF race results, statistics, rankings, US college times; anything I wanted to read about athletics. I read about the times being run internationally. I read it all. There was no Google in those days, but here was everything I needed to know on paper.

Obviously with Dad at Nike, I suddenly had access to Nike products. Initially I was too small to fit anything, so my run clothing was always too big. The running shoes fitted, but the spikes did not. I checked the Nike warehouse every week until they did. I was so impatient to run in Nike spikes. Despite the fact I could get any shoe free, I still cleaned my spikes after each run and always made sure my running shoes looked clean and fast.

I took everything to do with my run racing and training very seriously.

Wesley continued to provide me with opportunities to remain involved in sport. Each year we all had a fitness test that ran over three to four weeks of PE classes. There was a mix of strength, flexibility, aerobic and anaerobic fitness tests. Very traditional tests, like the vertical hang, where you tried to hang from a bar as long as you could with your eyes level with the bar; a sit and reach for flexibility; and a test to count how many sit ups you could do in a minute. One of the boys in class would generally fart in this last test, destroying the session and causing the PE teacher to demand a restart.

My favorite test was the twelve-minute run. Everyone knew it was going to be fast, and all the boys in my class who considered themselves good runners knew I was going to try and beat them. The best I ever got was just over 3,200 m on the grass track. I managed to win outright. Most of the boys in my class claimed they had to go to the toilet that day, as I ran away with the win.

Teachers at Wesley fostered my passion for running. Phil De Young was the Middle School Coordinator and a runner himself. Phil was one of the leading contributors to the success of the Wesley co-education vision. He was very supportive of my running. I would see him in his office on a Monday morning and ask him if he could run at lunchtime on Wednesday. We often headed out for a thirty-minute jog, meaning I could sneak in an extra run without Dad knowing.

In Year 7, with an extra year of training and dreaming about running, it was finally almost time for the Victorian All Schools Track and Field Championships. I asked the Athletics coach at Wesley for an entry form and took it home to Dad. We entered the 800 m and 1500 m event. All I wanted was a state medal. I had never had the opportunity to win a medal.

The 1984 Victorian All Schools Championships was held at Box Hill athletics track, a suburb east of Melbourne. I had to wear my Wesley uniform. The youngest age group was Under 15 and I was only 13. I had to go up an age group to get a start. I didn't care. Dad was finally allowing me to race outside the APS. I was happy.

I had the 800 m on the Saturday and then the 1500 m on the Sunday. In both events I came fourth. I missed a medal in both. I could not believe it. I told Dad it was because I didn't train enough, and he needed to let me train properly otherwise I would never get anywhere. I was so annoyed with myself.

Looking at the meet program I noticed that the following weekend there was an Under 15 (U15) 3000 m championship race. I showed Dad and he said he would call the Victorian Athletics Association (VAA — now Athletics Victoria, AV) office on Monday to see if I could get a start. I reminded Dad all Monday morning on the way to school, to make sure he did not forget. Fortunately, Dad made the call, but he was told the entries had closed. Being a Carney, Dad refused to accept 'No', and asked if it would really matter if another athlete was allowed to run. After all, didn't they want to encourage girls? Dad got me a start.

I will never forget the race. I had worked out 3000 m was seven-and-a-half laps of a 400 m athletics track. I had never run that many laps in an actual race before. At the start the girls all looked a bit serious. I asked Dad what I should do, and he said, 'just run'. I decided that meant run fast out from the gun and that's exactly what I did. I remember running the first 200 m and I was in the lead. I ran another lap and was about 40 m in the lead. I looked at Dad as I passed the 600 m mark as if to say, 'Is this right?' I saw him shrug his shoulders and he yelled, 'Keep going!'

Much to everyone's surprise, including the track officials, I extended my lead every lap and won the Victorian All Schools 3000 m championship race by around 100 m. I smashed the Victorian record by 21.56 seconds and clocked a time of 10 minutes 29.20 seconds.

I had arrived into the world of Track and Field, even if it was just the Victorian Schools Championships. It was big to me.

Adding to the collective incredulity of VAA officials, was the fact that I had no recognised coach or competitive experience. It was my first meet at the state level, and I was completely unknown to the athletics community. Unknown to me, once I crossed the finish line, Dad found himself fending off a number of established athletics coaches. Suddenly there was interest in me as an athlete. Dad still did not want me to train under a coach, because he was concerned I would over train and burn out.

I was extremely proud, because Dad said I ran well. Dad's feedback was always very important to me. I had managed to prove to Dad I could do more than just school training. Dad signed me up to the Box Hill Women's Athletics Club and agreed to let me train with them on Sundays. So, I had another win that day.

Me being me, I never missed a Sunday Box Hill Athletics Club training session. Sunday training at Box Hill was really sprint training. Dad was obsessed with me working on speed and technique as a junior. He wanted me to stay away from training volume because he saw this as far too damaging on a young body. These sessions were run by a guy called Perc Mann. He and his wife Iris basically ran the Box Hill Women's Athletics Club, which was quite separate from the men's club. The men's club was a very well established in the Victorian scene and unfortunately, I was soon to discover, quite chauvinistic. In the worst instance, the renowned coach who ran the men's club, Alan Barlow (the track is named after him), turned the lights out on me while I was training because the men had finished. At the time I wondered why it had gone dark, but when I saw Dad and Alan yelling at each other it was obvious what had happened. I didn't care. I carried on. I could still see the white lines in the dark, so it did not really worry me. Frustrated, Alan ended up locking the gate, and Dad and I had to jump the fence when I finished.

Fortunately, nothing managed to deter me from athletics. Including negativity. I soon developed a mistrust of officials though. Following my successful All Schools 3000 m Championship, I was awarded the Victorian Record, then had it taken back. Apparently, someone had not updated the book and I missed the actual record by a few seconds. I was annoyed, Dad was furious, and I started to loathe sloppy sports administration.

My 3000 m victory gave me automatic selection into the Australian Schools Championships in Brisbane at the QEII Stadium, the 1982 Commonwealth Games Track and Field venue. I had never run on a track like that before, in a real stadium. It was my first Victorian uniform and my first trip away as an athletics team member. I was by far the smallest and most inexperienced. All the other junior athletes seemed to have coaches, had done years of Little Athletics and knew what they were doing. I ran scared and did not run well. I bolted the start, taking off far too fast, and ran my 200 m personal best (PB) over the first half lap. With 2800 m to go, I did not recover and pretty much blew up from there. I learnt a lot. I learnt I still hated losing, regardless of who I raced.

Now I was a member of an Athletics Club, I asked Dad if I could also include my own training sessions between school sessions. Finally, he said yes. I was allowed to run a maximum of three or four kilometres. We worked out a course from home and Dad said I could run before school on Monday and Wednesday. I never missed a morning. I also worked out that given I was training less than all my competitors I had to be smart. I decided I would train harder. Every time I stepped out the door on those mornings, I ran flat out. Jane started coming, and sometimes Dad. Jane used to ask why we had to run flat out, and I used to tell her you get fitter that way. Dad was way off the back. He actually never beat me running, fortunately Dad was completely ok with that.

Sometimes, Dad must have not felt like running, so just to check on me he would drive his car while I ran along the footpath. He had a company car from Nike that had a digital speedometer, so I would yell out to him to let me know when I was running 15-17 km/h (kilometres per hour). I always thought that was a good pace to hold for a sustained effort. I had done a lot of reading on threshold running and I was starting to test my own training theories. I always enjoyed toying with the pain of running fast and seeing how long I could run and hold the pace.

After I had run and won my first 3000 m track event, I looked up the world rankings in the most recent *Track and Field News* to see what I needed to run to be competitive internationally. I needed to run around 2 minutes faster to be world class, and about 90 seconds faster to be a top Australian runner. I asked Dad when I could start training properly and he told me I had to wait until I had finished growing, so when I was about twenty. That seemed like ages away. I thought, surely, I could do something else to improve my running.

Noticing how light-framed the world's best runners were, I decided that if Dad would not let me train like everyone else, I could try losing weight. I thought my power to weight ratio would improve, and I would be faster. I decided the best way to do this was to skip lunch. No one would notice, and I could cut out a third of what I was eating. Obsessed with winning, I obviously did not consider all the side effects of this plan. I lost weight, a lot of weight. Wesley teachers were concerned, my parents were concerned. I gave myself my first running injury, a stress reaction in my right shin and was diagnosed with anorexia. Typical me, I pushed it to the extreme.

Fortunately, this dabble with eating control ended quickly. I got sick of being injured and very sick of being hungry. In this period though, I learnt that my mind was very strong and if I really wanted to achieve something, I was capable of it regardless of how much discomfort I put myself through. I also learnt if I did not adhere to good nutrition practices, I was going to constantly be injured and get nowhere.

Once I was over the stress reaction in my shin, I spent the rest of my school days running APS Cross Country and VAA (state level) Cross Country in Winter, and APS Athletics in Spring with VAA Athletics all summer. Wesley had become resigned to the fact that although I was very capable of being a first team player, I was not suited to team sports. I was given a sports exemption when there was no athletics and no cross country in that season of sport. This allowed me to dedicate myself to state competition running and prepare for the VAA Track and Field Championships over the summer. I raced pretty much every Saturday, either through the mud or around the track, depending on the time of year. I won a number of state titles and I also won many Victorian All Schools titles for Wesley, both cross country and athletics. The school athletics coach allowed me to start a new tradition and enter a team in the 4 x 800 m relay in the Victorian Schools Relay Championships each year so that Jane, Clare and I could run together. We remained unbeaten the entire time I was at Wesley. For the fourth relay team member, I always found someone from the school who was prepared to run two laps flat out. I always ran last just to make sure we won the Victorian title.

Nationally, I was a Victorian team member every year for both athletics and cross country. I was generally a top three place getter at the national championships in both disciplines. I was a recognized talent but had no coach. It was just Dad and me working things out. Although I was invited to various training camps, such as the junior distance camp at Falls Creek in 1986, Dad would not allow me to run the full program like everyone else. I was constantly frustrated with the limited training, always arguing with Dad that I could win if he allowed me to train more.

As I progressed though Years 8, 9 and 10, I started to notice I was different from everyone else in my year level at Wesley. Not particularly interested in social events, I looked forward to early nights on the weekend. I wanted to race Saturday, so Friday night needed to be an early-to-bed night and I finally convinced Dad I should run Sundays too, so I wasn't going to mess that session up with a late night either. I didn't ever view my commitment to running as a question of sacrificing my social life, it was what I wanted to do. I had plans, big plans, and nothing seemed more important to me than making sure I was able to train and race properly.

It was at school that I discovered my heart was different from a 'normal' heart. In science class, we all had to take our resting heart rate and record it for the teacher. When I wrote mine down at 39, the teacher asked everyone to take their heart rates again because someone in the class was being silly. We all did. This time I wrote down 36. I had been sitting for longer, so it had dropped. I was sent immediately to see the school nurse, because the teacher had concerns for my health. This was the first time I realised that perhaps physiologically I was different from everyone else and maybe this was why I was so good at distance running.

Towards the end of my school years, Mum and Dad, always the entrepreneurs, bought a bakery in Camberwell, a suburb east of Melbourne. It was a hard slog, seven days a week. Busy too. Dad was still at Nike, so Mum ran the bakery. We all pitched in on the weekends. The hard work paid off though. In 1988 we had a family holiday house at Noosa on the Sunshine Coast, Queensland, on the famous Hastings Street. Apart from being 'the' place to holiday for me growing up, it was also home to the Noosa Triathlon, the greatest triathlon event in the world, which I discovered a few years later. This event became my favourite, yet toughest, race to win.

For Year 11 and 12, we had to attend the original Wesley campus at 577 St Kilda Road, Melbourne, as senior students were not taught at the Glen Waverley campus. The senior St Kilda Road (Prahran) campus was a great place to finish school. As it was near the city, it seemed less sheltered from the outside world. My year level made quite an impact. One lunchtime we decided we were going to have a sausage sizzle to raise money for a charity or something. No one really knew what. We had everything set up but did not think out the location properly. Within twenty minutes, five fire trucks arrived at the school, sirens blaring. It became apparent we had set up the barbecue under the smoke detectors in the walkway. The school was fined a few thousand dollars and we were educated on 'appropriate planning'.

My success in sport grew to the extent that when I started at the St Kilda Road Campus in Year 11, teachers and students already knew me or know of me. I assumed it was my running ability that preceded me, not my behavior in class. My arrival at the senior college coincided with a staff appointment which undoubtedly further contributed to my development into a world class elite athlete. Matt Paterson was a new Middle School coach at the St Kilda Road campus. An athlete himself, he was also the former training partner of UK Olympic Champion and 1500 m World Record Holder Steve Ovett. Suddenly I had someone at school who knew what it took to become the world's best. I couldn't believe my luck. Before Matt started at Wesley, members of the staff informed him of my presence at the school. I had just won my first two national titles and was the current All Schools U19 1500 m and 3000 m national champion.

Matt's coaching was delivered with authenticity. He was the most influential coach I ever had, and he always trained with me. I learnt a lot from Matt, both as an athlete and as a coach later in my life. The tough, balanced, simple yet precise training sessions to which Matt exposed me, stayed with me throughout my career. I may have just been really, really keen to learn, and to finally have a coach, but Matt's influence on my understanding of the hard work and commitment required to achieve my dreams, contributed greatly to how I raced and to my absolute desire to win. After coaching me at Wesley, Matt commented:

Emma was clearly very ruthless and very driven. She was very talented and wanted to improve very quickly. Emma was desperate to get to the top and asked questions all the time. She would ask whether she was capable. Emma used to ask about my overseas experiences and what it took to become world class. She said to me, 'what does it take to become a world class athlete?' I said, 'It's a lot of hard work, luck, patience'.

With Matt's arrival at Wesley, I managed to convince Dad I should run Monday, Wednesday and Friday lunchtimes and do my speed sessions during school training with Matt on Tuesday and Thursday. For my lunchtime run days I would change into my PE gear, meet Matt near the Middle School gates, and run to the Tan. The 'Tan' in Melbourne is a 3.8 km gravel loop around the Royal Botanic Gardens, which is very popular with runners. It is about 2 km from the Wesley school gates, so we slightly adjusted the loop to fit in the three laps. Lunchtime was only around an hour.

It was a great run, but I was always in trouble when I returned. PE uniforms could not be worn in the classroom at Wesley. After lunch I usually had Economics and my Economics teacher always told me to go and change before entering his class. I decided to take a stand. When he asked me to leave his class to change one day, I refused. I told him I was trying to fit my training in around my school time and one day I was going to be a professional athlete. I must have either impressed him with my resilience or just shocked him, because I was allowed to wear my PE gear from that day on in his class.

Wesley required senior students to attend a one-on-one meeting with the school careers advisor to make sure we chose subjects for Year 12 that aligned with our career choices and desired university placings. I kept skipping my meeting, until one day I was bailed up by the careers advisor and dragged to her office. When asked what I wanted to do when I finished school, I replied that I didn't think she could help me. She responded:

'Emma, Wesley College is a school with vast resources, we can prepare you for anything.'

I was not about to set a plan B.

'Ok then, I'd like to be a professional athlete.'

With that I was told that I needed to have a plan. She told me while I should follow my dream, I also needed to make sure I was making the most of the investment my parents were making in my education. I am not entirely sure she fully appreciated my resolve to make it as an athlete, but I think she did have my best interests at heart.

'OK. I will study commerce, so I can invest all my prize money wisely. That can be my off-season career.'

I finished the meeting with subject preferences for a Commerce degree at either Melbourne or Monash University.

In 1989, my final year at school, I remained Cross Country captain, was also Athletics captain, and appointed a School Prefect. I struggled with the School Prefect role, because I was required to enforce some of the school rules. I was asked to do tram duty once. I had to make sure all the students boarded the tram 'appropriately' outside the school on High Street. It was impossible. I didn't try very hard though, because I also didn't like the tram conductors much. I, like the rest of the school, thought they picked on private school kids, so I wasn't really interested in making their job any easier. I just made sure everyone got on the tram and overloaded it so the conductor couldn't walk around and collect tickets. I then crammed myself on and caught the tram too.

Perhaps a little less celebrated, but highly audacious, I also managed to pull off a stunt that almost had me sitting my Year 12 exams off campus in disgrace. I had long thought that the PE uniform was not great for running. The school rowing team members were all allowed to wear clothing that was appropriate for rowing, but the school would not budge on the Athletics uniform. I decided to do something about it.

Every year, the Athletics season culminated in a meet at which each school competed for the APS Cup, the winner being the school with the highest point score at the end of the day. Wesley had not won the APS Cup ever in the girls' competition and it was decades since they won in the boys' competition. In my final year, with me as captain, I was pretty confident the Wesley girls could win the title. I thought it would be fantastic if Wesley not only won, but also had a new Athletics uniform. I asked Dad if he could get the Nike athletics international bodysuits, as worn by some American athletes at the 1988 Seoul Olympic Games, most famously by the flamboyant sprinter, 'Flo Jo'. I wanted a uniform that would be seen as elite and world class, but made up in purple and gold, the Wesley colours. I wanted a statement for my last run for Wesley, as captain and hopefully for an APS win.

Dad had the suits made and I distributed six of them out to girls I thought would win their events and made them swear to secrecy. Competition day arrived and I wore the bodysuit first, as the 800 m was always the first event. I won.

After my 800 m event, I put my Wesley tracksuit on and as captain I stood with the Principal of Wesley College Mr David Prest. He was an outstanding College Principal and was behind the success of Wesley's coeducational vision. He also liked a flutter on the horses and the Caulfield Cup always clashed with the APS finals. This particular year, he asked me if I thought Wesley would win.

'Yes. I think you should make sure you are back here by midday,' I told him.

He left promptly, and I suddenly felt more at ease, because we could now wear our bodysuits without the Principal seeing them.

Clare won her 800 m wearing a bodysuit like me. That was pretty much what happened. All those who wore the bodysuit, won their events. Some teachers didn't notice, some did. I don't know why I didn't consider the obvious fact that someone would tell the Principal. No one said anything on the day. Mr Prest returned in time to see the Wesley Girls win the APS Cup for the first time. As Athletics Captain, I secretly hoped this might distract from the bodysuits.

It didn't. I vastly underestimated how widespread the reaction would be. The impact of the bodysuits reached further than the College Principal's office. The story made the TV free to air Channel 9 news (all editions) and ran as a feature article in the main Victorian newspaper, *The Herald Sun*, for two days in a row.

I was also dragged into Tony Conabere's office (he was now Head of Prahran Campus) for a 'please explain'. My response was that I wanted Wesley to lead the way in sportswear, be cutting edge, win in style — I was putting forward anything that seemed positive. Unfortunately, he didn't buy my excuses. I had to write an official apology to the Principal, Mr Prest. If I refused, I would have to sit my Year 12 exams off campus at the Melbourne Showgrounds, 'with all the other schools'. As it turned out, fortunately, Mr Prest wasn't bothered. The College leaders were really just concerned that students would start inventing College sporting apparel as they liked.

Despite irritating the school executive, I was recognized for my contribution to Wesley College sport, as demonstrated in the following tribute, published in the 1989 College *Chronicle*:

> *Emma's enthusiasm and encouragement have undoubtedly lifted the standard of athletics at Wesley. She is an athlete with immense potential, and we all wish her well for the future. Emma has made an enormous contribution to athletics at Wesley over the years and we thank her for that.*

The day after the final Year 12 exams, a fire substantially damaged the St Kilda Road campus. Significant archival material was lost with the virtual destruction of the school library. There was talk that some of the Year 12 completed exams could have been burnt. This was a little concerning, as I thought I had finally finished my school studies. Fortunately, it was just a rumour. The damaged areas were rebuilt by 1991, but it seemed a little ironic that the year I finally completed my schooling at Wesley, it was almost burnt to the ground.

I achieved the marks for entry to my chosen University course, so Wesley succeeded in educating me academically. My education also prepared me for a life as an elite athlete. I understood how important it was to maintain a standard. I wore a uniform with pride and I also knew how to present myself professionally. Some very important principles required for world class sport.

On leaving school, I knew how to win, I knew how to bend the rules (possibly too much), I had my head full of dreams that most school systems would write off as impossible, I had ambition and tenacity, and I was not afraid to have a go.

Wesley had prepared me well.

3. Adding the Swim and the Bike

With school behind me, I entered a frustrating time in my sporting career. I actually began to doubt my ability and wonder whether I was perhaps a pretty ordinary athlete.

It appears I wasn't the only one to think this. In the winter of 1993 Victorian *Herald Sun* sports journalist Nic Bideau wrote about me as, 'one of those talented juniors that for one reason or another fail to fulfill their obvious potential', and described my running career since I finished school in 1989 as 'plagued with inconsistency'.

This was more than a little harsh but given Nic Bideau was a sports journalist who had applied unsuccessfully for a Sports Marketing Managerial role at Nike around that time, I assumed it was a dig at Dad. Being the daughter of a Nike boss, I felt a few people in the athletics fraternity didn't really think I was as good as all the Nike gear I was wearing.

Things were complicated in those first few years after school. Sometimes Dad's confrontational behavior didn't help. He always attended the local, Victorian and national athletics meets to support me, but also checked on his Nike sponsored athletes between my races. If he saw a sponsored athlete not wearing Nike or worse, wearing a competitor's brand, he was known to 'fire' them on the spot for breaking their contract. Some athletes who lost their contracts then became bitter towards me, because apparently it was my fault they didn't know how to treat and respect their sponsors. This period taught me a lot about sponsorships and relationships. Dad was always telling me that a truly professional athlete understands that when they have a sponsor, they must always wear and represent that company, and if they don't, then they run the risk of losing the mutually beneficial business relationship. I felt like I was caught up in the middle of everyone else's sponsorship problems and there was a lot of angst, but there was nothing I could do.

Dad wasn't all one way though. He gave jobs at Nike to a lot of athletes, making sure they were paid well, had flexible hours to suit their training and racing needs, and worked in roles that did not require them to be on their feet so that they could train well. Dad understood athletes but had no patience for fools.

Shortly after school, the newly formed Victorian Institute of Sport (VIS) awarded me a Track and Field Scholarship and I felt finally I was part of the athletics fraternity. I wasn't really. Matt Paterson was still my coach since leaving Wesley and he was highly sceptical about the support I would get. He told me, 'Nothing will get you to the top other than hard work.' He was right. Unfortunately for me, Matt returned to Norway to become their head distance athletics coach and I did not have a coach again until April 1991. I trained hard off programs Matt sent me and continued to push myself most days.

Outside of running, I started studying for an Economics degree, majoring in Accounting at Monash University, Clayton campus, south east of Melbourne. Jane was already at Monash, studying Law Economics with top class marks. She told me it was great fun at Uni. I hated it and it appears the University hated me. All my time at Wesley I hadn't failed a thing; at Uni I couldn't stop failing. I was so bored. It was torture to study, torture to attend and torture to travel there (it was a good hour's drive from Eltham).

Jane could see I was struggling, and suggested I try to get involved in the university life. I had a look at the Athletics club. I was told the University Games were a great event, because at the end everyone runs the 'Beer Mile', where you drink as much beer as you can in a mile run. I was appalled anyone would think I would do something so unprofessional during a race. I couldn't understand why anyone would enter a race to mess around: a race is a race, to be won. I took fewer and fewer subjects on, until I was doing just one subject a semester. It was going to be nothing short of a miracle if I ever finished my degree.

Despite Nic Bideau's harsh criticism, Matt's absence, and my own doubts, my running improved. For the first time, Dad allowed me to train properly and race distances over 5 km. Through the 1991 season I was generally the top runner in the weekly A grade interclub 3000 m (the highest weekly state level track competition) and shaved my PB down to the low 9 minutes 20 seconds range. I was the Victorian 3000 m champion for my age group and 1500 m runner up at the state championships. But I still was not running fast enough to be outstanding nationally, finishing third in the U20 3000 m titles at the end of the season.

Matt returned to Australia at a perfect time for a winter training build. I rejoined his group and finally started to train full time. Running twice a day, I gradually increased my weekly volume. I followed the traditional running program of Tuesday, Thursday and Saturday intervals and intensity sessions usually involving a track session at least once a week. Mondays and Fridays were 'recovery days' with easy jogs, still totalling 16 km a day. On Wednesdays I combined the two shorter runs into a single semi-long 16 km (10 mile) run, a standard threshold build. Sunday was long run day. Traditionally the long runs were on the trails at Ferny Creek in the Dandenongs, which was about an hour's drive east of Melbourne. It seems that every great Australian distance runner has trained in the area at some point in their career. The trails are soft underfoot, reducing the impact on the legs, but also very hilly. The undulating trails force you to be light on your feet, focus on technique and lift your running economy. Along with these key sessions, I also added daily 30-45 minute recovery jogs.

There were so many benefits to training with Matt at this time. He coached A-Grade male runners, who were much faster than me and pushed me. A training gem he added to my program was the concept of the 100 mile (160 km) week, sustained for six weeks. By the time I built up to this I was at a level of fitness I had never reached before.

I ran a little better at Victorian cross-country events over the winter. The season opener was always a road relay at Sandown Racecourse, a car racing circuit east of Melbourne, and I recorded the fastest time for the lap in 10 minutes 30 seconds. Two weeks later, I won the Victorian Open Women's 4 km Cross Country event at Longwood, about a ninety-minute drive straight up the Hume Freeway north of Melbourne. This was my first State Open Women's title. It was a sprint finish and I won by a tiny margin, but I beat some notable senior national level runners for the first time.

The other runs for the season were not particularly notable. With Dad now allowing me to contest the 10 km State Road Championship previously I ran that for the first time. But it was not fast, around 35 minutes. I didn't have the strength endurance to hold the experienced runners in the closing stages and struggled with the fatigue of my full training load. The leaders dropped me at about the 7 km mark. My performance at the Australian Cross Country Championships in late August was not spectacular either. I finished out of the placings with a time of 22 minutes 13 seconds for the hilly 6 km course.

In September 1991, I developed a serious back injury. It was really just an overuse issue which I ignored, so it became chronic. I was unable to train properly for weeks, almost ten. It was extremely frustrating. I tried the usual visits to physios and doctors, but nothing would release the problem until I went to see an old family friend who was a chiropractor, Nick Kiss von Soly. His wife had a market stall every Sunday at St Kilda Esplanade with Mum. Nick worked on re-aligning my spine, particularly my pelvis. I remained with Nick throughout my career, finding that chiropractic care was really important for me to avoid further back problems. Within four weeks all was ok again and I returned to jogging.

Around that time, I saw my first triathlon on TV. The 1991 International Triathlon Union (ITU) Triathlon World Championship was in progress on the Gold Coast. Perhaps because it was in Australia, it was being broadcast live on free-to-air television. Returning home from a run I found Dad watching the end of the women's race. All the competitors were running. When asked, Dad explained what he was watching, 'This is apparently the triathlon world championships.'

We both stood watching the women running.

'They don't look very quick,' I commented to Dad.

Dad said, 'No. But they have already swum 1.5 km and biked 40 km.' He continued, 'Their run technique is poor. You are better than these athletes.'

I couldn't help agreeing with Dad. It looked amateur.

A few weeks earlier, while I was struggling with my back injury, Dad had encouraged me to do some cross training and I had a feeling I knew what he was thinking. 'I don't think it is in the Olympics though Dad — what's the point?'

We pretty much left the conversation there. A Canadian athlete won the women's World Title that day; neither of us really wanted to hang around to see that.

To maintain fitness, I did attempt some cross training, as Dad suggested. I had no idea what I was doing. If I was supposed to run for an hour and couldn't run, I swam for an hour. Just laps, no structure. Some days I just got in the local 50 metre pool and swam a hundred laps. I thought 5 km was a decent amount of swimming.

During this period, I crossed paths with an old school friend: Marcus Galbraith. An OW (Old Wesley Collegian — the name given to past Wesley College students), Marcus was in the year above Jane at school, and the last boys-only grade at Wesley. He was in the Wesley boys' athletics team when I trained with them early on. I didn't know him personally, but his reputation as a sports-man and high achiever was well established, so I knew of him. In 1983, as a Year 9 student, he 'blitzed the field' to win the U15 800 m APS finals. Apparently, he lost a shoe in the process. He won a total of ten APS titles during his time at

Wesley. Naturally Wesley loved Marcus. He received many honours and awards, and he was Athletics Captain and School Vice-Captain in 1986.

Sometime after he finished school, he started to visit Mum's bakery at Camberwell, which was near his home. In a strange coincidence, Marcus and I earned the exact same Year 12 score, and both went on to study Economics and Accounting. Unlike me, Marcus continued on to achieve in his studies, graduating from Melbourne University with a Bachelor of Commerce and commencing work with the prestigious accounting firm, Price Waterhouse (PW), in Melbourne. It seems that we were very similar though, because boredom hit Marcus once he started at PW. Like me, he was more interested in sport. He quit after about a year, because he wanted to see how far he could go in triathlons, which he had just taken up. He particularly liked the sound of an iconic endurance distance event held at Hawaii every year, known as an Ironman triathlon. Hawaii was the home of the first Ironman triathlon, but by the time Marcus dropped into the bakery, the Hawaiian event had become the Ironman World Championships. The event involved a 3.8 km swim, followed by a 180 km bike ride and a full marathon. Marcus was training to see if he could qualify to compete in Hawaii.

That all made perfect sense to me. I think Marcus liked discussing his triathlon dream with me, because it was all normal to me. I saw nothing wrong with throwing in a respectable job to train for something he had never done before. When he dropped into Mum's bakery after some of his epic training sessions, he looked shattered. I would ask him what he had just done, and he would tell me he had ridden to Portsea and back (a 200 km round trip along the Bayside suburbs of Melbourne to the Port Philip Bay Headlands), or he might have run 20 km or more, or swum over 7 km. To me that sounded like a very enviable way to spend your days. Marcus and I trained together a bit. I joined in on some of his rides and swims and he started to do a few of the run interval sessions I did with Matt's group.

Christmas of 1991 came and went. My family spent time at our holiday home in Noosa, as had been the tradition over the past four years. Marcus raced the local triathlons through the summer as part of his Ironman preparation. On Australia Day — Sunday, 26 January 1992 — Marcus was killed on his bike while returning from a triathlon at Queenscliff, near Geelong. He was only twenty-three years old.

I was devastated. And I swore off triathlons. I didn't ever want to be involved in the sport.

I attended Marcus's funeral with Jane. It was a very sad day. Funerals were not meant to be attended at our young age. Marcus was one of those invincible students at school. Everyone wanted to be like him, good at everything. Outstanding at everything. At the funeral I spoke to his father Dick. I don't really remember what I said, but I do remember what his Dad told me.

He said, 'Emma, Marcus always thought you could be the best triathlete in the world.'

At the time those words hit me, like I had to hear them. I never forgot them. Marcus had amazing foresight, though I didn't know it at the time.

But I didn't feel like I was going anywhere in the first few months of 1992. I skipped the Australian Track Running Championships in March. I felt I had lost too much quality work with my back injury. I had not yet returned to full training volume and my times on the track were still not great. A relapse in April drove home the ever-important lesson that self-care, stretching, and proper injury prevention practices are really, really important. I needed to take better care of myself if I was going to be a successful, full-time, professional athlete.

At the start of the winter season I finally put a good race together, running third in the Victorian Open Women's 8 km Cross Country Championship. For two months I trained really well. At track sessions in July I made strong progress with 1 km times consistently under 3 minutes. But I raced poorly again at the cross country nationals in Nowra, NSW, in late August. Frustratingly, my racing just didn't seem to be progressing as well as my training. Dad raised the idea of me doing triathlons for cross training again. We had a look at the local races and decided I would try, just to see how I would go.

Nike had been dabbling in triathlon and committed to sponsor a Victorian series over the summer of 1992-1993. Dad signed me up for the second race of the Nike series, to be held in Elwood, a bayside suburb of Melbourne, on 20 December 1992. Having swum laps reasonably consistently throughout the year because of my running injuries, I thought the 750 m swim couldn't possibly be too bad. As it turns out, it was horrific. I exited the water several minutes behind the leading woman. I grabbed my trusty old Malvern Star 7-speed bike and rode flat out. By the time I finished the bike leg, I was only 1 minute 38 seconds behind the race leader. I had no idea of this at the time. To me the entire race seemed very messy. I was used to run racing either on a track or cross country, where you knew where everyone was all the time. All I could do on the day was swim, bike and run as fast as I could and hope for the best. Once I hit the run, not knowing my placing, I asked each girl I ran past if she was winning. Everyone kept saying, 'No'. Finally, I ran up to a girl and when I asked her if she was winning, she said 'Yes'. I said 'Good!' with relief, overtook her, and went on to win.

With a run split that was more than 2 minutes faster than any other female competitor in the field and faster than most of the men, I finished 40 seconds clear of my competition and won the race. Clare raced too and recorded the second fastest female run time, to finish third in the junior women's event.

It was a landmark moment for us. Tiffany Cherry, a good friend of mine from Athletics (school and club) also participated in the event. She was, like Clare and me, interested in this new sport of triathlon. Tiff recalls thinking on the day, 'Wow. Emma is a stand-out. She's really good.'

To be honest though, I didn't really think much of the race. Triathlon still seemed amateur and was not an Olympic sport. It was fun but didn't seem serious. Unknown to me though, Dad was very interested in triathlon.

It was perhaps two days later, when Mum, Dad, Clare and I were having dinner at home in Eltham, that Dad started a casual conversation about triathlon. He said he had been looking at some international triathlon results.

Dad recalls his research.

I explained to Emma that we had long used the differential in racing time of elite men's and women's times as a measure of Emma's progress in Athletics, in order to always have a clear measure of performance. An elite woman that achieved a performance time that was 9.5 per cent to 10 per cent slower than an elite male time was performing at a truly elite level, provided of course the male used as the comparison was a truly elite athlete. I compared Emma's times in the Elwood race in each discipline against published race times of a number of races, both internationally and in Australia for both males and females. What was very clear to me was that within the sport of Triathlon, women were not performing to that comparison measure we had always used, so, if Emma were to race 9.5 per cent – 10 per cent slower than men in races, she would be the fastest in the World.

I then compared the race splits of each discipline of Emma's Elwood race to race splits of the current (at that time) elite Triathletes, again internationally and in Australia. The run was simple because Emma was already a World class performer and was less than 8 per cent of the men's race times. Emma's bike comparison was more difficult because she was racing on her trusty old Malvern

Star bike. A good Australian bike, but her model was hardly built for racing fast. Despite this, her bike race time was very close to the 9.5 per cent margin. I also knew from the few occasions she had ridden that she was a powerful rider. She just lacked race skills and specific race training — and of course a race bike. It was therefore entirely logical to me that she would be competitive with the right equipment and bike racing skills. The swimming, of course, was the greatest problem at this stage, but as swimming was only around 16 per cent of a race time, it was the least important of the three disciplines and with a good technical coach and a lot of work, Emma would soon be competitive, or close to competitive.

My calculations were based upon the fact that Emma was already the fastest runner in Triathlon. It could be argued that Carol Montgomery of Canada could be marginally quicker than Emma on the run, but when comparing Montgomery's run times in a running race to her times in a Triathlon there was a significant drop-off, suggesting the bike leg had a considerable negative effect on her running performance. I knew Emma was a good bike rider, so all she needed was specific training by a coach that understood she was training for Triathlon. If that coach could be found, Emma clearly, in my biased father's opinion, would be the fastest woman in the sport of Triathlon.

Finally, to be the best in the world, Emma had to be at international standard in two disciplines and at state standard, preferably close to national standard, in the third.

The conclusion that Emma would be the World's best was therefore very simple and what was needed to achieve that was very clear to me.

- Running — Emma was already a competitive World Class Athlete.
- Bike riding — Emma had all the basic skills and strength to race internationally, but just had no interest in doing so. The right coach and good equipment were missing, but not an insurmountable problem.
- Swimming — Emma was totally uncompetitive and came from a family with no swimming pedigree whatsoever. A good coach was needed in a hurry.
- In essence Emma would be, in the sport of triathlon, the fastest for approximately 83 per cent – 84 per cent of the race time (the bike and the run), and be fighting to minimise damage in just 16 per cent – 17 per cent of race time (the swim), so she would clearly be in control for most of the race.

The final ingredients were the natural physical attributes, which Emma had by the bucket load, and finally the mental strength and resilience to want to be the best in the World.

Knowing Emma as I did, I knew she would relish such a challenge once the program was laid out in front of her.

Dad took me through this research very matter-of-factly. He was adamant that if I learnt to swim, I would be the best triathlete in the world.

'It's not an Olympic event though Dad,' I told him. The Olympics to me confirmed a sport as being authentic, real or something that mattered. But then Dad told me that he thought it would be an Olympic sport soon.

Suddenly triathlon seemed a little more interesting.

'I can't give up running.'

Dad agreed with this. He said my running was going to win me triathlons, because no one he could see could run like me. Dad had also looked at the triathlon season, and like athletics, the main international races were run through the northern hemisphere summer. He said I needed to race a full national season domestically, through the Australian summer, to gain selection for the Australian Elite Triathlon team. That sounded pretty normal to me. After all I had been trying to do this all my life with Athletics, racing for selection to the national team.

Dad already had a plan. 'If you compete through the 1993–1994 domestic summer triathlon season, you will gain selection for the Elite Triathlon World Championships in Wellington, New Zealand, in November 1994. I think you could win it.'

Now I was really interested, 'Win the World Title?' I asked.

'Yes. It seems Australia is the strongest country in the world in triathlon, particularly in the women. You will do well internationally if you do well domestically.'

I looked at Dad. He was dead serious.

'OK. Let's do it!' I said.

Clare was also listening. 'What about me?' she asked. Dad told Clare, 'If you do the same, you could win the Junior World Title.' Clare looked at me. I nodded, and she said, 'Ok!'

Mum joined in, '... and I will make sure you have the best nutrition in the world.' Mum had always done that for us, and we all are eternally grateful for her attention to what we ate.

At work the next day, Dad spoke to Raelene Boyle (Australian sporting legend, sprint champion, and long-time Nike athlete). Raelene was someone with whom Dad often discussed my athletic goals and ambitions, seeking advice. I think Raelene took me seriously, one of the few to do so at Nike. Most just saw me as the boss's daughter. She was very knowledgeable, and she also knew everyone in Australian sport at the top level. Raelene's brother Ron had cycled for Australia, so she knew and understood the finer details about cycling too. Dad told Raelene about his idea and asked if she knew any appropriate swim and bike coaches. She suggested he contact Alwyn Barrett for swimming and Harry Shaw for cycling. Both coaches agreed to take us for a trial training session.

Alwyn's trial was first. A former national breaststroke champion and also a national swim team manager, Alwyn ran a successful swim program with national level swimmers. Apparently, on receiving Dad's call, Alwyn thought Dad was probably asking the impossible and suspected that Dad was one of those over-obsessed fathers who wanted his children to achieve something he hadn't achieved in his own life. Dad managed to assure Alwyn that I was driving this, and I was serious in my pursuit of an elite sporting career.

Alwyn invited Clare and I to swim with her squad, the Aquastars, at the Bulleen Swim Centre. It was a fifteen-minute drive towards Melbourne from Eltham. Reportedly, Alwyn thought that we looked like 'superb athletes', given our physiques. We both looked fit and lean. Next to swimmers we looked even leaner, because swimmers tend to carry a little more body fat than specialist runners. I think our appearance gave Alwyn a false impression that we could swim. Once we started swimming though, it became obvious to her that we were not up to the standard of the national junior swimmers. About that first swim session Clare remembers:

She asked us to swim up and back and a minute-and-a-half later we weren't back. Asked us to get a kick board and kick and of course we just kicked on the spot, asked us to do tumble turns and we came up in the same spot.

I just remember struggling. It was so difficult, but we needed to learn to swim, because we were going to win world titles in about eighteen months. There was no time to worry about what we couldn't do.

Despite our debut swim performances Alwyn was impressed. She recalled that we 'continued to hang on for the remainder of the session'. She said I, in particular, 'did not miss a lap', that I was 'frustrated, but a real work horse'. In contrast to Alwyn's younger junior squad members, Clare and I were clearly disciplined and committed. Delighted with our work ethic fortunately, Alwyn agreed to 'give us a try'.

In coaching us, Alwyn aimed to provide constructive sessions, to ensure that we learnt the technique and understood the critical biomechanics of swimming. Most importantly, Alwyn ensured we didn't develop poor technique and simply just bash through the water. She focused on quality and stroke work, rather than volume, which meant that we weren't unnecessarily flogged in the pool to the detriment of our bike and run training. Clare and I were very fortunate that Alwyn was recommended to us. It was a very wise choice as she was invaluable to our swim skill development.

Alwyn had us swim training two hours a day, five days a week. The only days we didn't swim were Wednesday and Sunday. Saturday was sometimes dropped if we were getting a little too tired and needed a sleep in. The sessions required us to be on pool deck at 4.45 a.m., to be stretched, and in the water by 5 a.m. Clare and I gradually learnt to do actual swim sets with warm-up, main set and warm-down; not just to swim laps.

To Alwyn, Clare and I were not simply full of talk. Nor were we wasting our time or energy. Alwyn commented on my work ethic, dedication and focus:

Emma was a particularly coachable person. She listened. She worked. She wanted feedback. All the sort of thing you want from swimmers. When you have young swimmers it [usually] takes twelve months. She was totally dedicated to improving. Nothing was left to chance with Emma. If it is daylight you work, night you sleep. She was obsessive with her training.

She also said I had a 'wicked sense of humour', that I saw everything I did as fun and a challenge, not an impossibility. She said we seemed 'normal, loving girls' who were close to their family, but she also noted that I imposed strict limitations on my life. Improvement was all I cared about. Apparently, when Alwyn watched me compete in the 1993 Australian Sprint Course Triathlon Championships at St Kilda a few months later she, too, began to believe that I could be number one in the world.

With a swim coach on board, Clare and I next met our cycling coach Harry Shaw. Harry was probably about sixty-five years old, very fit and absolutely loved his bike riding. I never really asked Harry about his career, but everyone in the cycling fraternity knew and respected Harry Shaw. He was still racing when we met him, and I think he was always happiest while out on the bike.

Harry lived in Diamond Creek, the next suburb to the north of Eltham, which was of course very convenient for our rides together. I remember our first ride well. We rode from Diamond Creek out through Hurstbridge, past St Andrews and towards King Lake. It was a simple ride, of around 90 minutes and over 600 metres of climbing on hilly roads set in typical Australian bush. We didn't climb King Lake, instead turning at the top of the last hill prior, just after Wild Dog Road. I just followed Harry's wheel and Clare followed me. When we reached the last climb, Harry told me to ride ahead to the top, so I did. I assumed he just wanted to see how I rode. Unknown to me at the time, he didn't think he had ever seen a girl of my age and inexperience ride that well. He was impressed.

Following this 'maiden' ride, Dad received a call from Harry. He told Dad he would like to coach us, but suggested I forget triathlon and take up cycling, that I could be a world champion in the 3 km pursuit on the track, probably the road too. He believed that was almost definite and asked whether we were sure I could be a world champion in triathlon.

Dad relayed Harry's comments to me, but although cycling was an Olympic sport, it didn't interest me. To me, the big problem with cycling was that women did not have the same prestige as men in the sport. There was inequality in everything at that time: prize money, media coverage, prestige and sponsorship. I wasn't interested in being disadvantaged purely for being a woman.

Clare and I now had a swim, bike and run coach. We all sat down and put together a program. I was adamant that I maintain my running and try to qualify to represent Australia as an Athletics Australia team member. I couldn't give up on my childhood dream. To do this I needed to continue the key speed and interval run sessions on Tuesday, Thursday and Saturday. For my run economy and run conditioning I needed to maintain the long run and mid-week semi-long runs. Alwyn had me swimming Monday, Tuesday, Thursday and Friday with Saturday also a 'sometimes' swim day if I wasn't too fatigued from the week's training. Dad was adamant that, against everything we read about triathlon training, we should not ever practise running off the bike. He could not understand why in training we would need to practise running badly. We agreed my run training needed to remain of a high quality. I suggested I ride Monday, Wednesday and Friday, so key run sessions would remain on days without a bike ride and those runs with a bike on the same day would be done a minimum of 3-4 hours after the bike ride. The idea was that my running needed to remain clearly better than everyone else in triathlon.

Around the same time, I set up my bike position. Cyclists, I noticed, sat back on their bikes, using their quads for power. But that position left my legs heavy and overloaded. They felt tired on the days that I ran in the afternoon. On further research, I found that cyclists riding in a time trial position sat further forward on the saddle. I tried a more forward position and lifted my seat height. My legs felt less heavy because I was engaging my glute muscles more than my quads, leaving my legs more ready and able to run. To achieve a more even and efficient gear change, I also tweaked the gearing on the bike, with a 42-53 combination on the front and a full 11-21 on the back including the less common 16 cog. At Harry's instruction, I worked in the small chain ring initially and focused on pedalling efficiency. There was no structured time trial work, just good solid riding, learning the art of selecting the correct gear and sitting in the right position. The other key to my cycle training was limited volume, but always, always working in the hills. Similar to the long Sunday run in Ferny Creek we aimed to use a tough environment to push me to a higher level of efficiency and fitness as the key to outstanding performance. It was around this time we also met Peter Jones of Jones Cycles, the owner of a chain of bike stores in Victoria. Peter became a regular bike training partner and bike equipment advisor.

The underlying principles of the triathlon training program we put together was that it needed to be more challenging and more demanding than triathlon races themselves, we needed more intensity than volume in training, and I needed to out-prepare my competitors with regard to everything to do with triathlons. I learnt as much as I could about everything and everyone.

As is always the case with me, nothing is ever simple. With everything in place, my coach-athlete relationship with Matt became strained. Being a purist run coach he did not approve of all my cycling and swimming. I tried to explain that it was harder to recover from running because of the contact with the ground and that I could recover more quickly from a swim or bike session. As proof I pointed out that since I started cross training, I had spent four months training twice, sometimes three times, a day without injury. I had never had this consistency before. Matt told me that if I was distracted by triathlon, I would not fulfill what I had set out to do in track and field. I kind of knew what he meant. Triathlon was not my original goal in life, but all I ever really wanted was to be an Australian sporting champion and world beater, and if I had to change sports to triathlon I would. I didn't really have an argument with Matt at all, I respected him too much. We just drifted apart. I hoped maybe when I was world champion he would come around and see that I did the right thing for my sporting career. Instead I coached myself. After all I had coached myself my entire life so far. We continued on with the plan and my triathlon dream.

Matt was not alone in his concern. In October 1993, the VIS Track and Field Co-Ordinator, wrote to inform me that if I did not stop competing in triathlons and take my Track and Field Scholarship seriously, she would ensure the VIS removed me from the program. I remained adamant and assured the VIS I was serious about my athletics career. It was quite clear many in athletics did not approve of triathlon and did not view it as a viable sport. They wanted me to give up my triathlon idea, but I really believed I was about to win a World title as a VIS athlete.

To complete the plan, I wrote down a list of sponsors I wanted. I wanted Nike, but that was pretty easy with Dad as one of the bosses at Nike Australia. I also wanted Oakley eyewear, Trek bikes, a car sponsor, a major bank sponsor and nutrition. Dad agreed but pointed out that I needed an airline sponsor and all my race equipment covered. With triathlon that was three sports. I added Qantas to the list and researched the best equipment.

Dad chased up the sponsors for me. I was signed with Oakley almost immediately. Every single major race I have ever won I have worn Oakley eyewear. They became my signature, and to this day I still receive Oakley product. ZIPP wheels were also quick to sign me up. Both companies put me on a small base contract, with bonuses added for each win. I don't think I was expected to win quite as much as I did. My contract sizes grew exponentially over the next season. So much so, I went onto international-sized contracts with the US company owners.

I believed Trek bikes were the best available at the time and not many rode them in Australia. I always wanted to have a point of different as well as race faster than everyone I competed against. Dad wrote to Trek Australia and we were told they do not sponsor athletes, perhaps we should contact the head office in Wisconsin, USA. Dad did, and he was told Trek does not sponsor Non-Americans. I was offended. Who the hell discriminates against Australians?! I couldn't believe that was even a thing.

But I still wanted a Trek bike, so I decided to buy a frame, and use the components from my current bike (Shimano 101, entry level componentry). I needed to irritate Trek USA, and I needed to avoid giving Trek any exposure, because they were not supporting me. We decided to put black electrical tape over every Trek logo on my bike, so when I started winning, and especially when I won the

World Championships, Trek would get no free promotion from me. I just needed the AUD1,800 for the bike frame.

My best chance of a new bike was to win prize money at local triathlons. The plan for the remainder of the 1992-1993 triathlon season was to do well in Victoria and test the competition nationally. There was a really good Victorian triathlon series, with races at rural locations around the state. I signed up and raced in country towns such as Deniliquin (a NSW town close to the Victorian border), Hastings, Benalla and Cobram, winning them all and taking home the prize money of $500 for first in each race. I raced the Victorian Sprint Championships in Ballarat and messed up the bike leg to finish a close second. Jane won the prelude age group race that day, so there was a win in the family at least. With a season's-worth of prize money, I scraped together the cash for the new Trek bike frame. Peter Jones ordered it for me, and we set it up as I liked it. I covered all the logos, knowing that one day Trek USA would notice.

Over that first triathlon season, I also participated in a number of races that were part of a national triathlon series. In those days, Triathlon Australia (TA) had an established series that played an important part in providing consistent race experience, and clear development and elite pathways for all athletes within the sport. I believe the series made an important contribution to the strength and success of the Australian Triathlon team at that time. At the Australian Sprint Triathlon Championships, I narrowly missed the podium by four seconds. I had the fastest run of the day with an average pace of around 3 minutes 15 seconds per kilometre. The Australian Olympic Triathlon Championships, held in Geelong in early 1993, attracted a more representative national field, as well as the national triathlon and mainstream sports media. The televised highlights focus on the athletes who were leading the Daihatsu Australian Triathlon Series point score, such as Bianca Van Woesik and Rina Hill and world class triathlete Brad Beven. I exited the water six minutes down, and was out of contention, but managed to finish fifth overall, showing how strong my bike-run combination was becoming.

I first attracted national triathlon media attention both for my dramatic arrival on the Victorian triathlon scene over the 1992-1993 summer and also for an incident at the Melbourne Classic Triathlon, held at Patterson Lakes on the Mornington Peninsula in March 1993. I was reported to have sworn at a triathlon official, but still to this day, I remain adamant this was neither the case, nor my intention. I raced the 1.5 km swim and 40 km bike well. Bianca Van Woesik was the national series leader and travelled to Victoria probably thinking there was no competition. She could have a soft race for good prize money. Although she was a standout cyclist, I held her on the bike throughout the windy 40 km course. I knew that with a fast 10 km run I could have my first major scalp in triathlon. As I exited the bike to run transition at full pace, there was yelling, but I was focused. Apparently, I was being told to slow down; I am not sure why you would ever be required to slow down in a race ever. As I exited transition, someone grabbed my arm and I shook myself free and told whoever it was to get lost. Unknown to me, an official had grabbed my arm to read the number on it. I was not aware anyone could ever hold you in a race, this had never happened to me in athletics or cross country. At the same time, I was very focused on chasing down the one world-class Australian professional in the race, so I wasn't about to stop and check. I was about 2 minutes 30 seconds down on Van Woesik at the start of the 10 km run, and I believed I could run her down. According to reporter Roger Vaughan writing for *Triathlon Sport* magazine, I displayed 'outrageous running talent' as I made up the 2 minutes on Van Woesik who was also on fire and finished tenth outright.

I was told after the race I had been disqualified, and my hatred of officials who did the wrong thing by athletes and then penalised them just because they could, was reinforced. I appealed the disqualification, but the hearing was a sham because the medal presentations began about ten seconds after the appeal started. Dad made no friends with the officials that day, when it became obvious that they had no interest whatsoever in conducting a fair appeal.

Everyone in triathlon had now heard of Emma Carney.

The setback did not alter my triathlon plans. I concluded the 1992-1993 season determined to compete in all the races of the 1993-1994 national series across Australia and to qualify for the 1994 ITU Triathlon World Championships to be held in Wellington, New Zealand, on the last weekend of November.

Despite the widespread belief I could not combine running with triathlon, I also had a breakthrough track season in 1993 off the back of my first season of triathlon. I won the weekly A Grade 3000 m consistently, with times around 9 minutes 20 seconds. On 25 February 1993, I ran the prestigious NEC meet in Melbourne at Olympic Park. This was an invitation-only Thursday evening, twilight meet with only the best Australian athletes. Everyone knew it was important to run well there, as the Athletics Australia team selectors were watching. I had a light swim on the morning of the race as I didn't want to miss a pool session. On the start line I felt fit. I was in very good shape, and I knew it. I decided to just run along with the leaders. Later, I recorded the splits for each lap in my training diary:

200 m, 33.94 seconds;

600 m, 1 minute 47.16 seconds;

400 m, 1 minute 13.22 seconds;

400 m, 1 minute 13.99 seconds

(resulting in a 1 km split of 3 minutes 1.15 seconds);

400 m, 1 minute 13.54 seconds;

400 m, 1 minute 13.28 seconds;

400 m, 1 minute 13.14 seconds;

400 m, 1 minute 12.16 seconds.

I ran a total time of 9 minutes 7.64 seconds for 3000 m which was a PB and ranked seventh fastest ever in Australia over 3000 m at the time. I finished third on the night. It was a breakthrough run, and I beat most of Australia's top female distance runners.

Suddenly, now that I was running well, I raced with more confidence. Nike had a women's 5 km national three-race series late in the summer. I ran well in all three, running just over 16 minutes on the road and placing in the top three in each race, again against Australia's best distance runners.

About a week after the NEC meet, I received a call from Athletics Australia selector Pam Turney advising me I had been selected for the Australian team for the Seoul International Women's Road Relay to be held on 11 April 1993. An 'Ekiden' relay, teams of six runners would cover the 1988 Seoul Olympics Marathon course, with team members running varying distances between five and ten kilometers. Now an Australian team member, the VIS held off dropping me from their program, but their disapproval continued to bubble along.

Before long, I was off on my first trip as an Australian team member. The other team members were the best female runners in Australia, with a few younger runners like me being exposed to international racing for the first time. Jenny Lund, Kerryn McCann, Sue Malaxos, Maryanne Murray, Jackie Gallagher and Susie Power provided for a strong team combination. As it was my first trip away, the more experienced athletes took it upon themselves to show me how an Australian athlete should behave in order to continue the tradition of Australian athletics. I learnt a lot. Two days before the race, the race officials told us we were all to board buses to drive over the course. Each country was assigned a bus number and boarding time. I took the instruction very seriously and sat in my room checking my watch as the nominated time approached. I thought maybe I was on Australian time, because thirty-minutes later there was still no movement in my teammates room next door. I knocked and they told me to come in. Everyone was resting.

'Don't we have the course recce to go to?' I asked.

I was right. Suddenly everyone was queuing for the toilet and rushing around. Soon, the Australian team entered the lift to go down to the hotel foyer. Jenny Lund led the way. I had always admired her as an athlete. She was one of Australia's top 10,000 m runners. She stepped out of the hotel and straight onto a bus.

'Is this the right bus Jenny?' I asked.

She turned to me and said matter-of-factly, 'it only matters on race day,' before taking a seat at the back. We all followed.

With that an official ran on waving his arms. 'No. No. No Australia! Wrong bus!!' he yelled.

Jenny gave him a very disinterested look and told him we weren't doing any unnecessary walking, because we needed to save our legs to race. She also commented that all the buses go the same way, 'so who cares anyway'. Looking exasperated, the official gave up on us. We stayed put and Jenny turned to me and said, 'See, it never matters.'

As it turned out, the bus ride was a waste of time. After sitting in traffic, we made the Olympic stadium, but the entire Australian team was too bored to carry on. Jenny and a few others managed to convince the other countries on the bus that we should turn around. We all then convinced the bus driver to break rank and turn around too. After that trip, I understood a little better that being an Australian team member required quite a bit of rule bending and non-conforming. I liked that idea.

The last team to arrive at the official hotel was the Chinese team. When we all saw them for the first time at breakfast in the hotel, they looked formidable. I had never been exposed to athletes who looked like this before and couldn't help staring.

'How the hell can you compete against them?' I asked.

No one could answer me.

A lot of questions were raised about the entire team and their appearance. I learnt over time that you just have to race whoever shows up.

Race day came around. As the first runner on the team, I was to run 6 km, starting in the 1988 Olympic stadium. We all had to board the correct bus again, and this time I made sure I was on the right one. I started my warm-up as soon as we reached the stadium. As this was the first time I was competing for Australia, I decided to just run as fast as I could and not screw up, a very simple race plan and I figured I couldn't do any more than that. That is exactly what I did. The Chinese team member took off and the Kenyan ran as far as she could with her. I ran with the bulk of the field behind those two. It was fast. I just ran flat out for 6 km, with an official time of 19 minutes 49 seconds. We all managed to run under the old course record. I was recorded as handing over in ninth, but it was really just one bunch.

We were all really chasing a Chinese athlete who flew in that day, along with all her teammates. They clearly won, and a few months later the entire team decimated every female world record, from the 800 m up to the 10,000 m, in the Chinese National Track and Field Championships. The Chinese athletics team improvement was quite astounding, so much so it shocked the world. There were calls by the world's greatest female distance runners at the time to investigate potential doping. When Wang Junxia became the first woman to break the 30-minute barrier for 10 km, the great Norwegian 10,000 m world champion and world record holder Ingrid Kristiansen, was quoted as saying, 'How can a 20 year old improve her personal best by more than three minutes in less than a year, win the world championship and break the world record? Well she's certainly not eating porridge.' American Lynn Jennings, World Cross Country Champion, apparently broke into tears of anger when she learnt that Wang Junxia crushed the world record by 42 seconds. 'Something is wrong, and it is tragic for the sport,' she was reported to have said. I followed all this in the press and lost a lot of hope of ever being able to compete successfully in athletics. Suddenly triathlon was even more attractive to me as it appeared to be a clean young sport.

Back in Australia, Clare and I continued to run consistently well. In early May I competed in the Victorian Road Relay Championships and ran the fastest leg of the day, clocking 20 minutes 45 seconds for a hilly 6.2 km. For the first time in my senior running career I lined up for the state road race titles on 15 May 1993 as the outright favourite. I won the tactical 10 km Victorian Championship in a reasonable road time of 34 minutes 14 seconds, while Clare finished second. Our one-two family finish attracted mention in a variety of newspapers, even making it into the 'In brief' column of the *Herald Sun*. The then Wesley Principal, D. Glen McArthur, wrote to congratulate Clare and me. Looking to the future he anticipated that I would one day be 'Wesley's second female Olympian' (rower, Jodie Dobson, was the first, having competed at the 1992 Barcelona Olympic Games). Maintaining my winning form through the winter, I also won the state 8 km cross country championships in July.

At the same time, I started to prepare for the 1993-1994 domestic triathlon season. I needed to race well to gain selection for the Australian elite triathlon team for the 1994 ITU World Championships in Wellington, New Zealand. Dad and I decided that to truly be a force in triathlon, I should aim to be international level at two disciplines. It was clear my running was there, but my cycling was improving as well. Harry wanted me to do cycle races. I knew that racing always pushed me to a higher level of skill and fitness when incorporated properly into my training program, so I started to dabble with some tough handicapped road races. Contrary to popular triathlon coaching, I always found a tough road race so much more beneficial than a criterium race. Just the pure brutality of those hours in the saddle forced you to ride smarter and better for fear of being spat off the back of the bunch to trundle home alone. The old-style races had me hanging on and suffering all the way to the finish line and forced me to learn essential skills like how to read the wind direction, how to sit effectively in a bunch to minimize effort, and how to ride hard, recover and attack and go hard again. Relentless races, they left me feeling like my legs were being ripped off. Every time. I learnt so much though, those races helped develop me into the strongest, most fearless bike rider in triathlon.

Along with bike racing, I also used the winter season of duathlon racing to practise transitions and fast runs under pressure. Duathlon formats usually involve a 10 km run, 40 km bike, and 5 km run. Minus the swim, the winter equivalent of a triathlon suited me. My Duathlon racing was clearly ahead of anyone in Australia. With run times of 33-34 minutes for the first run, bike splits close to an hour, and 16 minutes to 16 minutes 30 seconds for the second run, I rivalled the men's finishing times and was unbeaten in the state duathlon series.

Brought together, my running, cycling and duathlon races made for a hectic winter schedule. I competed in and won at the Victorian Road Relay Championships on the first weekend in May, won the first race of the Victorian Duathlon Series on the second weekend, won the Victorian 10 km Road Championship the following weekend, and won the second duathlon on the last. June was slightly slower with a second place at the 4 km Victorian Cross Country Championships and a win at the third duathlon. In July I won the Victorian 8 km

Cross Country Championships and finished second at the 6 km cross country titles. I finished fourth at the New Zealand Cross Country Championships on a hilly course in August and won the fourth duathlon. Of course, I also won the final duathlon of the series in October.

During this time, I also maintained a full training schedule, with around 80-100 km running, 200 km biking and 20-25 km swimming each week. A traditional triathlon coach would say my bike volume was surprisingly low and my run volume was surprisingly high. I found that my run improved my bike, but too much bike destroyed my run speed and efficiency. All my riding was done in the hills, so it was intense. I also rode with a group of faster guys, so we were not doing unnecessary 'junk' kilometres. My training was very specific, and the bike racing fitted in well, mainly tough and intense work in unforgiving winds on dead country roads. People always asked about my training. To start with I was honest and told them my training volumes. I could see no one believed me, so I just started to make numbers up. I didn't really want anyone to know how little I was riding, because I liked to keep people guessing. Also, the balance to me was perfect and I didn't need doubt put into my head. I didn't want to be questioned.

After a winter of tough and consistent swim, bike and run training, and solid duathlon and cross country racing, I started the triathlon season at the famous Noosa Triathlon on 17 October 2013. I was on the radar as a possible triathlon worlds contender, touted as a 'dark horse', but I was still not considered too much of a threat as I was ranked fourth. I was not happy with my result on race day and I didn't think I raced well at all. My swim was poor, I navigated badly, struggling with the low sun reflecting on the water. I exited well down on the lead swimmers. Riding strongly, I got myself into the lead, only to feel ordinary on the run. I finished second to Jackie Hallam (a strong runner who was third in the 1993 Australian Cross Country Championships). We both finished well ahead of third-place getter and pre-race favourite Jackie Gallagher. The fact that I beat the top ranked athlete signalled to the triathlon world that I was an athlete to watch but I still hadn't won. I was annoyed with myself.

Following Noosa, I was invited to participate in the Pepsi Duathlon Cup in Rooty Hill, West of Sydney, after an easy win at the Australian Duathlon Championships in Kew, Melbourne on 24 October. It was supposed to be the first time Jackie Gallagher and I raced a duathlon head to head. Both from a running background, neither of us had been beaten in duathlon format racing.

The race never eventuated, with me winning and Clare finishing second. Jackie pulled out and went home early. It was becoming a bit obvious that the 'known' triathletes were beginning to avoid racing me. I didn't care. I always refused to comment and stayed focused on my plan.

Leading into the next major event, the Nepean Triathlon on 5 December, I had my first taste of the politics and unrest that existed in Triathlon Australia (TA). Ever since Dad, Clare and I had decided we were going to take the sport seriously, we read everything and anything about triathlon, what was going on, and who was who. We were on top of everything about the sport. In those days that meant reading all the magazines. There was no social media. I noticed a new professional triathlete's group was being formed called APTA (Australian Professional Triathletes Association). It seemed to me that all the professional (elite) triathletes were members of this group, so I thought perhaps I should be too. I told Dad about it and he contacted them. Dad recalls that he introduced himself 'as Emma Carney's Dad', but 'much to my surprise I was greeted with a very unenthusiastic and negative response.' His recollection continues:

> I was told the group had never heard of the name Emma Carney, that APTA took no notice of any Victorian race results because Victorian Triathletes could not compete with those from NSW and Queensland and they doubted Emma Carney would ever be good enough to join APTA. I said that she would probably race the Nepean Triathlon and received some sort of response along the lines that he would be interested to see her result but doubted she would be successful. I was extremely annoyed that an organization, self-anointed as the peak body representing the elite triathletes in Australia was so ignorant of any triathlon matters outside of New South Wales and Queensland and that the APTA representative was so dismissive to new triathlon talent.

Dad advised me of his conversation regarding APTA, and I decided there was absolutely no way anyone other than me was going to win the Nepean Triathlon that year.

The Nepean Triathlon is an iconic race, with a tough bike course near the foothills of the Blue Mountains in NSW, west of Sydney. I swam well enough to stay in touch with the lead swimmers, and then unleashed a bike leg that ripped the race apart. Confirming how aggressively I rode, the then Australian sprint triathlon champion, reported that:

Emma Carney caught me about 14 km into the bike, and just out of interest I timed her on a 6 km section through some hills. I couldn't believe it — she put about 50 seconds into me in that 6 km, and that was the last I saw of her. And it wasn't like I was going slowly. I managed about 40-42 kph and I was pretty happy with how the ride went for me.

By the end of the bike leg I had a 2-minute lead over pre-race favourites Jackie Hallam and Jackie Gallagher and put another minute into them on the run. I won by over 3 minutes and claimed the course record.

Following the race, APTA invited me to join but I declined. Dad had decided they were a break-away group from the official national federation (TA), and I didn't need them. Nor did the sport of triathlon. As Dad reasoned:

I thought there seemed to be a lot of odd rules in triathlon that were causing problems. Triathlon had traditionally been an individual event. That is, you swim, bike and run with no help from others. In following this ruling, the bike was supposed to be an individual time trial. The rules of the sport were that you needed to keep an area around you about 10 m long by 5 m wide so there was no gain from 'drafting' or riding in the slipstream of another competitor. You had 10-15 seconds to overtake another competitor and if you failed to do this, you would have a stop-go penalty issued by a draft buster (an official monitoring the race on a motorbike). There were so many obvious problems with this rule — cramped bike courses forced athletes too close together, athletes had different ideas as to the imaginary length of 10 m by 5 m around them and with competitors out-numbering draft busters, it really depended on luck as to who was caught and who wasn't.

Triathlon's world governing body, the ITU was also trying to prove to the International Olympic Committee (IOC) that it was a sport worthy of Olympic inclusion, and one requirement was that a sport could enforce its specific rules. As such, there was increasing pressure from the ITU to have the non-drafting rule dropped and draft-legal racing introduced. Les McDonald, ITU president was rightfully improving the professional nature of triathlon by creating an international federation that had control of its sport and its rules in the best interests in its athletes.

The unrest this caused in the sport among athletes and established race organisers was very widespread. To add fuel to the unrest, the World Triathlon

Corporation, who ran the famous Ironman event in Kona, was very against draft-legal racing. Groups such as this also believed the Olympics were not important, decided their event was bigger than the sport of triathlon itself and saw themselves as the international triathlon federation. Legal battles ensued and Ironman and the ITU threatened to sue each other three or four times. During this unrest break away groups such as APTA also appeared. It was madness. It was also very pointless in-fighting.

APTA didn't last long fortunately. It stifled itself with its own negativity and self-importance.

Dad and I decided to try and keep out of the politics as much as we could. I just wanted triathlon in the Olympics, and I didn't want to get involved. Both of us underestimated quite how difficult this would be as my triathlon career continued.

In November 1993, I was selected by Athletics Australia to represent Australia at an international event for the second time. The 'Chiba International Ekiden' held in Chiba, Japan, was highly regarded, and Athletics Australia always sent strong teams over. The first runner for Australia, Michelle Dillon, ran well to put us in the top group. Kerryn McCann ran next and cemented our position in second place, behind the Japanese team. Russia were in third. Race day was windy, really windy. I started my 5 km leg with a tail wind. That lasted for 100 metres. A 180-degree turn put me straight into a block headwind for the next 4.9 km. I decided I would run as I did in Seoul, just go flat out. I couldn't do anything about the wind, so I thought the best thing to do was ignore it. I took the changeover, used the first 100 m with the tail wind to control my breathing, then turned into the headwind and ran like I stole something. I ran as fast as I could for the entire race. I managed to record the fastest time for my leg and in doing so, pull away from the Russians in third and close the gap on the Japanese in first. The Australian team finished third overall, which was the best an Australian women's team had placed. Because I won my leg, I was chauffeur driven to the finish line and fortunately avoided the slow bus trip back to the hotel.

Interestingly, following the Chiba Relay race result, the VIS Track and Field Co-Ordinator wrote to congratulate me on my performance. I thought perhaps the VIS were going to accept me combining triathlon with athletics. Very naïve of me.

Maintaining a strong form, I mostly placed well in the Athletics Australia

Mobil Grand Prix events I contested over the 1993-1994 athletics season. On 28 January I ran a slow 9 minutes 36 second 3000 m in Canberra. I flew in too late and messed up my preparation, so I hired a car and drove to Sydney for a 1500 m Grand Prix two days later. I managed to run a more respectable 4 minutes 23.11 seconds. At the Australian Athletics Championships in 1994, I placed second against a very competitive field in the 3000 m. Athletics Australia then selected me for the 1994 World Cross Country team to go to Budapest in March.

At the same time, I still needed to compete in every national selection race on the Triathlon Australia calendar, just to make sure the TA Selection Committee knew I existed. I was not entirely confident they were looking at athletes south of the NSW border. At the first event held on 12 December in Port Stephens, NSW, the field was decimated by the tide on the swim leg, and I had the first mechanical problem of my triathlon career on the bike leg. I ran home hard to finish second to Jackie Hallam. I was annoyed with myself the entire trip back home to Melbourne. The second race of the series was held in Adelaide on 16 January 1994. I had a solid swim, tore apart the field on the bike and ran away from everyone to finish over 2 minutes ahead of second place. That was better! After fitting in the Athletics Australia Grand Prix events in Canberra and Sydney, I knew I had some run speed, so I felt confident when I lined up for the Australian Sprint Triathlon Championships in Canberra on 12 February. It consisted of a 750 m swim, 20 km bike and 5 km run around Lake Burley Griffin. I won my first national triathlon title easily. While on the run course, perhaps with just over 1 km to go, Rob De Castella was standing on the sidelines, cheering me on. I almost stopped in my tracks. I was amazed that he even knew who I was.

A week after the sprint triathlon titles Clare and I flew to Wellington, New Zealand, to race the Olympic distance national championships there. The race was to be run over the proposed 1994 World Championship course. We wanted to see what the course was like, see how we were faring, look at what we needed to prepare ourselves for, and just get used to travelling to Wellington. When Clare and I competed in the New Zealand Cross Country Championships the year before I finished fourth. It seemed that flying in on the Friday left me feeling tired. We decided to see whether flying in a few days earlier improved how we felt. We just wanted to make sure our preparation for the World Championships was perfect.

On race day, I found the swim in Wellington's Lambton Harbour really cold and choppy. I couldn't see the swim markers and lost time with my inexperienced sighting in the rough water. I found the course on the bike really suited my riding strength while the run was flat with no real concerns apart from wind. I ended up finishing second, but I learnt a lot from the experience. It surprised me that no other Australians bothered to practise racing the course.

Our next two races, the third event in the National Triathlon Series and the World Cross Country Championships, were both in mid-March. The triathlon was in Devonport, Tasmania on 13 March. We both got through the swim and bike, but during the run I collapsed apparently with food poisoning and finished in Devonport Hospital. Clare also threw up and then pulled out at almost the same place on the run a few minutes behind me.

With no time to recover we rushed back home the same day and started packing for the trip to Europe. The Athletics Australia team left for Heathrow London on Tuesday, 15 March. While the team recovered from the flight at Brighton, we had a small race for a bit of a hit out. The conditions were terrible. My Grandparents on both sides came to visit me at the team hotel and also came to the race. Grandad White, I think, still viewed Australians as convicts and didn't really hide his disappointment that I was racing for Australia. In contrast, Dad's parents, Grandma and Grandad Carney, were as I remembered them; completely in love with anything Australian. They chain smoked inappropriately as I raced.

On Sunday, 20 March, with the World Championships scheduled for the following Saturday, the whole Australian Cross Country team flew to Budapest, Hungary. We stayed just out of Budapest and trained lightly at an Olympic training venue until two days before the world titles. When we moved to a hotel right near the course, things became a lot more intense. The course was at Kincsem Park, which seemed to be a horse racetrack. It was flat, but at one end there was a massive tree lying across the course. I assumed that we were supposed to be able to jump over the tree, which seemed like it was almost up to my shoulders when I first saw it. After a bit of practice, I seemed to be able to clear it at speed. I just hoped I didn't trip on the approach.

Race day came around, and the Australian team officials briefed us on the race start. Each country was assigned a 1.5 m wide square marked out in chalk, in which all their team members had to line up. The open women's team for Australia had six runners. It was a tight fit with three rows of two runners. I was assigned to the front row for Australia. With all the countries lined up in their chalk boxes, World Cross Country Championships have a very wide start line, over 500 m. The first 1 km is generally a sprint flat out for positioning, and the remainder of the race is just a mad run for the line. A bad start can ruin your race immediately, but you can gain or lose 20-30 places over 10 metres at any stage of the race and even more places towards the finish. As a consequence, your only option is to run flat out at every stage of the race, which is what I did. I managed to finish 68th in a field of 147 finishers, which was a respectable finish among the Australians in the women's 6 km event. The race again proved that I could compete internationally and did not crack under the pressure of intense competition. I wasn't overly impressed with my result, but at least I was one of the stronger members of the Australian team.

It was the first time I represented Australia at a World Championship level, and I was given my Athletics Australia representative number AA #700. It was also the first time I spent such a long time overseas preparing for one event. I learnt a lot about tapering, adjusting nutrition with foreign foods and mental preparation.

Once back in Australia I had a month to prepare for the final National Triathlon Series event in Mooloolaba, Queensland. Interestingly, Erin Baker of New Zealand flew across to race. Erin was in the twilight of her career but had been a trailblazer in the early days of triathlon racing; a tough competitor, and intolerant to losing. She managed to beat me out of the water, then sat in a pack of male riders to stay away from me on the bike. I knew she was doing this because my cycling training partner Peter Jones was in that group of male riders, all drafting in a non-drafting race. She gained a lot of time and I had no possible way of catching her, although I did manage to get within 40 seconds of her by the finish. She won, and it became blatantly obvious to me you cannot enforce non-drafting racing. I have never really had much respect for her since.

At the close of the 1993-1994 triathlon season, Jane, Clare and I all qualified for the World Championship team. I was in the elite female team, Clare the junior elite team and Jane in her age group. It was time to fine-tune our preparation, so that we could take on the World Titles and win on debut on the international scene.

4. Rookie World Champion

Having been selected for the World Championships, it was expected I would race ITU events internationally, because that was what everyone did. I had no intention of doing this, instead opting to make my ITU debut at the World Championship itself. I wanted to keep working on my weaknesses without public scrutiny. Also, everyone knew a younger athlete racing and travelling the circuit can tire by season's end. I wanted to turn up to the world championships fresh. No other ITU race was as important to me. I wanted to win this world title, this year, and to arrive with maximum impact. I wanted to race the circuit as the World Champion in 1995, the following year. No one had done that before, debut and win a world title.

I liked that; stuff that hasn't been done before always appeals to me.

Dad was still working on sponsors, and it had come time to negotiate a Nike sponsorship. As Dad was a Nike boss, he couldn't exactly negotiate a deal for me. We engaged a Sports Management Company 'Advantage International' and my manager was Brian Cooney. Brian met with Nike marketing manager Ben Buckley. It was agreed I would receive a base fee, which would increase in year two with a bonus payment if I won the 1994 elite ITU title at Wellington. Dad always maintained that both Nike and my manager never really believed I would win, so the deal was seen as a bit of a joke, especially as I was also the boss's daughter.

They didn't know I had never been so serious. I was adamant I was going to win, I expected it.

I was meticulous in my preparation for the World Championships. Clearly the swim remained my greatest concern. My times were improving. By January 1994 I had reduced my 100 m splits by more than 15 seconds, equivalent to more than 3 minutes off over 1500 m in a standard Olympic distance triathlon. But swimming in a triathlon involved more than faster pool splits. Alywn believed that I needed to focus on the swim start, 'to be able to sprint for 200 m to keep up with the girls and sit on their tail.' My pool work was progressing well, but it was very different having to battle and fight in the first few hundred metres of an open-water swim event. It was also obvious I needed to develop open water skills and understand the various intricacies of tides, water chop, drafting and navigation. In triathlons with sheltered swims I exited the water under a minute down but on a bad day with water chop and tides I lost larger chunks of time. That was clear from the swim at the New Zealand National Championships over the Wellington course itself.

It was at this point of my preparation that a wonderful and generous man, Garth Prowd, provided me with some valuable guidance. I owe him so much with regard to my open-water swim development. I met Garth at the Noosa Triathlon in 1993. It is now the largest triathlon event in the southern hemisphere due to his efforts. At the time, Garth was toying with the idea of setting up an event company, because he could see the potential of combining multisport events with triathlon, starting with his beloved Noosa Triathlon.

Garth cared a lot for the athletes who raced his events. I can't remember who contacted who, but I expect Garth rang Dad one day and told him we needed to spend some time in Noosa learning the skills of open-water swimming. This offer to me was a no-brainer. Noosa is one of the nicest locations in the world, just an hour's drive north of Brisbane on the Sunshine Coast. I was always keen to spend more time in Noosa, but to have dedicated open-water swim training was an opportunity both Clare and I took on eagerly.

For two weeks from 19 June to 3 July 1994 we stayed in Noosa, with Garth working specifically on our open-water swimming. On the evening we arrived I showed Garth the program I had written for our stay. He took one look and told me I could fit my training in around what he had planned, and to be at his Sunshine Beach home at 6 a.m. the next morning. We would run through the National Park then swim. Trained well by my former run coach Matt, Clare and I diligently turned up 10 minutes early. He always reminded me that a coach should never be left waiting and told us that he would only ever wait 1 minute for an Olympic Champion and 2 minutes for a World Champion. As I was neither at this stage, I was always early for every coach.

Garth had a few mates assembled, who were going to give us a thrashing in the water. He had also dragged his twin daughters Sally and Megan along. They must have been only about twelve years old. I'm not sure their enthusiasm to run and swim at 6 a.m. was as great as their Dad's, but they got stuck into the session too. As Clare and I knew the National Park well we took off, once Garth explained where we were going. After about 12 km we all regrouped on Noosa main beach.

Pointing towards the Noosa National Park entrance, Garth said we were going to swim past there. It looked like a long way. Struggling out past the waves we managed to stay with Garth by following his feet. It felt like we swam straight out from the beach for ages. I had never swum this far in open water (outside a race situation) before and started to feel a little uneasy. I knew for sure Clare would be too. Looking to the right as I took a breath, I could see that we had passed the National Park entrance and were swimming alongside the last few beaches of the headland. I was concerned that we were running out of solid land should we need to abort the swim. I felt like I was swimming in the open ocean. Panicking, I jumped on Garth, pulling his legs and forcing him to stop swimming.

Garth looked surprised. Sally and Megan swam up to us too.

'Garth, where are we going?' I asked.

'Dunno, just having a swim in the ocean,' he replied. I remember being envious of how relaxed he was. I looked around and there were some buoys joined with rope between us and the shore.

'What are they marking?' I asked.

'Shark nets.'

'Garth, aren't we on the wrong side of them, shouldn't they be between us and the open ocean, not us and the shore?? What the hell, Garth?!' I yelled in a panic.

'I don't reckon they work anyway. They just kill turtles. We should check them.'

'I'm bloody scared of deep water,' I blurted. Clare agreed, so did Sally and Megan.

Garth then looked a bit perplexed. He told me that triathlon swimming was all in deep water and how did I think I was going to avoid swimming in it? I explained that I was fine in deep water in a race scenario, but I wasn't fine with swimming 'free range' in an ocean on the wrong side of shark nets. Realising that none of us were joking, Garth gave in to the four swimmers with him who wanted desperately to return to shore. I swam quickly, not wanting to be the slowest of the human shark bait I was convinced we had become. Back on the sand, Garth told me I swam fine. I don't think he realised I was swimming fast because I feared for my life. After what I considered to be an epic swim of survival, Garth focused on specific techniques closer to the safety of the beach. Whenever he ventured out a little further, we all jumped on his legs to stop him. It was a wonder we didn't drown him at times.

Clare and I learnt many new swim skills during our two weeks in Noosa. Garth showed us how to enter the water for a beach start. Wading through the water required large steps, swinging our legs out and over the water while using a wide arm action to maintain balance as we ran into the surf. We learnt that once wading became too difficult and we could no longer lift our legs high enough to wade (normally about waist depth), we were to porpoise dive through the shore break. When this was no longer possible because it was too deep, we were told to dive under the waves, and grab the sand to hold position and to simultaneously avoid being pushed back to shore by the relentless power of the shore break. Along with beach starts, we also learnt how to read the swell and time our breathing so that we filled our lungs with air rather than salty water. There were many other skills, like how to add navigation into our stroke effectively, when to kick to avoid the pull back of a retreating wave while swimming back into the shore, and how to body surf into the beach. Garth also taught us about rips (strong currents on the shore) and how to use sand banks and shallow areas of water to really get an advantage by running as far as possible off a beach start.

Dad recalls Garth updating him on our progress:

He told me that Emma and Clare were the best female athletes he had coached. He and his mates normally run hard enough to make sure those with them work hard prior to the open water swim. Garth said he wasn't able to run fast enough to keep up with them, and what was even more amazing, both Clare and Emma didn't even look like they had run more than a light jog while he struggled.

When we returned to Melbourne in early July, I felt a lot more confident with open-water swimming and had everything covered in my preparation. All that was needed now was consistency. Naturally, as is always the case with sport, there was a hiccup in my preparation. I managed to develop an injury. The final training block leading into my first major triathlon championships was heavily interrupted.

All my life I have had lower leg, calf and Achilles problems. This time it was an acute Achilles injury with inflammation, soreness and irritation in the area. It started with what seemed like tendonitis but just hung around far too long. Some basic mistakes led to the injury. Firstly, I think my calves and lower legs were tight due to the beach and sand running at Noosa. Secondly, I had been away from my masseur, Garry Miritis. Used by anyone in athletics who wanted to be anything, he kept everyone going and treated their injuries. Those in the know trusted no one else. His massages hurt like hell, and no one ever looked forward to their treatment, but no one missed their weekly torture.

I only really had overuse injuries when I didn't have a weekly Garry Miritis treatment as part of my routine, which was the case at Noosa. With the increased tightness of my lower legs and no Garry massage, my Achilles flared up. I dread and hate soft tissue injuries, I have always preferred to break a bone than stir up a tendon or muscle. Bones heal, tendon soreness hangs around for ages. There are conflicting views on how to treat them, but mine generally respond to little. I have tried everything: heel raises, hot and cold treatment, magnets, ice, decompression chambers, cortisone, anti-inflammatory creams and tablets, sleeping in a leg brace — everything. Even rest doesn't seem to work.

I first noticed soreness in the Achilles in late July and didn't run again consistently until mid-September. That was around 6-8 weeks off running, at a time when I should have been building for the November World Championships. This could have been a major problem, but I managed to deal with the setback well, because a year earlier I fortunately received some very good advice from the great Rob De Castella. He told me that as an elite athlete I should never wait until I was 100 per cent fit to race, otherwise I would never race. Managing problems and injuries was part of being a world class athlete. It was how I managed setbacks that would set me apart from everyone else. I took this on and focused on what I could do to prepare myself. Tentatively, I started light jogging in October 1994. As my major race approached, I started to add some carefully managed speed intervals to my run program. I remained on top of things mentally because fortunately, my preparation elsewhere was almost flawless. It wasn't panic stations, yet.

Just as I cautiously resumed my run training the VIS wrote advising that because I was competing in triathlons, they were stopping my Track and Field Scholarship. I wasn't taking my athletics career seriously enough for them. I was disappointed, unsure as to why the VIS didn't deem it worth supporting my goal to become a world champion. Dad told me to ignore the letter and respond only by winning the championships. I found the situation frustrating and sad. I had a lot of respect for Australian sport and I wanted to be recognised as a Victorian sporting champion by organisations such as the VIS. This was my first real taste of the backlash I would receive for simply being different from the norm, and for doing things my way.

My Achilles still didn't feel great, but we had planned to compete in two triathlons in the lead up to the World Championships. At this late stage, I would have to force myself into race fitness through them. I found racing always pushed me to a higher level of fitness; Dad referred to it as 'blowing away the cobwebs.' Clare and I flew back up to the Sunshine Coast for the Noosa Triathlon on Sunday, 30 October. We trained in Noosa for a week and Garth ran us through some more open-water swim sessions. I familiarised myself with the bike course while also treating my fragile Achilles carefully with the sand running. I felt pretty good, but I knew I was under done. Ideally, I should have had another race prior to Noosa, but anything earlier and my Achilles would not have survived.

This was the second time I contested the Noosa Triathlon. The experts still did not see me as the favourite, but for the first time I was invited to a pre-race press conference. Race day came around and the weather was warm. I swam well, rode ordinarily for me as I felt out of race practice, and ran better than the previous year. But I was disappointed with the result. My Achilles played on my mind all through the bike, and while I closed the gap on the leader — Sarah Harrow of New Zealand — I again didn't win. In hindsight, 'not winning' was probably a blessing in disguise, because everyone then wrote me off as a contender for the world title four weeks later. I told no one about the injury, so everyone thought a race fit Emma Carney was out there getting beaten into second.

In contrast to me, Clare raced well. She had a massive improvement on the previous year and finished fourth overall, the only other female to run within a minute of my time. She was obviously on track to win the World Junior Title, but TA still didn't seem to rate either of us. We were basically seen as team member fill-ins from Victoria, who really didn't know what they were doing.

Clare and I stayed in Noosa for a further week to work on our open-water swimming and attend a triathlon clinic with Dave Scott. Dave Scott is a big name in the triathlon world, one of the 'Big 4', including himself, Mark Allen, Scott Tinley and Scott Molina, who thrashed each other famously at iconic early triathlons around the world. On meeting Dave, he asked how I had raced, and I told him I came second and wasn't happy. Apparently, his thoughts on Clare and me were that we 'possessed raw talent' and 'the right mindset'; he believed we had what only 'a select number of athletes' have, the 'will power to prevail'.

The training camp was interesting. It was actually the first time Clare and I spent time with another triathlete and gave us our first chance to listen to the views of a coach with triathlon experience. I knew more about his rival, Mark Allen, as he had been a Nike athlete, but I respected Dave and read a lot about him as well. I was very keen to listen to his ideas about training, because he was a very successful and experienced triathlon competitor with a tough mindset. I liked a number of his sessions and incorporated some of his ideas into my training, although he focused more on ironman volumes. The respect he showed towards me as a triathlete was also great. He didn't dismiss me and my big goals. He understood them. It was nice, especially with such a big race coming up.

Returning from Noosa to Melbourne, I fine-tuned and sharpened my bike time trial work with some 40 km motor-paced sessions with Harry. We had to keep an eye out for Police patrol cars on Plenty Road near Whittlesea, because riding behind a motor bike is apparently illegal. Harry seemed to think that was a minor issue when a world title win was on the coaching agenda. I of course agreed with Harry's commitment to my cause. I was sure the Police would understand too; fortunately, we were never caught.

Two and a half weeks out from the World Championships, I managed to catch a cold and had a few forced days off training. I was told that athletes tend to become ill leading into major championships, as their high levels of fitness affect their immune system. I again concentrated on remaining positive, staying strong in my own self-belief. Light training was on the agenda, as my fitness wasn't going to improve but I could possibly become sicker if I pushed myself too hard. I recovered enough to race our last planned event. Part of the local series, it was a sprint triathlon in Brighton, a bayside suburb of Melbourne. I raced well, won easily, and spent most of my time trying to catch as many male competitors as I could out on the run.

I felt prepared.

Dad didn't tell me at the time, but at work one day during these final few weeks, Ben Buckley (marketing manager at Nike) asked Dad if he thought I would win the World Championships. Dad of course told him, 'Yes, definitely,' and asked why Ben asked him that. Ben explained that he hadn't taken the sponsorship seriously and hadn't budgeted for my bonus payment. Dad promptly told him to 'find it'.

On Sunday, 20 November, a week out from the World Championships, Clare and I flew to Wellington. Mum and Dad managed to convince Grandma and Grandad White to fly over from England to watch us race. Grandad had finally accepted that we were racing for Australia. Dad told him we would win world titles, so as you can imagine, he and Grandma wanted to see that, regardless of who we were racing for. They visited Australia first and Mum and Dad took them to Noosa as a bit of a prelude to New Zealand. Grandad actually warmed to Australia, was amazed the beaches had such nice sand (unlike the pebbles at many beaches in the UK), and referred to it as 'Paradise'.

The original Australian Triathlon team selected for the World Championships was announced way back on 19 May 1994. The men's elite team included Brad Beven, Tim Bentley, Miles Stewart, Simon Knowles and Matt Braban. The women's elite team consisted of Michellie Jones, Jackie Hallam, Bianca Van Woesik, Jackie Gallagher and me. Since then, the ITU had announced that Wellington would probably be the last world titles with a non-drafting bike leg, which caused a backlash among the established triathletes. I didn't particularly understand the argument, because if it was to be the last event of its type, I thought they would want to compete, not boycott the race. Regardless of the lack of logic, the stand-off gained momentum. One athlete alleged to be disappointed with the impending rule change was Australia's Michellie Jones. The current ITU World Champion, Michellie in fact won both the 1992 and 1993 World Championships. Michellie and I had not yet raced head to head. I think she was the first person in the world to work out I was going to be a tough competitor to beat. Of course, she was a hot favorite for Wellington, but she ended up pulling out, citing a foot injury. With Michellie out of the team (TA added first reserve Rina Bradshaw), I knew that when I won the race, everyone — including Michellie — would say I won because the current world champion was missing. I was disappointed. It was frustrating. I just wanted to make sure I was the reigning world champion when I did eventually race her. That was the best and only thing I could do now.

During the week leading up to the race, we trained by ourselves, and had a few team commitments. We were issued with our team uniform. My tracksuit was too big as usual, but the race suit fitted well, which was a nice surprise. Having run for Australia, I had worked out that if your uniform doesn't fit, there is not much you can do to fix the problem. To top the uniform off we were all given an Akubra hat. I was a little embarrassed by this, after all we were triathletes not bushmen. The Australian team stayed together at a place called Weir House. Clare and I roomed together and kept to ourselves. We didn't really know anyone else because we were so new to the sport. I was disappointed I wasn't invited to the official race press conference, but Dad reminded me I hadn't competed in an ITU race yet. I was still really surprised no one had worked out I was going to win. In my mind it was a definite result.

All I wanted to do during the week prior to the race, was swim the course every day to get used to it. A one lap course of 1500 m, it headed 500 m out to the first right turn, 250 m across and about 750 m back into transition. Clare and I swam it every day, practising in our wetsuits and getting used to the icy cold, messy

66

and very choppy waters of Lambton Harbour. I also rode the bike course most days, familiarising myself with each turn, climb, descent and flat section, looking for places where I could possibly ride away from my competitors. There was a decent climb called Brooklyn Hill. It was apparently going to break the field up. Compared to the relentless hills of Eltham and King Lake, it was a mere bump. The only concern was the wind. I liked tough windy conditions, but Wellington was experiencing some horrific winds that week, so much so, the ITU issued a warning a few days out from the race to avoid riding, because it was thought the gusts might throw athletes off their bikes. The run course was simple and flat, out and back twice along the waterfront. Again, the only concern was the wind. I knew I was fast in blustery wind though, because of my win for Athletics Australia in the Chiba Ekiden road relay a year earlier.

Race day arrived. Windy conditions were predicted, and the weather bureau was correct. I had already decided I wasn't going to worry about anything I couldn't control. The junior women's race started at 7.15 a.m., so Clare was off before me. TA had moved the elite men's and women's team to the International Hotel closer to the start, and we could watch the results of the day. I remember watching Clare race. The race start was almost at first light and the water in the harbour did not look at all inviting. I remember feeling a bit sorry for her. Regardless of this, Clare was focused. She swam well, exiting the water in fifth place. I saw her return to transition in the lead off the bike and then run away from everyone to win the Junior World Title. When she crossed the line, I smiled and knew I had to win now. We couldn't go home with half a job done, and I couldn't go home the family loser!

The elite women's race was the last race of the day, with a 10.25 a.m. start. Marshalling pre-race, I focused on what I needed to do, minimise the damage of the swim, bike hard and run harder. That was the plan. Nice and simple. My mindset was that if anyone could stay with me, they were going to go to hell and back, so good luck to them! My race plans were generally always like that.

The swim began with a sprint from a deep-water start. The messiest start possible. We all wore full-length wetsuits the water was so cold. This was to my benefit. Wetsuits made you more buoyant, and as I tended not to float very well, it helped. I remember focusing on the task at hand. Making sure I swam as fast as I could I fought hard to get on the feet of the front group in the swim out to the first turn buoy. I did and exited the water well, entering transition one (swim-to-bike) in the top ten.

Things were on track.

Out on the bike I got myself to the front as we headed out onto a highway section only about 5 km into the 40 km course. As I rode, I could tell my competitors were trying to work out who the hell I was. There was a 180-degree turn before we headed back towards the City of Wellington and the hilly section of the course that had the all-important Brooklyn Hill climb. I was riding with the current race leader Sabine Westoff of Germany approaching the turn. My presence threw her, and she looked at me puzzled, then rushed the turn, entering it too tightly I thought. When you enter a 180-degree turn tightly, you tend to exit badly and either potentially run out of road to complete the turn, or re-correct too tightly and bring yourself down. Sabine did the latter. Because I had anticipated the fall, I kept clear, rode wide and navigated safely around her.

I was now clearly in the lead, a little earlier than I had expected, but a nice surprise.

As I rode towards Brooklyn Hill, Sarah Harrow of New Zealand overtook me. She put herself in front of me, and I darted out of her slipstream, aware the Kiwis would love to have me disqualified for drafting. This was after all the last non-drafting world title, so competitors were still not allowed to gain assistance by sitting in the slipstream of other riders. Sarah was riding strongly, and I thought going a little too hard just prior to the major climb of the day. She gapped me, maybe putting 20 m between us. I had no idea where the rest of the field was; I didn't really care, and I wasn't going to waste time looking. I avoided looking behind me when racing.

At the bottom of Brooklyn Hill, Sarah was ahead of me. On hitting the hill, I immediately started to chew up her lead. She changed down to an easier gear, while I just stood up to climb. As a result, I remained in a larger gear and climbed a lot faster. On that all-important climb, I built a lead that was never challenged and rode the rest of the bike course flat out, descending fast and time trialling like my life depended on it. At the completion of the bike leg I had recorded the fastest time of the day. I entered the second transition with over a minute's lead.

With just the run to go, the race was really over. I ran hard, just to make sure I won and built up a lead which saw me with the world title by the largest margin ever in the history of the sport of triathlon. No man or woman, from the first World Championships in 1989 to 2009 when the World Triathlon Series (the World Championships became the World Series Grand Final, and the Grand Final winner was not necessarily the winner of the Series) was introduced, has matched my winning margin. I recorded the fastest run and bike split of the day and won by over 2 minutes. I managed to pull off what we had set out to do as a family just eighteen months ago. No siblings have ever been able to replicate the dual ITU world title wins to this day.

In my mind, I had planned everything about that day. What I hadn't planned was everyone looking at me as I ran down the finish chute. I felt really embarrassed. I had never had that many people look at me at once before, and I could hear comments like, 'Who is that?' It was an odd combination, reigning elite World Champion but completely unknown to the sport. Despite the upset, the triathlon world welcomed their rookie World Champion home.

While I took the win, Dad encountered something else for which we hadn't planned. The ITU generally issued passes to the finish area to the parents of athletes expected to win. No one expected either Clare or me to win, so Mum and Dad had no passes. Fortunately, Dad wasn't the type to be stopped by red tape. When Clare approached the finish line, he thought nothing of it and tried to enter the finish area. Security promptly stopped him. 'My daughter is about to win the World Title, it is unexpected, so I have no pass. Please let me in,' Dad remembers saying desperately. The large security guy didn't look too convinced but gave him the benefit of the doubt and told him to remain towards the back, away from the cameras. Dad just pushed past and celebrated with Clare. Of course, just a few hours later, as I approached the finish line, Dad was back. He confronted the same security guard, 'You won't believe it. My other daughter is about to win the elite World Title. No one expected it,' he tried to explain. He was right. Security didn't believe him. Fortunately for Dad, someone on the inside saw him and dragged him in. Much to the security guard's surprise, Dad wasn't lying, and congratulated a second daughter on her win that day. Apparently, Dad thanked him on the way out.

When I crossed the line, I gave Dad a hug and being an Aussie I promptly and purposely pretended I didn't know who New Zealand Prime Minister Jim Bolger was, just for a laugh. Fortunately, he found it funny too.

Unfortunately, and despite Dad's efforts, there wasn't much time to celebrate as I was taken off for post-event drug testing. It was standard policy for all ITU winners to provide urine samples for post-event testing for illegal substances. It took me ages to pee. I had obviously dehydrated myself racing. When I returned, the crowds had started to dissipate. My drawn-out drug test also delayed the post-event press conference, which was a problem, because suddenly everyone wanted to talk to me. I basically had my own press conference with the world's triathlon media. Everyone was surprised I had won. I didn't know why no one had picked up my obvious ability to win. One reporter actually said, 'Look, we don't know anything about you.' I didn't know where to start with that.

The official ITU presentations were the same evening. I met ITU President Les McDonald, and ITU Vice President Loreen Barnett for the first time. These two individuals were absolutely instrumental in the professional development of triathlon as a sport. At a time when international triathlon was full of in-fighting, Les and Loreen shaped the circuit into the Olympic Sport it is today. They were two quite different people. Les was the confrontational leader who wouldn't back down from a fight and Loreen was quiet and reserved and never raised her voice or said anything untoward about anyone.

Les could polarize people. A union leader from the north of England, he emigrated to Canada and was one of the pioneers to develop Whistler as a world-class destination for skiers, he himself being a great skier. I got along very well with Les, because he was very similar to my Dad. He stood for what he believed in, maintained high standards and was always, always committed to equality for women. His Grandma had been a suffragette and she drummed into him from a very early age that women must always be treated equally. As a consequence, Les had zero tolerance for inequality for women especially on the triathlon circuit. Les couldn't run the ITU on his own though. I don't believe the sport would have progressed as much as it did worldwide without Loreen Barnett as Vice President. I am sure Loreen spent a lot of time behind the scenes tirelessly 'steadying the ITU ship'. Combined, the contributions of both Les and Loreen meant that ITU triathlon developed into a professional sport, worthy of Olympic inclusion, and ensured equality in all areas for women; prizemoney, TV exposure, race distances, everything. Triathlon was thirty years ahead of the world in this regard. To end his legacy, Les McDonald was adamant that he would only pass the leadership over to a female leader. True to his word, he did; to Marisol Casado of Spain in 2008. When Marisol became President of the ITU, she was the only female leader of an Olympic Sport and became one of the few female IOC Members, proving that an organization built on principles of equality will retain those throughout time.

At this point in time though, I met Les and Loreen quietly with a brief 'Hello', as they welcomed me to the sport of triathlon. It was a nondescript meeting of triathlon leaders, for whom I would develop a deep respect over the next few years. What was most pressing to me at the time, was the fact that I was a little overwhelmed at the amount of attention I received everywhere I went. I had not foreseen this part of my world title win.

Clare and I returned to Australia to be greeted by national television cameras as we exited customs at Melbourne's Tullamarine Airport. We became the lead story in most free-to-air television sports news segments that evening. Nationwide, newspapers also reported on our results. We were flat out for the next month with media commitments, from TV specials, to print and all types of stories covering our world championship winning feats. We were also flooded with letters of congratulation. The recognition was nice to receive. Particular mention should be made of Australian Prime Minister John Howard writing me a personal letter of congratulation. Wesley College was also quick to again congratulate us, with letters from both the then principal Glen MacArthur and also Bruce Gregory, a long-time supporter from our school days.

I asked Dad to follow up on Trek USA, because I thought surely now that I had won a world title they would at least respond. I was correct. Trek did respond to Dad's letter, but just congratulated me and told me they were pleased I liked their bikes. I told Dad I really liked the feel of the Trek bike, and I was clearly riding the best in the world at that time, so I didn't really want to ride another brand. We decided I would continue to race on the Trek bike through 1995 with the Trek logo covered in black tape, to see if we could irritate them into sponsoring me.

Amongst the accolades, interestingly, was an article in Melbourne's *Herald Sun* newspaper, which claimed that I was a VIS athlete and stated that the VIS was very pleased with my result. Dad followed this up, asking if I had been dropped or not. He was told that perhaps the VIS could find some 'associated' support for my triathlon career. I went along with it. At the end of the day I just wanted to be a part of Australian sport and VIS recognition was important to me. Sporting scholarships were like validation to me. Obviously, given my result, I never really needed them though.

Despite the sign of approval from the VIS, I still managed to upset the Athletics establishment. Over the next few weeks Clare and I raced some local triathlons. On the evening of Thursday, 15 December, we raced the famous 'Zatopek' at Melbourne's Olympic Park. Zatopek is Australia's highest profile distance track meet and features the Men's and Women's 10,000 m Track Championships each year. We both ran just over 33 minutes, tired from a triathlon in Queenscliff four days prior. Much to my despair, Clare pipped me for a faster time, as we both struggled through the closing laps. It became clear that while the public liked us competing, Athletics Australia boss Brian Roe didn't approve our 'triathlon' appearance on the Track. Clare and I raced the event in our Nike two-piece tri suits with 'Nike' on the bum. This seemed to offend Athletics Australia and we were told we could be disqualified. With no ruling of this nature, the problem ended. Somehow again, though, I had managed to disrupt the authorities. In reality, with the triathlon world title in hand, it was inevitable that my involvement in athletics would diminish.

Unknown to me, my new sport of triathlon was a melting pot of discontent and power plays worldwide. As a newcomer, I was suddenly of interest to these power players and I was walking blindly into a firestorm.

5. Racing to Win

Winning a world title at my first attempt and at my first international race created some very odd problems. I wasn't completely new to being blasted into recognition; in a strange coincidence, I had done this ten years earlier (on a much smaller scale) when I won my first Victorian running title. In the eyes of the experts, I was an unknown who came from seemingly nowhere and won convincingly.

Now I had done this 'win from nowhere' on the world stage, I had taken a few organisations and groups by surprise. For the ITU it was a problem, their newly crowned female world champion didn't even have a world ranking. Before I appeared, it was generally a top ranked athlete who won the world title. I raced the World Championships with the number '157', the highest number I ever pinned to myself pre-race in a triathlon. Always planning ahead, Les McDonald was very interested in my racing plans for the 1995 season.

Each year, the ITU ran between ten and twelve top-tier 'World Cup' events, with at least one on every continent around the world. Points were awarded to the top twenty finishers at each race with overall rankings based on the seven best race results for each athlete across the season. The athlete with the most points in a season was ranked world number one and also the winner of the World Cup series. Athletes received double points for World Championship finishes and of course had the chance to win the world title. In 2009, the ITU renamed the World Cup race series the World Triathlon Series (WTS) and redefined the Triathlon World Champion as the athlete who won the year-long series of races. In 1995, fourteen years before this change, I planned to win both the World Cup series and the World Championships in my debut season.

At the time I burst onto the scene, the ITU, headed by Les McDonald, had just secured the inclusion of triathlon in the Olympic Games. Les needed to reassure the IOC that the ITU had control of the sport of triathlon and, very importantly, was supported by the world's best triathletes. In an effort to comply with the IOC requirement for enforceable rules, Les introduced draft-legal racing in the bike discipline in 1995. It was a well-known fact that the non-drafting rule was very arbitrary and would become almost impossible to enforce if a multi-circuit triathlon format was used to make triathlon more exciting for spectators. He copped a lot of backlash from established triathletes for this break from traditional triathlon practice. At the same time, an American group emerged with the aim of setting up a competing non-ITU 'Pro Circuit' and claimed that it had the support of the world's best triathletes (mostly Australian and American). The group had no interest in the Olympic Games, preferred to retain the traditional non-drafting race format, and posed a potential challenge to the authority of the ITU. The ITU did have a wider hold across the world, with backing in Europe, the UK, Asia and South America. By the end of 1995, the ITU had also secured a television deal with Pacific Sports Entertainment, part of Rupert Murdoch's News Limited group, ensuring that the ITU series of events and World Championships were broadcast globally by a leading news conglomerate. This global coverage was un-matched by any other triathlon series at that time.

Amongst all this controversy in the world of triathlon, I was a newcomer, and obviously a big-time performer. With me now in the mix as the current ITU Triathlon World Champion, Les wanted to see where I stood on all this controversy. Australia was the powerhouse nation in the sport of triathlon, but the emergence of APTA suggested a lack of full support for the ITU vision. Les didn't know me. No one did. And he wasn't sure which way I would go. He hoped I would commit to the ITU vision.

Les didn't need to worry, that was my vision too. I was exactly what Les wanted, a kick start for a new era of triathlon in which athletes race to win World Championships and compete in the Olympic Games.

We decided Dad would look after the planning side of things, I didn't have the head space for that. It was also important I wasn't in the firing line when disagreements appeared. I wanted to be able to concentrate on training to be the best in the world.

Les sent the ITU marketing manager Mike Gilmore to Melbourne Australia to meet Dad in early 1995. Dad gave his word that I would fully support the series. After discussion, it was agreed the ITU would ensure I was always provided with airport transfers to and from race venues, I had a private hotel room and all travel costs were covered. I had already managed to secure a Qantas sponsorship, so flights were predominantly taken care of (in the best possible way). All the ITU media surrounding events I raced were to include me and if there were any payments made for athletes to race, I was to be paid at least the sum of the greatest amount paid. It was also agreed my race number for the season would be '0' (zero) until I had raced enough races to become '1'. Everything was done on a handshake.

Mike asked Dad if I could support a race to be held in Derry, Northern Ireland. It was going to be a part of a public showing of the Northern Ireland peace deal. It was agreed that I would make my first appearance on the ITU circuit at that race in June 1995.

The Australian triathlon scene contributed to the consolidation of international triathlon, mainly due to the strength of the athletes on the international racing scene, and the innovations of race or triathlon series organisers, not because anyone at TA was in control of the sport. In this time, many individuals running the sport in Australia appeared to be triathlon fans or triathletes themselves. I had been exposed to the refined organisational structure of Athletics Australia and the long-established rules and regulations of the International Athletics Federation (IAAF), so Triathlon Australia in comparison appeared unprofessional at best, run by individuals on the fly. Odd behaviour from those at the helm included things like the then TA Chief Executive Officer, Tim Wilson, heading off for a training run or ride rather than watching or even showing much interest in the results of national triathlon series events as they were in progress. He also busied himself with self-serving irrelevant details, the most obvious being a change to his job title closer to the Sydney 2000 Olympic Games. He suddenly became the TA National Executive Director despite no apparent change in his work (for the purpose of this book I will refer to him as TA CEO).

Despite the sport's poor governance in Australia, Australian race directors set a high standard. There were many different Race Directors, but two standout race organisers were Garth Prowd who established USM (United Sports Marketing) in Noosa, Queensland and David Hansen who established Supersprint in Melbourne, Victoria. Every time I raced their events, I was on free-to-air TV and mainstream radio, even the local Supersprint races. Through the media exposure their races brought to the sport, triathlon was beginning to capture the imagination of everyday Australians.

A new professional triathlon series, linked to APTA, had also appeared in early 1994. Having encountered APTA during my first full domestic season I was already wary about them. Run by former triathletes and some businessmen from Sydney, they could see that the sport of triathlon needed leadership and saw the opportunity to become major influencers in shaping and marketing triathlon in Australia (and therefore possibly the world, given Australia's domination). Out of this group, a business called Online Sports emerged and set up a made-for-television triathlon series. A very successful national surf lifesaving television series already existed in the country, and through it surf lifesavers had become household names, legends to the Australian public. Every summer the nation tuned in to watch the innovative surf racing formats on TV. In early 1994, the owners of Online Sports took this concept, turned triathlon on its head and brought triathlon into the living room of most Australian households. Different formats were introduced: swim, bike, run became run, bike, swim; or three swim-bike-runs back-to-back, and so on. Australians loved it, and triathletes became very visible on free-to-air national television stations throughout the summer.

There was one major problem with the Triathlon Grand Prix series, and something that disappointed me completely. It went against everything Les McDonald and the ITU stood for, equality for men and women. The ITU only endorsed events that were equal to men and women in race format, prize money and TV exposure. In its first year, Online Sports did not hold a women's series at all. Suddenly the world's most equal sport for men and women became the most unequal in Australia, the stronghold of the sport.

In 1994, with just the Toohey's Blue men's series airing on TV, I forced myself to watch a few races, and I liked the concept. I had no possible way of competing though, because I was female. I had never been discriminated against so blatantly before simply on the grounds of gender. Fortunately, Australians noticed and under pressure, the organisers introduced a women's series in 1995, funded by a very small sponsorship deal with Cool Charm, a women's deodorant brand. To add a twist, Online Sports didn't entertain the possibility that I would win the 1994 world title, so I was overlooked for a contract and a start in the initial 1995 line up. My world championship win suddenly put the women's series into turmoil as Online Sports scrambled to me sign up.

Against this turbulent backdrop, another issue surfaced regarding my world title win. The triathlon world was divided in its view of me. Was Emma Carney the best in the world? Or was Australian triathlete Michellie Jones, who didn't race the 1994 world championships, the best in the world? Everyone had an opinion.

In those days in sport, the media tended to show two women vying for the top spot as a potentially toxic situation. Men could have gladiatorial battles, but women would generally be torn down. As women, if we had an opinion against the norm, we were hard work; if we showed ambition, we were greedy; if we showed emotion, we were too dramatic. In the case of the new emerging TV series, if we fought for equality, we were seen as disruptive and uncooperative. The media could have celebrated the fact that Australia had the two leading female triathletes in the world, Michellie and me. Instead, I felt our reputations were turned into a melodramatic media story beat-up.

Fortunately, when I signed with Nike, they provided some media training. A piece of advice that really stuck with me was never to comment on competitors as it will always be taken out of context. Taking this to heart, I refused to comment publicly about Michellie whenever prodded by the media, taking the air out of the story. Instead the interest moved to when we were to meet to race.

Cadbury, TA's major sponsor, paid for me to compete in the national triathlon series over the 1995 domestic season. Dad thought the National Sprint Championships on 8 January would be the most likely event at which Michellie would race me. It was near to where she lived in Sydney and likely that she would prefer to race me over a sprint course initially. Leading into the race, the media obsessed over whether Michellie and I would race. I was National Sprint Champion and current World Champion and Michellie was a two-time World Champion before I took triathlon by storm. We were both obviously the best in the world and we had never raced each other. All mainstream Australian newspapers were running stories, and everyone wanted to know the outcome. Michellie did not appear once prior to the race. She even had her identical twin rack her bike in transition and set things up for her. Unfortunately for Michellie, I wasn't in the least put off by the subtle games that were going on. I hoped she would race, because I loved racing. It didn't matter who I raced, I believed I would win.

Sure enough, Michellie was present in the line-up just before the race start. The swim was 750 m in a waterway with signs warning of sharks, in an 'only in Australia' situation. Michellie swam well and beat me out of the water by 30 seconds. It was never going to be enough to beat me though. The bike was a looped course over 20 km. One side was a climb and the other was a descent with a flat section near the transition area. Checking out the course before the race I decided I could use the descent to gain momentum with a big gear that would then catapult me through the flat section and up half of the hill. I would have to ride well technically to avoid braking and slowing on corners, but I thought I had enough room. I figured if I rode that aggressively I would decimate the field on the bike. There were four laps and I decided I would commit my attack at halfway.

My plan worked a treat. I flew past Michellie on the bike and built on my lead heading into transition two (bike-to-run). No one was capable of running me down, so I ran a solid pace to take the win but not bury myself: I wanted to keep something in the tank, because I had another triathlon scheduled for the following weekend in Canberra. Michellie crossed in second and graciously told the media I was strong on the bike, and then dropped a post-race clanger that she, 'was only about 80 per cent fit'.

I could see one win wouldn't be enough to shut down the critics. Nothing would ever be enough this first season as World Champion.

Things got ugly the following Wednesday. Online Sports held a press conference in Sydney to launch the revised Triathlon Grand Prix. With women involved, they had their major athlete signings present, but as they had overlooked me, the current world champion, there was an embarrassing and obvious hole in the line-up. I was the only undefeated Australian triathlete and my absence became a focal point. By the end of the press conference, Online Sports had accused me of not supporting TA, painted me as an athlete who refused to race domestically and round that up in a neat little package about me being too weak and not good enough to race Michellie Jones on a regular basis.

Following the press conference, I received a string of media calls asking my response. I didn't have one. I hadn't been signed to the series. The heat then returned to Online Sports. Dad received a contract offering a sign on fee that was less than 1 per cent (yes — one per cent!) of the top men's sign on fee. The offer killed the possibility of me racing in the Triathlon Grand Prix. Dad told me at the time, 'It is important you don't lower your standards to fit in. This is not about you. This is about equality for women.' He had a very good point. I seemed to be the only female triathlete who resisted this inequality. As a result, Online Sports often portrayed me as difficult and disruptive.

I still had the National Cadbury tour to contest and my next race was only four days later on Sunday, 15 January in the nation's capital, Canberra. I always found Canberra a tough location and felt tired pre-race. The water of Lake Burley Griffen was cold, and with wetsuits not permitted (the water temperature has to be below 20°C), I was going to struggle more than most. Cold water really zapped my energy, and I was always more vulnerable. I was never an athlete with much body fat so really felt the cold, both in the water and after being exposed to cold water. Out on the bike, in a wet pair of bathers and with the wind picking up, I struggled to warm up. To make things worse, I felt a little tired on the bike. I still started the run in the lead and crossed the line with over 50 seconds on Jackie Gallagher. Despite feeling very ordinary all race my hatred for losing ensured I still won that day.

My dominance in the 1995 domestic season continued with the Australian Triathlon Championships (classic distance 1.5 km swim, 40 km bike, 10 km run) in Geelong, Victoria, on Sunday, 19 February. I won the event by around 7 minutes and broke the old course record by 10 minutes. National TV stations, Channel 7 and 9, both covered the race and *The Age* newspaper claimed my time as a world record for that distance. TA executives called my effort that day the most impressive performance seen by an individual in triathlon.

Reverting to athletics the following Thursday, I competed in the Melbourne NEC Classic (a high-profile track meet), contesting the Open Women's 5 km. My legs were tired, and I felt flat, the residual from my triathlon four days earlier. I managed to scrape together a 16 minute 11 second, on the flat 5 km run, to finish in the top third of the field. No one seemed to care I was beaten. Channel 9 televised the run, and suddenly everyone was interested in how I was racing, whenever I raced.

My running and triathlon worlds intersected again in March. In late January Athletics Australia had announced its team for the Cross Country World Championships in Durham, England, including both Clare and me. It was rare for sisters to be in the one World Championships team selected by Athletics Australia. The race was scheduled for 25 March and team members were required to fly out on Thursday, 16 March. Clare and I needed to race a national series race in Devonport, Tasmania on Sunday, 19 March, so we requested a later flight out arguing that I had contractual obligations with sponsors. Brian Roe of Athletics Australia wasn't happy and was not prepared to ok a later flight. The issue was referred to highly respected distance run coach Dick Telford who approved the flight change. He also invited Dad to a National Coaching conference in April. It became clear that we had some very strong supporters in the Athletics fraternity, amongst a few critics in the hierarchy.

With Athletics Australia permission we travelled to Devonport for the next round of the Cadbury Triathlon Series. In a slightly old-school format, the women started 12 minutes before the men, with the men expected to mow the women's field down. I found the whole set up sexist and offensive and decided no one was going to mow me down. I swam well, out in second place, having sat close to the feet of swim specialist leader Deidre Grace. I rode hard over the 40 km, tough, undulating and windy course and ran the 10 km leg hard, keeping my distance from the chasing men's field. I managed to win the women's race by 7 minutes and beat all the men home. I think that was the last time the women started ahead of the men in Devonport.

Following the Devonport race, Clare and I flew back to Melbourne, only to fly out to London, Heathrow the next day. A long flight with very sore legs ...

Around twenty-eight hours later we joined the Australian World Cross Country Team in Durham, Northern England. It was freezing and our Australian tracksuits, which were as usual two sizes too big, weren't improving things much. Clare and I spent a lot of time in our room stretching and doing run drills in the hallway out of the sleet. The food was rubbish, so I decided to mainly focus on recovery.

On race day, my most disturbing memory was the lack of toilets at the start. The scene was horrific, I found myself dry retching as I warmed up and accidentally saw other athletes relieving themselves in the open. No one seemed to care who saw what. I managed to pull myself together for the race and finished in 52nd position. In any other race I would be appalled at this result, but it was higher than my placing at the World Cross Country championships the year before. This put me as second Australian across the line, so it was a good run.

Back in Australia, and back to the sport of triathlon, Clare and I were off to the last race of the summer series in Mooloolaba, Queensland on 23 April. The race would start with a wetsuit-free surf swim off main beach. I wanted to make sure I made all the right choices, to take advantage of the rips and currents on the way into and out of the water. If I got this right, I could come out with the swim leaders. Get this wrong, and I could make winning a lot harder. I asked some surf lifesavers for some tips, and fortunately they were spot on. I caught a wave in and exited in fourth, just off the feet of the front swimmers. Within 3 km of the 40 km bike, I took the lead and ran away to comfortably win the race by 5 minutes over Rina Bradshaw and Jackie Gallagher.

With my Mooloolaba victory, I took out the national series and won all the national triathlon titles I contested. I was also recognised as Australian Triathlete of the year. My domestic season had been successful.

While I spent the summer racing the official series, the Triathlon Grand Prix series had also taken place. Early on in the series, Online Sports owners ensured that their television commentators referred to Michellie as the current world champion, in an attempt, Dad and I assumed, to entice me to race. This type of negative motivation never worked on me. My management wrote to Online Sports to suggest they correct their commentators, because a legal battle would ensue if it continued. Halfway through the series, Online Sports contacted Dad and offered over twice the original measly amount for me to start the series. It was still grossly below the men's start fees, so my response remained a firm no. By season's end, Online Sports were talking to Dad about the 1996 series. Dad and I decided we would consider signing me up if the male and female race series prizemoney was equal; we didn't insist on equal appearance money as it was always going to be tough to prove.

Although the official season of racing domestically was done, there was still plenty of interest in triathlon on the part of the mainstream media. Channel 9 filmed Clare and me training and racing throughout the summer as they put together a feature story. I also made an appearance on the most popular Australian Saturday television show at the time, *Hey Hey It's Saturday*. The print media ran stories on us all summer too. Our profiles were growing, because we captured not just the sporting media, but also non-sports publications, such as *Business Review Weekly*, showing just how far our reach had spread throughout Australia.

Again, Wesley College also celebrated our successes and invited us back to the annual College Founders Day dinner, a dinner that celebrated the 'founding' of Wesley College attended by many Old Wesleyans (OWs). It was a nice sign of respect from a great Australian school.

Along with the Australian National series, and the ITU series, triathlons were run across the world by individual event organisers. Various international race organisers called Dad to lock me into events for the 1995 season. I was always concerned that too much racing would be detrimental in the long run. The big races were the focus. I wanted national and world titles, the top world ranking and world series points. Chasing prizemoney was dangerous. It often forced an athlete to race too much. With too much racing, overload and fatigue set in, and the quality of performance generally dropped. The body can only do so much. I wanted to earn money through sponsorship endorsements, because they provided me with a stable income. With performance bonuses added to contracts the idea was my income would grow exponentially. Prize money was the bonus on top of all this.

There were, however, some exceptions to this rule, and every now and then an extra race was added.

Following Mooloolaba one particular phone call set up nicely my second race against Michellie. As expected, she won the first women's Triathlon Grand Prix series, while I won the traditional TA National Triathlon Series (Cadbury Series). Importantly, to me, I had two more national titles, one from beating her in January. I also remained the only undefeated triathlete in Australia. Sydney event organiser Phil Bates called Dad following my win in Mooloolaba. He asked Dad if I would be interested in racing a Channel 9 Wide World of Sports (the most watched sports TV show in Australia at the time) feature race in Fiji on Saturday, 20 May. Both Dad and I had heard rumours of this event. We had also heard Michellie was signed on to race. Dad asked Phil for confirmation, but he was very reluctant to reply. As Phil struggled with a response Dad told him the following:

> *If Michellie is racing, Emma will be there. You must not advertise or tell anyone that Emma is racing, otherwise Michellie will pull out. I suggest you fly Michellie to Fiji before Emma and ensure she is committed to race, then fly Emma in.*

Phil agreed with Dad and the flights, accommodation, appearance fee, and prize money was finalised.

I was locked in.

I couldn't wait.

By the time I arrived in Fiji, Michellie was sitting down with Channel 9 doing her pre-race interviews. I think that interview was the first time she was told that I was racing.

I wasn't the most popular triathlete in town that weekend. It wasn't just Michellie who was annoyed with me. Most of the women in the race seemed to think me racing was unfair. I think they all calculated their prizemoney going into the event, and my presence messed their calculations up. The men's race had a strong field too, with some big names including Mark Allen and Simon Lessing, so it was nice the women's field was attracting more of the media's attention.

The race was set up around the grounds of the Sheraton Hotel in Fiji on Denarau Island. As it was an invitational race, the total field number was small, only 39 competitors all up. It was agreed there would be one mass start, with men and women together. This concerned me a little, because with men in the mix, Michellie could get greater draft assistance in the swim than me. There wasn't anything I could do, so I decided I just needed to be quick at the start. The bike was non-drafting (most of the athletes racing were old school) with laps of the road around the Sheraton, while the run was a few laps of the golf course.

I took it easy the day before the race. Dad flew in late on the Friday afternoon, eager to see me beat Michellie, so much so I had to ask him to settle down. It wasn't a done deal yet.

Race day was hot, and the start was scheduled for 10 a.m., which meant it was going to be warm. Someone had forgotten to organise a boat to take us all to the island for the swim start. One was eventually found, but it delayed the start by over half an hour.

Eventually we were underway, after a false start. I ran off the beach to hit the water fast, as everyone did. We had to head out to a swim buoy then turn towards the Sheraton on the main island. In my inexperience, I was thrown by a television helicopter flying low and messing up the water. I also hadn't checked the exit mark and I swam slightly off course. Little errors, but by the time I left the water I was almost 2 minutes down on Michellie. Annoyed with myself I took off on the bike and chased her down by about halfway. Michellie then sat behind me, making it difficult for me to ride away from her, so I just waited for the run. My run was strong, and I crossed the line, clearly ahead, in first place. I now had two wins from two starts and hadn't been beaten by anyone in the triathlon world since my world title win.

I assumed Michellie hated me even more now. She apparently lodged a protest that I drafted other riders to catch her, because she didn't believe I could ride that fast. In a funny twist, she was charged with a drafting violation while I received an all clear. It didn't really matter anyway. There was a post-race dinner, and Michellie and I exchanged the basic niceties. Neither of us really had much to say because we were competitors. For the rest of our careers, we shared a hatred for losing generally and a severe hatred for losing to each other. There was enough animosity between us to ensure every time we raced, we pushed each other to higher levels of competition. I truly believe it was good that we were racing at the same time. We actually benefitted from each other's presence on the triathlon scene. And it was good for the sport. It brought exposure to the sport in the mainstream media.

Following the race, I had a few days to enjoy Fiji. The day after the race, we had a free day at Beachcomber Island: pretty relaxing, although I managed to fit a run in when we returned. On the Tuesday, I helped Channel 9 film the 'hosting' segments for the Wide World of Sports. As this was the most watched sports television show that aired every weekend in Australia, it was a fairly big production. Channel 9 broadcast hosts and Australian television legends themselves, Ken Sutcliff and Max Walker, flew in for the shoot. Filmed on a sandy atoll off Beachcomber Island we had to wait, exposed, until the cloud cleared. They took shots from a helicopter flying overhead that made us look like we were marooned. I was given the job of holding up their cue cards. It was a very entertaining day, mainly because of Max Walker being his usual entertaining self. At the end of the filming, we all returned to Melbourne.

Back in Australia, I discovered that mainstream newspapers had covered the race, despite it being a bit of an 'exhibition' triathlon. Online Sports had also contacted Dad again, but still offered less than the men. A week after the race, the Channel 9 segment aired, with very positive feedback. It wasn't just triathlon that had captured mainstream media attention, it was women's triathlon that was getting prime time coverage.

As always, it wasn't all smooth sailing, with everyone on board with my success. There was another interesting dig at me from some in the athletics fraternity in early June. The Australian *Runner's World* magazine published a story explaining how cross training does not work, and triathletes are really athletes who cannot achieve anything in individual sports. The timing was suspicious, almost as if athletics officials feared that their athletes were going to start taking up triathlon because of my success.

I was still competing in athletics events though. Shortly after returning from Fiji, I flew to Brisbane for another Nike Women's 5 km road race and finished second. All of the top three women ran under 16 minutes and I raced athletes who were heading off for the Track and Field World Championships, so I was happy with my result. It was also a good hit out before I headed overseas for my first ITU event.

Due to the decision to make all ITU races throughout the season draft legal, a few established athletes including Michellie Jones refused to participate in the Triathlon World Cup Series and instead chose to focus on the American 'Pro-Series'. I had given the ITU my word that I would support them and make my ITU World Cup debut in Northern Ireland. Derry would be my first ITU race since the World Championships and my first race on the circuit. As I hadn't raced an ITU event since the World Championships, many were interested to see me race again.

Jet lag was always a juggle for Australian athletes racing in the northern hemisphere. There were two theories on managing jet lag: fly in and race within twenty-four hours or fly in ten days prior to race day and adapt. I didn't believe the first would work, and I didn't have the support to fly into Northern Ireland ten days early, so I left Australia on Monday, 12 June for the race on Saturday, 17 June. Dad and I decided almost a week would provide me with enough time to adjust.

Northern Ireland was as expected. Cold. The local organising committee had someone collect me from the airport. He seemed surprised I had a lot of luggage. He didn't seem to realise I needed a bike. He managed to get everything loaded in his car, which was — to my complete amazement — an old mini. I couldn't believe anyone would pick up a triathlete from the airport in a car so small, given the amount of sporting equipment we need to transport. Things were about to become weirder. As we were heading out of Belfast towards Derry where the race was, he said, 'Do you mind if I drop in on my mum? I don't get to Belfast much.' I told him I didn't mind, but I had flown all the way from Australia, and I wanted to have a shower and get some rest, could he be quick. In a strange turn of events, we ended up at his mum's house, eating shortbread and drinking tea, while she asked how long we had known each other. I suddenly realised his mum thought I was his girlfriend from Australia. On realising this, I cut tea short, and we left. I didn't have the heart to let his mum know we weren't an item.

Only in Ireland did that ever happen.

Derry was an interesting place. It was made famous for 'Bloody Sunday' (sometimes called the Bogside Massacre), an incident on 30 January 1972, when British soldiers shot twenty-eight unarmed civilians during a protest march. The ITU event was part of the movement towards a peace deal. This was one of the first high profile sporting events to be held in the area for many years. I had been pre-warned to travel to Northern Ireland only on my Australian passport, because British Passports were still very much hated.

Driving into town, the effects of the fighting in Northern Ireland were quite obvious. Footpaths on each side of the road were still painted different colours indicating which side the Catholics and which side the Protestants should walk on to avoid trouble. Police stations were still barricaded, and barbed wire surrounded them. I had never seen firsthand the scars that civil violence left behind. It was quite confronting.

The people seemed really happy to host the event. Pre-race there were school visits and in between training to be done. It didn't actually get dark through the night, because we were so far north in the world. It was supposed to be summer, but temperatures weren't really indicative of that.

I met Les McDonald properly for the first time in Northern Ireland. He was full of history about the place. While he was now a Canadian, he had grown up near where Grandma Carney had grown up, in the North of England. He was a similar character, being a hard worker and strongly standing up for what he believed in. He was also very astute about who supported his events and those who did not. This was the first of many, many chats I had with Les throughout my triathlon career. I developed a very strong respect for Les. He was a selfless man who gave a vision to and developed the sport of triathlon, from which athletes today still benefit.

Race day came around, and there was a sizeable crowd in what I thought were cold, damp conditions. The swim was freezing, just over 11°C in the water. We were supposed to swim 1500 m, but it was shortened to just over 1 km due to the water temperature and tide. As a result, the entire field all really left the water as one pack. Out on the bike, things were a little different. As a drafting race, we were allowed to sit in the slipstream of other bikes, but it was the first ITU race of its type. There was some arguing amongst the group, as the new race dynamics were tested. Some bossier athletes decided that some weren't working and yelled at them to do so, to share the workload. Athletes didn't trust those who sat on the back of bike packs and 'saved' their legs for the run. It didn't matter to me much. With the 10 km run to follow I believed I had the field covered. There was only one other athlete who I considered as a notably strong runner and that was Carol Montgomery of Canada. She was a 32-minute 10 km runner. In triathlon it is all very well being a fast track runner, but you must also be fit and strong on the bike so that it does not destroy your ability to run fast. Fortunately, as I would soon demonstrate, my bike-run combination was unrivalled in the world and I was able to outrun everyone. It was tough though. I was so cold I couldn't feel my toes until about 7 km into the run. Ignoring the conditions, I won by over 2 minutes and notched up my first ITU World Cup Series win.

The next day, feeling tired and sore from racing in such cold conditions, I flew out of Derry via Belfast to Bilbao, Spain. My next ITU event was in San Sebastian, Spain. I was looking forward to the warmer conditions.

On arriving in Bilbao airport, no one was there to collect me. Apparently, the race organiser had decided not to pick athletes up from the airport and, being so inexperienced, I had no idea what to do. The only person I could find who would speak English was at the British Airways help desk. Fortunately, I had the race organiser's phone number, so I asked them to call him to ask how I was to get to San Sebastian. On receiving the call, the race organiser told the British Airways employee to tell me to 'catch a cab'. So, I did — straight to his office, and gave him the USD250 bill!

The collection from the airport wasn't the only problem that weekend. The race organiser had ignored ITU instructions and given me the race number '82', not zero. More concerned with my recovery race preparation for the upcoming weekend, I left it to Dad and Les to work out via long distance phone calls.

Spain was fantastic, but also very different. I didn't realise afternoon siestas were actually a thing. Lunch and dinner were both difficult to organise because shops shut at 2 p.m. sharp and didn't re-open until 8.30 p.m. at night. I spent most of the time eating too late or not eating. Fortunately, the Spanish food was so good that when I did eat, I had too much to choose from.

Spain was a great place to race, and the crowds really supported the event. Pre-race, there was much discussion from the athletes that the swim at San Sebastian main beach looked long. Les asked me for my opinion and I replied that I didn't care, there was nothing I could do about it right now. He seemed surprised I was neither interested in getting into a discussion about it, nor deterred by everyone else complaining.

It was a beach start, out to a buoy, back into the shore, with a run around a marker, and back into the water. This type of broken swim was perfect for me. The more running involved in any leg of the triathlon, the better. There was also a decent run to transition for our bikes. As a result, I exited the water well and was in the lead on the bike within 10 km. There was a climb on the bike course, so despite it being a drafting race, everyone had to work to hold my wheel. Riding hard I managed to drop the entire field. The run was a formality and I won by over 5 minutes.

I returned to Australia, on the way home stopping overnight in England to visit Grandma and Grandad Carney. Grandma really was ill with emphysema and it was the last time I saw her. She still smoked, but in between each cigarette puff she took on oxygen to help her breathe. I spent the night trying to understand Grandma's logic of continuing to smoke while also on oxygen. We had a laugh together, with Grandad also agreeing none of Grandma's logic made sense. I felt really sad leaving them the next morning. Both looked very old and frail.

Clare was the next to race, heading to the ITU event in Gamagori, Japan on

Sunday, 9 July. Still a junior, she didn't let that get in the way of a great result. She finished a close second in her first senior ITU World Cup.

After I returned to Melbourne, I took a week to recover from the racing and travel, before putting together a month of solid training. Preparation for the next block of international races involved swimming over 30 km in the pool, biking 200-250 km and running 100 km every week. It was challenging because the weather was really cooling down in Melbourne. Late July, we headed to Canada and the US for more ITU events and the Chicago Triathlon, a famous American race.

On 29 July 1995, my twenty-fourth birthday, Clare and I flew to Montreal, Canada. Having endured another long-haul flight, we were both reminded just how far away Australia was from most of the places we had to race. We finally dragged ourselves into the Montreal Airport Hilton Hotel crashing into bed just before midnight, still on 29 July, despite travelling for over twenty-four hours. That was both the longest and dullest birthday I ever experienced. The next morning, someone collected us from our hotel and drove us to Drummondville, in Quebec, Canada, the location of the next ITU World Cup.

As the race was scheduled for Sunday, 6 August, Clare and I had a week to acclimatise. It was a hard slog. This trip, the jet lag hit me hard and I felt lethargic, tired and sluggish. Light swim, bike and run training all week with some short speedwork got me back into some sort of form, but I knew I had to race smart.

The race had a two-lap swim. I exited sixth. The bike was dead flat, so I didn't really have any hills on which to break free from those sitting in the bunch. It was really just a wait for the run. I felt sluggish, but arrogantly assumed I would outsprint everyone if I just stayed in contention. I did, but only won by 5 seconds, my smallest margin yet.

Clare and I stayed in Drummondville to recover and keep training. On Thursday, 10 August we flew out of Montreal to connect to Toronto for our next race destination, Cleveland, USA. It was the same story really. Good swim, strong bike and fastest run to win. It was important to win in Cleveland, because it was the approved site for the 1996 World Championships. My race was very strong, and expectations for my return the following year were high. I had a constant stream of radio and newspaper journalists calling to speak to me. My unbeaten run was beginning to get a lot of attention back home in Australia.

Our next stop, Nike Headquarters in Portland, Oregon, was all fun. In typical fashion, Nike flew Clare and me first class from Cleveland to Portland. Suddenly my tired and aching body felt a lot better. Amazing what a first-class flight can do for your recovery. Nike also organised a hotel in Portland and Clare and I managed a post-flight training session, although I still felt a bit fatigued.

Nike had always inspired me, and to actually see where it all started was very eye opening. As we walked onto the Nike campus one morning, we bumped into Phil Knight, the company founder. I met him in briefly in Australia, but as the boss's daughter, not as a Nike athlete. He stopped and said, 'You are those sisters from Australia, aren't you? Your Dad is MD in Australia, and you have won World Titles?'

'Yes. That's us,' I replied.

'Good job,' he responded.

It was nice to have not only been noticed, but also to have impressed someone like Phil Knight.

Nike loaded us up with a lot of gear. We were shown around the campus and trained at Nike Athlete facilities. It was every bit as awesome as you can imagine. Everything was the best you could get.

Clare and I spent just over a week at the Nike campus, flying out to Chicago on Thursday, 24 August. The famous Chicago Triathlon, part of the US Pro Triathlon tour, was on the last weekend of the month. It was a short flight in comparison to the distances Australians are used to travelling (only four hours), but stinking hot in Chicago when we landed. We had hassles at the airport, as the race organiser had promised a lift to our hotel, but no one arrived. To be honest, I hadn't expected the organisers to give me a warm welcome, given the race was part of the tour that rivalled the ITU series, but it was irritating in a city as large as Chicago. Clare and I negotiated an airport express bus transfer to the Chicago Hilton (spending some time working out exactly which Chicago Hilton we were actually staying in, as there were apparently a few), but had to buy two tickets each because we were travelling with bikes. I argued my bike wasn't sitting on a seat, but quickly realised that in America you get what you are given. There is no negotiating.

We finally arrived at the hotel just as Dad arrived. He had flown across from a sports expo in Europe to meet us. Having been travelling for a few weeks now, it was nice to have someone else take over the organising. I lay down while Dad went to a Chicago Nike store and then asked him to find a decent restaurant, because I heard meals in Chicago were better than typical American fare. I was a little tired of American-style massive portions of sub-standard food. Fortunately,

Dad did a great job organising dinner and I slept about twelve hours that night. I needed rest, with a race only three days away.

During the few days prior to the race we managed to find a pool to train in, ran the run course and drove over the bike course. I couldn't get rid of the constant tiredness but tried to get as much rest as possible between everything else I had to do. One pre-race requirement was an ESPN interview. I knew before I signed up for the race that Michellie raced Chicago every year and raced well. It was also a key race on the US triathlon calendar and attracted the top professional triathletes. For the first time all year, I was racing in a less welcoming environment, although the American Pro-Circuit did recognise me as a top-ranked athlete in the field.

Waking up on race day I knew I was tired, and I knew it was going to be a tough race. The 1.5 km swim was in Lake Michigan. Wetsuits were permitted. The weather was really warm, and the water temperature seemed too hot, but US race officials ran the event to their own, not ITU, rules. Drafting was not allowed on the 40 km bike leg out along the highway. The run was flat, out and back along the lake foreshore. It was expected to be windy. Chicago was notorious for this, and for hot, humid race conditions.

The day started badly. The hotel breakfast opened too late, and Dad managed to get himself lost walking to the transition area, confused by the road closures for the age group race. The Age Group race, with 5,500 competitors, was already in progress. Dad was carrying most of our essential race gear for us. Clare and I rode to the race start, as a semi pre-race warm-up, but it was a very messy preparation as we scrambled to find Dad. Fortunately, the elite race start was postponed until 9.30 a.m. The bike course was still too heavily congested for the elite race to start. I was surprised that a well-established American race could make such an obvious error on timing, but I was happy for the delay, given Clare and I managed to find Dad at 8.50 a.m.

The actual race didn't really improve for me. I still felt tired, and really stiff and sore. I swam ok to start with, but my back seized up. Same on the bike. I exited the water over a minute down on the leaders and with a non-drafting race it should have not been a problem for me to reel them in, but I was flat. When I hit the run, I had a 2-minute deficit, and struggled home for third place. My first defeat. I was annoyed with myself and irritated. I knew I was tired but underestimated how it would affect my race.

I was in a foul mood. As I was picking up my gear in transition, I was still fuming. Stuffing my wetsuit into my bag along with my other gear I heard someone calling out my name. I was over everything, but always replied to my supporters. I looked up and someone was gesturing for me to come over to speak to them. They seemed to really want to speak to me, so I trudged over, forcing a smile.

'Hi. Yes, I'm Emma,' I introduced myself.

'Hi, I'm Mary Munroe. I am from Trek Bikes USA.'

'Damn,' I thought. She just saw the worst race result of my career. I assumed I had screwed my chance of a Trek sponsorship.

'Oh, Hi,' I replied, un-enthusiastically.

Mary asked me if I could visit Trek headquarters the next day. It was only a short drive to Wisconsin. I looked at her, and suddenly I thought about how tired I was, and how another day of travelling would really kill me, all I really wanted to do was have a good sleep. Plus, my back was killing me.

'I will only come if you agree now that Trek will sponsor me,' I said.

Fortunately, Mary laughed and said, 'Emma, you have driven us nuts by winning so many races with our logo covered up. We want to sign you as soon as possible, so we can get our logo uncovered.'

I called Dad over and the details were set. Suddenly my worst day of racing so far had turned into a fruitful day after all.

The next day (Monday, 28 August), Dad, Clare and I hired a car and made the two-and-a-half-hour drive to Trek Bikes HQ. Mary Munroe was head of marketing and sponsorship and introduced us to the team at Trek. They showed us how the bikes were made, and the wind tunnel testing set up. We spoke about what I wanted, and I was measured, so they could custom make bikes for me in the future. I told Trek I wanted them for my entire career. As we were so far into the season I asked if I could have a new bike sent over to Australia around December, in preparation for the next season. I also asked if I could have a smaller frame than the one on which I had been racing, as I felt I needed a more responsive bike for smaller circuit racing. All was agreed. Dad negotiated payment, which started with a base fee and grew exponentially as I performed in major races and maintained my world ranking.

Finally, I had my Trek sponsorship. They told me I was the first non-American to be sponsored on a road bike and congratulated me on my effort to get their attention. We had a laugh, and I told them they should reply better to letters from Australian athletes.

It was great to have Trek signed up. The next day we drove out of Chicago and headed south to Zipp headquarters in Indianapolis, this time a three-hour drive. Zipp, in my opinion, make the best bike racing wheels. Developed as a business from nothing by Australian Andy Ording, I was keen to see how the wheels were made and also meet the guys who were going to supply me with what they referred to as my 'speed weaponry'.

Another interesting day. The detail behind each wheel amazed me. There was also a discussion about riding a Zipp bike they were developing, but although it felt great to ride, I was really happy to have secured Trek.

Time crept up on us. We had to drive from Zipp to Chicago Airport. We were cutting it fine for our 7.30 p.m. flight out and Dad drove too fast as usual. The police stopped us, but gave us a warning once they realised we were Australian. We managed to make the flight to LA, and transfer to our Qantas flight for Melbourne. Somewhere over the Pacific Ocean we completely lost Wednesday, 30 August.

Back in Australia, I struggled with tiredness and had some blood tests. They showed that I was low in iron, and a course of B12 injections were prescribed to get me back on track. Over the next month, I gradually felt better, but I think it was due more to the fact that I was back home, training to a routine and not travelling so much.

I had a few commitments before my next race including promotional appearances for sponsors. I had signed with Holden, to be the face of the Barina model car. I was slightly disappointed it was a Barina, but Dad assured me the extensive deal including television commercials was worth it financially. One of the first print advertising campaigns did have me a little unconvinced: it had a picture of me in a convertible Barina, with the words 'to cool off, Emma takes her top off'. I remember asking Dad if that was really the best line they could come up with.

Another pending commitment was really an honour. I was invited to the Sport Australia Hall of Fame lunch, where I was inducted into the Honour Roll along with legendary Australian cricketer, Shane Warne.

The next scheduled ITU race was the first 'test event' for the proposed Sydney 2000 Olympic triathlon. Sydney won the bid for the 2000 Olympics in 1993, and in 1994 the IOC approved triathlon as an inclusion on the program. Very importantly, the sport of triathlon was expected to play a leading role in the Sydney 2000 Olympic program. Host countries always prefer to open the games with events in which they expect success. Of all the Olympic sports, it was decided that the women's triathlon would be the first medal decided at the Sydney Olympic

Games. This was due largely to the success of Australian women in international triathlon, particularly my recent dominance in the ITU series. I hadn't lost an ITU event, and this type of domination and consistency was rare, really rare, in international elite sports. Another factor contributing to the decision to open the Sydney Games with the women's triathlon, was the fact that the race could showcase the famous Sydney Harbour, with the transition area at the Sydney Opera House forecourt. Planners dreamed of breathtaking images showing off the Australian setting as the triathlon was beamed to televisions across the world.

To prepare for the Olympic Triathlons, Victoria-based triathlon event manager David Hansen relocated to Sydney. He worked with the Sydney Organising Committee for the Olympic Games (SOCOG) to design the course and prepare for 2000. Very early on it was decided that it should test athletes in all disciplines. It would start with a tough swim in Sydney Harbour, which was expected to be affected by water chop. The bike included the surrounding hills with the aim of breaking packs up; taking competitors up Macquarie Street and into the Botanic Gardens a number of times. The run was predominantly along the foreshore, with some climbs and multiple loops designed to provide better viewing for the expected crowds. The hilly course suited strong bike-run athletes. It was perfect for my style of racing.

Given the importance and significance of the Sydney ITU event, I wanted to race it every year leading into the Sydney Games. Clare and I flew up to Sydney on Friday, 13 October and stayed nearby. This inaugural year, I was asked pre-race to provide feedback on the course, and areas I thought could be improved. There was also a press conference followed by a dinner in honour of the ITU at Chifley Tower. John Coates AO, President of the Australian Olympic Committee, invited me to attend. While it was an honour to attend a dinner in such company, I really just wanted to get to bed and sleep. I didn't race for the accolades or the dinners. I raced because I loved representing Australia and I hated losing. I had an important race that weekend, and pre-race socialising wasn't an important part of my preparation.

Saturday morning, the day before the race, I had an early ride over the course. We were to do six laps on the bike, and I wanted to ride a couple at speed before the traffic built up. This was always a difficult thing to do pre-race, especially for races held in the middle of major cities. Regardless, I was careful and managed a 45-minute ride. I liked the course. I could see with my strong bike riding ability I could do some real damage to weaker riders on the hills. Because of the nature of the course, it would be very difficult for anyone to ride as fast as me, even if they worked as a small group against me. A single strong rider could obviously hold her own on those tough hills.

Late on the Saturday afternoon I attended the pre-race meeting. These meetings allowed organisers to explain the particulars of the course and athletes to raise and address any issues. It was a fairly typical meeting, nothing too complicated, until right at the end when the ITU marketing manager Mike Gilmore stood up and announced that due to sponsorship problems, all prize money was to be reduced by 50 per cent.

I was disgusted, and also embarrassed this happened in my country. I immediately lost interest in racing, because while prize money was not my total income, I didn't think it was appropriate that anyone should receive a 50 per cent pay cut at such late notice. I told Dad I didn't think I should accept that, and I was seriously considering withdrawing from the race. Dad of course 'had an immediate conversation' with the ITU, and suddenly the situation was corrected. Full prize money was reinstated, and all athletes agreed to compete.

The first race over the inaugural Olympic triathlon course was held on Sunday, 15 October at 9.30 a.m. for the men and 9.50 a.m. for the women. Reportedly around 40,000 people crowded onto the Opera House steps and surrounding area that day to watch. Slightly before the women finished, Brad Beven of Australia won the men's event.

In the women's race, I had a solid swim exiting the three-lap course with the main front pack. There was one swim specialist off the front, but as expected she was caught within two laps of the bike course. Carol Montgomery of Canada was in my pack, and I always considered her as a threat on the run. Ideally, I would drop her on the bike to make things a little easier for myself on the final leg of the race.

Each race is a little different, and on this particular day, I was working quite well with an American who was also strong on the bike. At one point I rolled to the back and suggested to her we could break away. I knew she would take this offer up, because she was not a strong runner and any break on the field meant she had a better chance of coming second behind me. I told her when we next negotiated the turn at the Opera House before the climb up Macquarie Street, she should go first. I would slow the group, then jump across to her and we could break away. My plan was agreed upon, and I waited for the next descent towards the Opera House foreshore roundabout.

The tactic worked a treat. The group slowed as I took the turn with my brakes on, allowing the American to get away. I then jumped out of the turn. I timed everything so well that when I came past her on the hill, and I let out a whistle to let her know I was coming, I was moving too fast for her to react. I flew straight past her. I remember hearing her swear at me as I disappeared over the hill and out of her sight. I laughed to myself, carried on and decided to really go for it and rip the bike course up. Over the remaining three laps of the bike I pulled away from the field, riding solo, and hit the run around a minute in front. With me that far ahead, the four-lap run became an exhibition of Australia's dominance of triathlon, and the crowd loved it.

It was a nice win. There was a lot of positivity given the location, the double Australian win, and the ease at which I had taken out the race.

The next event on my schedule was to be my World Title defence, so after official press duties I flew back to Melbourne to prepare. The 1995 World Championships were to be held in Cancun, Mexico on Sunday, 12 November. I wanted to really focus on my final preparations and given the amount of travel required to get to Cancun, I decided to not race Noosa Triathlon on 29 October that year. Holden was a major sponsor of Noosa Triathlon and as a sponsored athlete, there was much discussion between Dad and Holden. They agreed that I should attend the event, but not race. I desperately wanted to race, but Dad was adamant that the ITU Championship defence was the priority, and I had had a long season of racing. It took a long time to recover from my last trip, and I really needed to avoid tiredness at this end of the season. In hindsight, I still wish I raced Noosa that year. I always enjoyed that event. I made the quick trip north for Holden, then returned to Melbourne. I copped a bit of backlash from some media outlets for not racing, and putting myself in 'cotton wool', but the focus was on my preparation for Cancun, not what others expected from me.

Clare and I set out for Mexico three days later on Wednesday, 1 November. Mexico is a complicated place to get to from Australia, especially when you are aiming to race well once you arrive. Juggling jet lag and tiredness was my priority. Clare and I had also been warned that it was important to remain diligent with regard to water and eating, as illness and sickness was a high possibility in Mexico.

We arrived in Los Angeles three hours before we left Australia, as is the case for Australians flying across the Pacific. We checked into a nearby hotel, arriving around 4 p.m. local time to find that Mum and Alwyn were already there. On Thursday, 2 November, day two of our journey to Mexico, we all left the hotel at 5 a.m. for a 7 a.m. flight to Houston and finally reached Cancun late in the afternoon.

Clearing customs was very laid back, a little too laid back if you asked me. As I showed my passport, the customs officer passed a comment along the lines, 'Oh, Australian. You here for a good time?' I was sick of travelling and out of patience and replied, 'No mate, a short time,' as I snatched my passport back. Fortunately, I was allowed into Cancun ok, despite my lack of regard for the customs guy's friendliness.

Outside, TA team manager Alan Elrick met us with our bags, and transported us safely in a van to our hotel. We stayed at a place called 'Aqua Marina Beach Apartments'. It was nice, but not five stars, so missing essentials like internal doors and windows that shut properly. There wasn't much to eat, and I was too scared to eat from street vendors, so I told everyone I was going to bed to rest.

We woke to a hot and humid bedroom. Apparently, the hotel didn't have power throughout the entire night and the air-conditioning had turned itself off. As Mum had brought some food from Australia, we had a bit of breakfast. I wanted to put my bike together, and make sure nothing was damaged during the trip. All seemed ok, but I went out for a ride to test everything anyway.

The main drag of Cancun wasn't exactly an ideal bike training location, but we didn't have much choice. I was pleasantly surprised by the courteous drivers, but the amount of traffic didn't really allow for a fast ride. Clare and I headed outside the hotel zone and along what appeared to be a highway. We found a stretch of road where we could hit some decent speeds, before reaching a checkpoint of some sort. I panicked when I saw a guy guarding the road with a gun over his shoulder and stopped when he waved us down. Fortunately, Clare and I had our Australian kit on, so we looked like tourists. Instructed in broken English to turn around, we did as we were told. An eventful first ride, but also successful; our bikes were fully tested, because we rode flat out back to the hotel, scared stiff by the guy with the gun.

The race was a week away, so Clare and I spent the days getting to know the course. The swim was in the ocean, with a shallow start and fairly long run out. This was to my advantage. It was difficult to train on though, as there were hundreds of little sting rays everywhere. Clare and I aren't particularly comfortable in open water at the best of times, so hundreds of sting rays really didn't help the cause. We found a local pool at a nearby health club and mixed our swims between the ocean and the pool. We ran early, to avoid the heat. While I believe it is good to adapt to the conditions, you do not need to keep testing yourself in the heat. I was surprised at the number of athletes doing the opposite and jogging around in the midday sun.

Cancun was an interesting place. Between training sessions Clare and I found it amusing watching the behaviour of people staying in the hotel. Every day, the guests were treated to a swimsuit fashion parade at the main pool. We watched this religiously, amazed at the poor taste of each contestant. It was like the early days of reality TV but in real time: so bad, you can't look away. Grocery shopping was also amusing. Mum loved it. In Mexico, most were a similar height to her, and she got really excited about going shopping and being able to reach everything on the top shelves.

We were staying in the hotel zone, which was typical of a tacky American holiday. Outside the zone was the real Mexico, which tourists were told to avoid. I was about to find out why. On the Friday before Sunday's race, Mum and Alwyn decided to go on a day trip outside the hotel zone. My preparation seemed to be going ok and I didn't think much of it at the time, but by the next day both Mum and Alwyn were feeling a bit ordinary. Both spent most of the day in bed. By Saturday evening I was feeling queasy and Sunday morning, race morning, I felt awful. Through the night I actually pulled the bed sheets over me, because for the first time since arriving in Mexico I felt cold. I played down how I was feeling. Not racing was never an option to me. I didn't even consider it at the time. It was race day, and time to perform. End of story, no excuses.

When I woke up, I tried eating something light, as race start was 8.45 a.m. I couldn't manage a thing. I spent the morning on the toilet, and tried to remain positive, telling myself, 'Oh well, as least race weight today is a little lighter.' Despite my attempts to remain positive, I felt weak and dehydrated.

Ignoring the signs, I took some Panadol and headed out to rack my bike, set up my transition and get ready to race. As I entered the transition area, the TA Team Doctor Dr Di Robinson ('Dr Di'), saw me and asked me how I was feeling. She used to check up on us all on race day. I told her I felt ill. She looked concerned and gave me some tablets, telling me they would help with the queasiness and also 'block me up'. I was a little apprehensive, because I always check any medication with the ASDA (the then drug agency which is now ASADA) banned substance list. The list is provided so that athletes can ensure that they don't accidentally take a banned substance. Dr Di assured me they were 'safe' to take, so I did. I felt a little better, but it was short-lived relief.

Unlike last year, we were introduced at race start. Clare was in the elite team, so we were racing each other. I was looking forward to getting started, knowing I had a short window before Dr Di's tablets wore off and I started feeling terrible again. The gun fired. With a start thigh deep in the water, I had the opportunity to dolphin through the shallow water and get to the front. I always liked this type of start, because it required fitness and the ability to use the bottom of the ocean to jump off. I started well. About halfway through the 1500 m swim though, I started to feel a little weak, with no real power or strength to my swim stroke. I could feel myself dropping back but forced the negative impact of this from my mind and continued to fight for my position. I exited the water 1 minute 20 seconds down on the swim leaders. It was further back than I wanted, but I was confident in my ability to get myself back over the 40 km bike and 10 km run.

There was a long run to transition, which again was something I preferred; the more running the better. Soon I was out, riding with a small pack. With no hills on the flat, looped bike course to break the groups up, it came to a chase. Riders worked together to reel in the athletes ahead. I felt awful, unable to push the gears I normally pushed. It impacted the dynamics of the race: with me unable to initiate a massive chase, progress was slow. I decided we would catch the leaders, but it was going to take most of the bike. I contributed as little as I could. My weakness on the bike worried me. I didn't want to use up the little energy I had if I didn't have to. At times I dropped to the back of the pack to throw up. I wasn't sure if it was sea water or me being ill. I tried to take on some nutrition but threw that up too. I started to realise I was in a bit of trouble. By the last 10 km all the race contenders rode together in a pack of about twenty-five riders. I started to really fade. At one point I struggled to hold the speed of the pack, which had never happened to me in a race before. It was obvious this world title was going to be decided in the run, and I just hoped I would feel better once the run started.

Once again, I transitioned well, and started the run in the lead. To everyone watching, it seemed business as usual. Unfortunately, in the typical unpredictable nature of elite sport, my body had other ideas. I ran well for 2 km and told myself that all I had to do was keep this up. After all, I had done this all season. Instead, over the next kilometre, I absolutely fell apart, overcome with a weakness and dizziness that absolutely reduced me to a survival creep home. I could do nothing as competitors passed me. Six to be exact. The finish of that race was the worst I had experienced, and every excruciating step was a nightmare. I was shattered both physically and emotionally when I crossed the line in seventh place. Unable to face anything, I kept walking straight back to my hotel room. I hated losing and couldn't pretend I wasn't devastated.

I was told I was a bad loser and just agreed with anyone who said so. 'Yes. I am a sore loser. I hate losing more than I love winning.'

98

What a disastrous end to the season.

We stayed in Mexico until the Monday, giving me a few days to mull over what had happened. I was a little angry with Mum and Alwyn for leaving the hotel zone a few days earlier, but it didn't last long. They were also ill, so much so they remained in bed for two days. Both of them said if I felt this bad on the day of the race, they didn't know how I even started. It didn't really matter to me. I constantly questioned whether I could have done anything to have finished better.

I received letters from Ben Crowe at Nike Australia and Nic Bideau (now an athletics coach) congratulating me on an outstanding season. Both letters reminded me I was always a world champion for life, you never lost that honour having won one. They told me that to finish seventh when so ill was really a respectable result. Nic Bideau's letter went further, telling me everyone respected my efforts and I was only feeling such overwhelming disappointment because I was a true champion and expected excellence from every performance. He was right, but it was going to take me a while to get over this result.

In hindsight, I should have been very proud of what I had achieved in such a short time.

I had just completed the best debut season ever in the sport of triathlon (this remains true to today). After winning the World Championship at my first international race just twelve months earlier, I had won every ITU event I contested. I was clearly the world number one triathlete on points and rankings and had collected the ITU World Cup title (which today is the World Championship title). I had lost the one race I didn't want to lose, maybe through no fault of my own, but that was the beauty of high-performance sport. There is no place for losing. I did not want to lose like that again. I just had to regroup and look forward to the upcoming domestic season of racing through the Australian summer followed by the 1996 ITU season. That is one great thing about sport. You can fix most of your problems with your next race. I decided this was what I was going to have to do.

On the way back to Australia, Clare and I stopped in San Diego to meet some sponsors. I knew I had to keep on top of the other side of my sporting career, my sponsorship commitments. But I just wanted to get back home. I needed to take a bit of a break before the domestic season started. Racing in Australia was always a priority for me, and I knew one thing for sure: I could not lose in Australia.

6. World Domination

My debut ITU season had gone to plan. I had been in the sport less than twelve months and won everything the ITU had on offer prior to Cancun. In today's World Triathlon racing calendar format, I would have also remained World Champion. Despite my dramatic and highly successful arrival on the ITU stage, I took the failure to defend my world title hard. It annoyed me, not winning one race wasn't good enough. With hindsight though, losing taught me a lot more than winning did. I began to realise things will not always go to plan in sport. My loss forced me to understand the process. After all, if sport was a smooth road to success, everyone would be world champion.

But in the last month of 1995 I really didn't want to think about all of that. During the year, I started to invest my prize money and sponsorship earnings and purchased two properties in Noosa, actually in the same street as Noosa Triathlon organiser Garth Prowd. As an athlete, I knew my race days would end at some stage, so I decided to invest in property. I never bought myself anything to celebrate a win like a lot of the other athletes did. I couldn't see the point. I wanted the rest of my life to be set up once I stopped racing and property seemed the most sensible thing for me to invest in. The last month of 1995 I spent time furnishing my places and organising one to rent out and the other to be my northern base so that I could escape there during the terribly cold winter months in Melbourne.

While setting up my Noosa base, I needed to get the Australian telecommunication company Telstra along to connect phones and, in those days, dial-up internet. I was training at the time the Telstra guy arrived and Mum was there to let him in. Mum told me later that when the guy arrived, he asked Mum if this was the place of 'the Emma Carney'. Mum replied, 'Yes, the triathlete'. The Telstra guy was so excited, he was apparently a big fan and named his daughter Emma after me. He told Mum it was an honour for him to set up my place, and I'm not sure if it was a fluke or not, but I had the fastest dial up internet in Noosa. I still reckon the Telstra guy hooked my place up to some supersonic Telstra hub somewhere. Disappointingly, I never had the chance to thank him, as he was finished by the time I returned from training.

It was late January 1996 when I finally signed a contract with Trek USA. It had been a long time coming. I had other bike companies, Zipp and Quintana Roo, also enquiring about me riding their bikes but I still wanted Trek. I placed the order for my new bike with a smaller frame size as organised. I was looking forward to riding a bike that was more responsive through corners. This was important as triathlons were shifting more and more to tight circuit criterium type bike courses.

Signing with Trek wasn't the only highlight of January 1996. I also called Matt Paterson, my first running coach from Wesley College. I asked if he could get over the fact that I was a triathlete, not a specialist track runner, and coach me again. Matt agreed. I was really excited to be working with a run coach again. I was always confident in his coaching, because he knew what running fast required. What also worked well was that Matt coached following the philosophy and coaching practices of predominantly middle-distance run programs; perfect for triathlon. Middle distance focuses on speed and endurance, keeping the intensity focus in training, something I believe is so often overlooked by typical triathlon coaches.

Before I could start ramping up my run training though, I needed to get over a calf strain I developed towards the end of the 1995 season. It cropped up in late November and was probably the result of a long season of racing and long-haul flights. The forced rest was a blessing at the end of the season, because my body was given time to recover.

During December and through January Dad, despite my scepticism, managed to come to an agreement with Online Sports. I signed on to race the Triathlon Grand Prix series but there were many issues to resolve. I wanted confirmation that prizemoney was equal for men and women. It was obvious that appearance fees were not equal, but we decided that wasn't something we could change alone.

There were all sorts of issues with the event sponsors and my own personal sponsors, which almost rendered me less able to race than my refusal to accept inequality for women. The situation was only going to get worse, because in 1996 I signed with National Australia Bank (NAB) while TA and the Triathlon Grand Prix series signed with St George Bank. NAB had signed me onto their newly created 'Team National', a group of athletes leading their field in various sports who were likely to be highly visible in the approach to the Sydney 2000 Olympic

Games. This was a part of their ambush marketing campaign on Westpac Bank who were aligning themselves closely with the Sydney Olympic Games organisers. St George Bank as major sponsor of TA and the Triathlon Grand Prix series, naively thought they assumed control of every athlete, but their sponsorship had no control over me personally. Both Dad and I could see that TA, Online Sports, and TA's connection with St George Bank's Di Ainsworth, were going to try and make things difficult by muddying up the sponsorship boundaries of my bank (NAB) and theirs (St George). Naively, we decided to give them the benefit of the doubt.

Another issue arising from my signing to the problematic Grand Prix Series related to what we were required to wear. Online Sports required all athletes to wear the same race kit, which my sponsors did not like one bit. We negotiated with my personal sponsors, but the logos were very small and hardly visible to television viewers. It was a very sticky point in negotiating the Grand Prix contract. I had more to lose by signing, because my personal sponsors were major players in their market and provided me with more opportunities both financially and through advertising campaigns than the TV series did. They paid me well, and I needed to live up to my side of the contract. I was a little worried. I didn't want to lose my value and reputation as an athlete worth signing, especially as I knew the organisers really didn't give a toss about me anyway.

Finally, it was announced I would be racing, but both Dad and I doubted whether the contract would hold. Required at the official press launch in Sydney, I dutifully attended then on the way out announced I was injured and would miss the first race. I hoped the organisers were annoyed, because I had little to no respect for them anyway. I missed the first race due to my calf injury but was ready for my Grand Prix debut in round two in late February.

My first race of the season was the Australian Sprint Championships in Melbourne on Sunday, 4 February. I would have liked a little more run training prior but reminded myself of Deeks' advice that you can never wait for the perfect preparation otherwise you will never race. I'm glad I took the gamble. I won easily and spent more time post-race signing autographs than the race itself. Race organiser David Hansen ran out of things for me to sign. Mum was curious as to what people were queuing up for and walked to the front to proclaim, 'Oh, it's you!' in front of everyone. 'Thanks Mum' I told her, much to everyone's amusement.

On Sunday, 25 February I raced my first Grand Prix event. It was held at St Kilda Beach, so I was racing in front of my home crowd. The format for the women was designed for fast and furious racing, with a 500 m swim, 14 km bike and 3 km run. The series put first, second and third athletes into coloured kit, and as I hadn't raced the first event I was in the regular red and white kit. Some swim specialists were emerging in the junior ranks and they had been signed on to try to add pressure in the swim. I exited slightly down but bridged across on the short bike. It came down to the run and I won easily from Jackie Gallagher with Michellie Jones a distant third. My win put me into the second-place, pink-coloured kit for the next round.

Following the first two races of the domestic triathlon season, I remained in Melbourne and got stuck into some run training with Matt. Some of my favourite training sets reappeared in the Tuesday track session, like the six 600-metre efforts, with a 200-metre float jog between. We put together some great training sessions, and I was back running sub-3-minute 1 km repeats on the track, sub-1-minute-50-second 600-metre efforts, and sub-68-second 400-metre efforts. The quality of my run training improved under Matt's watchful eye and I started to feel good running again. With my return to run form, confidence in my ability to race well grew also.

My next race was round two of the Grand Prix series in Canberra, a traditional 1500 m swim, 40 km bike and 10 km run triathlon with a twist. The first 20 km of the bike was non-drafting, while the last 20 km drafting was allowed. Very odd, but the organisers were trying to be creative in their triathlon racing formats. I swam very poorly, suffering in the cold water of Lake Burley Griffen. Being the strongest triathlon bike rider in the world, it took only 10 km to catch the lead bunch during the non-drafting first half of the bike course. At the 20 km mark, drafting was permitted, and we all rolled around looking at each other. No one was prepared to try to break away. I decided I would just wait for the run, because I felt I was the strongest runner in the field too. Towards the end of the bike, one athlete went off the front, but I didn't care because she was a poor runner. At the bike to run transition Australian triathlete Jackie Gallagher took off in hot pursuit of the lone athlete out the front, while I approached the run in a more controlled pace. She quickly gained 80 m on me and everyone watching assumed I was beaten, but I had other ideas. I wound my effort up with the intention of negatively splitting the 10 km (running the second 5 km faster than the first 5 km). This worked well, and at 7 km I was in the lead, eventually opening this up and winning by a large margin. With two wins from two starts, I was now leading the series.

The following week I turned down an opportunity to drive in the Celebrity Grand Prix (the real one, racing Formula 1 cars). To take part, I was required to spend a week at Sandown Racecourse in Melbourne obtaining a CAM's (car racing) licence. I didn't want to miss a week of training. I had races to win.

In hindsight, I should have taken up the offer of car racing, because on Friday, 8 March, I fell off my bike in training and cracked my left scapula (shoulder blade) a third of the way across. That of course put me out of the rest of the triathlon series and most of the domestic summer of racing. The only positive thing was that because I had only cracked it a third of the way across, I just needed to wear my left arm in a sling, and it would heal. Told that I needed to rest for six weeks, I decided I would use all my patience and give it four.

Swimming was out, running was out (too much pressure on my shoulder) and bike riding was limited to indoor alternatives. With nothing to do, I decided to get away to my place up in Noosa. The fourth round of the Grand Prix series was on at Twin Waters, just south of Noosa, on Sunday, 17 March. Channel 10 asked if I would commentate both the men's and women's races. It was nice to be involved but irritating to watch. The race lead was mine, and I told the race organisers I should have been wearing the leader's yellow kit while commentating.

A week later I flew to Sydney to commentate the next round of the Triathlon Grand Prix, at the request of Channel 10. It was then that Online Sports showed their true colours. Owner Damian Bray told Dad and me that he had requested I be removed from the commentary team. They claimed Di Ainsworth, who was in charge of the St George Bank sponsorship, was not happy I was sponsored by the rival National Australia Bank. This had been the case from day one, and we asked why it was a problem now. No reason was given. Apparently, Reebok had also required that the transition area be called the Reebok Changeover. These were all concocted problems, because in reality they were not my problems. The problem lay in the fact that St George Bank had negotiated sponsorship with TA and the Triathlon Grand Prix series, not me as an individual athlete. Both Dad and I knew this would blow up: it was just a question of when. I believe Reebok were just bitter with me because Dad was one of the heads of Nike Australia and the sportswear industry was cutthroat. It was clear that the problem was my obvious association with competing brands. Again, I was different from everyone else, which gave me a distinct presence, but also ruffled feathers. Frustrated, I told Dad I didn't want anything to do with the series and we left.

It was a good lesson to learn. When things are toxic, it is not even worth trying to fit in. I was always going to have problems with a triathlon series that expected everyone to be the same. I wasn't like everyone else, and I didn't want to be. I wanted to be the best in the world, and to be that I needed to be different. The Triathlon Grand Prix series was not endorsed by the ITU, so was run without established process or protocol. The organisers were not required to look after athletes, and they didn't care about equality or anything other than making money from the sport. Both TA CEO Tim Wilson, and TA President Bill Walker didn't seem to mind an independent business venture taking control of the sport of triathlon in Australia, so it was up to the athletes to fend for themselves.

At a later stage, Di Ainsworth requested a meeting with Dad and asked to buy out my NAB sponsorship. She was, however, surprised at the fee required, having come to the table with nothing to offer. I wasn't sure what she expected, but she seemed to think I would just fall into line. The meeting was futile. At the end of the day, I didn't want to be like everyone else and wasn't going to change my mind either, no matter how much they ostracised me. I wanted my image to be quite distinct and I also wanted to be supported with mainstream advertising through my sponsors. My public profile was growing fast because of this approach.

I walked away from the toxic Online Sports organisation and asked Dad to avoid dealing with people like that in my career again, or if he did, to not get me involved in the process. I didn't need that much negativity in my life. Being an athlete was brutal enough.

Online Sports continued with their passive aggressive behaviour towards the sport of triathlon and launched an International Grand Prix Series in late March. It was apparently going to take on the world of triathlon racing. The men's race series was 'supported' by three women's races, and I was named in the line-up. This was of course completely untrue, as I wasn't even signed up to their Australian series for the following year, let alone an international series. News filtered through to Les McDonald regarding the announcement of the International Grand Prix series and, aware of the discrepancy between the men and women's series, all ITU travel support was withdrawn from those athletes. Online Sports was told to remove me from their line-up immediately.

For their part, the ITU brought in an independent consultant to review the sport in preparation for the 1996 season, with the aim of maximising ITU control worldwide. Graham Lovett was engaged through Pacific Sports, a subsidiary of Rupert Murdoch's News Corporation. Graham advised Les McDonald that to ensure both Michellie and I raced the ITU series, we should both receive a USD50,000 appearance fee for the 1996 season. It was a deal done in complete secrecy, and as Dad pointed out to Les, it was going to be a waste of ITU funds.

'Emma is always going to race, and Michellie will take the money, then race when she feels like it,' Dad told him.

'I know, but no one listens to me,' Les lamented to Dad.

Les was against appearance money payments and the ITU has never paid them to athletes. He believed it was unfair and athletes should always race hard for their payment through prize money, not receiving a payment simply for showing up. He was so against this particular payment to Michellie and me, he refused to allow Graham Lovett to use any of the ITU's money. Instead the money came from Pacific Sports. The payments were made, and Dad was correct in his prediction. I raced and Michellie never showed all year.

With regard to my sponsors, problems were beginning to crop up with Nike Australia. I was really just being treated as the boss's daughter, and still sitting on base entry level contract dollars. I met with Nike Australia sponsorship manager Ben Buckley late in March, but it was looking to me like I needed to go to a sporting goods company that saw me as a world class athlete in my own right and not in relation to the boss.

By this time, I was able to return to full bike and run training. My scapula had healed well, but swimming was still a problem. I couldn't overload the shoulder blade due to the pain. It wasn't until mid-April I was able to swim pain free. Unfortunately, at that stage, my right knee was becoming increasingly sore. I never had knee problems before, so it was a completely odd injury. I noticed swelling around the patella and thought maybe I somehow knocked it. After almost a week juggling the pain, swelling and treating it with ice, I could manage the injury, but couldn't get rid of it. Being a runner, I thought I might have worn my running shoes in an odd way. They seemed perfect. Dad then suggested I look at my bike shoes. I looked at the cleats (attachments to the bottom of the shoe that clip into the pedals) and noticed the cleat on my right shoe had moved. The small change would have forced my knee into a slightly different position, affecting the way my knee tracked. Once I replaced the cleats, the problem subsided, but it took a couple of weeks for everything to settle again. Having an injury scare again forced me into becoming really diligent with all my equipment.

The knee injury also forced me to miss the 1996 Australian Triathlon Championships. It was a disappointing time. I had suffered a number of injuries over the domestic season, and most had not really been through training, rather mistakes.

By May I had fully returned to training and moved back to Melbourne from Noosa to make my final preparations for the 1996 ITU season. But before I left, the cracks in our relationship with Nike deepened. Dad felt strongly about having a 'think globally, act locally' strategy, whereas many US Nike executives just wanted to Americanise the world of sport. Dad took Nike into Cricket and Nike objected. Dad aligned Australian sporting heroes with the brand in Australia and US bosses didn't recognise them. The result was there were personality clashes and major disagreements. Dad was never someone who just fitted in; rather, he stood by his principles. It seems I adopted that character trait from him.

All this blew up in the first week of May. I decided I was going to back Dad and asked him to find me a sporting goods sponsor who would support me properly. I needed a company who respected me as an athlete. I also couldn't work with a company who had fallen out with Dad. It just didn't feel right.

On Wednesday, 8 May, I flew out to Japan for the first ITU race of the season. Held in Ishigaki, located in the Okinawa Islands, the area was renowned for its beautiful beaches and tropical, laid back lifestyle. To get there required quite a few flight changes, and the ITU booked me onto a JAL flight, which did not connect smoothly with the Qantas domestic flights. I stayed overnight at the Kansai International Airport Hotel, before flying out just before midday Thursday, 9 March to Ishigaki. Despite the overnight connection, flying to Japan was always so much more pleasant than the long-haul flights we as Australians had to endure when racing in Europe or North America. Jet lag was also never an issue with only a two-hour time difference.

The flight to Ishigaki Island from Kansai Airport was packed with most of the other athletes. The island had a very laid-back atmosphere, nothing really like the bustle of more renowned Japanese cities like Tokyo. Being a race on a small island the entire town was excited about the event. A large convoy of buses and trucks greeted us when we arrived and took us safely to Hotel Miyahira, where we all stayed.

I spent the next two days familiarising myself with the race layout, training on the swim course each day, riding the bike course and getting to know the run. The swim consisted of three laps in the local harbour (Tonoshiro Fishing Port). The water was warm at 25°C, and pleasant enough to swim in. The main problem I had was the number of sting rays in the water. In race scenarios, I really didn't care what I swam over; in practice swims I did. I was a lot more comfortable with the bike course. It was predominantly flat and technical through the town of Ishigaki. The Southern Gate Bridge, a steep bridge near the harbour and the swim course, offered the only hill. We were required to ride this loop seven times, so I thought the technical areas and the constant climbing and descending on the bridge in the wind could really create some problems for the weaker bike riders. I knew that if I worked hard in these tougher areas, I could stop large bike groups from forming. I was a little worried though. The weather was unpredictable, with frequent little tropical storms. If one struck on race day it would make the bike course very slippery. The run was similar to the downtown section of the bike, with five laps in the opposite direction. If I was able to get a break on the field, the tight course would allow me to get away and out of sight. Once I was out of sight, it would be harder for anyone to catch me. My race plan was set.

Race day was Sunday, 12 May with a 3.30 p.m. start. The wind picked up through the day, which was going to affect the bike. I had a good swim, exiting the water only 40 seconds down on former German national swim champion Ute Mückel (she swam so fast, her times were the same as the men for the first lap of the swim!). She worked well on the bike with another German athlete off the front of the field. I bided my time for a lap, found my legs, then jumped across to form a group of three. By attacking hard to join the leaders, I knew I would take the riders in my group by surprise. No one was able to go with me. At the front of the race, we built a lead of just over a minute heading into transition two (bike to run). To back up my fastest bike split of the day, I put together the fastest run of the day to cross the line over two and a half minutes ahead of second place, Australian Jackie Gallagher. Another Australian, Rina Hill, finished third to make it an Australian trifecta.

The next round of the ITU series was in Gamagori, in central Japan. With only a week between races, recovery was my priority. I was good at gauging how my body felt, but generally I was tired and sore up to the Wednesday following a classic distance triathlon. Light training was really all I needed. I also had to factor in a day's travel back to mainland Japan and the usual pre-race requirements of press conferences and media commitments.

Gamagori is set in a more traditional, built up region of Japan. The race itself was set in and around a dragon boat racing stadium. The swim was surrounded by grandstands, with the bike and run exiting the stadium and returning each lap. It was a fast, flat course, with the heat the main concern. Race day was Sunday, 19

May, and it was hot. Fortunately, it never really bothered me. I always thought it was one of those things you couldn't change, so it was never really worth worrying about. I also think racing in the heat is one of those unwritten mental games you just have to master, especially if you race an endurance sport in summer months. Needless to say, I raced the event well and won.

Now that I was largely unbeaten on the ITU World Cup circuit, there was increased interest from everyone. It wasn't just the glamorous world of sponsors and mainstream media, but also out of competition drug testing. As a dominant athlete, ASDA (Australian Sports Drug Agency now ASADA Australian Sports Anti-Doping Authority) required my whereabouts to be constantly monitored so random drug testing could be done at any time while on Australian soil. This meant often I would meet someone from ASDA either arriving at my training venue or at home, just as I was heading out for a swim, bike or run. I had to provide a urine sample before I could leave to train or finish training. It happened a lot more regularly, which made me wonder just how 'random' the testing was.

My run of injuries through the Australian summer now appeared to have given my body an opportunity to really freshen up for the international season of racing. Following the Japanese races, I put together a really solid block of training. My run times were consistently fast, with 1 minute 45 seconds for 600 metre efforts, 65-66 seconds for 400 metre efforts, and 30 seconds for 200 metre efforts. It was clear that I was running well and with more speed and better technique than most of my competition. For my swim training, I was still working with Alwyn and also French triathlete Benjamin Sanson while I was away from Melbourne. I continued to work on maintaining my start speed, stroke rate, kick fitness, and holding form. Swim speed over 200-300 metres was still a priority, as that was where the swim leg of the triathlon was really set up, the first few hundred metres of the race. My bike riding was strong as always, a natural result of the consistent riding through the hills, and winding backroads surrounding the family home in Eltham. To this day, I still have not found a better area for bike training than those relentless hills surrounding Eltham.

On Wednesday, 12 June, I headed off overseas again for the next round of the ITU series. This time we were racing in Paris, with the transition area on the bridge over the river Seine, just adjacent to the Eiffel Tower.

Training and preparing for a triathlon in the middle of Paris was not the easiest thing to do. I managed to get some short rides in and found the best way to ride a bike in Paris was to ride without hesitation, take up a lane and look like you know where you are going. You fit in well in the hectic traffic then. I found a pool to swim in and there were plenty of parks to run in, but given the long flight over from Australia, rest and recovery was really what I needed most.

The race in Paris was odd. There was much concern about the quality of the water in the Seine, the site of the swim, but the race organiser did not really show much concern. In preparation for the event, I had a doctor in Melbourne give me a number of shots to make sure I didn't get sick swimming in filthy water. There was a current, and we were taken further upstream in little boats to ensure the swim was 'difficult enough', whatever that meant. The race organiser kept trying to reassure us, saying, 'Look, I see fishies. See the water is not that bad.'

All I saw though was one big dead fish floating upside down.

'Do you have any live fish?' I asked him, but he didn't seem to understand the question.

My negativity towards the dirty water reflected in my swim time, and I exited a little down. Fortunately, I was able to ride the bike course well, using the technical cobbled areas and also riding the head and tail winds to my advantage, and jumped between groups to get myself to the lead pack. The race finished in a similar fashion to all my ITU races so far. I won by almost a minute, running away from the field following a fairly bunched ride. I ran more than 40 seconds faster over 5 km than anyone that day and felt strong throughout. I was happy with the race and also pleased to keep my unbeaten run intact. It was a very memorable race, given the location, but all I wanted to do was get back to my hotel for a shower once I crossed the line. I felt like I had swum in sewage, and I was sure I could smell pee on my skin through my sweat.

Following the race in Paris, I flew to Montreal for the next ITU race in Drummondville, Canada. With an afternoon flight out of Paris on Monday, 17 June, I had time to enjoy a real Parisian café, something I could very easily get used to on my post-race recovery days. My glamorous day peaked at breakfast though, as I endured a six-and-a-half-hour economy class flight to Boston before connecting to Montreal. My tired and sore legs struggled in the cramped conditions. My Qantas sponsorship had spoilt me.

An official event car collected me at Montreal airport. Along the side of the car was a life size picture of me winning the event last year. Awkwardly I climbed in and looked through my own silhouette as we drove down the highway to Drummondville. I was exhausted by the time I checked into my hotel room at 11.30 p.m. and finally got to bed.

I had a week to prepare for the next race. Recovery was again my priority along with rest. I trained on most parts of the swim, bike and run courses during the week, but I was familiar with Drummondville having raced and won there the previous year. The entire town was interested in the race, and each evening there was a party at someone's house or media-related pre-race function to attend. All in all, there were more functions than I preferred. As always, rest, recovery and remained key to my race preparation.

The women's race was scheduled to start at 2.15 p.m., about fifteen minutes after the men. There was a rule that male competitors would be pulled off the course if the women caught them. Quite an incentive to go fast, I thought. Threatening rain luckily held off long enough for us to complete the course. Wetsuits were not allowed, but it was very borderline, with the water temperature in the lake at 20°C. Looking at the start list, I was concerned about one athlete, Canadian Carol Montgomery. Carol was a classy runner, having represented Canada at the World Cross Country Championships and also at the 1994 Commonwealth Games in the 10,000 m track event. I hadn't raced Carol much, but looking at her results in triathlon, the bike seemed to negatively impact her run times. She didn't have a great win record over Michellie Jones either, so I assumed that, to beat Carol, you needed a tough bike ride. My problem at this race was that it was dead flat, and no one would really be interested in working with me, because everyone knew I would drive the bike hard to tire Carol's legs for the run. I decided I needed to race smart and remain aware that the race would be won with a fast run.

My predictions were correct. Groups formed on the bike, with all the contenders in the front pack. It came down to the run. Carol and I ran hard that day. It was only my stubbornness and hatred for losing that got me over the line first. I ended up beating Carol across the line by only around thirty seconds, putting a surge in at the 7.5 km mark. Carol and I were both more than a minute faster on the run than any other female athlete. I almost broke 34 minutes, clocking 34 minutes 8 seconds for the 10 km run leg. Third placed Jackie Gallagher was over a minute behind me, with the rest of the field lagging further.

The next round of the ITU series was in Bermuda. It was only a week away, so again recovery was really important. I pulled up really sore in the legs from the fast run in Drummondville. I had a few days before travelling again, so I rode, swam and ran the soreness out of my legs with some easy sessions. At the same time, my consistent racing must have made its way back to Australia and a number of radio stations, including Triple M Melbourne and 2UE Sydney, called me to follow up on my most recent win.

On Thursday, 27 June, I flew out of Montreal to New York and from there to Bermuda. I had some difficulty clearing customs in Bermuda because I couldn't provide an address for my accommodation. I always expected the ITU to organise my accommodation, and for someone to meet me at the airport. I finally cleared once the race organisers had been contacted and provided customs with an address. It was a long day by the time I reached the unknown location, a homestay with a local family. I arrived late, and felt really awkward disrupting them, but my homestay family (Cathy, Bill and their son Robert) didn't seem to mind. With a focus on recovery I swam each day and rode over the bike and run course fairly easily. Except for an athlete briefing, I spent the majority of my time trying to rest my sore legs. This really meant watching TV on my homestay's couch or lying in bed with my legs raised up on pillows to help the recovery process.

On race morning, Sunday, 30 June, I had to actually get myself out of bed early for the first time in a while. The swim started in deep water, in the Harbour just off Front Street, Hamilton. I always thought it was quite a tough way to start; treading water, waiting for the starter's orders. I had a really clean start and could see that I was close to the front pack. With a huge effort I managed to get into the draft of the front pack and settled into a hard but comfortable swim. The lead swimmer was only eleven seconds ahead as I exited the water, so I started the bike in the front pack. I felt surprisingly ok and ran away with the win. My winning time was fast that day — I recorded the fastest bike and run legs and even more importantly, I was less than ten minutes behind the men's winning time, showing how strong I was now racing.

On returning to my home stay, a nice ride through the very picturesque coastline of the small suburbs of Bermuda, I was met with admiration from my adopted family.

'You never told us you were the best in the world Emma!!' Carol said to me in amazement.

I just laughed. 'Maybe I was just lucky,' I replied.

With the race done and won, it was time to explore Bermuda. My homestay family took me out in their boat and showed me just how amazing and beautiful Bermuda really is. I flew home the next day, via New York and Los Angeles. It was great to board the Qantas flight at LA and to be greeted with Australian accents. Having lost Tuesday somewhere over the Pacific in some time zone black hole I arrived in Brisbane on Wednesday, 3 July. Garth Prowd organised a car to pick me up and take me to my place in Noosa. I enjoyed an easy week of training in Noosa, before returning to Melbourne.

The easy week extended out to another week, as suddenly it seemed I was the athlete whom everyone wanted to interview. The television and print media, and sponsors, all wanted my time. Dad had also held discussions with adidas clothing and footwear company, which somehow involved adidas Germany, so it was an international deal. I received a stack of adidas gear to train in while the negotiations continued. Changing clothing sponsors was not a problem, but to me changing a shoe sponsor was fraught with danger. I had run in Nike all my adult life, and my body was used to the 'last' and fit of the shoes. Adidas was a leading shoe company, but it was going to be different for my body. I needed to start wearing the new product as soon as possible so my body had time to adapt slowly. I knew my Achilles were fragile and triggered easily. Fortunately, the adidas shoes felt good. Even better, the deal was struck within six weeks and soon I was a full blown contracted adidas International athlete.

Barely a week after arriving home I decided to head back up to Noosa. Melbourne in July does not generally have the best weather for training. I don't mind the cold too much (within reason), but rain makes bike rides downright miserable and dangerous. I decided I would return to Noosa in the second week of July and start my full training load there.

Initially I felt a little tired, but as I eased back into things I felt better. I always preferred the familiar sessions in Melbourne but managed to replicate them in Noosa. My bike and run form soon returned. I also joined a swim squad at Nambour pool, with head coach Dick Orbell overseeing my swim program. In Noosa, I had the added benefit of doing some open water swim sessions, which was not at all possible in Melbourne through the winter months unless you wanted to die of exposure in the freezing Port Phillip Bay.

Everything was going well until Thursday, 15 August. I had a slightly sore throat for a few days and then, after a poor night's sleep, woke with a persistent cough. I still swum that morning but could not complete my run session in the afternoon. My chest felt tight and breathing was difficult. I dabbled with my training for the next week. I knew full well I could not really get any fitter for the World Championships on 24 August, but I could get sicker.

Unfortunately, that is exactly what I did. I developed what I thought at the time to be a serious chest infection. Light training was all I could manage.

I left for Cleveland on Sunday, 18 August. Most Australian team members were at a TA training camp, under newly appointed head coach Brett Sutton, but I wasn't interested in attending. Brett generally trained every female athlete I raced from Australia, except Michellie, and I did not want to start training alongside my competitors. Earlier in the season, TA CEO Tim Wilson told Dad he expected me to 'fit in' with the program and attend TA camps, but begrudgingly also acknowledged that I 'seemed to be progressing well'.

Without a thought of not contesting the World Championships, I lined up at the start on race day. I hadn't told anyone from TA, including the team doctor, that I wasn't well because I didn't see the point. My attitude was that I was a professional athlete and I needed to perform.

The women's World Championship started at 8 a.m. It consisted of a three-lap swim, eight-lap bike and four-lap run. The swim was a tight circuit — too tight — and being three laps was very rough. Rough from flying fists, not water chop. There were too many swimmers all fighting for clear water in such a small circuit. I exited uncharacteristically off the pace for my season of racing so far. On the bike I struggled through periods of tiredness, but still bridged all gaps and brought the field together. All the main contenders were in the one bike pack, so it was clear as we approached the bike to run transition that as usual the strongest runner would become World Champion.

On any other day, I would have clearly handled the situation well. Today was a different story. Today was a nightmare; the tough side of losing. A world title that should have been won so easily but lost so painfully.

From the first step of the run I felt awful but grabbed the lead almost through habit. I hung on for as long as I could but just ran out of energy. Each lap I did the best I could, but I was weak from my illness. Brett Sutton started to yell out splits to me, something he had never done in the past, and something only my Dad ever provided. I told him where to go, frustrated with his sudden interest in me, as if trying to justify his TA Head Coach appointment. I only slipped to second, but to me, I might as well have come last. It was only on the last lap and the top of the last hill that I lost the lead. My compatriot Jackie Gallagher beat me ever so slightly for the first time ever, and boy did that hurt. Jackie enjoyed every minute of it and she never let me forget it.

There was a compulsory 1 p.m. press conference and all the attention in the room was turned on me, with questions as to why I didn't win. Pre-race, I was expected to win, and the room was shocked I had been unwell. No one had been told of my illness. I explained that I did not want anyone to know pre-race as I didn't want to make any excuses. I spoke as little as possible because I felt like I was going to explode with a mix of disappointment, despair and anger. I think I can say confidently that I am the world's worst loser. I have no time for losing, and I have no ability to hide my disappointment when I lose. I skipped the evening presentation, flying back to Australia instead. Les reprimanded me for being a 'bad sport' once I landed.

'Yes, Les. I'm a bad sport. I hate losing,' I told him as he berated me down the phone.

'You need to represent good sportsmanship, Emma,' he told me.

'Give me a break Les… When was the last time you enjoyed losing?' was my response.

Les conceded that was a very solid reply.

I honestly did not understand why everyone was so amazed at my behaviour. That was two years in a row I had not won a world title because I was ill. Again, I was devastated. I did not race to lose. Ever.

Since starting on the ITU circuit in June 1995, I had nine World Cup starts for nine wins.

Undefeated.

By contrast, from three World Championship starts, I had 1 win, 1 second (ill), and 1 seventh (ill).

I was world number one, but my world championship title record was letting me down.

There were different possible explanations for my 1996 world championship result. I thought perhaps the long-haul flights contributed to my illnesses. I was not convinced though. After all I picked up the chest infection in Australia. TA was beginning to pressure all athletes to attend training camps during the international season to reduce the amount of travel. The glaring problem was the fact that I would be training with my competitors. I preferred to do things differently and privately. I did not want them to get to know me, to perhaps find a weakness in me, or to discover a way to beat me. Dad was of the same opinion. Unknown to me, TA President Bill Walker met with Dad to discuss the possibility of me training under the guidance of Brett Sutton. He reasoned that the only reason Jackie Gallagher beat me at the World Championships was because she did less travel and had a sound training base. Dad, being Dad, did not take this well. He corrected Bill Walker by reminding him I had been ill.

115

The pressure on me to conform was intensifying because TA stood to receive increased funding aimed at developing medal winning athletes for the Sydney 2000 Olympic Games. It was obvious that if I trained with TA appointed coaches, TA could claim my wins on the ITU circuit as theirs. The more success TA had internationally, the more funding TA received from the Australian Sports Commission (now Sport Australia). Word got back to Dad and me that TA justified the success of their program in a report, purely on the grounds that I was beaten by an athlete who attended their camp. I understood TA needed to maximise their program funding but would have appreciated someone at least showing interest in my personal wellbeing not only as an athlete, but as a member of their team. Fortunately, I had a thick skin.

Dad was quietly furious, and was also concerned about the pressure on me to fit in. Here I was, the most dominant and successful triathlete in ITU history and TA wanted to change things that were clearly working for me.

Meanwhile, I was still ill. I took myself to Noosa to see if the warmer weather would help me shake off the remains of the chest infection. Two weeks after the world championships, still feeling off, I saw renowned Sports Medicine doctor June Canavan, based in Mooloolaba. June tested my lung function, and I was at less than 60 per cent capacity compared to a test done earlier in the year while healthy. On reporting the results of the test, June made some comments that haunted me six or so years later. She told me that while it was amazing I was able to race three weeks earlier and place second in a World Championship with what must have been less than 30 per cent lung capacity, at best, what she feared was the 'long-term physiological damage this effort would have had on my body and vital organs'. June confirmed that I did not have a mere chest infection, instead I had a chest virus. She was quite surprised I was able to race at all. June tried to simplify things and told me I was like a Ferrari or a top thoroughbred racehorse. I was finely tuned and needed to be kept in top running order to remain fast. Anything slightly off and I will damage myself permanently.

I listened to June's words, but I was beginning to feel that the worst of the chest problem was gone. I knew exercising through a virus was dangerous, and I thought I had taken adequate steps to allow myself to recover. I remember asking when she thought I could train fully again.

June asked if she could speak to Dad about my condition. I said that would be a good idea, because Dad helped me plan my training and racing. Apparently, she asked Dad to take all necessary steps to ensure I never again raced while in such a bad physical state, because a virus of this type can cause damage to vital organs, particularly the heart. June explained to Dad that this damage would not show up at the time but would certainly manifest itself at some stage in the future. She only hoped that I hadn't already damaged my heart by pushing myself to second place at the World Championships a few weeks earlier, a feat that was remarkable under the circumstances. Dad recalled June's comments later:

June called me, and explained that if any damage had been done to the heart, it would be absolutely minimal initially, but with scar tissue the heart would need to work harder and with each extreme effort there would be more damage. This would accumulate and initially cause an imperceptible decline but worsen over time. Following this conversation, I spoke with Emma and we took time to make sure she was well before racing again. She returned to racing well, and we assumed Emma was ok.

In order to regain my health, I wrote the whole of September off, withdrawing from all ITU events. I remained in Noosa where it was warmer. Even in the later winter months Melbourne was cool. My training times improved by early October and it looked like I would be able to return to racing for the last few rounds of the 1996 ITU circuit.

In early September, with the adidas International contract signed, I received more gear than I had ever received in my life. I was on a 'significant contract', but the amount of product surprised me. It was getting ridiculous. At one point I needed a swim towel. I was sent thirty. To this day I still have too many adidas swim towels. Dad wasn't at all surprised and told me that by providing more gear than I needed, adidas knew I would have enough to replace absolutely everything I owned. All my life I had access to the Nike Australia warehouse, but never had I received so much gear at once. It showed how serious adidas were. It was actually nice to be working with a company that took my sporting career as seriously as I did.

Adidas had signed me but didn't have a tri suit for me to race in. With a few more ITU events left in the 1996 season, I had a bit of a rush to get some appropriate race gear. All sorts of bathers and tri suits were sent backwards and forwards from head office in Melbourne to me in Noosa, before I found a pair that suited triathlon racing. The suit was printed up, but it was a rush job. The traditional three stripes were screen printed down the side of the suit but they were somehow smudged. Adidas asked me to 'just wear them', so I did.

The next round of the ITU series was in Auckland, New Zealand. It my first appearance since coming second at the World Championships and I ran away with the win. It was nice to be back.

A week later, we were back on the Sydney Olympic course for the next round of the ITU Series. Despite my loss at the World Championships, I was still in demand and had to do a live cross to the Channel 7 national show, 'SportsWorld'. This commitment ate into my warm-up a little but was a non-negotiable requirement for adidas.

Jackie Gallagher was there as the newly crowned world champion, so I decided there was no way I was going to have her, or anyone, near me at the finish. I raced well, out of the water with the main contenders, with the swim specialists around forty seconds ahead. I broke away on the bike after a lap and recorded the fastest bike and run of the day to win by over two minutes. It was nice to be back winning, but also bittersweet, given it was obvious I should not have lost the world title just over a month earlier.

Although the next race, Noosa Triathlon, was my favourite annual event I still hadn't won it. It was time I did. Following the Sydney ITU race, I headed to my place at Noosa to prepare. Race day was Sunday, 3 November and I woke up the evening before with stomach problems and queasiness. I hoped it would be gone by the morning. We called in June Canavan and she gave me some meds, telling me they would make me feel better. She said that I could race if I could get some fluids in and felt strong enough but advised that I make the decision as close to the race start as possible. I took her advice which meant going through the process of racking my bike and warming up. Things didn't improve and Dad told me I needed to pull out. He told me I needed to race to win and it was just silly if I was ill and unable to do that. I pulled out just before the start. Immediately accused of pulling out due to sponsorship clashes between the race and my personal sponsors, I left Dad to deal with the fall out and went home to bed.

Monday was spent with adidas, who wanted some 'file shots' for an upcoming new product release. It was a long day, which didn't help much with my recovery from the stomach bug.

The ITU invited me to a Women's-Only Triathlon at Amami Ōshima Island, in southwest Japan. So, the following Thursday, I flew out from Brisbane early in the morning, stayed overnight at a hotel near Kansai Airport and continued on to the island the next day. The hotel at the race was very traditional, set just off the beach. The island was very picturesque, with clear waters and offshore reefs. It seemed to be traditional early Japanese style living with none of the hustle or bustle of the cities. I asked our translator if she could take us to a supermarket so I could get some water and food that was less fishy. I felt a little unmotivated as the race was sprung on me last minute. I was already mentally prepared for my end of season break. It was surprisingly difficult to get myself going again.

On the Saturday evening prior to the race, Les McDonald pulled me aside and asked me to 'not win by too much'.

I looked at Les and said, 'What?'

Les then explained to me he thought if I win by too much it would embarrass the Japanese. I told Les I had no idea what he was asking, and I had a reputation to perform to. I told him I didn't know what 'half racing' was. Les rolled his eyes at me and walked off.

We had a midday start on race day, Sunday, 10 November. I was still not as focused as normal as the official racing season was over. The swim was fairly straight forward in the still waters of the bay, the bike was a tough hilly course with a strong headwind in parts, which suited me very well, and the run was a hot 10 km. I built up a lead of three minutes off the bike and added another two minutes on the run to win by just over five. When the second competitor had crossed the line Les said to me, 'Five minutes? Thanks for following my request to not win by much.'

'No worries Les,' I laughed as he stormed off, assuming Les would forgive me.

Later that evening at the prize presentation ceremony, I was given an apparently very valuable bottle of Saki and a roll of Kimono material. I was told that too was very valuable. Unfortunately, on the bus ride back to the hotel following the prize ceremony, the Saki bottle was opened and consumed by us all and the Kimono material was held out the back window in an attempt to re-enact the famous scene from Australian movie, 'Pricilla, Queen of the Desert'. Both items were lost on the night. Fortunately, my prize money was wired electronically to my bank account in Australia, so I didn't have the temptation to throw that out the window too. I don't remember much of the remainder of the bus trip, but I do know I threw up at one point narrowly missing Les McDonald.

Very dusty the next morning, I decided I would be first to breakfast, in an attempt to pretend I was one hundred per cent fine. I was first there. Les was second. Les sat opposite me and looked me in the eye and asked me how I was feeling.

'Fine,' I replied.

Nothing was ever said of the incident, as everyone slowly came down for breakfast. There were a few sore heads, but I remained adamant I was fine. It hurt on the inside though!

Earlier, before the race, Les spoke to me privately about a number of male athletes and ITU executives who were challenging his policy of equal prize money for men and women. Some of the men were pushing to receive more prize money, arguing there were more of them and they also raced faster so it was more exciting. I was annoyed to hear this was still an issue and even more disappointed when Les gave me the correspondence in which the athletes put forward their request.

Les asked me to write to one of the people campaigning for unequal prize money, a fellow Australian team member, to outline my disappointment that an Australian male would not support female equality. I had done so before leaving Australia. Les also asked me to collect female athlete signatures supporting equal prize money. At breakfast, I handed him the petition with the signatures I collected over the weekend. He seemed surprised I had been productive through the previous evening, given my antics.

'This is so important Les. Let me know what else I can do.'

Fortunately, equality prevailed and the ITU did not buckle to the chauvinism that threatened a sport that maintained equality many, many years before other established sports even considered it.

We left Amami Island after breakfast. After a five-hour wait at Kansai Airport, we boarded the flight for Australia. Finally, my 1996 racing season was done.

With racing over, it was time to lighten the training load and spend time with my sponsors.

I travelled to Perth, for the official announcement of the 1997 ITU Championships to be held there in November. Back in Melbourne, Clare and I were invited to attend the opening of the Myer sports store. We were driven to the door in a limo along with AFL footballers and runners. I presented my racing flats to the Myer Managing Director in front of a large crowd of people. It was reportedly the largest sport store in the Southern Hemisphere. The next day I was picked up from Eltham in a limo again, to do a radio interview at the store with Triple M Melbourne. Surprisingly I was asked on air why Dad had left Nike. I dismissed the question with something along the lines that Nike had lost their best employee, refusing to enter into a discussion. I'm not sure how anyone would ever think I would diss my own Dad.

Early in December, adidas flew me to Los Angeles to shoot the first of a series of television commercials. Adidas Australia head of Marketing, Rob Mills, and I flew Qantas Business class. We stayed at The Georgian Hotel in Santa Monica, a short drive from the shoot location. Part of a marketing campaign for new shoes called 'Feet you Wear', adidas brought in a number of other key international athletes to shoot advertisements for the product launch as well. Legendary tennis player Steffi Graff shot her commercial at a different location the day before me; hers, naturally, was on a tennis court, while mine was at Santa Monica Beach. The Olympic 10,000 m champion Haile Gebrselassie was also involved in the product launch and his commercial was filmed at the beach, after mine.

I had to be 'on set' early, at 6 a.m. The beach was quiet, but to set the scene of a barren run in sand, an old car was placed on the foreshore. I had my own trailer. Initially, I wasn't sure why, but realised there were quite a few shoe and clothing changes. There was also a make-up van and another trailer for catering. It was quite full on. Nothing like anything I had ever done before.

The shoot took a while. The day started off overcast and as the skies cleared all the camera lenses had to be changed. With around six cameras this seemed to take a while. During the morning shoot they filmed me running on the beach. Following lunch, I was on the bike, and later in the evening we finished with some open water swimming in the surf. I froze as the voice overs were shot while the sun was setting. I had no script, because the producers wanted me to be spontaneous. Rob fired a string of questions at me and I tried to reply with one-liners. The one that stuck and ended up in the advertisement was, 'My feet are my life'. I spent many months copping flack from others telling me I needed to get a life.

After a full day, and with the sun completely down, I was really pleased to hear the producer announce that we were done. I was surprised how quickly the crew packed everything up. We were invited to the end of shoot drinks, but both Rob and I were tired, so we didn't stay long. We had to fly back to Australia the next day.

I ended the year with my first major international adidas commercial shoot, a contract with a large Australian bank (NAB), Holden running the mainstream print campaign featuring me, and plans for a Holden television commercial as well. I remained undefeated on the ITU circuit and World Number one for the second year running.

1996 had been very good to me.

But I still hadn't won my world title back. I planned to fix that in 1997.

7. A Creep in the Camp

The next year for me was a big year. I raced well, very well.

My results were so good, all thoughts of the dire health warning given to Dad and me by Dr June Canavan the previous August were pushed aside and forgotten. Some feelings of tiredness did start to slowly creep into my body, but elite athletes are always tired.

In 1997, TA had the benefit of increased federal government sport funding through the Australian Sports Commission Olympic Athlete Program (OAP) due solely to the sport of triathlon's upcoming debut as an Olympic sport. This funding was designed to support athletes and coaches preparing for the Sydney 2000 Olympic Games. With OAP support TA funded a squad of athletes with Brett Sutton as head coach. I didn't really think the appointment would affect me in the slightest, because I was predominantly self-managed, working with my own expert coaches and groups. I was also Melbourne based, with training stints in Noosa. I didn't want to train with my competitors and despite TA putting pressure on me, I had no interest in working with Brett Sutton.

As had always been the case, I wasn't convinced that triathlon coaches were what I really needed, and I certainly wasn't convinced about Brett Sutton as a triathlon coach. To me he appeared to be a failed swim coach who was now applying his swim coaching theories to bike and run coaching, thereby applying the volumes and recoveries wrong for biking and in particular running. Brett had a reputation for overtraining athletes. Some athletes who managed to survive his training regime did put together some good races, but so many didn't. From what I heard his training methods were damaging, both physically and psychologically. Given this, I was disappointed in his appointment by TA.

Despite what was going to be uncovered later in the year, 1997 started like any other for me. January and February were solid training months, with sponsorship commitments. I had various contractual requirements with adidas. The main one in January being a Myer department store opening in Melbourne with Steffi Graff, the world's best female tennis player at the time. The store opening was big. Both Steffi and I had bodyguards to protect us from the massive crowd and, to be honest, it took me a little by surprise. I wasn't entirely comfortable with that type of crushing attention.

Early February, I shot a television advertisement for NAB in Sydney. It was again a decent sized production requiring all day filming, both at sunrise and sunset. The location was alongside Sydney Airport, making it seem barren and isolated with views across the water. I was also required to shoot some still photos which were to be used for billboards nationwide and promotional material in NAB branches across the country. At one point during the shoot, the head of the campaign asked me what my day looked like. I thought for a few seconds and said, 'swim, bike, run, eat, sleep'. That became my quote for the campaign, and I was really quite apprehensive that anyone would find that at all interesting.

During this time, I still struggled with Achilles problems and started some treatment with an osteopath in Sydney, Kay Macpherson. Kay had been work-ing on a problem Clare developed with her hamstring and lower back. Kay had a very specific treatment regime, requiring intense massage and body realignment along with exercises to correct the muscle imbalances in my body that were caus-ing the constant lower leg injuries. I thought perhaps I needed to improve my strength and conditioning routine with some finer muscle balancing exercises. After a small break from running while I had this treatment, I was soon back jogging again.

While nursing my body back from this injury, I competed in a couple of national mountain bike races and managed to finish on the podium a few times. I was very aware though that mountain bike racing was great for developing my technical bike skills but came with the risk of injuring myself in another crash like I did the previous year. I really didn't want to write off my summer with another injury. Each time, in a bid to protect my body, I would get off and run rather than ride the really technical areas of the course.

Early March I was again invited to drive in the Melbourne Formula 1 celeb-rity race. As a Holden sponsored athlete, I was expected to drive this year. So, 3 March, I diligently attended the week-long training course at Sandown Raceway. Each member of the celebrity challenge had to gain their CAMS (Confederation of Australian Motor Sport) racing licence. We trained in race modified cars with roll bars and modified seating and were provided with custom-made car race suits complete with fireproof undergarments, a helmet and racing shoes. With all this equipment, I assumed I was safe, so spent the week driving like a maniac. We practised slalom driving through cones, and I hit most of them. We practised starts and I just sat and smoked my tyres. When we raced laps of the course, I just tried to brake later than everyone else, thereby shooting through corners out of control. I was black flagged by officials, but I didn't really care. The instructors called me into the pit and told me I was a dangerous driver in a race car.

'Yes, I know,' I told them.

'I'm a triathlete, not a driver. We are all dangerous out there. Isn't that the point? Bad driving?'

I frustrated the hell out of my driving instructors, but I was having way too much fun to back off.

As you can imagine, race day came along and I wrote my car off within one lap of the Albert Park racing circuit in Melbourne. I had a slow start, having too much fun smoking my tyres on the start grid. I managed to recover slightly but ended up T-Boning another driver who was in a spin. This completely destroyed the front of my car and blew my oil tank. I was towed off the track ASAP.

With the celebrity drive out the way, I was looking forward to getting my triathlon training and racing routine back. I raced the Devonport Triathlon in Tasmania on 23 March and won easily. I felt good, a little out of race practice, but it was another dominant showing in Devonport for me. While in Tasmania, I made some store appearances in Launceston, about an hour's drive south of Devonport, for adidas. This delayed my return to Melbourne by a day, but I needed the rest after the tough racing.

The 1997 ITU season started in April. The first round of the series was again in Ishigaki, Japan. As always, I did a little local race before leaving for Japan, to get my body moving fast again. I felt good and the Melbourne weather gave me a tough race with choppy water and winds to contend with. I won by a large margin and really spent the morning again trying to run down as many male competitors as I could.

I flew to Sydney, then to Japan on Wednesday, 9 April, equipped with a new Trek bike and a half newly-designed adidas race kit. I had been working with adidas designers to get a suit put together. It was still in prototype stage, but I just took what had been done so far. We flew JAL on a plane that still had a smoking section. I felt like I lost a lung on that flight, despite being seated in the non-smoking section. I missed flying Qantas.

My flight was fairly uneventful, until customs at Narita airport decided to put my bike through the X-Ray machine. My bike case was a hard case, because

I wasn't particularly confident the airline baggage handlers noticed the 'fragile' stickers. I hoped that the hard case would get smashed more than the bike on international long-haul flights. The case was a little larger, and on this occasion too large for the x-ray machine. I stood there watching about ten Japanese customs officials struggle with my bike. They finally wrestled it out and I asked if they wanted me to open it for them to have a look. They all ignored me and just let me go through customs. I think they no longer cared what was in it. With an overnight stopover at Haneda airport, and two more flights the next morning I finally reached Ishigaki. I was staying at the regular ITU Hotel, Hotel Miyahira, with a stack of other athletes from around the world.

The familiarity of Ishigaki Island was nice, and I spent the time up to the race with some light training to rid the travel soreness from my body. The pre-race press conference was on the Friday, 11 April, two days out from the Sunday race. It was a clunky press conference with translators working hard to keep us all up to speed. Les was obviously bored and passed me a note saying, 'Up your kilt Carney', to distract me just as they started to direct questions towards me. Following the press conference, we had the athletes briefing, which was normal procedure. At the completion of the meeting, it was announced that the ITU required everyone to sign an athlete's agreement for the 1997 season. That's when everyone complained. It seemed every athlete in the room refused to sign it. Les found me and asked me what I was going to do, explaining that athletes are required to sign agreements in most sports, and up until now the ITU was behind Olympic sports in this regard. He said it was for the betterment of the sport and just enabled the ITU to use athlete images to promote ITU and triathlon. I told Les I would run it past Dad, but I just wanted to race so I would most likely sign by the afternoon.

As it turned out, Les was right. I signed the agreement. There was one other female athlete who signed without any pushback, and that was Carol Montgomery of Canada. Most of the Australian, NZ and USA athletes held off signing, so the ITU informed them they would not be allowed to race. In response the athletes became even more aggressive. I was there to race so kept clear of the confrontation. Instead, I busied myself preparing for the race. As expected, every athlete had signed the agreement by race day. It seemed obvious to me this was going to be the outcome. I never understood why the athletes behaved so irrationally leading into an event, it was such a waste of precious energy.

Amongst the angst surrounding the signing of the ITU Athlete Agreements, something else cropped up, which irritated me personally. A female competitor who was a part of the USA team, was claimed to be the next 'Emma Carney'. I took immediate offence and purposely never learnt her name. My teammate, Jackie Gallagher, told me that this athlete had run a number of world class marathon times and was in the mix for USA Marathon selection. What particularly irritated me was the arrogance of thinking that someone with a strong run could beat me in triathlon, a sport that required skill in three sports. To be a truly world class and dominant triathlete on the world circuit, you needed to be internationally competitive in more than one discipline. I did not believe for a moment that an athlete who could run marathons only would beat me in a triathlon, regardless of how fast she could run.

What made things fun for me was a new ITU rule requiring athletes who were lapped on the bike, to be immediately disqualified. I made it known that I was going to attempt to lap the athlete who was heralded as the 'next Emma Carney' out of as many races as I could during the 1997 ITU season. I wanted it to be known that there was only one Emma Carney, and that was most definitely me.

I was ready to race hard by 13 April, given all the upheaval leading in. I had a very good race, strong in all three disciplines, and as a result won easily. As was always the case in Japan, the royal family was present. I was quite a way ahead of the field, so I had time to bow to the royal entourage just before I crossed the finish line. Les told me I won by too much again and was ruining his sport by dominating. I told him he should put that in the Athlete Agreement if he wanted me to follow his instruction. He also asked if it was true that I was trying to lap athletes out of races.

'Only those who claim to be me, Les,' I told him.

As I left the race area, I noticed there was a large group of people wearing white T-Shirts with my face on the front — the image of me winning the previous year. When I approached them, they all cheered and held up signs. I suddenly realised I had my own Emma Carney fan club. Awkward, but also very humbling. I received my own fan club T-Shirt, signed a heap of others and shook a lot of hands.

On the Monday following the race, I flew out of Ishigaki, arriving back in Australia on Tuesday afternoon. I flew into Brisbane and drove up to Noosa, because the Australian Triathlon Championships were in Mooloolaba, Queensland the next weekend. TA gave me race start number three. Dad was livid.

'You are clearly world number one and still your national federation won't recognise your status!' he ranted.

I didn't really care anymore and reasoned with Dad.

'Dad, we don't conform. I have sponsors who conflict with TA's sponsors, and I am clearly supporting the ITU. I am going against the norm of most athletes. This is an attempt to irritate us. Don't worry about it. I actually find it easier to race harder when barriers are put up to try to stop me.'

I didn't need external recognition. I didn't expect any support from TA either. I had lost hope of that a long time ago. And I was happy with how I was going.

Given the previous week, I had a light week of training. As tended to be the case following race and travel, my Achilles pulled up sore, so swimming and biking was the initial focus. I managed to get my body moving again by later in the week taking on some treatment and careful running. Australian mainstream media interest in me was intensifying. I had various interviews leading into the race and Channel 9 was filming a 'Wide World of Sport' feature story over the weekend and into the following week, so I had camera crews following me around.

TA held the pre-race press conference in Brisbane. Oddly, TA announced at the conference that Mooloolaba was going to host the next eight Australian (standard distance) Triathlon Championships, and also claimed that the weekend's race would boast the best national championship field ever. According to TA the 'big six' were all racing: Michellie Jones, Jackie Gallagher, and me in the women's race and Brad Beven, Greg Welch and Miles Stewart in the men's race. No one seemed to have checked in with 'the big six' though, because within twenty-four hours, it was only Brad and me standing, with Michellie a no show, Greg Welch ill, Miles Stewart injured and Jackie citing a 'lack of energy'. TA, with their 'big six' down to a lonely two, at least picked the winners of each race. Brad Beven won easily on a day of pretty ordinary weather, and I won easily exiting the water in fourth, rolling around on the bike, only waiting for the run to clear out. It was nice to win another national title, and nice to have back to back weekend wins.

I didn't have much down time after the Mooloolaba Triathlon, because I was off to New Zealand to race the next round of the ITU series in Auckland the following weekend. This was my third weekend of racing in a row, two of them international. I knew I was going to be tired. I reduced my training dramatically, with the focus on just trying to remove all remaining stiffness and soreness from my body. I slept in each morning, and just took everything as easy as possible. Dad made the trip to New Zealand with me, just to make things a little easier. Travelling with a bike and luggage always took more energy, so with Dad there I took a step back and let him do the heavy lifting. From the outside, small things like that seemed irrelevant, but I wasn't just flying to NZ to take part, I wanted to win, and I needed to do everything to make sure I would.

As it turns out, Dad's efforts were rewarded, and I won. Qantas was the event sponsor, and someone must have been a triathlon fan, because on the way home Dad and I flew first class. I returned to Melbourne in extreme comfort and ready for a few light weeks of training.

Melbourne was having its driest April on record. This meant I actually had a really pleasant late autumn training block at home. I put together some tough interval run sessions with Matt and equally tough bike rides around the hills of Eltham. My swimming was feeling good, so I was pleased with where I was at.

With a long season ahead, I put a weekend aside to do some instore appearances for adidas in Sydney and appear on the NSW Footy Show. Adidas arranged the appearance as part of the launch of the 'feet you wear' television commercial we shot in LA late in 1996. I was a little apprehensive going on the Footy Show. Being from Victoria I really didn't follow the National Rugby League (Victorians mainly follow Australian Football), so I decided I needed to appear like I knew what I was doing. For the appearance, adidas provided two clothing options: full tracksuit or a windcheater and shorts. I could choose. I decided that, because the Footy Show hosts, all men, wore suits and tie, I should dress similarly. So, against the norm of an athlete, I wore a corporate outfit, with skirt, jacket and shirt. Those who saw the interview and knew of my clothing decision all believed that because of what I wore, I was actually taken seriously as a female athlete. It was an interesting experiment. I never dressed down again in male dominated media appearances.

Adidas was also pleased with the interview and did not show any irritation about me not wearing their pre-selected tracksuits. At another store appearance for adidas the next morning I again needed help getting through the crowd. I was surprised at the number of people who recognised me. I wasn't completely comfortable with the attention, doing my required appearance for adidas and asking to be taken back to my hotel asap.

Over the next few weeks my profile lifted enormously. Adidas promoted me hard and suddenly everyone wanted to know more about Emma Carney. NAB and Holden ran television advertisements simultaneously as well. All were in free to air prime time slots, so I was becoming a household name. Triathlon feats were no longer the focus. Instead everyone wanted to know how I became me; how I grew up; what I ate for breakfast; and even which parent gave me my sporting talent, my Mum or my Dad (that last question has never been answered, and my parents also will never agree, claiming it was their family that provided me with sporting talent). Details of my personal life were also sought after: my simple existence of training and racing I think actually both surprised and disappointed many who hoped my life was full of exciting hot dates to fill their gossip columns.

Before traveling overseas again, I headed to Noosa to get some open-water swim work in. I flew with Ansett, an airline that collapsed a few years later, with an upgrade to first class. An obvious benefit of having a higher profile now. While in Noosa, Dad called to warn me that Brett Sutton in his role as TA Head Coach would drop in on my morning swim session and have a 'quick discussion about things'. I didn't particularly want him at my training session and checking what I was doing. I didn't trust him or his visit, especially as he personally coached most of my competitors. Also, while I had never met Brett, I had heard about his apparently excessive training regimes and I didn't like what I heard. I agreed that athletes needed to train hard and be challenged, but I believed a coach should also educate athletes to be independent, and not totally reliant on their coach. After all, in triathlon you have two hours where you have to make decisions in a race on your own.

Brett appeared one morning at a swim session with Dick Orbell's squad at the Buderim pool. He spent some time talking to Dick on pool deck. At one point he told me he thought I was a 'good swimmer', as if I was seeking his approval. Nothing could be further from the truth. I had already decided I wasn't going to say much, because I didn't want to engage in conversations with him. He also told me I needed to learn to work harder and also learn to train 'on the edge'. The comments proved he did not know anything about my training regime, and he was obviously attempting to prove he could offer me help as a coach. I wasn't so easily led and just listened — I wasn't going to be drawn into a discussion on what I did for training. It was a nondescript meeting, and I left as soon as I could.

I only had another solid week of training before leaving for the next ITU race in Monte Carlo, Monaco, on 29 June. Clare was finally fit and flew out with me. It was an epic trip over, a massive long-haul flight followed by disjointed connections and then a cramped drive to our final location. When we flew into Nice, France, Les was waiting at the airport to collect Clare and me. He asked me how I was, and I replied, 'knackered'. Les told me to get myself to the hotel and get some rest, because Michellie Jones was racing.

'Les, I don't care, I think it's good she is racing. We need it for the sport.'

Les agreed, but said, 'she won't turn up tired Emma.'

Les was right. I needed sleep.

As seemed to be the case leading into ITU races, athletes were kicking up a fuss about new regulations and the mandatory Athlete Agreements they were required to sign. There were also athlete uniform requirements now, reducing the number of sponsor logos permitted on each athlete's race kit. Most other professional sports had these rules already, but this was new to triathlon. Many existing triathletes on the ITU circuit didn't like the change, arguing they would lose the ability to earn money. They failed to understand that having fewer sponsor logos on the front of their race kit, would force the value of sponsorship space up, ensuring they actually made more money from each sponsor as a result. Not many seemed to see this benefit initially. Pre-race athlete protests were becoming the norm. As always, by race day athletes had signed all the documents and everyone was on the start line.

This was the first time Michellie and I were to race head-to-head on the ITU circuit. Unfortunately, my day couldn't have really gone any worse than it did. It was a very ordinary day all around. The race started late at 11.55 a.m. Out in the swim, at the first turn, I managed to get myself caught up on a loose rope on the swim buoy, but I couldn't really blame my loss on that. I was tired and out of sorts. I exited the water down by just over a minute, but with the bike over the same technical course the F1 cars normally negotiate, I was up with the leaders by the halfway point. There was a nasty crash which knocked three athletes out of the race and a puncture prior to the hairpin turn, which I managed to negotiate my way through. Despite my ability to avoid problems that my competitors threw at me, I was uncharacteristically slow in the bike to run transition and could not find my rhythm. Michellie slowly put time into me each lap of the run as I struggled with tiredness and lethargy. To be perfectly honest, Michellie clearly beat me. I was livid.

I absolutely hated losing, the indignity of losing was an insult to me. With hindsight (and this is hindsight from around twenty years later), it was good for the sport. Suddenly everyone was discussing who was better: Michellie Jones or Emma Carney. Michellie had turned up to the ITU for the first time in three years and stopped my dominant reign of thirteen straight victories from thirteen starts. It was an odd coincidence that my winning streak was stopped at thirteen. The ITU had recently stopped issuing the number thirteen to athletes because athletes who had raced with the number often reported bad luck. Les promised to remove it from all start lists and to this day there is still no number thirteen in ITU racing. It was also this number that stopped my winning reign, and I was in a foul mood for weeks. Not even a dinner at the entrance to the famous Monaco Casino or congratulations from the Prince of Monaco could shift my mood.

I called Dad in Australia and told him I needed to race again asap because I didn't want the stench of defeat to permeate my soul. I was disgusted with myself. I was insulted. My reaction wasn't surprising, I judged all my self-worth on whether I won or lost. In today's environment with attention to athlete wellbeing, this attitude would ring all the 'expert' alarm bells. But to me this was normal. To me it was perfectly 'healthy'. After all, if I didn't win, I honestly thought I was wasting my time, my sponsors' time and my supporters' time.

I flew out of Nice the next evening, determined to balance out the loss with a win at another race.

The next round of the ITU series was in Gamagori, Japan. Normally the time zone changes, and long-haul flights would have stopped me from backing up a European race with an Asian race. In normal circumstances, I would have been more cautious of the jet lag and lethargy that excessive air travel causes. But, right now I didn't care.

Rather than come with me, Clare decided to go to the TA training camp in Hahn, Germany, to see what it was like. TA was putting a lot of pressure on me to attend and Clare wanted to have a look. I trusted her judgement. If it seemed sensible, I would also attend. But first I needed to win a race. I wasn't going into a TA camp with a loss as my last race.

My first flight took me to Heathrow, London. There I discovered that I was twenty-four hours early for my connecting JAL flight to Nagoya, Japan. There was no earlier JAL flight, so I was stuck. I checked myself into an airport hotel and found myself becoming increasingly more irritated for stuffing up my flight connections, accentuated for also losing a race a day earlier.

I caught my flight to Japan the next day, but everything still annoyed the hell out of me until I got to the start line in Gamagori, Japan. There was no way I was going to lose this race. Still fuming, I won comfortably. However, in doing so, I pulled a stunt which until now I never really admitted to. There was talk, but I never conceded I actually did this.

It all started in the mandatory ITU athlete briefing the day before race day. These meetings were set up to allow athletes to air any issues they may have regarding the race and to also ensure all athletes understood the course and the race rules. I never really contributed much to these, preferring to get them done as soon as possible so I could get back to preparing myself to actually race. This particular time, I contributed. Over my few years of racing, I noticed in ITU races that the drink stations were predominantly set up for right-handed competitors. It irritated me a few times, and really irritated me the previous week in Monaco where I was beaten. I suggested to the technical officials in the briefing that it was slightly unfair that the drinks were not handed out on both sides to competitors, so that left-handed athletes could drink using their dominant hand. Everyone in the room laughed at me and the technical officials told me I was being silly. I was never one who responded well to being laughed at, but decided instead of kicking up a fuss, I thought perhaps I would see if I could force a change with a visual example of exactly how hard it was for a left-handed person to grab a drink when ITU triathlon aid stations are set up on the right.

The race really went as planned. I was slightly down after the swim, rode hard to catch the leaders and then waited for the run. The bike to run transition was hectic, with most of the field together. The run was four laps, and at the end of the first lap I was about 20 metres ahead of the entire field, on my own, with everyone chasing hard. It was really hot, being summer in Japan, and very humid. At the completion of the first lap of the run I could see the aid station set up ahead, as usual on the right-hand side of competitors running past. All the drinks were meticulously laid out on a table, prepared for us to grab as we ran past. Immediately annoyed again about everything being on the right, I decided to make a very clear point. I aimed to grab the first drink on the table, then I dragged my arm through the entire table, almost knocking every drink over in the process. I didn't flinch or look. Instead I accelerated with my drink in hand and carried on to win easily. Apparently behind me there was chaos, athletes and officials in a panic with the aid station in ruins.

When I crossed the line, Les came over to me looking annoyed.

'Emma, there has been a protest and you may be disqualified,' he told me.

'What for?' I asked.

'Destroying an aid station,' he replied.

'Les, show me the ITU rule on that.'

Les said he didn't think there was one.

'I couldn't control my right arm. I am left-handed and was running flat out. I didn't have time to focus on controlling my non-dominant hand,' I added to my case.

Les walked away and never said another word about it.

The ITU also started setting up aid stations with drinks on both sides in their races. (The ITU Technical Official race handbook now has a rule regarding drinks at aid stations under the subheading 'Run course aid station procedures and operation plans' under which 11.4.11(d) states that at all ITU events, 'Volunteers must be ready to serve left-handed athletes'.)

I was happy on both counts. I actually did think the aid stations would now be fairer. More importantly though, I could now go into the dreaded TA camp as a winner.

Dad had flown to Japan to meet me. He wanted to make sure I was ok, picking up that I was being really hard on myself for losing in Monte Carlo. He completely understood where I was coming from, but also knew I was under pressure from TA, travelling and managing things alone and still pretty inexperienced on the world circuit. We discussed the TA camp. I still wasn't convinced that training with my competitors was really something I should do. Dad also agreed. We both had the view that to be better, you needed to be different and training as a group was not focussing on a point of difference. It was quite the opposite. We discussed my defeat in Monte Carlo, and I said I believed it was a combination of poor training in Noosa compared to Melbourne and tiredness from jet lag. If I was to remain in Europe at the TA camp, we could see what a European base did for my preparations. There was an ITU race in Sweden in the next month, then Hungary and also Bermuda in September. We agreed I would go for two weeks leading into the event in Sweden and reassess from there.

With my attendance announced to TA, I flew out to Frankfurt, Germany, the closest airport to the TA camp in Hahn. Dad headed back to Australia. At the airport, JAL allowed me into their lounge and also seated me in the upper deck, front row with a lot of leg room. It was a twelve-hour flight, so it was a nice set up. Flying to Europe from Japan gives you similar gains in time as from Australia, so I arrived in Germany the same evening. Rob Pickard from TA met me at the airport. He was the TA High Performance Manager and attending the camp with his wife and two young kids. I knew Rob vaguely, but never really spent much time around TA staff before. To be honest, I didn't really trust them.

Hahn was just over an hour's drive from Frankfurt airport, depending on how fast you drove along the A60 autobahn. The TA training camp was in an old US army base set up during the cold war, when the invasion of West Germany was thought to be a real possibility. It had been deactivated as an army base in

1991, but there was evidence of the army presence still. The TA team stayed in some apartment blocks located close to a synthetic running track and various running trails through the neighbouring forest. My first impression of the place was shrouded in apprehension. I just didn't like staying with my competitors. And I didn't like Brett Sutton either, I didn't trust him. I was pleased Clare was there to meet me.

Brett greeted me when I arrived. He had claimed a room downstairs, next to the only room that had a television. I expect he took that room to keep an eye on the athletes. He seemed happy to have me there, telling me I gave his camp 'credibility'. I didn't know what to say to that. Most of the athletes were sitting watching a German television program on a couple of couches, so obviously everyone was literally just watching TV. Clare took me upstairs and showed me around. We were three flights up. Each flight had a living area off to the left and the right. Each living area had two bedrooms, a living room, kitchen and bathroom. Clare had chosen the top living area off to the right. We were alone at the top, with the living area to the left empty. We could pretty much retreat to privacy, which Clare told me she had been doing a lot. Apparently, no one wanted to be at the top because there were too many stairs to climb, but we thought it was perfect. No one had a reason to come up other than to visit us, which I hoped would be never.

'Brett is an arsehole,' Clare told me. 'He messes with everyone's head, especially the girls.'

'Really? Keep away from him then, we can do our own training,' I reassured her.

Clare seemed pleased I had arrived and had saved me some dinner.

'We have to be ready to go swimming at 7.05 a.m.,' she told me. 'I'm going to bed now.'

'Brett is a complete arsehole to me at swim training,' she said as she left the room.

I didn't like the sound of that at all. I never warmed to abusive coaches. I was a strongly self-motivated athlete. I needed technical and well-structured coaching, not yelling, abuse, screaming or mind games. I also didn't want my little sister to be treated like dirt.

As it turned out, I had every reason to feel concerned.

Initially the camp seemed ok. TA must have told Brett I was only planning on attending up until the ITU Stockholm event, so he was reasonable to me in the first few weeks. The sessions he prescribed were different from anything I had done before. Very repetitive with lots of volume in the swim, bike and run disciplines. Speed was not important, and I was often told to slow down in running sets. I never had a coach tell me to slow down before. There was no recovery or treatment provided which I thought was very unbalanced. Just an emphasis on training volumes. There was a large group of Australian triathletes at the camp, both male and female. Neither Jackie Gallagher nor Michellie attended. It was odd that Jackie didn't attend, because Brett was her long-time coach. I learnt later that she only trained with Brett intermittently. At the time I suspected that Brett was just trying to work me out and then see if he could train his athletes, Jackie being one, to beat me. It seemed a bit strange that he was both the TA Head Coach and personal coach to some members of the team.

A week before the Stockholm race, I fell ill. Almost every athlete attending the camp caught the same bug. It was like a bad chest infection that knocked us around for a week. When I came down with the illness, I refused to take any medication that the coaches were handing out to athletes. I was well aware that cold and flu tablets were banned by ASDA and I was never going to take a tablet I couldn't recognise or before reading the ingredients on the packaging. Brett was really annoyed with me and confronted me over the issue telling me I was the only athlete who had refused the medication he offered. I told him I didn't care.

'What if it was banned? What if ASDA came along here and did an out of competition drug test?' I asked. The Australian cycling team was moving into the apartment block across the driveway. An ASDA visit wasn't completely out of the question with two Australian teams in one location. Brett said that was 'highly unlikely'. I was not prepared to take that risk.

I was livid that a TA coach was pressuring me to take something that was most likely on the banned list.

As he left my apartment, Brett told me I would not recover as quickly as everyone else and my stubbornness showed I was not committed to my sport. I just ignored him, unable to understand why he would ask me to do something so stupid.

When we arrived at Stockholm, again there was controversy surrounding the event as yet another ITU rule change was announced; this time relating to equipment. Athletes were told their clip-on aero bars had to conform to new regulations. (Aero bars are used to get yourself into a more aerodynamic position on the bike and are very traditional to triathlon racing). If their bikes didn't conform, they would not be allowed to race. Basically, the rule required aero bars to be shortened so they did not protrude further than the bike brake levers. Triathlon officials believed that shortened aero bars would keep athletes' hands closer to their brakes. This was seen as a move to make the bike leg safer as drafting was now permitted and triathletes were riding closer together. Apparently, the cut-off date for compliance was the Stockholm race. TA didn't seem to think a massive bike rule change was important enough to tell their athletes, so we were all caught out. It was chaos at the Athletes briefing, and again Les copped it.

It didn't really matter to my race, I felt awful and pulled out about a third of the way into the run. I had my first ITU DNF (did not finish). I felt extremely weak and tired and shouldn't have raced, given my illness the week before.

Brett Sutton, still annoyed with me for refusing to take his self-prescribed medication, told me I was soft for pulling out. I effectively told him where to go and reminded him he was not my coach. Fortunately, Dad flew to Stockholm to watch and was concerned that I was again racing off the back of an illness. He was still concerned about Dr June Canavan's warning the previous year. He explained later:

Emma did not look at all good racing, she seemed flat and I pulled her out of the race, concerned she would just carry on and push herself to a top performance. In my mind, I remained concerned for the damage Emma was capable of doing to herself, because she could really push herself so hard to perform all the time.

The next race on the ITU Calendar was in Tiszaújváros, Hungary on Sunday, 10 August. Dad asked me what I thought I should do: stay in Europe or return home? Adidas wanted me to do some photo shoots in London in about a month, so it made sense for me to stay in Europe. I agreed. I was currently run down, could minimise my travel and get back into shape for the next race if I stayed put. I was confident I could remain in control of my training if I returned to the TA camp. I wanted to make things simple with regard to the problems with tiredness, illness and excessive travel. Going home was an emotional indulgence and would not help my performance. Dad agreed, because up until now, I had made sensible decisions regarding my training and preparation. As Dad remembers the discussion:

Emma seemed to be happy with staying in Hahn at the TA camp. I told the TA President Bill Walker to make sure Emma was looked after. I didn't trust Sutton — there was something odd about him — but with Emma and Clare both at the camp they seemed to be able to retreat from the group together and

look after themselves. Emma needed rest between races, so minimising travel
seemed a good idea at the time. Of course, I thought TA would be true to their
word and look after Clare and Emma.

The next few weeks following my return to the TA camp in Hahn was the
strangest mix of abusive coaching, damaging mind games and manipulation of
athletes to which I have ever been subjected or ever witnessed. There was nothing
I could really do apart from remain silent when we were told the day's training
sessions. I refused to allow Brett Sutton to break me.

As the days passed, it became apparent that Brett was now going to make it
almost impossible for me to do my own training sessions while remaining at the
camp. It also became apparent that Brett's method of training was to work on an
athletes' weakness, bring it to the forefront of their mind and then make them
vulnerable and reliant on him to remove this weakness. He focused the majority
of this destructive coaching on the female athletes in the group. He would openly
tell every female athlete they were genetically fat, because they were female, so
they needed to train harder than the men. The first time I heard him address
the girls with this I said, 'What did you say?' Brett turned to me and said, 'Not
you two, Emma and Clare. You are not fat. I will train you more like the boys.' I
wasn't sure if I should be further offended by that comment.

Brett was true to his word though. The female athletes on the training camp
were put through absurd volumes of training. I wasn't privy to the finer details
of others training, mainly because I kept my discussions to a minimum. There
was talk however of athletes running one hundred 100 m on the track, and fifty
400 m repeats only to do the same the next day. It was ludicrous.

While prescribing excessive training sessions, Brett would also manipulate
athlete's minds. No one was allowed to question a session, and if they did, the
session volume was increased, or they were ridiculed to their face and behind
their backs as 'weak' or 'soft'. It wasn't uncommon to run twenty-five 400 m
repeats one day with fifty 200 m repeats the next. Clare and I were amazed that
everyone thought this was ok, to smash yourself daily on a running track. We
came from the coaching world of quality over quantity and fast track running, not
volumes and volumes of slower reps. I always ran my best off a middle-distance
run program, whereby quality running was nurtured. I was quite confused by
Brett's approach. He would tell me I was running too fast to get the volume into
my legs.

The bike training was of course equally insane. Brett managed to find a 1.2 km loop and then insisted we time trialled for an hour on this one particular loop. The surrounding areas of the camp were perfect for riding, but Brett minimised any type of normal training. He preferred to screw with your head. I was often sent out to time trial for an hour and required to show him the results of the time trial on my bike computer. One particular day I managed just over forty laps and he made a big fuss. A few of the male athletes asked me if I had cheated.

'What? Why would I cheat in training, what is the point in that?' I asked them, puzzled.

'We haven't done forty laps, we don't believe you,' was the reply I received.

I didn't really care what anyone did or didn't believe. This is what Brett loved to do, have everyone obsessing with others training, and then trying to pull apart someone else's performance. I didn't engage with this type of negativity. It was another part of the toxic culture on that camp. There was a complete lack of empathy for everyone's wellbeing.

Swim sessions were toughest for me. This was not my natural discipline. Brett would abuse what he called the 'weak swimmers.' I was thrown into that category and rather than argue I just swam hard every single day. An easy day finished off with one hundred 25 m sprints with a band on (feet tied together with no flotation) as a warm-down set. We would swim until we had headaches. Quite often after swimming for hours Brett would drive off in the team van and leave us to run the 16 kilometres back to camp. I never complained, never asked when we were going to finish and never ever let Brett crack me.

Food was another avenue through which Brett could inflict mental abuse. To add to his quite vocal opinion that all female athletes were genetically fat, he would enforce non-sensical rules on the girls. Brett believed girls became fat when they ate food from different food groups together. His idea of a food group however was absurd. For example, he saw chocolate as a food group, ice cream as another. Clare and I couldn't believe the athletes took this advice on. It got so bad, on one of the athletes' birthday, Brett told them they could all go out for ice cream. He said if they wanted to eat ice cream however they had to have it for dinner, not just dessert. As a result, they all went out and gorged on ice cream. Clare and I refused to attend. We were not there to play Brett's mind games.

I was unlucky enough to have my birthday during camp, so Brett's present to me was to swim one hundred 100-m repeats in a 25-metre pool. It took two-and-a-half hours, swimming 100 metres, resting, and going again every 1 minute

30 seconds. I quietly got the session done. The birthday fun didn't end there. Brett gave me an afternoon 'special' session consisting of ten 1-mile repeats on 6 minutes 30 seconds. I held 5 minutes 30-40 seconds for every mile. I could not believe what I was hearing, but I didn't flinch and just ticked off the reps in my mind and on the track. I covered 18 km on the track that day following 10 km of swimming. Absolutely ridiculous.

That evening, as it was my birthday, Brett said I could go out for ice cream. I declined the offer. I was not playing his stupid games with food too.

Another disturbing focus of his manipulation of the female athletes was personal note writing. Brett would hand out secret handwritten notes to athletes. From what I could see, only the female athletes received them. I was the only female athlete who did not receive a regular note. I have never been one to be left out of things, so one day Brett was slyly slipping notes to female athletes when I yelled out, 'Hey Brett, where's my note?!' Brett looked at me and said, 'You don't need one.'

I wondered why.

A few weeks later, Brett did hand me one of his notes. I opened it up and it said in his messy, scrawled handwriting, 'You are the real deal.'

I chucked it in a bin as I walked off the pool deck, hoping he saw me. There was no way I was going to succumb to his mind games in that way either.

I spent most of the down time resting and recovering from absurd training sessions. I also decided to pretend I was ok with the training loads, because it became obvious that Brett was trying to crack me. He wanted to see me hurt, cry or break down. He wasn't going to get any of that out of me. I was one of the lucky few female athletes not to crack, physically or mentally. I had worked with tough coaches before, but never witnessed a coach break so many athletes. Most female athletes left the camp with some type of injury. Training techniques were constantly being concocted so athletes could train through injuries. Brett didn't believe in resting an injury; an injury was just the sign of a weakness in an athlete's body according to Brett. I have also seen the ongoing mental impacts of Brett's coaching, as athletes carry the psychological scars of his abuse through their private lives, well past retirement from triathlon. To this day there is widespread belief amongst many of the top triathletes from that time, that Brett Sutton's abuse contributed to a high-profile Australian triathlete's suicide.

I look back on this time and wonder why I didn't leave, why I put up with the abuse. To be honest, I am disappointed I stayed, but I felt at the time that if I did leave my competitors would view me as 'soft'. This was absurd. I wanted to show I could survive everything. Although I had a number of races and sponsorship commitments in Europe, I could have relocated myself to a more constructive training environment. I also had a lot of pressure from TA to remain at the camp. The entire period was destructive and awful. I regret ever attending this TA-organised training camp.

The next ITU World Cup was on Sunday, 10 August, at Tiszaújváros, Hungary. Dad was on his way to a world sport expo (he was now head of sportswear brand Fila in Australia) and decided to do a detour to Hungary to check on how I was going. I met Dad at Budapest airport and we boarded a bus for the three-hour trip to Eastern Hungary for the race.

The town of Tiszaújváros was very friendly and welcoming to all the athletes, everyone for miles around seemed to have an interest in triathlon that weekend. The crowds were big, and the support was massive. Dad brought a bag full of autograph cards printed up by adidas and after an hour signing with the crowd I ran out.

I spent the days leading into the race familiarising myself with the course, as was my pre-race routine. Heavy rain in central Europe had resulted in localised flooding and fast-flowing rivers. The race swim was in the Tisza river, so the water was moving really quickly. It was obvious we needed to be really diligent in the way we swam the course; keep close to the bank when swimming against the current and swim close to the middle of the river when with the current. The swim was going to be tough and the bike was technical. There was a 5-km flat section into town, followed by a number of loops through the town which were all technical following the street layout. The bike ended at a second transition area. The run was also looped through the town, flat and possibly fast.

On race day, I managed to have a horrific swim, missed the gun and it was all a mess from there. I got out of the water to hear Dad yell, 'Three minutes!' I realised I was three minutes down on the leaders out of the water and I remember thinking, 'This is going to hurt!'

Not once did it occur to me that it was impossible to win from here.

I grabbed my bike and time trialled the 5 km into town. I felt strong and in control, so I really buried myself. When I hit the town and the technical street areas of the course, I decided I would avoid braking on the corners to try to maintain speed and also eat into the front bike group's lead. I then remembered a conversation I had earlier in the year. My bike tyre sponsor was Continental

Tyres. Greg Rule was the Australian agent and when I picked up my last lot of racing tyres, I asked him out of interest about how far you can lean on a bike tyre before losing control. In response to the question, 'Can you corner on the wall of these tyres?', Greg replied, 'Yes, of course you can Emma, these are Conti's.'

That day in Tiszaújváros, I decided to trust my tyres and lean into the corners as much as I dared. (I later told Greg Rule his advice was correct, the tyres did hold corners well even when you pushed the bike to the wall of the tyre, and he said, 'Bloody hell, Emma. I was joking. You can't do that!')

Regardless of whether I could or couldn't, I did. I managed to pull in every athlete ahead of me and was in the lead bunch with a lap to go on the bike. I had rectified my appalling swim by outracing the entire field on the 40 km bike course.

Completely fired up, I was also prepared for a tough run. The Hungarians had a very good female triathlete Erika Molnar, who they expected to beat me. She was a very tough runner and was always going to put in a solid run for the Hungarian crowd. Erika and I ran shoulder to shoulder, with me getting a slight edge over her with about 3 km to go. I sensed my slight advantage and forced a break in Erika's stride beside me. I pushed on to run away with a slim margin at the finish. Somehow, I managed to win the race that was impossible to win following such a poor swim.

Following the morale-boosting trip to Tiszaújváros, I returned to Hahn camp and Dad came with me. He had some time between business meetings and wanted to see the training setup. In a very strange coincidence both Rob Pickard and Brett Sutton disappeared the entire time Dad was around. It was almost as if they were avoiding something, or someone. Both Dad and I should have picked up on this and left on the grounds that the TA staff were weird at the very least.

While Dad was around, we called his mum — Grandma Carney — for her birthday. I spoke to Grandad on the phone and he asked where in Germany I was staying. I told him it was about 120 km out of Frankfurt.

'Do they have any bridges?' Grandad asked me when he heard my location.

'Yes. Why Grandad?' I asked.

'I bombed the hell out of that place,' he said. 'We tried to blow every bridge up in the area.'

Grandad never really spoke about WWII. That was the only thing he ever really mentioned to me about it.

While Dad was with me, we discussed my upcoming race plans. I didn't really have another race for a few weeks, so I asked if he thought I should do the

World Duathlon Championships in Spain. (I had won the Australian Duathlon Championships in June which gave me automatic qualification). Dad agreed. I also suggested I should do some local European Triathlon Union (ETU) races as well. While I won in Tiszaújváros, my swim showed my weakness. I wanted to work on my strengths and also the problem areas. Dad reminded me it was the flooding river and my inexperience that gave me a poor swim but said a few extra races wouldn't hurt. He called the ETU and asked for a start at the Geneva race on Sunday, 24 August, in two-weeks' time. Dad recalls our conversation, and his discussion with the ETU representative:

Emma and I discussed racing the ETU Geneva race during our time in Hungary. Emma was feeling a little tired with the ridiculous Hahn camp and wasn't sure she should race. My advice was to ignore Brett Sutton, back off the training a bit and sharpen up to race Geneva.

I called the race organiser in Geneva and was greeted with Bonjour, and a flow of French which I didn't understand. I asked if they spoke English and the reply was in French. The person at the other end of the phone obviously thought I was English because apparently, I sound more English than Australian over the phone.

I then said, I am sorry I don't speak French because I am from Australia. With that the reply was, 'Ahh, Australie, how can I help you?'

She was then extremely helpful and when I told her that I was Emma Carney's father she was so pleased Emma wanted to race that she willingly provided a good appearance fee, excellent accommodation and meal allowance money. In return she wanted to be able to confirm Emma's entry there and then, that she would appear at the pre-race media briefing and would make herself available for thirty minutes or so for the local Geneva media.

A few other athletes from the Australian Triathlon camp decided to do the Geneva ETU race as well, so we took a team van and drove across to Switzerland. Despite driving fast on the autobahns, we still arrived late and missed the start of the pre-race briefing. When I walked in the entire meeting screeched to a halt, as everyone stopped and stared. I had never raced an ETU race and it became obvious the organisers and athletes were impressed I had chosen to do so. I apologised to the room for being late and sat down. Following the meeting I spent more time with the media before being shown to my hotel.

During the race, I swam well, third out of the water, and worked hard on the bike. It was an old format of racing, with a non-drafting bike leg. I felt strong on the run and won easily. The only real incident on the race was the bike dismount line. In triathlon you are required to dismount your bike before a line outside the transition entrance (you cannot ride into transition). Usually this is a painted or taped line. In this particular event, the race organiser put a plank of wood down, probably thinking it would prevent anyone from riding through the line. I always came in fast and dismounted my bike at speed, running as soon as I hit the ground. With a plank of wood seen at the last minute, I jumped it and my bike hit it hard only to fly in the air. I yelled out, 'Why can't we use paint, guys??!!' picked up my bike and carried on.

Late August, adidas Head Office in Germany asked me to travel to London to take part in a shoot promoting a new material they were to launch. Brett told me he did not give me permission to go. I refused to be drawn into an argument and also pointed out he was completely out of line thinking I required his permission to do anything. I would be away just over twenty-four hours and adidas was a very important sponsor of mine. I hadn't had a day off training for months, so a day with my sponsor was very reasonable. Brett was obviously frustrated he had absolutely no say in what I did or did not do because as a result, the days leading into me leaving, he set training sessions that were more absurd than normal. I just took the volumes on and showed no reaction.

On 27 August, I hired a car and drove myself to Frankfurt airport. Adidas flew me business class to Heathrow, where I was met by German marketing representative Daniel Gottschell. We made our way to the hotel, 'Sydney House', which was a boutique hotel in Chelsea, London. The hotel was extravagant, I thought. Perhaps the best hotel I had ever stayed in. It was the complete opposite from the training camp environment I had just come from. It was nice to enjoy some comfort and luxury, having spent the last few months in a training camp run by a megalomaniac who connected the need for luxury and comfort to a sign of weakness. That evening, I had dinner with adidas marketing executives, along with Portuguese Marathon champion Alberto Pinto, also an adidas athlete flown in for the shoot the next day. Breakfast the next morning was provided at the time you requested. I thought that was very impressive, so I ordered an 8.05 a.m. breakfast just to see if it came on time. It did and seemed posh enough for the Queen.

Following my fancy breakfast, I had a 10 a.m. shoot. Adidas was promoting a new sporting material claimed to enhance performance by 12 per cent. From the mock-ups of the shoot, I could see that I needed to provide the photographer with a perfect lunge. In the advertisement I would appear to be lunging over the advanced seam of a garment. I didn't think that sounded too difficult, put the adidas gear I was required to wear on and started the shoot. Unfortunately, it wasn't as simple as it first appeared. Apparently, the photographer wanted a certain look on my face, that is, of a tired athlete. I am hopeless at acting, so I wasn't able to provide the look until we were close to 2 p.m. and I was actually physically tired from so many lunges. My legs felt wrecked when the photographer finally decided he was happy. As I left the shoot, I felt sorry for Alberto Pinto, who was required to do reps up a small ramp built in the studio. I expected that was going to wreck his legs even more. On my way out I spoke to tennis player Surgi Brugera who was forced to do repeated serves and was complaining of a sore arm. With very sore legs, I flew out of London that evening, arriving at the TA camp at about 10 p.m.

About a week after the shoot, my lower back seized up. My back has always required regular chiropractic care. I had received no proper treatment while on the TA camp. With hindsight, it wasn't really surprising. I tried to juggle my training, but it was just far too painful. Sharp pain too, the type of stuff that cripples you and stops you in mid stride while running. I simply couldn't train. Brett wouldn't allow me to stop. He told me I needed to keep training because it was a sign of weakness to give in to injuries. He said he always viewed me as a tough athlete and instructed me to get on the indoor bike trainer for four hours to prove it. I remember looking at him and thinking, 'what an idiot'. I thought it over in my mind and decided, as there was nothing else to do, I would get on my bike and roll easy to see if my back loosened up.

I took all my stuff downstairs and set my bike up in the TV room, turned the TV on and tried to turn my mind off. I sat on the indoor trainer and watched Lady Di's funeral for four hours. It was depressing viewing fit for a depressing training session. That evening, Brett told me he would massage my back. Brett's idea of a massage was weird. I kept my running gear on, because I didn't trust him. I lay on the couch in the TV room, hoping another athlete would wander in. Brett basically ignored my back and ran his hands lightly over my legs.

'What are you doing?' I asked him.

'Massaging your back,' Brett replied.

It was so weird it made my skin crawl. I got up and left.

I missed the Duathlon World Championships in Guernica in early September as a result of my injury. Clare was also injured through Brett's training (she developed Plantar Fasciitis and could hardly walk) and still raced but struggled to finish fourth. That would have been an almost certain one-two World Championship for Australia. No one from TA ever asked or followed up to find out why Clare and I were both forced to pull out, especially after having developed injuries at their training camp. I just don't think anyone at TA cared and Brett was certainly never made accountable for the damage he did to athletes.

By September, most of the racing was over, many athletes returned to Australia, injured, and the TA camp was quieter. Clare left before me. I was one of the last to leave the camp, even outstaying Brett himself. Rather than go straight home, I travelled to Hamilton, Bermuda, for the next round of the ITU series. I was actually so pleased to be on my way home I felt a lot happier. It was nice to be able to sleep in again and get ready properly for a race. It was nice to be away from that toxic culture and negative, passive aggressive behaviour. It was just nice to be able to enjoy myself and not to be ridiculed for not training while constantly punishing myself.

I was familiar with the race in Bermuda. Everything suited me. The swim was easy to navigate, the bike had a tough little hill on which I could rip the field apart, and the run was dead flat out and back. I felt strong racing. I raced well and won by five minutes.

What I particularly enjoyed about the race was the fact that the American athlete touted as the 'next Emma Carney' at the beginning of the 1997 season had had a tough year. In Bermuda, true to my word, I lapped her on the bike course and had her disqualified from the race. I managed to catch her when I had just 200 m left of the bike leg. I could see her up the road as I completed the last lap of the bike and was forced to sprint to catch her and lap her out. I recall looking across as officials pulled her off the course, she gave me a black look and was never seen again at an ITU event. In hindsight, I now see how ruthless this was, but in my mind, I had sent out a very clear message. Don't enter the sport of triathlon, claim to be something you aren't and expect a welcoming ceremony. Sport only has one winner. Triathlon only had one Emma Carney, and I wanted it to remain that way.

While I was in Bermuda, dear old Grandma Carney passed away. She had been suffering from emphysema for a few years and it finally got on top of her. Grandma fought hard and she fought in her own way too. She continued to smoke right up to her death, despite doctors telling her that the smoking caused the illness. I don't think she ever believed them. She puffed on a cigarette in one hand and dragged on oxygen through a tube she held in the other. One day when she was swapping her oxygen and cigarette, she accidentally lit the oxygen, forcing Grandad to chase the flame along the tube, stamping out the flame before it hit the oxygen bottle and blew the house up. Typical Grandma Carney chaos. It was a really sad time, because Grandma was such a favourite of the entire family. Grandad Carney, understandably, was devastated.

I flew home Tuesday, 23 September. It was so nice getting on my Qantas flight and hearing the Australian accent again. I was travelling light this time, because I had been away from home so long, I was sick of all my clothes. I threw everything out and gave some things to local kids. All I had with me was my bike, racing gear and the essentials I needed to get back to Australia. I couldn't wait to get there!

8. The Perfect Score

Once back in Australia, there was no 'down time', as the last three races of the 1997 season were important ones: the Sydney ITU World Cup, Noosa Triathlon and the ITU World Championships in Perth. I agreed to attend a TA training camp based at the Australian Institute of Sport (AIS) in Canberra mainly because I found the AIS inspirational and I wanted to train at the best facilities in the country with the best athletes, coaches and sports scientists. I was young when the AIS was established and grew up holding it in high regard. Triathlon, with its recognition as an Olympic sport was now supported by the AIS and this meant TA could hold camps there and use the facilities. I thought TA never did enough of this, engaging the best sporting experts in all areas of elite sport in Australia.

Clare and I organised to arrive at the AIS on Tuesday, 30 September. We had an afternoon flight, because Don Burke was coming over to do a TV segment on our garden. Don Burke at the time hosted a television show in Australia called 'Burke's Backyard'. It was a very high rating gardening show on Channel 9. Each week, as a part of his show, he went and saw a celebrity's garden. What was particularly embarrassing about the segment was that it was aired the following weekend. Clare and I were in the dining hall at the AIS with all the athletes at dinner when we came on the large screen TV. Clare and I left dinner early that night as all the AIS athletes there watched in amusement.

On the afternoon that we arrived at Canberra, a bus was waiting to pick us up and sitting in the bus were all the TA athletes. I thought it was odd that everyone came, but I assumed everyone flew in at a similar time. Some TA officials informed us that head coach Brett Sutton would not be around for a few days, because he 'had to go to the Gold Coast for something'. That announcement seemed odd. Couldn't he organise himself to attend the camp? But to be honest, I was pleased to hear that he was absent; the less I had to do with Brett Sutton, the better. Clare and I had dinner at the AIS food hall and had an early night.

The first morning at camp, Brett was absent again. TA officials and support coaches were acting very strangely and very vague about the training plans for the day. I was quickly irritated, because I needed to train but I wasn't allowed to do my own training, as I thought I would. I started to talk about returning home but was told I was not allowed. Fortunately, my car sponsor Holden organised a car for me to use while I was in Canberra, so I picked that up. I now at least had an option to leave, as home was only a seven-hour drive away.

After our first morning swim session, we were all called into a meeting. There we were told that Brett Sutton had been arrested by the Federal Police two days ago on several counts of misconduct with a minor. I seemed the most surprised and shocked at the news, making me think that perhaps everyone else knew of this part of his shady past. I was immediately concerned as to what I was going to do for training. Were we all waiting for him to suddenly be freed? I was told that my reaction was selfish, and I needed to show support for Brett. I was confused as to how I was suddenly the selfish one.

'I need to know what we are doing for training, otherwise I am going home,' I remember saying.

TA officials told me that I was not allowed to leave the TA camp under any circumstances, because we needed to show support for Brett. He had been extradited to the Gold Coast to face an initial court hearing, where they expected him to get bail. TA was going to support him in this, because he was an important part of their Olympic campaign. We were then told that our training locations were most likely going to be off the AIS campus, because the AIS did not support TA in its protection of Brett Sutton. I was really annoyed then. I wanted to leave and somehow tell the AIS I agreed with them, so that I could continue to use their facilities.

It was an awful scenario. I just wanted to cut ties with all this unnecessary baggage that wasn't mine and prepare myself for the remainder of the season. I had three very important races coming up. I didn't need this. I left the meeting, called Dad, and told him Brett Sutton had been arrested. Dad couldn't believe it and called TA to get to the bottom of what was going on.

Dad recalls the conversation:

I spoke with CEO Tim Wilson because TA President Bill Walker was unavailable. I had a conversation with Bill sometime later when I bumped into him at a race.

Tim Wilson just brushed off the whole incident and told me that Brett Sutton had an affair with an underage girl years ago. He told me something along the lines of, 'The whole thing will blow over in a few days or so.'

He then very concerningly cautioned me to tell both Emma and Clare to keep the matter confidential. I told him it was not for him to conceal or sanitise the facts, and his duty was to act in the best interests of TA athletes. I also told Tim to never try to threaten Emma or Clare into maintaining silence. He told me again that neither Emma nor Clare were allowed to leave the AIS Camp and to do so would lead to disciplinary action.

I couldn't believe what I was hearing and told Tim that Emma and Clare would leave whenever they wanted to and that he personally, and the rest of TA, had failed in their duty of care towards them and every other female athlete.

Meanwhile at the TA camp, training was all over the place. TA organised some coaches from Sydney, but they were obviously just provided with Brett Sutton sessions. We had a track running set that was too long and intense and a recovery swim session in which everyone swam too hard.

News flowed through to us throughout the day regarding Brett's progress on becoming a free man. He obtained bail, which was fully supported by TA. In the meantime, the AIS informed the media and in response TA told us all we must refuse to comment, if contacted by any media source, or risk disciplinary action. It also became clear that it was the AIS that allowed the arrest to take place. I felt very fortunate the AIS stepped in. It was quite clear that TA would never have cooperated with police investigations. With the AIS statement, news of Brett Sutton's arrest made the mainstream media, even hitting the TV screen in the AIS dining hall. For the first time in my career, I was embarrassed to be a triathlete. TA remained adamant Brett should be supported, and all the athletes had to show a united front.

Despite their support of Brett, TA did have to bow to the pressure of the AIS and the media. His head coaching role was reduced, but to everyone inside TA, he effectively remained in charge. With Brett banned from the AIS campus, and the AIS distancing themselves from TA, training became a disjointed, dysfunctional disaster. We could no longer train using the AIS facilities. As a result, all TA training became centralised around the hotel Brett was now staying in. We ran a 2 km loop he found and rode loops around the exterior of the AIS campus. I was increasingly frustrated that we were not allowed to run on the AIS Athletics track and ride properly using the great surrounding roads of Canberra. Swimming was the discipline that was really badly affected. Banned from the AIS, we had no pool. TA organised for us to have an hour in a nearby 25-metre pool in a suburb called Kayleen. Compared to the 50-metre world class training pool at the AIS, the Kayleen pool represented the other extreme. It was heated for beginner swim lessons; too hot for elite level training. We were only allowed two lanes, so it was absurdly crowded. We were also forced to swim only in the late afternoon. Everything about the swim training set up was wrong.

There was now no one I could talk to about the situation, not that it would have helped. TA was not just supporting Brett; he was now our main contact with them. They also tried to make us move to the Hotel where Brett was staying. I didn't want to be kicked off the AIS property. It was becoming absurd. Training effectively was becoming impossible.

An incident following swim training really pushed me over the edge. Brett pulled me aside and told me I needed to take protein supplements. I told him I wasn't going to start taking supplements. I didn't trust them, didn't agree with them, and I also didn't want to bulk up. Above all, I told him, I was not going to risk failing an ASDA drug test, because everyone knows supplements can never be cleared to be clean from prohibited substances. I could therefore fail a drug test and I wasn't going to risk that. Brett questioned my commitment while I wondered whether Brett was trying to sabotage me as an athlete.

Since arriving in Canberra, I felt that Jackie Gallagher's return to the training group was a little suspicious. She and Brett, as they were long time coach and athlete, spent a lot of time talking things over and watching me train. Jackie started to avoid the swim training sessions I attended, while I was not allowed to leave the camp and had to go to the swim sessions. Brett also concentrated on his personal athletes, Jackie Gallagher and Loretta Harrop, working on their run specifically and trying to get them into shape. They both specifically needed run training, because both were out of shape in comparison to me on the run.

I didn't like the way things were playing out, and, most importantly, I was in total agreement with the stance the AIS was taking about Brett. I did not want to show my support for TA officials, because I believed they were completely wrong in their support for someone of this character. I decided I needed to get out of the camp, because it wasn't good for me in any way. I was over it.

I managed to conform for about ten days before telling Clare I had had enough. It was on Monday, 20 October that Clare and I packed all our gear into my Holden sponsored car. Because Clare was coming too, we had two bikes, two bike cases and all our training luggage. Clare looked at me and said we were never going to get it all in the car.

'We bloody well have to, and we have to do it quickly before we are seen,' I replied.

It took about fifteen minutes to cram everything in. We did an amazing job. I kept telling Clare to keep a lookout for any athletes or TA coaches who might see us. Just as I was shutting the doors Clare said quietly, 'Oh No! Its Brett.'

I turned around quickly to see Brett walking up the driveway towards the athlete residences.

'What are you doing?' Brett asked.

I actually thought I should be asking that of him. Wasn't he banned from the AIS?

'We are leaving Brett. Dad has organised some things I need attend in Sydney.' This had been our pre-planned line should we get sprung escaping.

Brett then put his hand on the car and told me I must not leave. He said it was a sign of weakness not staying with the group. Also, very alarmingly, he told me that this could affect my Olympic selection.

"What are you talking about?' I stopped and looked at him.

'We need to be united,' he told me.

I kept busying myself with a few remaining items. I didn't want any more of Brett's control over me. Clare was already in the car. I got into the driver's seat and started reversing.

'You will regret this Emma!' he yelled out.

'Such a creep,' Clare muttered.

'Dirty creep,' I added.

We drove off with Brett glaring at us.

Clare and I drove the two and a half hours to Sydney, so happy to be free from the horrible situation at the TA camp. We drove straight to Kay's house in Sutherland, just south of Sydney. Our very reliable and great friend Kay told us to stay with her while we got ourselves organised.

As it was, we only really left the TA camp three days early, because the rest of the team left later in the week for Sydney as well. The next round of the ITU series was in Sydney on Sunday, 26 October. It was an important race, given it was over the Sydney Olympic course, and so far, I was undefeated. We transferred to a hotel near the course on Friday and met Mum and Dad there. Dad said he received a letter from Brett. It was so badly written Dad could hardly understand it, but it spoke about how important it was that I remained with him as my coach.

'But I never was coached by him,' I said. 'I was attending a TA camp, as required.'

'Exactly,' Dad told me. 'I will speak to [TA President] Bill Walker. This is absurd.'

On the day of the Sydney World Cup, the atmosphere was boosted by a very large crowd on the Sydney Opera House steps. It was a really nice change from the situation I had been in for the past few weeks. Brett Sutton was lurking in the crowd, wearing his cheap suit. He told me he always watched a race wearing it because he was 'at work'. Brett avoided me because I kept Dad near me when warming up and preparing for the race. I certainly didn't want to speak to him.

My race went well. Race start was at 9.30 a.m., so it wasn't a terribly early wake up. Up until now the swim started in deep water, but this year started from a new pontoon. I swam hard off my dive and exited the water on the back of the front pack. The American team had a few specialist swimmers, who were slightly ahead, but the front pack was where I needed to be. I rode strongly and made my way through the field to the leaders. I caught the swim specialists and formed a group of four. With me doing the bulk of the work, we built a lead of two minutes over the rest of the field by the completion of the bike course. I was clearly the strongest runner in the group, so I knew I could further extend my lead in the final leg of the race. On the run I felt good and won by just under 3 minutes. I was now undefeated on the Olympic course and showed that I could perform well there.

From nineteen ITU World Cup starts, I now had a tally of 17 wins, 1 second, and 1 DNF.

And I was happy to be away from all the recent TA problems. Or so I thought.

Following the race TA CEO Tim Wilson, rather than congratulate me, told Dad I was required at a press conference later in the week, to be held in Sydney. He told us if I did not attend, I would be fined $5000 and also removed from the Australian World Championships team. I thought this was completely out of line, because I had never skipped a press conference, so wondered why he thought I was going to skip this one. I organised myself to stay in Sydney for two more days, attend the Press conference and then head north for the Noosa Triathlon. The next day Bill Walker, called me to ask me not to attend the press conference, because St George Bank preferred I didn't. I ignored the request. By this stage, I did not think TA could have acted any more unprofessionally than they already had. It was appalling. Little did I know what was to come...

While all the confusion regarding the press conference was taking place, Brett Sutton wrote Dad another letter, which he left creepily at the hotel reception. In his scrawled handwriting and terrible spelling, he seemed to be saying that Dad was being selfish in having me work with my sponsors, and that my focus should be on training harder. Neither Dad nor I could believe what we were reading.

The following day, I attended the 10.30 a.m. press conference after completing a bike trainer session in my hotel room. On arriving, I noticed TA had provided everyone with shirts. I asked the TA CEO Tim Wilson for my shirt and he told me he didn't have one for me. I thought that was a little odd, but just carried on. The press conference was pretty standard, if long, taking two hours. The most notable thing was that TA finally had their 'big six' in one room: Michellie, Jackie Gallagher, Brad Beven, Greg Welch, Miles Stewart and me.

Once it was over, we, the 'big six' athletes, had a group photo shoot with renowned, legendary sports photographer Delly Carr. Because I wasn't provided with a TA shirt, everyone had to put their AUS race kits on for the iconic photo taken on the steps behind the Sydney Opera House.

Once all official requirements were over, I rushed off to catch my flight to Maroochydore. The Noosa Triathlon was on Sunday, 2 November, and I wanted to win my favourite Australian race. I spent the week preparing as normal. Dad received yet more letters from Brett. I couldn't believe it. They were rambling rubbish, explaining that I need Brett and not Dad to get me ready for races. It was like Brett suddenly felt a weird need to control me. I am not sure why he would think I would ever train with him. Brett also called Clare and sent a fax to me telling me he thought I would win Noosa. I suggested to Dad that perhaps we needed to get a restraining order out on Brett. I didn't want any more of his mind games.

Up until now I hadn't managed to win Noosa Triathlon, coming second twice and missing a few years due to injury and illness. This year I wanted to win. Jackie Gallagher was also racing, as was Clare. My race went well. I swam strongly, with only a few swim specialists exiting the water ahead of me. On the non-drafting bike leg, I felt a little flat, but because it was non-drafting, I was able to ride through the field and then away from any chasers. My run was strong, I backed off halfway through and still ran just over 34 minutes. Following the race, just after I crossed the line, an official approached me and told me I was disqualified for drafting. I asked him what he was talking about. I had been riding alone all race, way ahead of the field. I then asked what number they had recorded. They said 110. I said they had the wrong athlete; I was number 101. As it turned out Clare was 110. I walked away and left Dad to appeal the decision.

Dad recalls the incident:

I was walking past the sport expo tent area as Emma was close to finishing, just behind transition, when a draft buster (a draft buster is a Triathlon official on a motor bike who monitors athletes riding out on the bike course), parked his bike, walked past the Expo and called to a couple of other draft busters, 'I got them both.' This guy then saw me and quickly walked the other way. I smelt a rat and went to look for Garth Prowd, the race organiser, to let him know the Triathlon Queensland (Tri Qld) officials were potentially up to something. As it turned out, Emma won the race and called me over to sort out a false accusation of drafting. The men's favourite Simon Lessing was also DQ'd. I had a huge fight with everyone and anyone who was around.

The Appeal was not settled for an hour or so, with Clare being reinstated. The officials even suggested that they would withdraw Clare's DQ and instead DQ Emma. I told them that even in a Kangaroo Court in Timbuktu that would not stand up and if they tried to do so, I would sue TriQld, their officials and demand costs when the Appeal was won.

The only person involved in TriQld that thought the incident was funny was Garth Prowd, because he enjoyed TriQld Officials making fools of themselves.

As it was, Simon Lessing was disqualified for crossing the road centre line, but Australian Craig Walton had clearly beaten him to the finish line anyway. Once all threats to disqualify both me and Clare were withdrawn, the final results for the women was Clare third, Rina Hill second, and me first, with a new course record of 1 hour 54 minutes. This was then claimed to be the fastest recorded time ever for a female over a triathlon of that distance (this time has never been broken over the Noosa course).

I was happy I had finally won Noosa, and also done so in record time. I now had a bigger race to win, the World Championships in Perth in two weeks.

I flew out to Perth, Western Australia two days after the Noosa Triathlon. Mum and Dad flew over with Clare and I and Jane also came across. We all stayed in an apartment at the accommodation organised by TA, as part of the TA group. The area was perfect for training, and I got to know the bike and run course really well. TA required me at the official press conference on the Thursday prior to the race, and I attended obediently. Leading into the race all press images of me released by TA, were from the Online Triathlon series, with the St George logo on the kit. It was quite petty.

I left the TA press conference early and adidas had a private press conference, where all media were invited to interview me alone. My personal press conference was better attended that the TA one, and it was nice to know that no one was trying to sabotage me. The past few months, I had felt unsupported and that TA had been working hard to try to destroy me and damage my progress with my sponsors and my standing in the sport. Adidas had a number of large mobile billboards in Perth for the week before and after the race. They featured a huge picture of me running with the words, 'No Overtaking - Emma Carney in Perth for the World Triathlon Championships'. It was quite overwhelming to see a huge billboard of yourself. At the completion of my press conference, it was announced there was now a forty-eight hour close on any media commitments, so I could prepare for the race uninterrupted.

Just as we were closing up, a journalist asked me one more question. He said he had prepared two articles. One stated I was the best triathlete in the history of the sport, and the other article outlined how I choked at every World Championships. He asked, 'Which one will I be sending off to my editor, Emma?'

I looked at him and said, 'Let's wait and see'.

With that, my press conference closed, and I was able to prepare.

Race day rolled around. I felt pretty happy with where I was at regarding fitness and training. I knew the course inside out and naturally had looked through the start list and sussed out my competition.

Race start was at 10.30 a.m. I got up at about 5.30 a.m. and went for a short fifteen-minute run to wake my body up. I felt good. I avoided reading any newspapers and kept all TVs off in the hotel. I didn't want to know what anyone's opinion was of me so close to racing. Mum, Dad and I drove to the race venue at 8.30 a.m. I had the usual requirements pre-race: athlete check in, body numbering, and transition entry and setup. There were several athletes warming up on trainers on their bikes in transition. I decided not to. I didn't want to possibly heat up my race tyres and cause a blow out and I also didn't want to mess with my race wheels. At 9.30 a.m. I started my warmup. Brett Sutton appeared while I was jogging out along the run course, so I crossed to the other side of the road away from him. I certainly did not need him and his baggage so close to my race.

I remember spending some time with Dad and Garth Prowd pre-race. Mum had gone to the VIP tent. She was always a little nervous before the big races.

A large number of athletes entered the water for a swim warmup. I decided not to, as it was very possible that I would be too cold following a swim and would not be able to warm up again. Pre-race marshalling was at 10.10 a.m. and I noticed that most athletes were shivering while waiting for the start, so I concluded that I had made the correct decision.

The race announcer started calling us up to the start line, beginning with top ten order. I was first out and chose my place on the start.

I got a fairly good start but copped a massive kick to the face about 50 metres into the swim. My left goggle felt jammed into my eye socket, but I just ignored it. At least they were still on my face I thought. Swimming fairly well, I stayed at the back of the front pack. I knew the swim specialists were off the front trying to get as much distance as they could between themselves and me.

I was behind about one minute thirty seconds when I exited the water and ran the fairly long swim-to-bike transition hard. Michellie was just un-racking her bike when I arrived, so I thought if I nail this transition, I will be with her a short distance into the bike. Jackie was also in transition with us. Just as I hoped, I managed to ride out on the road with them.

At this stage of the race, the swimmers' usual tactic was to hit the start of the bike hard, increasing the gap between them and the rest of the field, and gaining a psychological advantage as well. The swim is the slowest discipline in triathlon, and because it is immediately followed by the fastest discipline, the bike, small time gaps out of the water could appear much larger once the athletes had all transferred to the bike discipline.

The particular bike course had a tough hill about 1.5 km into the ride, and I used it to consolidate my position. I was on the front of the chase group the first time up the hill, and I decided to ride down the leaders. I didn't waste any time trying to get anyone to help me, I didn't care. I was very aware Jackie and Michellie would do as little work as possible, hoping I would tire for the run. I decided the sooner I caught the leaders, the sooner I could back off too. I could see that Brett Sutton's plan was to have his two athletes work against me, Loretta Harrop was to work hard out front and Jackie was to sit on me and out run me. He forgot one thing. I'm not stupid and I know how to race.

The bike course was five laps, and I worked hard for four. By then I had reeled in Loretta Harrop and American Barb Lindquist. That was their race effectively over. Heading into the bike-to-run transition, Michellie decided she was going to enter first and took the narrow transition entrance too fast. She collided with Frenchwoman Isabelle Mouthon's bike, stepping onto her rear cluster and cut her foot. I avoided the tangle and to be honest didn't have much sympathy.

I had another smooth transition and was first Australian out. I decided to dictate the pace and noticed no one was attempting to overtake me. I took this as a lack of confidence from whoever was chasing to beat me, so I kept running hard and settled into a quick off-the-bike pace: for the first kilometre, I apparently ran 3 minutes 4 seconds. The run was two laps out and back. The crowd lining the run course was massive. Apparently over 100,000 people turned out to watch. Being a crowd made up predominantly of Australian supporters, it was going mad. I realised why everyone was screaming so much at the first 180-degree turn of the run, the first time I could see who I was running with. I was leading, Jackie Gallagher was in second, and Michellie in third. Australia was one-two-three!

At this first turnaround, I could also see Michellie was slightly dropping off the pace and it was really just down to Jackie and me. As we headed back towards the end of the first lap, Jackie moved up to run beside me. We now had a tail wind. At no point did she run past me, so I assumed she did not think she could beat me. I wasn't feeling particularly strong, but I knew that given the poor year of racing Jackie had had, she would be pleased with second. I also knew I wouldn't be able to live with myself if I came second again, so I had to win. In the end I think that was the difference: what we were both prepared to do.

As we approached the 5 km mark, the crowd was deafening. I picked Dad out on the side, and I realised I would not be able to hear him, so I looked over my Oakley's to have eye contact with him. Dad's face told me I was going to win, so I gained a lot of confidence. While I never thought Jackie was a better triathlete than me, I respected her running ability, and her ability to race hard and tough. I had surged at 3 km and Jackie responded. Jackie surged at the last turnaround, at about 7 km, and I responded. Heading back to the finish area, we were running side by side. On the last leg of the run, there was a right-hand turn into a short dog-leg. Jackie and I turned together. Facing us was my adidas billboard towering over the crowd. I took one look at that and thought, 'Bloody hell. If I don't win, I will look like an idiot!' At about 1 km to go I again surged, and I felt Jackie struggled to respond as well as she had been. I turned the screws further and felt a gap slightly open. We now had about 800 m to go. I decided to start winding it up and was running flat out. The crowd had gone mad, and it was actually a little difficult amongst the noise and chaos to see where to finish chute turn off was. I just kept running flat out until I saw an official direct me right. I stepped onto the grass finish chute and ran the last 100 m to the line in front of an incredible crowd.

I crossed the line 12 seconds ahead of Jackie. Michellie was third, I have no idea how far back. We managed to do what the crowd wanted: a one-two-three finish for Australia.

The rest of the afternoon was a hectic time. I had doping control, and that always takes ages. Sometimes it can take hours. There was also the post-race press conference and a stack of phone interviews set up by adidas. The men's race followed ours, so I headed to the VIP tent to see if I could watch a bit of it. Everything was hectic. Everyone was excited.

Brett Sutton tried to come over to speak to me at one stage. I turned my back to him and told Dad. Dad glared at him, so he quickly disappeared. I wanted him and all his baggage out of my life. Some TA officials congratulated me, CEO Tim Wilson and President Bill Walker, they kind of had to.

After a brief presentation for the crowd, I started to make my way back to my hotel. I was exhausted but I was required back in a few hours and needed a shower and a little break from everything. It was close to impossible getting through the crowd. Finally, back at our hotel, I could relax. I enjoyed a champagne with Mum, Dad, Clare, Jane and Kay who had also made the trip over. Funnily, to me it wasn't so much a celebration of joy, it was more relief. I had finally won my world title back again. Despite winning though, I still wasn't completely satisfied. After all I hadn't won by much. I preferred a more dominant performance.

I had a shower and changed into my AUS team kit in preparation for the awards party. A steady stream of calls continued to come through from the media, and I left Dad to organise my schedule of television crossovers for the next day. Dad also arranged with TA for me to arrive at the party close to the end. It became obvious to everyone I would need help with security to get me through the crowd. I waited outside while my security was called. When it was announced I had arrived I couldn't believe it. I had always received such tremendous support from Australian triathletes and the Australian public, but this was overwhelming. I never felt the pressure from a crowd so intensely before. Every single person in the large presentation area seemed to want to congratulate me. The crowd surged forward, and I was pushed onto the stage to a massive wave of applause, cheering, and ecstatic screaming. It was very humbling. I said a few words and signed whatever people threw at me. After forty-five minutes security helped me leave.

Unknown to me, Dad bumped into TA CEO Tim Wilson while I was on stage. As Tim approached, Dad assumed he was coming over to congratulate him on my win. Instead of the expected positive greeting, Tim told Dad that although I was clearly better than anyone else in the world, because I always raced as an individual and did not race as a team my inclusion in the Olympic Team for Sydney was very doubtful. Dad said he was flabbergasted at the comment, and asked Tim why on earth he would say that. Tim replied that Brett Sutton had put together a strategy for TA and he was convinced that following the ITU rule changes to drafting on the bike it was certain that triathlon would develop very quickly into a team sport, just like cycling. Dad reminded Tim that in the two years since the introduction of the draft-legal bike-leg policy, team racing had not developed, and I had completely dominated every year. Tim continued regardless and told Dad that Brett was way ahead of all coaches and TA expected he would coach athletes to race as teams and prove again how good a coach he is. Dad couldn't believe what he was hearing. At that point, the security guys approached Dad to tell him I was getting ready to leave, so the discussion ended there.

As we left the presentation, Dad did not mention his conversation with Tim to me. Dad always tried to shield me from the negative situations and attitudes, especially with TA, and especially at a time when I should be celebrating. They weren't helpful. Instead they were insulting and hurtful. We all piled into the car and drove out to Subiaco for a quiet meal. Even out there I was constantly recognised and stopped.

Without the knowledge of the negative undercurrents from TA, I was really pleased with my day. I could easily tick off the past twenty-four hours as the most challenging yet rewarding of my life.

Dad and I were both of the view that 1997 was a great year overall. My track record was looking better now:

Nineteen ITU World Cup starts: 17 wins, 1 second, and 1 DNF;

Four ITU World Championship starts: 2 wins, 1 second (ill), and 1 seventh (ill).

I also won the ITU World Cup series for the third year in a row. I managed to do this with a perfect score, given your seven best results plus your world championship result adds up to your end of year world cup score. No one in the history of triathlon had ever before or has ever since repeated that feat.

9. Everyone is a critic

My achievements were recognised outside ITU circles. I was again runner up in the Australian Female Athlete of the Year awards. It seemed that every time I won a world title, the great Australian 400 m champion Cathy Freeman did as well. As a result, Cathy won the prestigious accolade over me twice.

In the American triathlon fraternity, despite the ongoing battles with the ITU, *Triathlete* magazine finally awarded me the coveted 'Triathlete of the Year' award. It was a begrudging award, given that, 'Emma Carney delivers … FINALLY,' was set alongside the article announcing me as the winner. It was nice to know, now that I had won more ITU races than anyone, the Americans recognised me as the world's best triathlete. It seemed three years of dominating the sport and three world championship medals from four world championship starts had finally won them over. They had a bit of a swipe at me claiming I finally 'rose to the occasion against the heavy-hitters' and 'no big names were at the '94 Worlds'. The really weird thing about the entire award was that I was never invited to attend and accept it, as other triathletes were. Odd. Although it was seen as a prestigious award in the past, it had lost a lot of credibility. The magazine had not awarded me the 'Rookie of the Year' award in 1994 when I burst onto the ITU scene and won the world title at my first attempt and first ITU event. There was animosity between this group and the ITU, so it wasn't surprising that I was copping flack. I had only ever supported the ITU series of events.

With all the recognition, press interest and sponsors, the summer following such a successful ITU season was busy. I always took the time between the end of the international racing season and the beginning of the domestic season to fit in a lot of my sponsor and other public commitments. Among my sponsor requirements over the summer was the launch an adidas T-Shirt line with my picture. I banned Dad from wearing one.

Due to all the commitments, I spent summer in Melbourne. I was closer to my key sponsors and, despite the reputation Melbourne has for poor weather, the long hours of daylight and reasonably consistent dry heat it was perfect for training. Melbourne training had always prepared me well. I knew it worked. After all, that was half the battle of being an elite athlete, finding things that worked really well for you.

A few weeks after my World Championships win, Dad told me of the conversation he had with Tim Wilson at the awards ceremony in Perth. It concerned me that TA were so spiteful and disruptive towards me. I didn't really understand why I was such a problem for them. I knew I didn't conform, but does that really turn a national federation against you? I seemed to polarise people just by simply being me. I wasn't a 'people pleaser' and I didn't accept the status quo. What I did do was race to win. Wasn't that my role in all of this?

We discussed the threat Brett Sutton made when I left the AIS after his arrest and how he told me that leaving would affect my Olympic selection. Now the TA CEO was telling Dad outright that I wasn't part of the plan. This had now been mentioned at two quite separate instances in time. The common link was the creep himself, Brett Sutton.

The Brett Sutton fiasco continued and still does to this day. Dad received a call following my 1997 World Championship win from the Federal Police. There were multiple claims against Brett Sutton, and he pleaded guilty. The investigation was stalled by the fact that no one in TA would comment or provide any information about his treatment of women athletes as TA Head Coach. Not the TA Board members, not the CEO Tim Wilson, not the President Bill Walker, and none of the athletes he coached. A high-profile female athlete and a high-profile male athlete both provided character references for Brett Sutton, at TA's request.

Stumped by their support for Brett, a Federal Police Officer called Dad to see if we had any evidence that would give them something to work with. I did not because I kept Brett at an arm's length at all times. The Officer explained that due to the lack of cooperation by TA, Brett's sentence would be greatly reduced. The ITU at least was suitably horrified and banned Brett from ITU events. The ban still remains in place. TA bowed to the pressure and had him removed as a TA coach. The British Triathlon program also banned him. In response, Brett set up an international training camp with the support of former TA High Performance Manager, and Hahn camp staff member Rob Pickard, a long-time supporter.

Around this time, Dad asked TA President Bill Walker if he knew of Brett's shady past when he was appointed as Head Coach. To Dad's amazement, Bill admitted that he and TA staff withheld knowledge of Brett's behavior when they appointed him. Bill attempted to justify this behavior by stating that the overwhelming opinion of the TA hierarchy was that Brett was the best triathlon coach in the world and there was no other coach capable of ensuring Australia won the women's gold medal at the Sydney 2000 Olympics.

On recounting this story, Dad recalled telling Bill he was disgusted that both Clare and I had been put under pressure to attend a camp where Brett Sutton was largely left unsupervised around female athletes and that Bill scoffed and replied that he didn't need to worry. Apparently, Brett was too scared of Dad to, 'try anything on with Emma and Clare'. That comment again amazed Dad, because he could see the TA officials didn't seem to even remotely understand the seriousness of the situation and their absolute lack of concern for athlete welfare at the time. Bill Walker then turned the conversation around, according to Dad, and said that Clare and I left TA 'embarrassed' and 'unsupported' when we left the AIS camp. It was fortunate that the other athletes remained at the AIS as a unified group. Dad reminded Bill that only Brett's athletes stayed and that we left only three days earlier than everyone else.

During the same conversation, Dad decided to casually ask Bill Walker how he felt about team tactics in triathlon. Bill said he absolutely agreed with it and that Australia was going to adopt that strategy.

'Even when Emma has been the most dominant athlete in the past three years?' he asked Bill.

'Yes,' was Bill's very short reply. It was a closed topic.

The conversation ended. Dad never liked Bill, while I always thought he was ok. I had no idea at the time quite how much he was using his position to undermine me as an athlete.

There were other signs that my relationship with TA was becoming more complicated. TA increased pressure on me to work with a TA-accredited coach. Obviously, Dad and I had always been sceptical of coaches and Dad shielded me from coaching at a young age. I developed my own coaching ideas through contact with some very skilled individuals who coached as specialists in reach discipline, and by reading, watching, and understanding the skill of racing. By the time TA was forced to notice me, I had an independent mind that absorbed the logic of sport, training and development in a holistic way. I was self-sufficient, referred to specialist coaches for advice, and used Dad as a sounding board. This seemed to unnerve TA and go against what they expected of their athletes. Various individuals at TA including the President,

CEO, High Performance Manager and former head coach Brett Sutton, were critical of the input I received from Dad. It was clearly an issue for TA. During 1997, CEO Tim called Dad to notify him that only accredited coaches would be permitted in certain restricted areas at races and as he was not accredited, he would be excluded. Dad pointed out I was the only athlete to be affected by this new ruling. Tim agreed, but said that was the decision going forward. In response, Dad signed himself up for a level 1 triathlon coaching course and became accredited. From then on, I nominated Dad as my coach and continued to predominantly coach myself.

The Olympic Athlete Program offered funding support for coaches that met the qualifying criteria. With his qualifications done, Dad was nominated as my coach and Dad advised Tim. Some months went by and no grant payments were received. Not a cent. Dad called Tim Wilson and he told Dad the scheme had been discontinued and no grants would be paid. Dad and I were surprised but accepted Tim's reply.

In January 1998, I raced and won the state triathlon championships in Ballarat, a town an hours' drive west of Melbourne. As expected, I won easily and unchallenged from the gun. Unexpectedly though, the trip to Ballarat brought further proof that TA didn't care if I won the World Championships or had a perfect ITU score. Instead, TA seemed to be actively working against Dad and me.

While in Ballarat, Dad had an interesting conversation with the then President of Triathlon Victoria (Tri Vic). He had approached Dad and asked why I had nominated Brett Sutton as my coach under the Olympic Athlete Program. This was the program that Tim Wilson said had been scrapped. Dad of course told the Tri Vic President that I didn't nominate Brett. Annoyed and puzzled as to why Brett's name was down as my coach in documentation for a scheme that supposedly had been ended, Dad called the Australian Sports Commission the next day. He spoke to the contact for the program who advised that TA had submitted the relevant documentation, nominating Brett Sutton as my Coach. That meant that several grant instalments had been paid to him. Dad immediately had Brett's name as coach replaced with his own.

Following the conversation with the Australian Sports Commission, Dad contacted Tim Wilson. Tim immediately denied he ever told Dad the OAP had been scrapped, suggesting that the forms must have been completed by a temp in the TA office during a busy time. This didn't stand up, because the Australian Sports Commission told Dad that TA was required to fill out the grant forms and Tim Wilson needed to authorise them. Regardless of this discrepancy in the explanation for Brett's name being put down instead of Dad's, Tim went on to try to justify the misallocation of funds by stating that Brett was effectively my coach because I had attended the TA training camp in Hahn the previous year. Dad reminded Tim I had been pressured to attend. It was absurd and completely wrong to suggest that Brett was my coach.

The conversation ended with assurances that the details would never again be adjusted, and Dad was officially my coach, but the whole episode added further to the growing distrust that Dad and I had for Triathlon Australia.

All this was happening while my busy schedule continued. Over the next month, I had commitments in Sydney with my sponsors Holden and NAB. The Devonport Triathlon was the next race on the calendar, just a week after Ballarat. I returned there to a slightly different course, but with the same outcome. I felt a little out of race fitness, but won fairly easily, a few minutes ahead of the field after a strong bike and run combination.

For the first time in my career though, I really began to notice that I was tired all the time. Not a typical tiredness where a good night's sleep could get rid of it, but a tiredness where I would very suddenly lose energy. It was difficult to pinpoint, so I ignored it. A bad habit of mine: ignore it and it will go away. Probably. It never did though, and from 1998 nothing was ever the same again. There was no longer a 'normal' for me. Tired was my new me, my now normal.

My perfect score the previous year meant that neither Dad nor I considered the warnings Dr June Canavan made in 1996 about a possible deterioration of my heart function. Dad recalls his thinking at the end of 1997:

Given that Emma raced so dominantly, the dire warning from Dr June Canavan was completely removed from my thoughts. Emma was so dominant and so far ahead of the rest of the world, to consider she was racing with a heart problem seemed completely wrong. It seemed Emma was fine.

With intermittent travel, training loads and abnormally late nights due to functions, I thought perhaps some occasional feelings of lethargy in races were really just tiredness due to changes in my routine. I didn't feel like I needed to back off my training, but I did monitor things more carefully and consistently myself. As an athlete, there are little things you can do to make sure you are giving yourself enough rest. I used to record my sleep hours in my training diary, take my morning heart rate and also had regular blood tests to make sure I wasn't running myself down too much. There were no really big changes to any of these indicators, so I felt reassured it was just out-of-season-routine tiredness. I knew my norms. I worked well off eight or nine hours' sleep a night, my morning heart rate was generally sub-33, and my blood tests were compiled and read by my doctor, so any abnormalities there would be picked up. With hindsight, the tiredness was really the first noticeable sign of an undiagnosed heart condition, but I didn't consider that perhaps there was actually something wrong with me physically. I only ever thought that possibly I was developing a mental weakness. It was more a feeling. I am not convinced that the improved attention to athlete wellbeing and monitoring of today's training environment would have helped me through this phase of my career. My behaviour was part of my character, part of me. I was wired to work hard, fight obstacles and never buckle. I took on adversity as something to overcome, not a reason to ask for help.

Despite feeling tired more often, I raced throughout the Australian summer and I raced well. I easily won a local race in Portarlington, just outside of Melbourne, and also a local event in Brighton, a bayside suburb of Melbourne. Between the various triathlons domestically, I ran some 10 km road races in late summer, recording 33 minutes 30 seconds in one without a proper training taper, so my running was ticking over nicely.

My weekly training volumes were still consistent. I swam around 25-30 km a week, rode 200-250 km a week and ran 70-90 km a week. I maintained a focus on quality in my key swim, bike and run sessions and still managed some good training times in all three disciplines. On top of this regular training, I did my strength and conditioning work, plyometric exercises and maintained everything with a weekly massage with renowned masseur Garry Miritis. My workload was sensible, as far as an elite athlete's training load can be sensible and because I was training in Eltham, there was quality to my key training sets. Because my training was going well, stupidly, I started to consider maybe I was just going a little soft. I doubted myself.

Early March I drove in the Celebrity Grand Prix in the Melbourne Formula One event at Albert Park. I managed to overshoot a corner at the southern end of the track, hit the grass, lose control of my car, over correct and slam straight into the wall. For the second year in a row, my car was a write-off and I was towed back to the pits, much to the disgust of my driving instructors. Again, they told me I was a danger to myself when I race cars. I didn't think anyone should be at all surprised, because I honestly thought that was what I had been asked to do: race a car flat out. What did they expect?

As usual I flew out to Japan in April for the ITU season opener at Ishigaki. The event was growing each year, and this being the third year, I so far had been the only female winner. The local community was very much behind the event, and my personal fan club had grown to a sizeable group. Leading into the race the hotel informed me they had received requests for me to go and meet the group one evening. I discussed the situation with Les McDonald and let the hotel know I would meet them Sunday evening after the race.

On race day, I had a good start but felt an awful weakness flush over me, reducing my ability to swim, about halfway through the first lap of the two-lap swim. I hung on and battled to remain as close to the front of the field as possible. Once out on the bike, my technical bike skills allowed me to reel in the swim leaders and I ran fast to win for the third year in a row. Australia took a clean sweep in the women's event, with Jackie Gallagher second and Michellie Jones third.

Clare was the next Australian across the line at Ishigaki, with the third fastest run split of the day, but she was no longer racing for Australia. Over the summer, TA High Performance Manager Rob Pickard wrote to Clare to tell her she was not good enough to receive starts in top-tier ITU races for Australia. It was an absurd claim against Clare. Thirteen Australian women were selected for the upcoming Sydney ITU race, so it was really obvious TA would rather try to destroy Clare's racing career than give her a start. As we were all born in England, there was nothing to stop Clare from racing for Great Britain. Ishigaki was Clare's first race in GBR colours, and Clare showed TA how nonsensical their claim was, beating every other Australian team member apart from the two others on the podium with me.

Not only did Clare prove their mistake, following her lead, four more athletes transferred from the Australian team to the GBR team. There were also a string of other athletes making changes to represent other countries.

On returning to Australia, I needed to rest up for the next ITU race, the Sydney Olympic test event. So far, I was undefeated in Sydney. It was a perfect record to have on an Olympic test event course. The expectations around the Australian Triathlon team with the Sydney Olympics only two years away was really building. As the only undefeated athlete on the course, the demands on me leading into the event were again complicated by TA. Pre-race, they accused me of missing the official TA press conference. They notified every athlete about it, except for me. It wasn't really surprising. The press conference was organised by Andrew Fraser, who was part of the group who put on the Online Sports triathlon series. Not exactly fans of mine. I was disappointed by this constructed accusation, because I always made myself available for the Australian media and I never intentionally missed a press conference. On arriving in Sydney, I had private press interviews as soon as I reached my hotel. One reporter informed me that Michellie Jones had been announced as a non-starter and asked what I thought of this. I replied I was pretty sure she had never confided in me with regard to her race schedule, so I didn't know why she wasn't racing. Again, I refused to be drawn into questions about my competitors, instead focussing on questions regarding myself and my race. I was not going to be drawn into any contrived disputes with my competitors.

The Saturday prior to the race we had our mandatory athlete briefing, at which it was announced that the first leg of the race would most likely be a non-wetsuit swim. Apparently, the water temperature was borderline 20°C, so the ITU requirement for a non-wetsuit swim came into play. I didn't think much of it. I did prefer a wetsuit swim, because it was my 'weaker' discipline and the wetsuit allowed me to swim higher in the water, but as it was a ruling that I couldn't change I didn't bother worrying about it. Interestingly, in ITU events of today, the water *and* air temperature are now considered before deciding on a wetsuit ruling, because athletes are exposed to both.

Race morning for me was planned around a 9.30 a.m. start. I had my alarm set for 5 a.m. After a light breakfast of toast and black coffee I did a small sharp warmup on the bike trainer in my hotel room and made my way down to the race site in front of the famous Sydney Opera House, at around 8 a.m. The weather had turned cold and there was a strong cold southerly wind blowing. There was much discussion amongst the athletes about whether it was still a non-wetsuit swim: it seemed too cold. I made the decision to do a full land warmup, believing that if I got into the water then stood to be marshalled, my body temperature would drop too low and I would not be able to warm up again for the race start. I was pleased with my decision, but despite staying dry and keeping my clothes on for as long as possible, the length of time it took for the pre-race marshalling left me exposed to the cold wind for too long. As we were all in the same situation, I tried to ignore the cold.

I had a good start, but at about 450 m in I just felt cold. I battled on, but once out of the water in the wind it was even worse. Normally I would have been at the front of the field on the hilly, technical course (and in previous years I was). I rode the first lap well, then pretty much stopped dead, frozen, and hardly able to move. Dad yelled at me to stop. At first, I ignored him. I completed another lap of the course, but once away from the crowds, I pulled out. Dad came running over and told me I should have stopped earlier. Clare had not even made one lap of the bike she was so cold.

I needed some clothes to get warm. There was no medical assistance, because I was out on the course when I stopped, so I made my way back to the hotel alone. Dad collected my gear from the transition area and no one from TA asked where I was. The complete lack of care by my national federation slightly amused me.

Fortunately, the following day, the media was very supportive of me. I was surprised and thought perhaps I always jumped to the wrong conclusion. Jackie Gallagher won the event in my absence, but no one from the media asked my opinion on this, which was a pleasant surprise. There were reports the race needed a lot of work, and there were reports by the BBC in the UK that the race was a shamble, because I had been forced to pull out.

At the end of the day, it didn't really matter what everyone else thought, I was disappointed. I really didn't need this right now, especially when I was beginning to feel there was something off. I now had a blemish on my record at the Sydney Olympic test site. This alone didn't sit well with me.

The following weekend I had a good hit out in a 10 km road race, running sub-34 minutes on a hilly course, but again felt flat. I told myself I hadn't tapered for the event, but everything felt sluggish. I wasn't sure if I was being too hard on myself, but I felt I was underperforming. Not a thought, again, of the warnings from Dr June Canavan, because I was still clearly the best triathlete in the world.

The national championships were held the following weekend in Mooloolaba. That meant my family and I all stayed at my place in Noosa for a week. As was becoming a tradition, I did some more training with Garth Prowd in the ocean. It was nice to be back in the beautiful surrounds of Noosa again. In order to avoid the fiasco of missing the press conference again, Dad made a point of asking Andrew Fraser for the details. Later in the day, Andrew Fraser rang me to see if he could do a personal interview with me. I asked why he didn't wait to ask me at the press conference. He replied rather casually that he, 'couldn't make it'. I couldn't believe it. Andrew accused me of skipping the press conference the week before, despite not notifying me of it, and now he simply couldn't be bothered to attend himself. I felt like I was losing brain cells dealing with this lot.

I spent the rest of my time pre-race quietly avoiding anything to do with TA and preparing myself.

Sunday, 10 May was race day. The weather was perfect. I woke at 6 a.m. for a 10.35 a.m. race start, fifty minutes after the men. I opted to stay in Noosa (just to be at my own place and sleep in my own bed pre-race) so I had a thirty-minute drive south to Mooloolaba. I had a poor start. As is always the case with an ocean swim, there is a little bit of pot luck with the wave sets and swell. I messed my start up, but also it seemed that Brett Sutton organised his swimmers to take Jackie Gallagher out through the swell. I ended up exiting forty seconds down. The bike was eight laps and I caught the main bunch by the third lap. I decided to stop my chase with the main bunch, leaving the swimmers off the front to burn themselves out. As long as they didn't pull away, it didn't matter if they remained 30-40 seconds ahead. I was very confident I could run them down. Brett was out on the course, dressed in his cheap suit and looking his usual creepy self. Instructing anyone he thought could beat me, he yelled 'cover her' or 'hold her wheel'. I ignored his antics and his obsession with trying to get his athletes to beat me and just focussed on what I had to do to win.

I rolled in at the end of the bike, making sure I didn't rush myself and run someone else's race. I wanted to warm into the run, stay in control, assess things, then wind it up. After about 300 m I admittedly lost patience with being patient and decided to let rip. I took the lead quickly. By the end of the run, I had put around ninety seconds into Jackie Gallagher, who placed second. There must have been some angst remaining from the Sydney race result, because painted on the road were the words 'stick it to her Emma!' That was one of my most memorable national triathlon titles, given the poor race result leading in and the very dominant performance over the field.

I returned to Melbourne that evening, wanting to return to a training routine I knew worked.

With my high profile, triathlon was getting a lot of free to air television coverage domestically. I had a number of TV interviews in Melbourne. In one weekend alone, a delayed telecast of the Nationals at Mooloolaba aired on Channel 10, and Channel 9 had a 'triathlon special'. It was a real growth time for the sport, and everyone really wanted to be involved. This time was really a missed opportunity for TA to grow and develop the sport properly; it was simply missing some strong leadership to keep it on track and help reach its full potential.

The week after Mooloolaba was quite a momentous one for the ITU. Les

McDonald settled with the World Triathlon Corporation (WTC), who ran Ironman triathlon. For the entirety of my triathlon career so far, the ITU and WTC had been suing and counter suing each other with regard to ownership of the sport of triathlon worldwide. This settlement was good for triathlon, because constant infighting between the two major bodies was only ever going to slow progress of the sport as a whole.

Mooloolaba brought the domestic season to an end, and I resumed a full training load as part of my preparation for the remainder of the ITU season. Clare left Australia a week before me. Now she was racing for GBR she needed to race the British National Championships. Dad organised for Clare and me to stay in Switzerland at the home of Zurich ITU Triathlon race organiser Anne Marie Gschwend and we planned to meet there in two weeks.

As was the case with my Qantas sponsorship, I flew Business Class to London, so it really was not much of a struggle. I really worked on eating clean and staying clear of coffee and chocolate to minimise my caffeine intake, so I was able to sleep through most of my long-haul flight. I landed in Heathrow at 5.45 a.m. with time for a shower, before my 7.45 a.m. connection to Zurich. There, I attended the Zurich race press conference, collected the car Holden had organised for me and made my way to a place called Bollingen, about a one hour drive out of Zurich. This was where Clare and I were going to stay for the next few weeks.

Bollingen was as picturesque as Switzerland can get. Our accommodation was on a lake where Clare and I could swim, although there was also a local pool down the road. There were good roads to ride with plenty of hills and also trails for running and a run track. It looked like Clare and I were set up well for a solid block of training.

That is how sport plays out. You think you have everything covered and thought through, and then everything falls apart. I raced the Zurich World Cup and felt terrible from the gun. Clare didn't race at all — she had been ill in the UK and never recovered. I got through the swim and bike in Zurich but was far from good form. I pulled out of the race about 1 km into the run, totally flat. It seemed I had caught whatever Clare had.

With Clare ill, and me now ill and not finishing the race, we called Dad in Australia. He said it was just a flat spot, I needed to remain positive and get myself well. Clare decided to go home. I knew it would be tough alone, but I thought going home would be like giving up. With hindsight, I should have returned with Clare, because my next ITU race was in Gamagori, Japan.

Gamagori was a poor race result for me, so much so, it was my worst result ever at that point. I swam ok, only thirty seconds down on the lead swimmers. This would have not been a problem for me to bridge had I been feeling ok, but I felt weak on the bike and then ran terribly. Despite my poor result, I received a standing ovation when I finished. It was the first time I had been beaten in Japan. It was quite humbling. I felt I had failed, yet the crowd told me there was still admiration.

Dad had flown to Japan to help me prepare for the race. I was pleased he did, because when we returned to our hotel, there was yet another letter for Dad from Brett Sutton. The letter, in Brett's almost illiterate handwriting, told Dad that he was ruining my career by stopping Brett from coaching me. Dad was livid and told me he was going to take out an intervention order, because this needed to stop. I asked Dad not to, I was sick of all the animosity. There was no way I was ever going to train with Brett, and I didn't know why he had this false idea that I would. Perhaps he was being told by TA to coach me, I didn't know. I was disappointed I wasn't being protected from this person.

At this point I should have returned to Australia. After two poor performances by my normal standards, I really needed to get myself winning again. For the first time in my career, I wasn't living up to the expectation of being world number one. I needed to work on myself again. The problem was any changes I made, I felt like I was giving up. For all the benefits of my education at Wesley College in Melbourne, I had never really been taught how to lose; how to handle losing, how to 'fail well'. After all, I never had lost a race at school. My triathlon career so far had been pretty much all winning too. For the entirety of my sporting career, when I really, really wanted to win I generally had. Nothing prepared me for losing. I assumed it was me, I didn't speak about how I was feeling. I just battled on. Not once did I consider a health problem was developing. With hindsight, this noticeable drop in my performances was clearly the early manifestation of a heart condition.

I searched for answers. Looking at the race results, what seemed very odd to me was the fact that I was not being beaten by athletes who were going faster, I was simply racing slower. Triathlon is a sport where courses obviously differ from one race to the next, some are hilly, some flat, some saltwater, some open water with chop. One constant in triathlon, however, is that the men and the women always race the same course. The true constant therefore was to look at women's race results and to compare the difference between the men's and the women's race finishing times. When I was racing well, I managed to finish within ten minutes of the men's finishing time. Now, with my current poor performances, I was finishing down the field in races where the female winner was more than ten minutes outside the men's finishing time. Therefore, it seemed quite obvious to me, I was underperforming. I was not being beaten by faster athletes. I was not being beaten by better athletes. For some reason I was suddenly getting slower.

What made things more confusing was the fact that I was still training well. I had a look at my training and had a look at my races. Training was ok. I just really struggled in races when a sudden burst of energy and effort was required, such as the swim start or when I attacked on the bike. I was experiencing terrible overwhelming surges of fatigue about two to three minutes into the swim. A triathlon swim always required a dive and sprint to the first buoy; an all-out effort of about 200-300 m. But it was becoming extremely difficult to perform, due to the wave of fatigue causing me to back off and then just try to get through. It destroyed any ability I had to remain close to the lead swimmers and front swim pack. Not only did I lose ground, but my loss of pace also put me in the path of other competitors, who just swam over me. On the bike my trademark efforts jumping packs or jumping from a chase group to the lead group, were missing in races. When fatigue hit me hard, it prevented any major pace change. I wasn't as consistent as I had been. Some days I was still dominant, sometimes not.

Working through the problem with the swim start, I decided perhaps my warm-up was not sufficient. Perhaps I was not able to perform because my body was not ready. I also reduced the warm-ups I did in swim training, to try to simulate what I expected from my body on race day.

Before I left Australia, I had gone to my doctor for all my regular blood tests, as always monitoring my body. I was advised that I was again low in B12. I thought that perhaps that was affecting me; my Iron levels were fine. Doctors regularly criticised my training, saying that my tiredness was due to overtraining (this is where training load is too great), but I was not entirely convinced of this, because my tiredness was not constant. It hit me hardest at the start of a race and at any major effort in a race. I convinced myself that my training tiredness was at this stage still predominantly the normal tiredness an elite athlete deals with most days. Deep down I knew there was something wrong, that no one could pinpoint for me, and nothing could clearly show me what.

I had another disappointing result at the next ITU series race, in Corner Brook, Canada. It should have suited me, with a hilly bike course and run. I struggled and finished eighth. My confidence was taking a hit, and again I thought maybe I had gone soft. Following the Corner Brook race, I was required to attend a TA camp in Remoray, France, near the French-Swiss border. Without the presence of Brett Sutton, the environment allowed me to train without scrutiny.

During the camp, I raced some local ETU races. One was in Nyon, France. I felt ok and managed to win, but to be honest, if I hadn't been able to win a race like that, I would have thought my situation was pretty dire.

The TA camp moved down to the team hotel, 'Au Lac', for the World Championships in Lausanne on 26 August. It was a Wednesday, and it was only 75 km away, mostly downhill. A few of us decided to ride down, while team management transferred our luggage. On the way, I noticed the gear cable to my front derailleur was slightly frayed at the end. I tested my gears, and all were working perfectly. I decided the cable was just slightly frayed because the cap had fallen off, not because it was worn. When I arrived at the team hotel, I spoke to the TA team bike mechanic about it, but told him I did not want the cable replaced, because I did not want to race on a new cable that could possibly stretch mid race and cause my gears to jump. The course was very hilly and far too heavy on gears to risk a new unstretched cable. The mechanic told me he could stretch a cable and replace it. I told him I didn't want to race on untried equipment, asked him to just replace the tyres on my race wheels and gave him all the stuff required for the task. I assumed he would do as I asked and didn't think much of it. I considered the conversation to be normal, the sort of conversation you had with your bike mechanic prior to an important race.

Oddly, I was then told by TA team management that my bike was not permitted in my room and had to remain with all the Australian bikes. I was immediately concerned. I always kept my bike in my room, because it was so vital there was no tampering with it. I questioned the decision and was reassured all bikes were going to be watched by security. Not happy with the decision, I had no real choice. I left my bike with the team mechanic and met up with Mum, Dad and Clare. Kay was with them. She had decided to fly over as well and give me some pre-race treatment for the race.

When I collected my bike from the team mechanic, I found that against my instruction he replaced the gear cable on my bike. We had a short argument, and he told me he knew what he was doing. I told him I hoped so, for his sake. I took my bike for a test ride on hills and flats, and all seemed ok.

Over the next few days, there was the usual course familiarisation and formal pre-race requirements. The location for the race was pretty much as picturesque as Switzerland gets. Lausanne is located on the edge of Lake Geneva and seemed to me to be where all the world's most affluent and beautiful people lived. The weather was perfect, and with a tough hilly bike course, I was actually looking forward to racing again.

Race day was Sunday, 30 August. The elite women's race start was 3.30 p.m., so I had the morning to prepare. It was nice having the time pre-race. I decided the breakfast at Mum and Dad's hotel was nicer than mine, so I headed over to join them. I also didn't really want to hang around those I was due to race later on that day. The weather was perfect, the wind had dropped, there was no sign of rain and the temperature was good for racing. Our bikes had to be in transition by 11 a.m. As I rode down to the race site, I tested my gears again. The cable seemed ok, but I wasn't really riding hills or testing it under extreme pressure. I decided I couldn't worry about it and hoped the mechanic was correct, that he did know what he was doing. I dropped my bike off and jogged back, feeling good.

Dad picked me up from my hotel at 1.15 p.m. and when we arrived at transition, a wetsuit swim was announced. The water temperature in the lake was below 20°C. That suited me. Everything seemed to be falling into place.

Pre-race, we were allowed to warm up in the water, but not on the course. Twenty minutes prior to race start, we had to exit the water for introductions to the crowd. It was to be a deep-water start, with a line that was to be lifted by the starter. Watching the start of the men's race the day before I decided it was best to sprint to the line from shore, as the starter fired the gun pretty much straight away.

If the starter followed the same procedure, I would have had an almost perfect start, but as it happened, today was not going to be my day. We were all called back and held by the starter for a long period of time. By the time we started, I was cold and experienced all the fatigue and energy difficulties I had been having recently. It was a poor start. The swim course consisted of a 1,000 m loop, followed by a 500 m loop. I exited the water around sixty seconds down, but the bike course was very tough, so it was not a major concern.

Out on the bike we had four laps. Half of the course, on the way out of town, went up; and the other half, on the way back to transition, went down. The final section of climbing out to the top point of the course had a sharp pinch with a 17 per cent gradient. I felt strong on the first lap and made a lot of progress on the field. I was not only out climbing everyone, but I was also descending and cornering well. I used all my gears, maximising my climbing and descending speed. I felt good.

As I made my way onto the second lap of the course, I heard an odd noise from someone's bike. I didn't think much of it, until I tried to change into the small chain ring as I approached the hilly section. My derailleur wouldn't move. I looked down and could see the cable had slipped through.

Without the ability to get out of the big chain ring, I couldn't get through the hills. I leaned down to manually push it across, but it just flicked back. The bunch rode away from me.

I couldn't believe this was happening to me.

I climbed off my bike and threw it across the course.

I then removed my helmet and threw it into some nearby bushes.

Then I threw my bike shoes across the road.

I was just getting to the end of my tantrum when an official came over to me. He asked me very politely if I could stop throwing my equipment.

'What?!' I yelled at him, completely frustrated.

'I have just received a message from Les McDonald, and he is sitting with Juan Antonio Samaranch (the head of the International Olympic Committee) in the transition grandstand, watching the live feed. Les is trying to prove that the sport of triathlon is mature enough to remain in the Olympic family and the coverage of you destroying your equipment is making this message hard to argue.'

I listened, stopped my antics and walked off slowly to find Dad.

I saw Les on the way and he asked me why I made such a spectacle of my withdrawal from the race.

I couldn't believe he was serious, and told him it was not planned, it was more a reaction to the frustration of someone stuffing up my world title defence. I had high expectations of myself, regardless of the recent disappointments, and that wasn't going to change. I also asked him if he had seen the Australian team mechanic.

Les left me to it. Dad was adamant my bike had been tampered with. I wasn't sure what the reason was, but that was a course I should have won on easily.

I faced the media, as everyone wanted to know what had happened. It seemed most had assumed I would ride away from everyone today and win my third world title. But at the team hotel, no one from TA asked how I was. Australia dominated the women's race, taking out gold and silver, so no one was particularly disappointed for me.

I never heard from the bike mechanic, and I don't think he ever returned to be a part of the TA team again. It was unfortunate all around. He was a good mechanic, but old school, and I don't think he realised triathletes, like cyclists, also knew a lot about their bikes.

Following the Lausanne disaster, I took a break with my family in Grindlewald. I wasn't much fun, but I needed a break. By the end of the week away, I am pretty sure everyone needed a break from me.

After the break, I raced the local Neuchatel ETU race and won easily. I then flew off to England to race the London Triathlon. I won this easily as well, but it was more a chance to catch up with relatives. Grandad Carney made the trip to watch the race. He looked old, but he told me he was very proud of me and liked what I had done with the name Carney.

I tore my calf a few weeks later and missed the next ITU round in Cancun, Mexico. Jackie Gallagher won in my absence and claimed to be the best in the world again. In November, there were two more ITU events in the southern hemisphere: Auckland, New Zealand and Noosa, Australia. I raced the Auckland event and finished fourth. It was a flat course, and I felt flat again. The women's race winner was over thirteen minutes behind the men's time, so it wasn't fast. I was just slow. Noosa Triathlon I didn't even start. I was ill again.

In 1998, I didn't win the World Series for the first time in my career and I was also no longer world number one. I had dropped to four. My worst ranking ever. Dad and I had a look at my season. It was still a very good season by normal international racing standards but had been very average for me. We thought perhaps I needed a group to train with, as many of those I used to train with in Melbourne were not as invested in training now they were older. I thought perhaps training with male athletes would provide a similar training environment to what I originally had in Melbourne at the start of my career. With hindsight, I underestimated the perfect training environment I had in Melbourne, particularly the rugged area of Eltham. Nevertheless, as an athlete you always look for more, and how you can do things better. Currently I wasn't performing, so I felt I was failing. I think the combined confusion as to what was wrong with me and having no clear explanation as to why I was suddenly racing slower led me to make a big change. Wanting predominantly males to train with, because I didn't want to train with competitors, I thought about moving to Cronulla, just south of Sydney. The area had a good reputation for triathlon training, and Clare got to know the area while she was receiving treatment from Kay and liked it. Kay said we were welcome to spend some time at her place if we wanted to try it out. We started to consider a move to Sydney as a training option.

With the international season of racing over, I spent some time with my sponsors again. In November, NAB invited me to an employee end of year celebration in Bali, Indonesia. While it was another trip overseas, it was, this time, a holiday. It was also nice to meet and get to know the people who had been supporting me over the last few years through my NAB sponsorship. Early December adidas had me in Melbourne to promote some products, and we planned out my responsibilities for the summer.

TA invited me to the AIS mid-December. It was actually a positive move from TA, and I was happy to go, especially given there was no chance the AIS would allow Brett Sutton to attend the camp — nor allow him anywhere near any of us there. I never really had the chance to work with the experts at the AIS, so I really made the most of their expertise. I spoke to biomechanists, physiologists, nutritionists and strength and conditioning experts. I had largely worked all this stuff out by myself so far, working with specialist coaches and reading as much as I could, so it was nice to have these conversations. I tried to learn as much as I could. I also did some VO2Max running and power tests on the bike. There was discussion of me riding with SRM cranks to measure power while I raced.

The VO2Max tests showed I could get my heart rate to a threshold level of 176 bpm. This is not a particularly high heart rate max, but I was able to race at 165-170 for most of the two hours of racing, so I was able to push myself extremely close to max for sustained periods of time. Along with this, it was also discovered I had a very high lactate threshold. Lactic acid build-up leads to that horrible feeling you get in your muscles during a physical effort that forces you to slow down, also known as basic human self-preservation. When you have a high tolerance for this, you slow down at a later stage than others, allowing you to go harder — or faster — for longer. My lactic tolerance was extraordinarily high, so it was believed I could race and train at close to my maximum heart rate with little to no lactic acid build up, thereby remaining faster for longer than my competitors were able to maintain. I never really saw myself as talented or gifted, but for the first time I had some facts and results showing I was wired for endurance sport. It also seemed to suggest that the argument put forward by some people about me over-training wasn't relevant. My body was not the same as everyone else's. Whatever the problem, it was a sign that something had changed with me.

Amongst all the discussions, I didn't mention my feelings of tiredness. I couldn't really work out how to explain it. I did ask to have some injury screening done, especially with my ongoing Achilles problems. There was also discussion about some altitude testing to be done at a later stage. I got as much as I could out of my visit to the AIS and felt a little better about things. I put my bad season down to a flat period. It was temporary. One 'down' season of racing can be easily turned around, and I thought I could work towards a better 1999.

10. Playing a Poor Hand Well

In my eyes, 1998 had been a complete disaster. In sport, to be a success you need to win. I didn't want 1999 to be more of the same.

I felt better after visiting the AIS but looking ahead to the 1999 domestic and international seasons, things still didn't make sense. The overwhelming problem was that while I was underperforming, I still remained competitive internationally and still qualified easily for the Australian elite triathlon team — the strongest triathlon team on the planet. It was a very frustrating time. I was not being beaten by new or faster athletes. Instead, my 'winning edge' was no longer as reliable as it had been. I didn't always have that 'edge', 'spark' or whatever it is called where I could do whatever was necessary to force a win. If I was honest, it was more than that. I was feeling tired. Really tired. Sore and aching. Dizzy and lightheaded now even at times between training. Breathless after sudden intense efforts in races.

I had no logical explanation as to why I was feeling these things. I was five years into my triathlon career. Was I just suffering from accumulated fatigue, just race weary? Perhaps my critics were right, perhaps it is unsustainable to constantly race to win.

Being predominantly self-managed regarding training loads and planning my program, performance drops were not something I processed well. I took on failure, which was what I considered anything but a win to be, as requiring a need for some changes and perhaps a different training regime. At the start of 1999 I had not yet accepted that the tried and trusted response of increasing the training load, or the quality of the training might not provide the answers. They did not, and no matter what I did things just did not seem to improve.

Dad and I had decided I should at least try training in Sydney. Clare and I moved to Cronulla before launching into the domestic season. We swam with a renowned tough swim coach based at Carrs Park in Kogarah. He was very old school in his approach and loved to be 'hard'. He would bang on about how tough everyone was in the old days and how we should all be thankful he bothered to coach us. If his sessions didn't crack you, his harsh comments would. He used to yell abuse from the pool deck, with a coffee mug in his hand, although I'm sure there was something stronger in the mug than just coffee.

Despite his idiosyncrasies, everyone swore by his training methods and sessions. 'Do two months of this stuff and you will be flying,' everyone told Clare and me. We did two years of it, and never swam so badly. Every week, we were subjected to the same sets.

Friday — sixteen 400 metre repeats on 5 minutes 30 seconds.

Tuesday — sixteen 200 metre repeats on 2 minutes 45 seconds.

And Saturday — a 45 minute band-only session, or a random set of one hundred 100 metre repeats on 1 minute 30 seconds, which he called two and a half hours of 'fun in the sun'.

It was relentless suffering in the pool, and you could never pass comment. If you did, the session would start again, with him yelling at us, 'You are lucky I care this much, to train you this hard.'

Clare and I would look at each other on the odd occasion we were allowed a break. I remember one day saying to Clare, 'I'm not sure if my goggles are leaking, or I am crying.'

'I am definitely crying,' Clare replied.

It was horrible. The type of coaching that fills you with self-doubt. The sessions were too hard, forcing you to wonder if you were tough enough, and the verbal abuse was just plain rude, forcing you to wonder if he was right. For some reason though, I put up with it. I stayed and turned up every day. I wasn't performing, but I wasn't going to give up either. I was stuck in my own little nightmare.

This period of excessive training in the pool I believe further contributed to my already manifesting heart condition. It was just as Dr June Canavan had predicted three years earlier, the pressure on my heart from the continuous workload slowly increased the accumulated overall damage to my heart.

While the swimming was tough, the bike and run sessions were also not what Clare and I used to do. In Sydney, we trained with more volume. Our Wednesday ride became a group ride with other triathletes from the area. They were entertaining sessions, given the guys we were riding with. But they were too long (given we were racing only 40 km in triathlon events), 120 km rides from Sutherland Shire to Wollongong and back via the Mt Keira climb. Running, I tried to maintain my track sessions and interval training, but that was where I was having the most problems with my feelings of lethargy — with top end speed and basic efforts.

While I wasn't performing to my best, I wasn't talking about things still, so everything just bubbled along. My profile was growing, with adidas posters and NAB billboards in prominent places around the country. I was constantly recognised in the street, something I never really felt comfortable with. Things looked great from the 'outside', but they really were not.

Online Sports tried to get me into their race series, but they did my head in, so I gave it a miss. Michellie pulled out of the series late February too, citing illness. All the racing was becoming difficult, especially for Australian athletes, as our domestic season was on while athletes in the Northern Hemisphere enjoyed their 'winter break'. I raced some national and local Victorian races, winning fairly easily. I was still fit, but no longer felt strong or fast. I felt flat. In late March I raced a 10 km road race in Melbourne, managing 33 minutes. It was a respectable time on a windy day. I felt ok, not great, and considered again whether maybe I had just gone 'soft'.

One physiological problem was quite easy to identify. Over the summer, my Achilles really flared up, particularly the left one. I think it was the biomechanical outcome of my poorer running form through the 1998 race season. I was constantly battling with soreness and tendonitis kept creeping back in. I could usually keep on top of anything too serious through massage, constant icing, treatment and various injury prevention exercises but I also looked for other ways to try to get my running pain free again.

I was filmed running when at the AIS, and it was suggested perhaps I should see a podiatrist to see if my foot plant could be improved. I wasn't convinced I needed orthotics, because I had never worn them, and I wondered if the filming had been done at a time when I was limping with sore Achilles anyway, so it was not really a true representation of my running style.

Despite my reservations, and being an elite athlete always seeking more, I decided to go along to a recommended podiatrist to see if there was a solution. I was set up with some orthotics and told to start to wear them walking at first, then jog, then run. This was meant to be a four-week process. After running in them, I started to get a sore right foot on the lateral side. It wasn't a sharp pain and was not easily pinpointable, so me being me, I ignored it.

As usual, Clare and I flew out to Japan in early April for the Ishigaki and Gamagori ITU races. Clare met the British team and I flew with the Australian team. Except for the previous year in Gamagori, I'd had much success at both races and knew the courses well. With increased Olympic program funding, TA arranged a full team, with staff support. Emery Holmik was the newly appointed Olympic Program Manager, which I think was the equivalent of the present-day TA High Performance Manager. We also had a Team Physio, Peter Stanton, and Team Masseur, Brad Higgins. With the extra TA support, one would expect the trip would have been a little more enjoyable, but my season was about to go pear shaped and it was still only April.

As Clare and I checked onto our flight, the Qantas check-in staff recognised me. Both Clare and I were flying business class, but as we were checking in, we were told the flight was not full and we could identify other Australian triathletes on the passenger list to be upgraded to business class as well. I looked at the list and hesitated. I had no problem with upgrading any of the male athletes, because I didn't have to race them. I did have a problem with upgrading the female athletes as I did have to race them. If they turned up more jet lagged than me, that was a good thing. 'These are the athletes, thanks for doing that,' I said as I handed the list back, with only the male athletes highlighted. Clare looked at me and I shrugged.

Once on board, Clare and I sat quietly while everyone else took their seats. There was much excitement amongst the men's team and disgust from the female team members. One particularly outspoken female teammate yelled at me, 'Why are you sitting up there, Carney?' I shrugged and replied, 'I always travel like this,' avoiding eye contact. Clare just busied herself with her massive business class seat and concentrated on not laughing. Neither of us ever told anyone, except Dad. Needless to say, Dad was impressed. After all, he disliked my competitors more than I did.

We had a stopover in Nagoya, endured flight delays and slow connections, and arrived in Ishigaki at 4.30 p.m. Thursday, 8 April, the following day. I managed to get a swim and run in before my 'fan club' arrived at the hotel to see me. There in the hotel foyer was about thirty very excited people, all wearing T-Shirts with my face on them. It was quite humbling, but also really funny. They were so excited to meet me, and I had no idea what they were saying. There was a lot of commotion for a while and then I asked the hotel staff to ask them to meet me after the race so I could spend time with them properly.

Pre-race, Michellie and I were both invited to the press conference and we struggled through it. Neither of us really wanted to answer questions on each other but did so diplomatically. We both got out of there as quickly as we could. I prepared as I had each year, getting to know the course and familiarising myself with its precise details. It was slightly different this year. Previous years we swam in the harbour and the bike made a few laps of the town before the second transition near the town hall. This year, the second transition had been scrapped, so we returned to the harbour for the bike to run transition and the run went over the steep bridge and back each lap. It made the run tougher, so I couldn't see a problem with that at all. I had the constant, dull, nagging soreness in the outside of my right foot despite having removed the orthotics but didn't really think much of it.

Sunday, 11 April was race day. The weather was hot, and it looked like it was going to remain dry. Our race time was 1 p.m. Normally I did a light jog pre-race, but my right foot was a little sore overnight. I didn't want to stir it up for the race.

A large crowd gathered for the race, and my fan club positioned itself near the start, so it was quite noisy. I took my place on the pontoon and chose the shortest line to the first swim buoy. All the fast swimmers elected to do the opposite and took the other end of the pontoon. They wanted to keep away from me. Up to this point I had also been slightly suspicious that the top ten athletes in different colour swim caps were easily targeted for a beating. Other countries could make things difficult for me, with lower-ranked athletes crowding me while their better-ranked athletes swam away from me. I spoke to Les about it, but he told me it was good for television. This particular race confirmed in my mind that I was being targeted by athletes from certain countries while other members of their team could get away from me. (The ITU later scrapped the different colour swim caps, as it became common knowledge that this was happening.) In the middle of the rush to the first buoy, a terrible wave of weakness came over me, and I was forced to back off. The combination of my position and my lack of 'go', badly affected my swim start.

Losing ground in this way fired me up. I was fuming. I left the water that day with slightly cracked goggles from a kick to the head, and very cracked patience with the swim cap rule. I was also furious with myself and dealt with it by fighting back. The swim was two laps and on the completion of the first lap we ran around a marker on the shore. I looked to see how far behind I was and decided that if I really swam hard, I could get back onto the main front pack. The swim specialists I thought were too far ahead now. I just needed to minimise the damage. By the completion of the swim, I had made it to the back of the main pack. As I ran to my bike, I heard we were 1 minute 20 seconds behind the swim specialists, American Barb Linquist, and Australians Loretta Harrop and Nicky Hackett. I didn't particularly think any of them could run, so felt ok where I was.

As I ran to my bike, the uneven sand under my bare feet really accentuated the soreness in my right foot. I was surprised at the sharpness of the pain. Out on the bike, it was a multi-lap course. I put up a bit of a chase, but subconsciously I was beginning to concern myself as to how I was going to run. My foot was really painful to ride on. With me not chasing hard, the dynamics of the bike group changed. No one was prepared to chase the swimmers off the front if I wasn't. As a result, my group lost time and I entered the second transition (bike-to-run) close to three minutes down. With a shoe on my foot, I had a dull but bearable pain. I started the chase and hoped the pain stayed dull. I could run on that. The hill over the steep road bridge and back allowed me to run away from the large group I had been riding with, but it also added pressure to my foot, especially on the downhill sections. On the last descent on the bridge, I felt something in my foot 'go', and the pain suddenly became excruciating. I told myself I didn't have far to go, pushed the pain out of my mind and managed to finish fourth, thirty seconds off second place and ahead of everyone who had been in my bike group, including renowned run specialist Carol Montgomery from Canada. On crossing the line, I had to get my right shoe off. I asked the finish staff for ice and dulled the pain while I waited for Clare to finish. I was annoyed I hadn't won and hobbled back to the hotel to get off my feet.

The Australian team was to remain in Ishigaki for the next few days because the training was a lot better than our next race location, Gamagori. I struggled through the evening with an aching foot, before deciding I needed to see the team management for treatment. I had an early swim and an attempt at a run, but the pain in my foot was really too much to ignore. I didn't really like disclosing details of my injuries to the TA team management. I felt like no one was particularly confidential and I really didn't want everyone to know, especially with a race the following week. Despite my apprehension, I knew I needed treatment. This was above my pain threshold.

I told Olympic Program Manager Emery Holmik I had a sore foot and he told me to go and see Peter Stanton the Team Physio. When I entered the physio room, I walked with one shoe on and one off, as shoes were now becoming a problem for my foot. I was surprised to see Peter, the Australian physio, treating an athlete who had recently started racing for the GBR team. I turned on the TV and watched tacky Japanese television shows while I waited. After about fifteen minutes, it was my turn for treatment.

I climbed onto the treatment bed, now with both shoes off, and started the usual pre-treatment conversation. I filled Peter in on how the pain had progressed over the weekend. Peter had a look at both feet and said my right foot seemed tight, so he would do some 'manipulations' on it. With that, he pulled my foot around to pinpoint exactly where the pain was coming from. I was in real pain at times and squirmed around on the treatment bed. After about twenty minutes, the next athlete came in for treatment, so I was passed on to masseur Brad Hiskins for 'loosening' treatment. When Brad finished massaging my foot and calf, Peter said he wanted to 'free up the area' a little more and pulled around with my foot again, focussing on the sore area for another twenty minutes. I was sent off to ice my foot and elevate it.

I could hardly walk back to my room and putting my foot on the floor was absolutely excruciating. I told Clare I was not walking anywhere for the rest of the day. I was in too much pain.

The next morning, I went for a ride with a few other triathletes. We rode around the island, about three hours easy. My foot was sore when I woke up but seemed ok once in my bike shoe. It was painful cornering, but the stiffness of the bike shoe really protected it from too much movement. I managed to convince myself it was ok, until I got off my bike and walked up to see the physio for more treatment.

Peter asked how it was feeling and given I had been riding, assumed he could continue with pulling my foot around. I asked him if the area that was sore was an area known to develop stress fractures and he replied, 'yes'. He said he didn't think it was a stress fracture though and continued to work on freeing up the area. The pain really became bad when Peter lifted my leg, put my sore foot into a flexed position then leaned on it with his bodyweight while moving the outside of my foot around pushing and pulling on it. He told me this would ease up the tendons in my foot and the pain was expected. I believed him, but I honestly felt ill it hurt so much. I suffered in silence, assuming he knew what he was doing.

With the treatment over, I could hardly walk again. I managed to get to the pool for a swim, but even kicking hurt my foot now. I spent the rest of the day in my room icing my foot and watching tacky Japanese TV.

The Australian team was due to leave Ishigaki for Gamagori on the Thursday. We flew out in the afternoon, giving us all time to do some light training. I could not run, bike or swim now the pain was so bad. I spoke to Emery about pulling out of Gamagori and he told me to see Peter again. Peter took a brief look at my foot and said he was pleased with how it was progressing. I couldn't believe my ears. I thought it was getting worse. I now couldn't wear proper shoes and had resorted to slides which allowed my foot room with no pressure apart from walking.

The flight out of Ishigaki was 11.15 a.m., with a stop in Okinawa before arriving in Nagoya at 5 p.m. Gamagori was a further one-and-a-half-hour bus trip from there, and with a few other athletes flying in at 6 p.m., we had a bit of a wait at the airport. I could no longer walk properly, so I called Dad thinking I should just fly home. This was hopeless. Dad agreed.

I walked to find Emery having a meal in the airport and told him I thought I needed to go home. I couldn't see how I was going to be able to race in three days. Emery again told me to see Peter. Wandering around the airport with an excruciating sore foot, I managed to find Peter and he told me he thought I should test the foot tomorrow with a run rather than fly back to Australia. He convinced me he had a taping method he thought could get rid of the pain. Emery came over to join the conversation and told me he had just been to the international terminal and there were no flights home tonight anyway. I believed both of them and boarded the bus.

Once at the hotel, I had some more treatment on my foot from Peter. It was so painful, but I trusted he knew what he was doing. Dad called me later that evening. He said he had organised a flight home from Nagoya and asked why I hadn't called him back. I was surprised and told him Emery had told me there were none available. Dad then asked me if anyone had scanned my foot or organised one now that we were in a large city. I replied that I had no idea, all the treatment was to 'manipulate and free the area' and that Dad should ask the team management. I knew that Doctor Di, the team doctor, was to arrive the following evening. Dad told me that was too late, I needed treatment now.

The Friday before the race, I told the team masseur Brad Hiskins at breakfast that my foot was still really sore. Asking me what was wrong, he appeared to have forgotten treating me a few days earlier. I couldn't believe that a member of the Australian medical team could forget I was injured. I was really disappointed that no one seemed to think it was a problem or concern that I couldn't walk. We all left the hotel to walk ten minutes to the pool for training. I again suffered in silence and made it to the pool. Swimming, it was painful pushing off the wall. I managed the hour-long swim and got myself back to the hotel. To walk now made me feel a little sick. Having broken bones in the past, I knew a broken bone often made you feel sick.

I went to see Peter and told him again that I thought I needed to go home.

Peter said he could cut a hole in the inner layer of my race flat, so my foot would not have pressure on it when I ran. Optimistically, I got my race flats out for him to destroy. It didn't work. I tried walking in them and hit the roof with pain. Peter then told me he had a great taping method. He taped my foot and told me to go for a jog.

Outside, I lasted all of one step. I was now in so much pain I couldn't even make myself put my foot down. I returned to the treatment room and told Peter I wanted to go home. Peter told me as it was a Friday and there was no point, because I wouldn't be able to get treatment until Monday in Australia. He simply didn't seem to care. I dismissed the comment and hobbled off to find Emery. Emery altered my flight to one that evening. I asked him how I was to get to the airport. He told me he heard the trains were really reliable. I again couldn't believe what I was hearing. Train stations in Japan have steps down to the platforms. I strongly suspected that I had a broken foot and here was the TA High Performance Manager suggesting I, with a broken foot, lug my bike and all my luggage up and down numerous steps to catch trains to Nagoya airport.

I walked off to find Les. I knew he would care. I found him in the hotel foyer and told him my predicament. He contacted the Japanese Triathlon Union (the Japanese national triathlon federation) and they organised me a lift. Peter taped my foot for the flight home, although I removed it as soon as I boarded the plane. My foot was throbbing. As I left, I could hear Les yelling at Emery in the hotel foyer, instructing him to ban Brett Sutton from coaching Australian Team members and telling him Brett was not welcome at ITU races.

The Qantas staff allowed me to sit in the cockpit as we descended into Sydney. It was an amazing experience. Having driven up from Melbourne, Mum and Dad met me at the airport. As the CEO of sportswear company, Fila, Dad was a major sponsor of the National Rugby League team Melbourne Storm. They were playing in Sydney that weekend, and their team hotel was at Brighton-le-Sands, right near the airport. As it was a weekend, Dad thought the team doctor was the best I could find before Monday. I disembarked the plane and Dad took me to see the doctor immediately.

Both the Melbourne Storm Team Doctor and Physio looked at my foot and said I needed a scan. After obtaining a request for a scan from TA's Doctor Di, we were able to make an appointment with Dr Ken Crichton for the same day. We fought the traffic over to the north shore of Sydney to see him. A leading specialist used by the Australian Ballet, he was an absolute expert in foot injuries.

He was excellent, every bit the expert everyone told us he was, and organised an MRI scan for that afternoon. Contrary to what I had been told by TA officials, it was possible to have treatment in Australia on the weekend after all.

Less that twenty-four hours later I was diagnosed with an 'extensive stress fracture of the 5th metatarsal'. I was told to stop all weight bearing activity, including walking on my foot, and to get myself some crutches immediately. It was clear that the sudden pain I felt running down the hill during the Ishigaki World Cup must have been when the bone snapped. My fourth place under the circumstances — outrunning the field with a broken foot — was an outstanding effort.

Monday, I returned to see Dr Crichton, to find out how bad the break was, and unfortunately it was so bad it showed clearly in a normal x-ray. To treat the injury, my right leg was put into a cast from the toe up to the knee. I was told the injury was so serious it could be career ending. When I asked Dr Crichton if I could do anything extra, because I needed it to heal, he told me about a bone growth stimulator he often used on injuries like this. He organised one for me and two weeks later I had the device fitted. I had two holes cut in the sides of my cast for the electrodes. A battery powered device that sat inside my cast generated magnetic pulses between them. To maximise effectiveness, I needed to keep it connected twenty-four hours a day, every day. I only removed it to swim or shower. It was an expensive device at $4,500, but very successful at healing bone breaks.

Wearing my plaster cast, I sat out the Sydney ITU World Cup. Michellie won from Loretta Harrop in a time that was slower than my first three races there. I watched from the VIP tent and turned down Les's offer of presenting the medals to the female placegetters. Les and I had a little argument about true sportsmanship, and I asked him if he would present the medals at an ironman event. We agreed to disagree. I returned home very annoyed with my injury.

Clare raced at Sydney but pulled up with a sore foot. She had a scan the following day and to our amazement had a navicular stress fracture in her right foot. The treatment was the same as mine with plaster from toe to knee. Clare and I were now both on crutches, with our right legs in plaster. We provided much amusement to everyone, so much so we were asked if we were making a joke of my injury.

Well and truly injured, Clare and I were only able to swim. That meant daily doses of verbal abuse from our swim coach. I trained hard in the pool, some weeks clocking up sixty kilometres of work. My cast floated slightly, so I swam with a pool buoy to float both my legs and avoid putting my back out. My foot was constantly wet inside my cast and Clare and I had to share the hairdryer after each swim as we tried to dry our feet. We were useless getting around or doing anything. Fortunately, Mum relocated to Sydney to help us.

On 31 May, the last day of autumn, and just as the weather in Sydney was turning really cold for winter, I had my cast removed. My right leg had a lot of muscle wastage in the calf area and my Achilles was quite sore almost straight away. With only twenty-four hours out of my cast, Dr Crichton ordered me to have another x-ray. I was horrified to see the break was even more pronounced than it had been before I went into the cast six weeks earlier. I was told this was normal and that it looked good. Small bumps were visible along the bone showing that it had repaired itself. Dr Crichton told me I needed to remain on crutches for another four weeks and keep the bone growth stimulator on. I was not to run for at least another month. To be honest, I was too frightened to run on it anyway. I could start riding but stay away from big gears for two weeks. I could roll on a stationary bike, so I did so every second day, then daily as my foot showed it could handle the work. It was really important so stayed away from stressful and pounding work on my foot. It would either heal well now or need pinning. Obviously, I needed to avoid the latter. Clare had her cast removed two weeks after me and remained on crutches too.

As my time in plaster and on crutches lagged on, I missed the rest of the domestic season including the Australian championships in Mooloolaba. I wasn't able to defend my national title. It seemed I was going to miss the ITU season as well. The injury was so serious, we didn't really know if I would ever recover fully. It was the end of June before I could walk without crutches. The ITU season was in full swing and I had missed every event except for the first race in Ishigaki. To say it was a frustrating time was an understatement, and in my frustration, I became increasingly annoyed with the aggressive treatment of my foot in Japan at the hands of the TA medical team.

I kept up with the race results. With me out of the picture, the dynamics of the races had changed. The swim specialists were managing to stay away, like Ishigaki when I was unable to chase hard on the bike. No one was chasing, allowing time gaps to blow out by the time the athletes hit the run. The swimmers off the front meanwhile were a tight knit group, used to working together and becoming more and more confident.

My world ranking was now four, but I didn't bother to look. I didn't want to further depress myself. I couldn't do anything about my predicament, so there was no point worrying. I maintained my fitness as best I could and that was all I could do.

As I was still unable to run, I decided I needed to water run. I wasn't really sure I knew how to do it effectively, so I drove to the AIS in Canberra to work with Australian water exercise expert Chris Nunn. Chris took me through a number of water-running techniques, and it seemed that although my heart rate didn't get as high, there were a lot of biomechanical crossover benefits specific to running. If I worked as hard as I could in the water, I would exercise the right running muscles, and be ready for when I could actually run on land again. I needed to remain positive and it gave me confidence on how to maintain some sort of running fitness. It was the best I could do.

In July I dabbled with sand walking. I wanted to strengthen my foot, with some movement underneath it. I contemplated doing some dune running once I got the all clear and asked Herb Elliot, Australia's greatest miler, about his sand dune training. Herb was helpful and told me he thought sand running was quite an aggressive workout on the foot, so I needed to be careful. He gave me other various training tips and exercises. I particularly liked his one piece of advice that there was no single thing that made a champion, it was everything put together.

By the end of July, I was able to jog lightly, but still apprehensive I could re-break the injury. With the World Championships in September, I decided to do some races to force some sort of fitness into me. Training is all very well, but it is racing that really lifts your fitness. My first major race was the City to Surf in early August. One of the largest fun runs in the world, with around 50,000 competitors (at the time), it consisted of an undulating 14 km run from the Sydney CBD to the famous Bondi Beach foreshore. The course was a good test of my foot. It was either going to hold up or break. All the top distance runners competed each year, and I enjoyed a preferred wave start with them: this enabled us to run fast and ahead of the masses. I ran ok (given my preparation), finishing third in 53 minutes 22 seconds. I felt terribly out of shape, but pushed myself hard. My legs ached for days, but fortunately no problems developed in my foot after the almost one hour of solid pounding.

TA CEO Tim Wilson by this time had contacted Dad to see if I would be fit for the World Championships. He told Dad he had a reserve athlete in mind and needed to know if I would race. It was almost as if he hoped I wouldn't be ready. Dad assured Tim that I was going to be in the World Championships start line.

It was disappointing that TA Olympic Performance Manager Emery Holmik never once called or checked in on my progress. They showed an amazing lack of interest in me or care for my recovery, one of their top athletes.

With the test of the City to Surf event out the way, it was a mad rush to get ready for the World Championships, while also trying to remain sensible with regard to training loads on my still fragile foot. I needed to do a triathlon to get back into things, but the only race that really fitted in was the annual Chicago Triathlon. I flew out on 25 August for the race on Sunday, 29 August. I needed to maximise the time I had to train in Australia.

Chicago attracted a lot of the big names, who were all in the middle of their main race season. I was always going to struggle, especially flying in so close to race day. I needed a tough race though, so I just got stuck into it. It was hot and windy, as usual for Chicago, throughout the race. I swam badly and felt weak at the start when I really needed to push hard. Out on the bike I rode strongly for 20 km and got myself to fifth, before feeling weak again. I managed one of the fastest rides of the day, despite this and made up a lot of the lost time from the poor swim. The entire 10 km run along the Chicago foreshore, I felt really race rusty but managed to get myself from fifth place to fourth by the finish. Due mainly to the fact I didn't win, I was annoyed. But I was pleased that my foot held up to a full triathlon, my first since April.

Following the Chicago race, I headed to the TA pre-World Championships team base in Hull, just across the river from Canadian capital, Ottawa. The setup was really quite good, I was impressed. I had my own room, with full cooking, washing and drying facilities. As soon as we arrived, a few of us headed to the nearby lake and did an open water swim to get rid of the travel stiffness.

I had ten days in camp and did as much training as I could without flattening myself with tiredness. There was no real point in freshening up because I had only been running a month. I did most of my run training with the guys at camp, so I was pushed (often dragged) into some sort of run fitness. I could feel myself improving, but the World Championships were fast approaching. Mum and Dad arrived a week into camp and I did a few run sessions under Dad's watchful eye. I distinctly remember doing a track session where I finally ran some fast 400-m repeats, because we both knew that I needed to find my run form.

On Wednesday, 8 September, the Australian triathlon team departed Hull for Montreal. I really felt I had run out of time to prepare adequately and had to hope that the fitness I had when I left camp was enough. World Champs were only three days away, and I expected myself to perform. I wasn't prepared to leave without a medal, regardless of my year and my terribly interrupted preparation.

With the Sydney Olympic Games only a year away, there was a lot of media interest from Australia. The Australian triathlon team was strong and dominating the world circuit. It was expected that the Australian women's triathlon team was going to deliver the first gold medal of the Sydney Olympic Games because the first event of the whole Games, was the Women's Triathlon. Ron Reed of the Melbourne *Herald Sun* newspaper was in Montreal to interview some of us. He told me he wanted a photo of the first three Australian finishers for the story he was putting together for the weekend feature. So, if I wanted to be in the picture I needed to, 'Do this'. He put it to me as if being in the top three Australians was going to be a tough ask after my year out.

As was my set routine, I prepared myself on the course and became familiar with corners, gradients, wind directions: everything and anything I knew could impact my race. The event site was around the Montreal Formula One track, with the swim in the 1976 Montreal Olympic rowing site. To be honest, I was disappointed with the course. It was flat with wide corners, so there was little opportunity to really break packs up on the bike. The run was also flat, so it wasn't really a course where someone with strong bike and run skills could tear up the field. It was not the type typically used for a major championship, as it didn't require a lot of skill to race. The weather was temperamental leading in with warm and cold days, so race day weather was hard to predict. I was never really going to worry about the weather though, because it was something I couldn't control. I would race to whatever conditions were presented on race day.

On the Saturday evening before race day, I met Mum and Dad for dinner. Mum appeared without Dad and she told me he had been called off to a meeting. Dad had recently signed the TA team to a FILA deal, and TA CEO Tim Wilson was constantly screwing up the deal with the wrong signage, incorrect press releases, and not having athletes in the FILA sponsored clothing for official TA functions. He always seemed to mess things up to the detriment of the sport. It became quite obvious to us as to why TA never secured long term sponsorship deals with large companies. Anyway, to have Dad called off to a meeting the night before the World Championships, as Mum told me, was very believable. He did seem to take a long time, so I said to Mum I wanted to eat dinner as I needed to rest up for the race tomorrow. Just as I said that, Dad walked into the room with Jane. I couldn't believe it. Jane decided that, as she had been at every world championship I won, she was obviously my good luck charm, so she flew over from Australia. It was one of the nicest and most thoughtful things anyone has done for me. Jane was also correct: she was my good luck charm.

World Championship race day finally arrived. So far, from five starts, my World Championship track record was good with wins (two) when illness, or mechanical issues didn't get in my way. For as long as I had a world ranking, I was number one, before dropping to four this year with only one race, due to a foot injury sustained during the first race of the ITU season. I had a lot to be proud of, and I was not going to let anyone beat me without a fight. Obviously, I wanted to win, or to medal at the very least, but to be honest, with less than four weeks training, and not enough quality training I had no idea of my form. I was really just resigned to the fact that what I did on race day was totally up to me and what I wanted out there. Whatever happened, it was going to hurt because I was going to fight to the line.

The weather turned out to be almost perfect for racing. It was sunny, not too hot and the wind was light. Race start was at 1.30 p.m. I liked the idea of an afternoon race, as I thought it allowed those mentally weaker to over think things and mess their race up. I also had time to prepare myself with a jog and light ride. Prior to race start, all the athletes had to have their race suits, bikes and transitions checked off by officials. It was time consuming and a lengthy process which annoyed me pre-race, but at least we didn't have to rush.

Fifteen minutes before race start, we gathered near the swim pontoon. The course was one large rectangular loop, well-marked and great for the spectators to view as we were simply swimming up and back on a rowing venue. Having dropped in my world ranking, I had the indignity of being introduced as the fourth Australian behind Michellie, Loretta Harrop and Jackie Gallagher, which I of course loathed. I at least could choose which swimmers I wanted to be near on the start pontoon. It was actually beneficial to not be first on the pontoon for once, because race start rules stated that once you selected your position, you could not move. For the first time, I could see my competitors when I chose my spot on the pontoon, a surprising benefit from being ranked lower than I had ever been before.

The race was soon underway, and I swam well to the first buoy. Loretta and another Australian Nicole Hackett were off the front, with American swim specialist Barb Lindquist just in front of them. They were obviously going to try to build a lead in the swim, build on the bike and hold on for the run as none of them were particularly good runners. We all knew this was the plan, I was also aware that because the course was flat and did not require bike and run skill, the plan might work. I was also not fit, so the renowned swim specialists' chances where pretty good that day.

Knowing all this I needed a good swim, and it looked like I was having one until about 500 m. Suddenly I felt awfully weak. I managed to back off a little and try to hang on. Understandably, I lost ground but still managed to exit the water with the main swim pack of about twelve. The swim specialists were just over a minute ahead, but a good solid chase would have destroyed this lead on a normal day for me. Today I couldn't do the bulk of the chasing on the bike, as I generally did, because I simply wasn't fit, and I didn't know how I would go on the run. As a result, we as a group didn't really make an impact on the swim specialists off the front, so it came down to the run.

Off the bike I felt ok, not great, but it was manageable. Everyone seemed to be running faster than normal to me, but I assumed it was just a sign I was not race fit. I decided regardless of whether I ran fast or slow it was still going to hurt, so I might as well run as fast as I could. Jackie Gallagher ran the best off the bike and took off leading us all, in pursuit of the swimmers. Michellie and another Australian Jo King (who won the 1998 World Champion in Lausanne where I DNF'd) both ran past me together. Whether they tried to intimidate me by running past together or whether it was a fluke, it did annoy me. I wasn't going to be the fifth Australian today. I hung on, hoping I could last, yo-yoing off the back and clawing my way back, going through strong and weak patches of energy. I just kept myself focussed. 'You need a medal today, Emma,' was all I told myself. While I tailed Michellie and Jo, we were all making our way through the field until only Loretta and Jackie were ahead of us. Sitting on the back I could see the entire field: Loretta, Jackie, Jo and Michellie and me. Five Australians in first, second, third, fourth and fifth. To be honest, I felt awful. Unfit, slow and lethargic. With 2 km to go, Jo put in a few surges. Each effort didn't really amount to much, so I assumed she was not overly confident to take on Michellie and me. Michellie on the other hand, I knew would wait for a sprint. I had done my homework on my competitors and knew them well. Over the years, Michellie had won all her sprint finishes, but I noticed that no one had ever tested Michellie out on a long sprint to the line, they had only attempted to outsprint her with about 100 m to go. I didn't want to enter a situation where she felt confident, so I always planned that any sprint finish with Michellie, I would go from almost 1 km out from the finish line. She would have to really hurt to beat me.

The finish was dead straight, and at the end of an 800 m stretch. I measured it a few days earlier in preparation for the scenario in which I now found myself. When Jo, Michellie and I made our way onto this last 800 m, I decided to make a move. I was confident Jo would not have a change of pace. She was coached by Brett Sutton and he was never good at developing speed in an athlete because there was too much volume in his training. Michellie on the other hand was going to be tougher to crack.

I took off. As predicted, Jo dropped off immediately while Michellie reacted. I was confident in my run-racing pedigree and went harder still. The finish line was fast approaching. I never allowed myself to look back over my shoulder at my competitors. I believed it showed fear and I liked to create the idea that I feared no one. With about 200 m to go, I could see Michellie slightly to my side and kicked again. The crowd was really noisy, and it seemed to add to the desperation of both of us as we surged for the finish.

Dipping at the line, I beat Michellie by 0.04 seconds to grab third and the bronze medal. It was the only time in my life I was proud of a race result that was anything but a win.

The response to my result that day was quite overwhelming. Mum and Jane were near the finish, and both were crying. I told Jane I only got a medal because she was there. Dad was a few minutes away as he had been out on the course watching. I had apparently been written off many times during the race but kept managing to stay in the hunt for a medal. Jackie Gallagher was nice enough to say my performance was probably the most impressive of the day, because I looked beaten so many times. TA's management also congratulated me. Tim Wilson told me my race was incredible, Emery Holmik for the first time congratulated me for a race result and told me he didn't know how I did it, and team Masseur Brad Hiskings said it was the gutsiest triathlon performance he had seen.

It was a great day for the Australian team: the entire TA camp was on a high, with the women finishing first (Loretta Harrop), second (Jackie Gallagher), third (me), fourth (Michellie Jones), fifth (Jo King) and, less celebrated sixth team member, Nicole Hackett, losing a lot of ground in the run to finish 23rd. No other country in the history of the sport to the present day has ever been able to reproduce the dominance we showed as a country that day. It was fantastic to be a part of such a dominant performance.

Mum, Dad, Jane and I went out for dinner that night, and for the first time in a long time, I felt good about a race result.

I had two days to recover and train lightly before I flew out to London, UK for the London Triathlon. I spent the week in the city of Bath, a two-hour drive West of London and used the training facilities at the Bath University, which were pretty well set up for triathlon. I caught up with Grandad Carney for dinner one evening, which was nice to do, although it was sad Grandma was not there also. I had never had dinner with Grandad without Grandma before.

Being Australian and racing in England, I thought it was especially important I beat anyone racing for GBR, despite all my English relatives watching. I exited the water with all the main English athletes, put in a massive turn on the bike, dropped them all and then worked hard to remain off the front. I built a substantial lead heading into transition two for the start of the run, eventually winning by two minutes. With the race out of the way, I caught up with some of my relatives who had come to watch.

To close out the 1999 season, I still had the Duathlon World Championships later in the year and also the Noosa Triathlon. Duathlon worlds consisted of a 10 km run, 40 km bike and 5 km run. I never contested the Duathlon World Championships before and wanted to for years. I was usually pretty hard to beat in a duathlon, as the fastest run/biker in triathlon. But this year, with my lack of form, I knew I could possibly be beaten. My main rival was Jackie Gallagher, who was running better than me currently. She won the silver medal in Montreal while I won the bronze. Jackie loved to beat me, and I loved to beat her, so one thing for sure, we were both going to try to rip each other's legs off.

The Duathlon Worlds this year was in Huntersville, North Carolina. At the ITU pre-race press conference on Thursday, 14 October, most of the Australian athletes turned up not wearing their team gear. It was the same at Montreal. TA and its athletes were not adhering to the FILA sponsorship deal. It was like the old days when Dad used to come down to the track and yell at athletes for not wearing their NIKE gear. Dad walked out of the press conference and emailed TA CEO Tim Wilson: he was pulling the FILA sponsorship for the continued breaches. Dad was furious.

'I try and support those buffoons, but it is impossible,' he told me.

I told Dad they probably didn't want a company where he was CEO as one of the main sponsors. He was wasting his time anyway. FILA had also signed Melbourne Storm, and the team had just won the NRL grand final.

'Just stick with the Storm,' I told Dad, 'Triathlon is far too complicated.'

The World Duathlon Champs were on Sunday, 17 October. Race start was at

12.30 p.m., so it enabled a relaxed wake up time and warm up. There was much apprehension regarding the weather. Hurricane 'Irene' was moving up the coast from Florida and we were told by the weather bureau that this was going to cause a rain depression in the Carolinas on race day. Fortunately, it seemed the weather forecast was wrong, and the rain depression moved over the ocean, leaving us with showers and dark skies to contend with. The weather didn't bother me, race day is race day as far as I was concerned.

The Duathlon Worlds were not as big on the calendar as the Triathlon Worlds, but the field was a decent size. Jackie and I just hammered the first 10 km. There were a few athletes with us, but no one of any concern. Jackie entered transition one (run to bike) with a ten-second buffer over me. I wasn't the least bit fazed because we had 40 km on the bike and there was no way I couldn't bridge ten seconds. Jackie and I were joined by a GBR athlete on the bike, so we had a tight knit group of three off the front. We built a three-minute lead over the field heading into the second transition and 5 km run. Jackie and I ran shoulder to shoulder for most of the last run, but my lack of run fitness cost me time over the last few kilometres. Jackie won, thirty seconds ahead of me. Given my year of injury, a silver world championship medal wasn't too bad. Nevertheless, as was always the case when Jackie and I raced each other, one of us left the race site decidedly pissed off. Today it was me.

I flew back to Australia the next day. Once in the Qantas club, I was able to catch up with the Australian newspapers. There was an interesting article written by Louise Evans of the *Sydney Morning Herald* reporting that TA was going to narrow its Olympic Athlete Program (OAP), as selection for the Sydney Olympic Games was fast approaching. It was reported that the women left in the program would be me, Jackie Gallagher, Michellie Jones, Loretta Harrop and Joanne King. Female athletes dropped from the funding would be Rina Hill and Nicole Hackett. I am not sure how accurate this article was, because when selection came around, everyone seemed to be in the mix.

I returned to full training but suffered through the excessive swim training on my own. Clare went into hospital for a hip arthroscope. She had been struggling with leg pain and hamstring problems and TA team doctor Dr Di suggested the hip needed a 'clean out'. After coming out of hospital, Clare was back on crutches and unable to do much again. Poor Clare, at least I could help her this time.

Noosa Triathlon was on Sunday, 7 November, so I had a few weeks to prepare. My main concern was the lethargy I was feeling again and trying to get rid of it.

While I put it down to the overseas trip for the Duathlon World Championships, I knew it was the same overwhelming tiredness I felt last year whenever I required a bit of extra effort from my body. It wasn't normal, and it completely fatigued me. I wasn't about to miss Noosa though. It was my favourite event. This year, Garth Prowd negotiated with the ITU to hold the elite race as a separate ITU World series event. The traditional course was altered to a looped course along Noosa Sound, so it was more spectator friendly than the traditional out and back bike and run courses. Garth asked me to pre-record a segment for a kids' television show in Brisbane on the way up and attend the Kids Triathlon on the Saturday. A Channel 7 television crew also followed me for two days doing some pre-filming for a show about the lead up to the Sydney Olympic Games. It meant that I had a lot of distractions leading into the race and not much downtime. It was becoming a problem. I had commitments I wanted to uphold, especially in Australian races, and Noosa was such an important Australian race. I generally always prepared for the Noosa Triathlon with a big schedule of commitments.

When it came to the event itself, I raced poorly from the gun. I was tired. At the time, I just thought I had done too much pre-race or maybe my lack of consistent training through the year due to the broken foot had finally caught up with me. Whatever it was, I struggled, and finished a disappointing second.

Through December, I had more media and sponsor commitments with adidas Australia and adidas International. Camera crews filmed me training for most of the month, working on projects, stories and advertising material leading into the Sydney Olympic Games. One shoot involved adidas athletes from around the world, performing in a Garden of Eden type scene. I was to be at the front of the shot on my bike and I needed to look like I was working hard. I suggested to the producer I just set up an indoor trainer and they could shoot what they liked. They agreed and I managed to get a really good workout done in the studio. Everyone seemed surprised how long I trained on a bike for. The rest of the marketing campaign involved a trip overseas, but that was in the new year.

I did one more major event on 19 December in NSW, the Australian Long Distance Triathlon Championships. I won easily and added another national title to my record.

I took a small break following the race, because the upcoming domestic season was important, very important. After two years performing well below my best, I needed to get back to my world dominating form. Olympic selection was the focus. As it turned out, my body was not the main problem in the year 2000.

Never, in my wildest dreams, would I have guessed quite how screwed up the Olympic Selection process would become.

11. When No One Won

As the Year 2000 approached, experts warned the world that a class of computer bugs related to the formatting and storage of calendar data for dates beginning in the year 2000 (called the Y2K bug) would halt the world in its tracks. As the world — city by city — gradually entered the new millennium, and nothing and no one dropped off the face of the earth, it seemed we were all going to be ok.

It seemed the year 2000 was going to be just another year.

It turned out the year 2000 was not just another year for me. I was hit by something worse than a computer glitch. In the year 2000 I lost my reason, my purpose, my life-long dream and as I saw it, I lost my identity.

Until this point, I knew that I would go through life and some people would not like me, would not want me to be successful, maybe even wish I was dead. Whatever — the feeling was probably mutual. In my own naïve little world, I always thought if you performed in sport, things worked out. In my world, what I achieved in sport also defined who I was and what I was. Things were simple: you won or lost, your day was good or bad, your sponsors stayed or left.

With triathlon's debut in the 2000 Sydney Olympic Games, the sport had to work out how to select Olympic teams. The Australian triathlon team was the strongest national team in the world and TA was in the box seat to collect the first Olympic gold medal of the Games. The women's triathlon was the opening event and therefore the first chance to win a medal for Australia. Given the dominance of Australian women in ITU triathlon throughout the 1990s, everyone was confident that the women's triathlon team would set up the home ground Olympic Games with an opening event win.

Like all national sporting federations, TA appointed a panel, named the Triathlon Australia Elite Selection Committee (TAESC), to choose the members of the Australian Olympic triathlon team. The TAESC had one job: select three male and three female triathletes, according to the TA selection policy, and nominate the athletes to the Australian Olympic Committee (AOC) for inclusion in the Australian Olympic Team.

The original TAESC line up included TA Olympic Program Manager Emery Holmik as the Committee Chair, Tennis Coach and APTA founder Marc Dragan, retired national level triathlete and APTA Athlete Representative board member Maureen Cummings, and retired triathlete and swim specialist Nick Croft. Triathlon ACT President Bill Baker later took on the role of TAESC Chair, in place of Emery Holmik. This group was odd at best, and in reality, failed dismally in their role.

As athletes, we were provided with the apparently transparent selection policy, and were required to sign the Athlete Acknowledgement Form, if we wanted to race and be considered for selection. I diligently signed my form on 28 February 2000. Presumably, all Australian triathletes in the mix for Olympic selection did likewise around a similar date. The selection appeared clear. We all knew we had two selection races: the Sydney World Cup (Sunday, 16 April) on the Olympic Course, and the Perth World Championships (Sunday, 30 April) a few weeks later. Win either of these events, and you gain automatic selection. This was the best scenario. Australians were expected to win these events. The athlete who didn't win, but performed the best over the two races, would be the third member of the team. If no one won a race, it was all about determining the top three Australian athletes from their performances in the two races. The selection races were the only way of getting into the Olympic Games.

Quite straight forward.

Very important.

Absolutely necessary to get right.

Despite pressure to do so at the time, I have never spoken publicly about the Sydney 2000 Olympic Triathlon Team selection. Below is my story.

My first scheduled race for the year 2000 was the Oceania Championships in Gisborne, New Zealand. My flight out of Melbourne was scheduled early on 1 January and as no one was sure if the Y2K millennium bug would mess up flights, given the date, we were advised to get to the airport early.

We had two flights, the first from Melbourne to Auckland, then Auckland to Gisborne. The connecting flight from Auckland to Gisborne was not fun at all. Mum dubbed the plane, 'the pencil'. It was long and narrow and to find your seat you had to bend over and creep down the aisle. There was a total of about eighteen seats all up and once it got going it was really noisy. It didn't do turbulence well, so I was really very relieved to arrive safely and stand on firm ground.

We arrived in Gisborne about 6 p.m. local time. It was a nice place, with an atmosphere of a small coastal town. There was evidence of a pretty big New Year's Eve party from the night before. Gisborne is the most easterly city in the world, and it was the first to see the sunrise of the new millennium.

I checked into my hotel with a day to check out the course. I felt flat but thought maybe I was tired from the travel and just ignored the feeling. I had a race to prepare for and knew I would always pull something together.

Race day was Monday, 3 January. It was a late start, at 5 p.m., so at least there was no early wake up. I had breakfast and an easy sixty-minute ride to make some final checks of my bike before a light jog.

The race was a beach start with a good long wade out. A run into the swim would suit me normally. But I felt cooked. I felt the training with my swim coach flattened me with too much volume and no quality speed work and it was obvious that too much swimming was more than just damaging my swim. Lacking speed, I exited the water just under a minute down on the lead pack of six. What started out as an ordinary day got worse. The bike leg was dead flat, out and back four times. There was a roaring headwind on the way out and a semi cross wind on the way back. Normally I would have relished the tough conditions, but today I didn't have my usual power to jump packs forward through the field. My chasing efforts were also all in vain. The lead swim pack gained a draft advantage from official motorbikes too close to the front. Today in World Triathlon racing, motorbike officials and camera crews are not allowed to sit in front of athletes to stop the possibility of bike packs gaining the motorbike slip stream advantage. Also, the men's race started only thirty minutes after the elite women's race, so both the men and the women were on the bike course at the same time. The lead pack managed to somehow get onto the draft of the men passing and no officials stepped in to stop it. As a result, I lost a further minute and started the run two minutes down.

Out on the run, I was pleased with how I ran for the first time in a while and managed to cross the line in second by the race finish. To be completely honest though, I was disappointed because I didn't win. At the same time, I didn't think it really was a fair indication of how I was going. There were too many outside factors that affected the eventual outcome. There wasn't much I could do but just accept a defeat.

The day after the race, I returned to Australia and was greeted with a swim session that would break anyone. My swim coach asked to speak to me and told me he needed to take control of my bike and run programming. I told him that hell would freeze over before that happened. I asked if we could do some speed work in the water and he told me to find another swim coach. I asked why he hadn't let me freshen up for the race in Gisborne and he told me he didn't think I should have raced. I told him he was my swim coach, not my manager, and he absolutely had no say in my racing career. The arguments and yelling were doing my head.

We did agree on one thing though: I needed to find a new swim coach. Simply being flogged unnecessarily was no longer something I was going to put up with. I had been working with him for a year now and my swimming was worse than ever. There was no technique work, no speed work just hard excessive volume in the pool. The excessive workload provided few gains. It just took energy away from my bike and run and it was my strong bike and run that always made me unbeatable. I felt I had lost the focus of our original plan back in 1992 when Dad and I first took on the sport of triathlon.

Dad and I made a time to speak to another swim coach at the Sutherland Leisure Centre, just near to where I was living. This coach was also tough and worked with a top squad of national swimmers. He didn't offer much advice other than to train hard. I was a little worried his squad was too high a standard for me, given the quality of every swimmer. When he agreed to take me on though, I decided it was an opportunity to get back to improving my swim technique.

Changing swim coaches did nothing for me though. I just moved to another coach who also refused to provide me with anything other than volume delivered with abuse. The last thing I needed was volume. I needed speed work, technique work and some sharp, specific tough swim sets under pressure. Triathlon swimming is not swimming, triathlon biking is not biking, and triathlon running is not running. Coaching requires balance, tailored to each triathlete. A coach needs to understand the underlying strengths that triathletes brings into their discipline if they are to coach successfully. Triathlon is vastly misunderstood by many coaches who specialise in one discipline. This lack of understanding and over prescribing of volume in my program was killing me. Literally.

In this time, I should have just returned to Melbourne. I should have returned to what I knew and removed the stress of trying to work with coaches who really didn't understand me or the sport. Bike and run training in Sydney did not compare to Melbourne either, so I didn't respond as well. The less than ideal training and my broken foot interrupted my 1999 season, but I finished fourth in the opening ITU event and third in the World Championships at the end of the season. My foot was better, I knew I was world class, and the world knew I was. I should have seen that I needed to get out of a training situation that was not helping me to reach my peak form.

Late January I headed to Melbourne to shoot a television commercial for Holden. It was pretty cheesy. I had to ride a gold bike alongside a gold car. It was along one of the main streets in Melbourne's CBD, so it was a little embarrassing too. I just hid behind my Oakley sunglasses and kept my helmet on, but unfortunately it was pretty obvious to Melbourne commuters that it was me, given the number of 'shout outs' I received while shooting.

While in Melbourne, I raced in Geelong and finished second. When I really wanted to bike and run fast, I again felt tired. My first two races in this particularly important year were hardly encouraging. The next race was the Australian Sprint Triathlon Championships (750 m swim, 20 km bike, 5 km run) in Wollongong, NSW, on 13 February. With a national title on the line I decided I would just push myself regardless of how I felt. With this mindset, I managed to exit the water with the main bunch of eight athletes. I rode strongly and then built my confidence to clear out on the run. I won easily. I rode back to Sutherland following the race, happy that I had won another national title. Thoughts of my recent second-place result were pushed aside. I was still competitive. I was back winning, so things seemed ok.

Two hours after the sprint championships, I rolled into my driveway and started packing to head overseas for an adidas television commercial shoot. Adidas International was preparing the Sydney Olympic campaign in Spain, so I was required to attend the shoot. Adidas Australia athlete marketing head Jimmy Tansey and I flew first class with Qantas from Melbourne to London. I had never flown first class on a long-haul flight before. I was upgraded on flights out of Auckland, but they were never really long enough, I didn't think, to really get yourself stuck into the benefits. With a long-haul ahead of me I relaxed in my Qantas pyjamas, picked out movies to watch, and enjoyed a flat bed, 34,000 feet above the earth. The bed was so comfortable I was a bit annoyed that I slept most of the way, missing the opportunity to enjoy fully my first-class benefits.

Arriving at Heathrow, London actually feeling ok for the first time in my life after such a long flight, I connected with a flight to Barcelona, Spain, followed by a helicopter to the site of the shoot. The specific location was a large equestrian centre on the Spanish coast. Adidas was shooting two commercials, an equestrian one and a sailing one. They were the only two Olympic sports for which adidas did not produce equipment. We were supposed to look hopeless. I had no idea about horses, which meant that I was perfect for the equestrian shoot.

I arrived at the hotel the night before the shoot, as did all the other adidas athletes flown in from around the world. At dinner I sat with Haile Gebrselassie, the world and Olympic 10 km champion from Ethiopia. With so many adidas sponsored world number one athletes, it was an interesting meal. Despite being from all over the world, we all really behaved very similarly, ate well, went to bed early, and got up extra early to fit a training session in before the shoot started.

Filming started punctually the next morning. It was a complicated shoot list with a large number of athletes involved. Each athlete was provided with an adidas tracksuit, so producers working on the shoot could identify us as the athletes. Each of us always had someone to accompany us. With the television crew and the equestrian staff, it was busy. My role was to walk into the equestrian stadium holding my bike over my shoulder and look confused. I was pleased I didn't have to say anything. I was told I would be notified when they were ready to shoot my particular segment, so I decided to head off for another run. Fortunately, Haile also insisted on a second run, so had done the groundwork to enable me to head off without adidas worrying about me disappearing for too long.

The process of securing about thirty seconds for the commercial took two full days to shoot. I got to know a few of the other athletes as we spent a lot of time drinking coffee at the catering van, all dressed the same in our adidas gear. I was surprised chatting to other athletes that triathlon was seen to be very hard. There was also a high regard for triathletes. Quite different from the attitude to the sport when I first picked it up. I never considered triathlon in this way, I had just seen it as something I could be very good at and worked myself hard to be the best.

As my bike was required for the commercial, I also travelled with my wind trainer and did some riding. It was just the swim training I missed for the two days of the shoot, but the interruption to training was over quickly. Soon I was heading back to Australia, first class with Qantas again, and this time a little more refreshed to enjoy the in-flight perks. I landed in Australia on Saturday, 19 February and headed straight to the pool to get my swimming arms back.

After a week of light training I headed to Devonport, Tasmania for the next race of the National Triathlon Series. Unfortunately, the race organisers altered the course and the bike and run were a lot flatter. This was always going to suit the swim specialists, as the hills used to break up the bike packs quicker. I didn't swim well because my position at the race start became very congested. Again, I felt weak, was forced to slow, and found myself caught up in the tangle of the main swim group. By the time I exited the water I had slipped to the chase pack and played catch up from there on. I slowly reeled the swim specialists in and caught all but two off the front, who gained some advantage from the lead motorcycle. It is pretty much impossible to catch a group of cyclists who are being motor paced. I pulled them back to just over a minute at one point and in normal circumstances I would have been able to run this deficit down. Unfortunately, it wasn't to be, and my run was not strong enough to get me back to the lead. I finished fifth.

Post-race I was disappointed. I shouldn't have raced. I had just come off an overseas trip and should have rested. Dad dissected the times in the race and showed me that the winner was three-and-a-half minutes slower than I was two years ago when I raced on the old, tougher course. No one was going faster. I just had an ordinary performance and I needed to get some rest to allow myself to think clearly again. Dad pointed out that if I wasn't jet lagged and I started the race in a better position on the line, I would have exited the water closer, had a stronger chase and won despite the leaders being motor paced on the bike. I felt a lot better about things, but it was still disappointing.

I was involved in a junior triathlon event in Melbourne the next day, so I flew out of Tasmania early on Sunday morning and spent the day starting triathlon races with Garth Prowd. I felt very tired by the end of the day. On the way back to Tullamarine airport that evening, Dad and I agreed that I needed to back off from all the extra commitments. I had another NAB event that week, sailing on the Harbour in Sydney, and a Landcare photo shoot the next day. So another week was to be interrupted with media and sponsor requirements. We agreed this was to be the last week of commitments.

With the Olympic trials fast approaching I also needed to sort out my training situation. I started to consider returning to Melbourne. After an early start I had another horrendous swim set. My swim coach said that as I hadn't trained last night, I needed to catch up. I was surprised at his attitude. Just because I hadn't swum didn't mean I hadn't trained. I just kept my mouth shut and trained as hard as I could. The next swim session was a time trial that was longer than my race distance. It was obvious I was being forced to do too much swim volume. Swim coaches were doing my head in. Not only was I being flogged in the pool, but they refused to factor in all the other training I was doing outside of their sessions. This swim coach was a dictator not a listener. I missed the technical and constructive training sessions with Alwyn Barratt, from which I benefited greatly at the start of my career in Melbourne. Speed is the name of the game in triathlon swimming and I did not see why I was being forced to stray away from that. With the benefit of hindsight now, it is obvious I should have trusted my gut feeling on things more. I am not sure why I didn't return to Melbourne. I think I just doubted myself.

On Sunday, 12 March, I had the next national series triathlon in Canberra. This time I swam well, exiting the water slightly behind the lead pack. Out on the bike I had terrible blisters on my feet. Adidas had sent some new shoes to race in and I trained in them over the past week, to wear them in. All I had done was give myself massive blisters on both feet. They looked like stage four burns, ripped open and exposing red, raw skin. Seeing how I was limping, Dad hauled me off the course, telling me that if I kept running in that condition, I would give myself an injury.

I was livid with myself.

I was making stupid mistakes with start positions and now equipment choices. Dumb, dumb, dumb mistakes I should not be making this far into my career.

We drove back to Sydney. The car was very quiet. Dad suggested I take it easy for the next fortnight leading into the Australian Triathlon Championships at Mooloolaba on Sunday, 26 March.

I had won many national titles in Mooloolaba and knew the course well. I went into the race with the messiest preparation I ever really had. I won the national sprint title earlier in the season, so there was form, but had made some silly mistakes in races since then. I tried not to dwell on them. After all, I liked racing in Mooloolaba and last time I raced there I won by five minutes.

As was always the case, I stayed at my place in Noosa. Noosa gave me a break from everyone. I really did not have anything to do with TA anymore. They managed to keep Brett Sutton in the coaching loop somehow and I felt he was working hard to undermine my credibility as an athlete. I attended the pre-race press conference on the Friday prior and the pre-race briefing on the Saturday. Between these requirements I swam, rode, and ran over the course so I was well prepared.

Race day came around. The women's race start was just after 10 a.m. The weather was pretty good, warm with a head wind over the bike course as was generally the case in Mooloolaba. The swim this year was one large loop of 1500 m. The one looped course generally favoured the swim specialists because there was no extra wading in and out to the shore as there is with multi-loop swims. I swam well and was at the front of the chase pack, exiting the water about fifty seconds down on the two swim specialists off the front.

Out on the bike, the chase pack once again had a real disadvantage because the two lead riders were getting a massive assistance from the surrounding motor-cycles (a lead official and a bike with a cameraman). There was no rule in place at this stage of triathlon racing, and often the lead motorbike sat in front of the lead-ers taking shots for TV and clearing the road of any hazards. It always amazed me this could go on. I became increasingly annoyed with the race officials: some laps when the motor bike was not in front of the leaders, we were holding them or making up time, but when the bike was back on the course, we lost twenty seconds in a lap. By the end of the bike the two leaders had two minutes on the chase pack. It was absurd.

Still, I could run down a two-minute gap to the swim specialists on a normal day. I was the first out on the run after the bike and chasing down the leaders, when suddenly I felt the awful weak feeling wash over me. Exhausted, I just about stopped moving forward. I forced myself through the run, collapsing across the line. I was dragged into the medical tent and lay on a stretcher hooked up to an IV drip for close to two hours. Nothing was really established as to what was wrong with me, so dehydration was the conclusion. I still finished in the top ten.

I dragged myself to the TA Awards Dinner that evening and picked up the Australian Triathlete of the Year Award. I didn't want to attend, I still felt exhausted. I just wanted to go back to my place at Noosa and sleep. With the Olympic Trials two and four weeks away, I needed to alter my training. A bless-ing in disguise, the Mooloolaba 'disaster' finally forced me to accept this. I was fit, training hard, but racing inconsistently.

I returned to Sydney and fired yet another swim coach. I suggested to Dad that perhaps I needed to either return to Melbourne or organise a solid train-ing partner that would be at every session to work with me. Clare had not been training consistently so it wasn't the same as when we first started and trained together. One of the elite male Australian triathletes, Jason Metters, sent me an email on the Thursday following Mooloolaba saying that my performances didn't make sense. I was better than all my results and he wanted to help me by being a solid training partner for all sessions going into the Olympic trials. I told

Dad we should take him up on the offer. A tough training partner was perfect for me. I was fit, I just needed 'sharpening up' for the Olympic Trials. I had finally started to receive the Olympic Athlete Funding (OAP) from the Australian Sports Commission. I suggested we pay him, so it was worth his while to turn up.

Together Jason and I planned my training sessions. I knew what worked for me historically and he also had some good training ideas. We adopted swimming sessions that were specific to triathlon. I wanted to focus on speed in the pool mixed with some threshold sets. We designed sessions around the hectic nature of the triathlon swim start. For the bike and run I returned to the training that I knew: intervals, threshold and working at pace. Jason was a great training partner on the bike. He was so much stronger being a guy, especially in shorter max efforts. My run always came together with my confidence, so that progressed well. For the first time in a long time I felt a little more confident in my training.

Another major change I made was to remove all early starts. I felt like I needed sleep. I didn't need to be waking at 4.30 a.m. for a 5 a.m. swim. My body needed rest and recovery just as much as it needed work.

Sunday, 16 April was the date of the first Olympic trial. The Sydney ITU World Cup was held on the approved Olympic course. Many countries also nominated this event as a selection race, so there was a lot resting on the results for everyone. Automatic selection to the Australian team required a win. If you didn't win, you needed to finish in the top three Australians over the course. History clearly showed that I was the fastest female athlete over the course ever, but my last two races here had been a DNF (hypothermia) and a DNS (Did Not Start due to my broken foot). Effectively I had never actually been beaten on the course. I was still one of the best in the world though and still national champion and a medallist at the most recent world championships. I also made some very strong improvements in my training and confidence over the last few weeks leading into the race. I felt a lot fitter, less tired, and had a level of optimism I hadn't felt for a while.

To my competitors and observers, I was an unknown factor. Many had written me off due to my recent poor results, which were not a display of my usual dominating performances. Everyone also knew though, that I was mentally tough and if anyone could perform through sheer determination and grit it was me. With Olympic selection on the line, I knew I could find something.

With races this big, the worry of a mechanical failure, flat tyre or some event that affected your race outcome was always a slight concern in the back of your mind. TA had provided a clause in the selection policy they called the 'Disadvantaged Athlete Clause' that you were able to call on if you suffered a disadvantage related to an unplanned race scenario which adversely affected your race outcome. TA informed us leading into the selection races that we were required to report any incidents of this nature post-race to TA medical staff or TA staff. While the clause appeared to provide athletes with protection, as it turned out, TA worked with their lawyers to apply a completely different interpretation of the purpose of the Clause during the selection process.

The Athlete Disadvantage Clause wasn't the only disaster to happen leading up to the Olympic Selection event in Sydney. A day prior to the event, Brad Beven was knocked off his bike, and ended up in hospital, missing the trials. I emailed him to see how he was, and he told me no one from TA had contacted him. I couldn't believe it. I was surprised even Brad was treated with such contempt by TA officials. I thought it was just me.

With all this bubbling in the background, the Australian fans turned up in their thousands to watch us all thrash it out. By the time the race was underway, thick crowds of supporters had gathered on the Opera House steps and along the bike and run course, despite a little light rain. There was a lot of expectation for the day of racing ahead. Triathlon in those days had a high profile.

The race started fine. Unknown to all of us racing to win that day, Australian swim specialist Loretta Harrop dived into the water and pulled out shortly afterwards. My swim was good, more than enough for me on a course with a tough bike and run. The minute gap between myself and the leaders when I exited the water was manageable. Out on the bike I rode well, reeling in the leaders and moving through the field as a normal race scenario played out for me. Just as I completed the second lap, making my way around the roundabout turn near the Sydney Opera House, my rear wheel skipped wide on a surface made slippery with the light rain. I was moving fast with the speed of the descent giving me momentum into the turn. While I managed to stay upright, I smashed my hand into the barricades. To complicate my injury further, someone in the crowd held out a large sign made of stiff plastic which I also clipped with my hand on the way past. The double whack to my hand was painful and I dropped to the back of the bike group. My hand was swelling already. As I climbed back up Macquarie Street to start the next lap, it was increasingly painful holding the handlebars, changing gears and braking. Being my left hand, it affected my ability to use the rear brake, which is the brake most used especially on a course like this. I also struggled to change chain rings, as the big-to-small chain-ring lever is on the left-hand side of handlebars as well. This hampered my ability to attack the climbs and descents. As a result, my bike leg was absolutely screwed. I could no longer chase hard. I had no choice but to do as best I could with minimal gear changes and poor ability to brake effectively and safely.

Without me working properly on the bike, my pack made no impact on the lead pack for the rest of the race. It was a nightmare. I did as much as I could, but there was no way I could ride fast and aggressively when I couldn't change gears, brake or manoeuvre my bike safely. I had to wait for the run.

Out on the run, I wasn't my best. I was ok, but stupidly my hand still hurt. I was telling myself, 'You don't run with your hand, just get moving.' I wasn't sure if I was just being soft again. I just ran as best I could and finished thirteenth.

Michellie Jones won, so gained an automatic selection. She raced well, really the only Australian who did. Nicole Hackett finished sixth, falling through the field the longer the run went on. Joanne King hung on to my group on the bike as I slowed and finished two places in front of me. I was fourth Australian. Loretta Harrop was a DNF in her predetermined plan to dive in and get out, and Jackie Gallagher bombed out to finish third from last.

On crossing the line, I sought Dad out. He sent me to the official TA team doctor, Dr Di Robinson, for treatment on my hand. She checked for broken bones and told me the swelling made it inconclusive. She then dismissed me with an ice pack. I asked for the incident to be recorded because it affected my ability to race, a true Athlete Disadvantage Clause claim. Unknown to me at the time, she either negligently failed to record the fact I required assistance at the post-race medical tent, or the evidence was subsequently lost or destroyed by TA. Dad and I sought out Emery Holmik to inform him of my hand to ensure the incident had been reported to more than one TA official. On returning to our hotel, Dad also emailed Emery Holmik, because he never trusted anyone from TA.

Over the next two weeks, I built on my confidence for the second and last Olympic selection race. I was now training daily with Jason and progressing well. I felt a lot better. Without the excessive swim load I was able to find my run and bike form. To this day, I really don't know why I didn't plan my own coaching away from the aggressive swim coaches earlier.

The second trial was in Perth, Australia on Sunday, 30 April. I liked Perth. After all I had won my second world title there in 1997 in front of one of the largest crowds ever gathered for a triathlon event. The course was slightly different from that I had won on, but was still very familiar. The swim was in the Swan River, we biked up to Kings Park, and ran along the foreshore.

Leading in I felt good, under control and ready to perform. Pre-race there were the usual requirements, ITU and TA press conferences and pre-race briefings at which the course was explained to all competitors. The women's race was first and there was a lot of apprehension from everyone, as again most countries were also using the race outcome as Olympic Selection events.

I swam ok. I was only 35-40 seconds off the main contenders. Swim specialists Barb Lindquist of the US and Nicole Hackett were off the front, as was the case in the Sydney World Cup two weeks earlier. Usually, neither ran well enough over 10 km to hold off the field, especially if the bike leg had some hills. With the hills on the bike course in Perth, it was unlikely they could hold onto their lead over the entire 10 km of the run. I worked hard on the bike and was within striking distance heading into the final leg of the race. Prior to the race I decided I wasn't going to try and play smart with any selection rules, I was just going to race and make sure I beat everyone who beat me in Sydney. Michellie was already automatically selected, so she was not really a concern. The Australians I needed to worry about were Nicole Hackett and Joanne King. Nicole was in the lead going into the run but wasn't too far ahead. I expected she would slow as the run progressed as she always did. Joanne King, the only other Australian to beat me in Sydney, was off the back of the field and a long way out of contention. Loretta Harrop didn't start the race this time and it was common knowledge she had a serious injury as a result of Brett Sutton's aggressive training regime.

I started the run well and increased my pace as I moved through the field. A multi-loop course, I could keep an eye on things ahead and could see I was running down the swim specialists. Nicole Hackett was in the lead, but — as expected — she was slowing down as the distance into the run grew, while I was whittling away at the gap.

As the field approached the start of the last lap an official opened the finish chute and the field started to make their way towards the finish line. I panicked: what the hell?! We hadn't run the full 10 km. I needed the last lap to get the most out of my run leg advantage.

There was nothing I could do, as the entire field followed the instruction of the official. I ran down the finish chute to cross the line in seventh, having completed the supposed 10-km run leg in 26 minutes. It was absurd. Nicole Hackett collapsed on the line and was declared the winner, with Carol Montgomery from

Canada closing in on her, just seconds behind. Carol recorded 25 minutes for her run. Michellie placed third. I was the next Australian.

If the technical error was ignored, Michellie, Nicole and I were obviously the best three performers from Australia over the two selection races. Loretta hadn't even started the second race, and had only swum 100 m in Sydney with no intention to finish, because she had a serious injury. Jackie Gallagher didn't record a finish in Perth and was third from last in Sydney. And finally, Joanne King bombed out in Perth, finishing almost last.

Selection was now in the hands of the TA Elite Selection Committee, and the team was to be announced in the next week. I didn't like the fact that I hadn't gained automatic selection but, due to the technical error affecting the outcome of the Perth race, neither had Nicole Hackett. I didn't realise athletes who were too injured to race were in the selection mix, but then again, I had never faced such an arbitrary selection process in my life.

Selection for the Olympic team is technically first made as a nomination by TA to the Australian Olympic Committee (AOC). The AOC then accepts or rejects those nominated. I was notified of my non-nomination via a call from Dad, who himself had received a call from TA CEO Tim Wilson on 5 May 2000. I couldn't believe what I was hearing when I answered the phone and I half hoped it was a sick prank he was playing on me.

'What a mess', 'what a disaster', 'what a failure I am', were my immediate thoughts.

I couldn't think straight, yet Dad was telling me I needed to appeal. Dad always thought clearly under pressure and he went on the tell me all appeals for non-selection were required within forty-eight hours of notification of non-selection. He was adamant, 'This decision was unfair and unjust and against the selection policy.' He told me I had clearly qualified and selection must have been biased.

I told Dad to do what he thought was best, but I always feared organisational and institutional power. Dad's suggestion of bias reminded me of the words, 'this will affect your Olympic selection,' from disgraced coach Brett Sutton in 1997 when I was leaving the AIS training camp. Maybe they were a warning that the selection process would not be as clear cut as I expected. Maybe it was because I wasn't part of a plan Brett Sutton had concocted. Maybe I was just not wanted.

Dad remained firm.

'The Australian legal system isn't corrupt Emma,' he told me.

At this point Dad was talking about an appeal process within TA, but he was also thinking about the Court of Arbitration of Sport (CAS) if the TA appeal went nowhere. We both naively thought of the CAS as a real court, but it turned out that it was quite separate from the Australian legal system.

Unfortunately, Dad and I were not to know this at the time. We were both of the opinion that we should defend what we believed I had earned: a place on the Australian Olympic team. Dad immediately sent an email entitled, 'Appeal — Nomination for Selection to the 2000 Australian Olympic Team', to the TA CEO. The contents of the email were as follows:

> *I refer to your facsimile dated 5 May 2000.*
>
> *Pursuant to clause 7 of Part 1 of the Selection Agreement and clause 4.1 of Part 4, Annexure C of the Selection Agreement, I give notice of my appeal against my non-nomination to the AOC.*
>
> *I note that the fifth paragraph of your facsimile states "…Please note that the grounds of any appeal must be in writing and forwarded to me within 48 hours of the announcement (time and date noted above)…" In accordance with Clause 7.1(3) of Part 1 of the Selection Agreement. I shall submit the grounds of appeal within 5 working days of this notice of appeal.*
>
> *Emma Carney*

With that, my Olympic appeal was launched.

My sister Jane, a Senior Associate at Freehills (a leading law firm in Melbourne), spoke to Jonathan Forbes, who was a Senior Partner and Head of Sports Law at Freehills (also an OW) and asked him if he would represent me in my appeal. Jonathan agreed and Dad met him and Jane that afternoon to consider and identify a prospective barrister from a shortlist of three senior and very competent QCs. The standout QC was Peter Hayes, and a meeting was organised. Prior to the meeting, and in accordance with the appeal process, Jonathan prepared the appeal document. The process also required that TA CEO Tim Wilson respond to Dad's initial email notifying an appeal would be launched, before this process could start. Tim had already gone to ground. This was only the start of some appalling behavior by individuals within TA and those involved in the entire process.

Dad, Jonathan, and I met Peter Hayes in his chambers the next day. Peter was an interesting character with a dishevelled appearance, portly in stature with piercing eyes behind his small circular glasses. He immediately launched into me asking a series of questions, many of them before I had finished answering the previous one. It was like he was grilling me on whether I believed I really did qualify for the Olympics. I told him that as an athlete you expect to qualify for a team according to a selection policy. You do not expect back door access to an Olympic team. I had prepared for two selection races and was working towards a peak on 16 September 2000. My performance in the selection races had provided me with qualification. At no point did TA indicate you could be selected by not racing selection races. The selection was wrong.

With that reply the QC was satisfied that I believed in my case and was committed to my appeal. Then he stopped, changed his whole demeanour and told me he believed there had been an enormous injustice against me. He had done some background reading so that he could understand the issues and he would be delighted to represent me in my appeal.

That was my legal team assembled.

With a very strong legal team behind me, I was told to continue to train and prepare myself for the Olympics, because from all angles my non-selection was not consistent with the selection policy. Two days after sending TA my notice of appeal email, the TA CEO called my phone to notify me it had been received. I couldn't bring myself to answer it and handed my phone to Dad. Dad, always my protector and seeing how broken I was, asked for a receipt in writing via email and told Tim to never call me again. He never did. My lawyers followed up with an email to TA confirming that I was not a point of contact anymore. Only my lawyers and Dad could be contacted.

My legal team was concerned with the damage an Olympic Appeal can do for an athlete's reputation. I told them I would not speak to the media under any circumstances. I never have, until now.

What happened over the course of the months leading into the Sydney 2000 Olympic Games and the first Olympic Women's Triathlon just about destroyed me. I have never been able to really process this time in my life, and still today I do not allow my mind to revisit this time. I believe my involvement in coaching and athlete wellbeing is strong today because I do not ever want athletes to have to deal with the heartbreaking process I had to deal with alone.

Les McDonald, the ITU President, sent me a fax saying:

Emma don't give up on your Olympic dream just yet. There is many a slip twist cup and lip. Be patient, be strong, be happy. Lots of things can happen between now and the 16th, Les.

It was nice to receive, but the ITU could not help me now. Olympic selection was up to the national federations, and I was beginning to think that mine had an agenda that did not include me.

12. Lord of the Files

When I was in about Year 9 at Wesley College, we read *Lord of the Flies* by William Golding, for English class. I thought it was a really good story until I realised what was actually unfolding. It was all about the disastrous attempts of a group of private school boys at governing themselves while deserted on a tropical island. It was the first time I considered man's inherent savagery.

Throughout my Olympic Appeal ordeal, I felt like I was a character in that story. I felt like TA deteriorated into this same state in its disastrous attempts to govern and manipulate people and outcomes within its own sport. It was such a toxic time when I felt that I was just surviving and trying to keep myself together.

I was not able to process it at the time. The specific details of my Olympic Appeal against non-selection were only really known to my Dad and my legal team. Bond University Historian and Assistant Professor Jane Hunt has studied the records of the Appeal and provides below a step-by-step account of the process my Sydney 2000 Olympic Selection Appeal followed. I have included both of their accounts here as they explain my non-selection in two different ways: Dr Hunt as an academic and my Dad as someone who was there and part of many undocumented conversations.

I asked Dr Hunt to contribute to my autobiography because I knew she would provide a factually correct account of the Olympic Appeal. The piece is, in my view, the only independent record of the Olympic Appeal. As a professional historian and author of the history of triathlon in Australia, there is no one more qualified than Dr Jane Hunt to write a record of events and outcomes of my Sydney 2000 Olympic Appeal.

'A Dream Thwarted: Emma Carney's Non-Selection
to the Sydney 2000 Olympic Triathlon Team' — *Dr Jane E. Hunt*

Athletes and triathlon administrators first began to think about Olympic Selection policies in 1996 when the International Triathlon Union (ITU) became concerned about peak athletes defecting to the International Triathlon Grand Prix. The ITU declared that all athletes would accumulate points through participation in ITU World Cups from the beginning of 1997. A problematic idea it was later abandoned. Instead collective national team performances at ITU events over the 1999 season determined whether one, two, or three athletes would represent any given country at the Olympics. National federations appropriately shouldered the responsibility for determining the composition of their respective Olympic teams.

TA began developing Australia's Olympic selection policy in September 1998, sending an early version to all Olympic Athlete Program (OAP) athletes and coaches for comment. The draft identified the 2000 Sydney ITU World Cup and 2000 Perth ITU Triathlon World Championships, both scheduled for April, as selection races. Emma Carney's copy of the draft only reached her days before the reply was due. She faxed Olympic Program Manager Emery Holmik requesting an extension and saying that at a glance the, 'elements of the draft selection policy [were] confusing, vague and ambiguous.'

Struggling with mysterious waves of fatigue, Emma's 1998 season did not reflect her previous international dominance in ITU triathlon. She understandably hoped that the TA Olympic Selection Policy would take performance history into consideration. Holmik did not seem to share her view telling her that, 'the Olympics were all about performing on a particular day.' Holmik pointed out that the selection policy did offer an exception to this principle so that, 'no athlete is disadvantaged by factors outside their control.' Appendix A of the draft provided for the possibility that an 'extraordinary incident' during the selection races might, 'have a significant effect on the overall result.' This caveat presented the first clue that the selection policy might be characterised by ambiguity and unresolved inconsistencies.

Originally Holmik hoped to finalise the selection policies for 1999 and 2000 World Championships, and Olympic Triathlons by the end of 1998, but he distributed another version of the Olympic policy to interested parties for comment in February 1999. David Carney remained unimpressed. Possibly he was thinking about the illnesses and incidents that he believed prevented Emma from securing world titles in 1995, 1996 and 1998 when he proposed that the policy should include specific provision for 'injury, illness, mechanical problems or interference,' rather than Holmik's general 'extraordinary incident'. In November 1999, TA tabled a summary of the Olympic selection policy at its Annual General Meeting, confirming that a copy had been forwarded to all OAP athletes 'for planning purposes'. The summary affirmed the centrality of the two selection races to the final policy and introduced an automatic nomination provision for any Australians who won either event. Athletes who finished among the top three Australians across the two races would be considered for the remaining places on the team. The summary did not include the details of what became known as the Disadvantaged Athlete Clause.

Annexure C of the final Selection Agreement signed by TA and the AOC on 23 December 1999 outlined the Olympic Nomination Criteria. Based on the deliberations of the Elite Selection Committee (TAESC), TA would nominate three women and three men to the AOC. The AOC would then formally select those athletes, if approved, for the Australian Olympic team. Clause 2.2.11 of Annexure C made allowance for athletes who were 'disadvantaged due to a pre-existing injury or illness or an incident [that] occurs during the race.' TAESC would instead consider athlete performances at ITU World Cup races staged since the start of 1999, as well as the 1999 and previous Triathlon World Championships.

The final Selection Agreement appeared to embody hopes of fairness and reflected aspects of the feedback provided by the Carneys during the drafting process. Yet its provisions rested on numerous assumptions and unclear or inconsistent logic. As the Australian triathlon community was about to discover, it provided opportunity for many interpretations and allowed the Selection Committee considerable discretion in determining how the document should be read. In particular, the precise legalities of the Disadvantaged Athlete Clause were unclear to athletes and TA personnel. Even the members of the TAESC applied the clause in inconsistent and contradictory ways. Finalised and distributed in the closing days of 1999, less than five months before the Sydney World Cup, the Selection Agreement also contradicted its own clear and objective requirement in Clause 4.3 of Annexure 1 that the national federation, 'develop the Criteria no later than 12 months prior' to the 'first nomination event'.

The belated finalisation of the Agreement meant that athletes did not know prior to the 1999 ITU season that their World Cup performances might be considered as part of the selection process if the Disadvantaged Athlete Clause came into effect. It failed also to provide a detailed mechanism for comparison of the selection race performances of athletes who finished the Olympic Trials with the past performances of athletes who did not. The environmental circumstances surrounding any triathlon are inevitably unique, meaning that comparison on equal terms can only be made of athletes competing on the same course under the same conditions. Even if the Selection Committee ignored the Olympic Trials and compared athlete performances at the same races across the 1999 ITU season, the late release of the finalised selection policy meant that the athletes in question had no formal advice that their 1999 races might be used to determine their Olympic selection. Nor did they have the opportunity to trigger the relevant Disadvantaged Athlete Clause at those past events in order to flag that they were not competing on equal terms with other athletes should the TAESC refer back to that particular event when considering nominations for the Olympic team. No one — not Emma, not TA's support team, not the TAESC — had reason to consider the possibility that Emma's fractured foot at Ishigaki in 1999 might have prevented her from competing on equal terms with fellow Australian Olympic hopefuls. No one had reason to flag the implications that the injury-induced interruption to Emma's 1999 ITU season had for her Olympic selection chances. Gaps existed in the provisions of the Olympic nomination policy, with the potential to impede consideration of team selections on equal terms. Those gaps enhanced Selection Committee discretion and the potential for selection decisions to be swayed by personal or institutional bias.

Unaware of the policy's lack of clarity, the very full ranks of world class female and male Australian triathletes prepared to deliver stand-out performances at Sydney and Perth. To achieve selection the women in particular needed to race at their best: world champions needed to beat world champions in order to make it into the top three, while there were many rising stars who also hoped to propel themselves into the spotlight at just the right time. A lot was on the line at the first selection race, the Sydney ITU World Cup, not just for Emma but also for the other Olympic hopefuls from Australia and around the world.

On race day Emma had a deficit to make up after the swim, but it was not alarming. She rode well initially. The main drama on the bike leg involved a crash at a tight, right-hand bend in which Emma bounced off plastic barricades. She stayed upright but her left hand took the brunt of the impact. The incident impacted on her ability to brake and change gears efficiently, reducing her ability to drive the pace of the pack as they chased the riders ahead. Nursing what 'Doc Di' later verbally referred to as strained ligaments in her left hand, Emma finished in thirteenth place.

Of the other Australian contenders, Michellie Jones finished first and secured an uncontroversial automatic nomination to the women's Olympic team. Nicole Hackett crashed heavily but had not yet qualified for the Perth World Championship team, so re-mounted her bike and made sure she reached the finish line. Sixth overall, Hackett was the second Australian woman and secured her place on the World Championship start line. Jo King crossed the finish line seconds ahead of Emma, making Emma the fourth Australian. Jackie Gallagher finished in twenty-fourth place, and Loretta Harrop pulled out early in the swim leg.

Loretta Harrop did not approach the Sydney World Cup with the confidence of a reigning world champion, as she had been suffering persistent and severe pain in and around her right knee for weeks. The medical personnel who attended to her injury while she trained in New Zealand prior to the Sydney World Cup, attributed the pain to bursitis and fat pad impingement. Harrop's manager, Diane Ainsworth, forwarded statements from the medical experts to TA on 12 April. Both advised against her participation in the first Olympic trial. The following day Holmik wrote to Ainsworth, having been politely reminded to do so by her, acknowledging receipt of the statements and carefully indicating that he understood them to mean that Harrop would be unable to compete in the Sydney World Cup. During the same week Ainsworth also forwarded medical statements regarding Miles Stewart, who had been hospitalised with a severe bout of tonsillitis. The TA media team put out separate press releases announcing the withdrawal of each athlete from the World Cup, Stewart's on 14 April, the Friday before the race. By Sunday 16 April, both athletes had changed their mind. According to Stewart, TA representatives advised him that, 'he needed to start the race being held on the Olympic course [in order] to be considered under the sickness/illness exclusion clause.' As numerous triathlon and mainstream media articles reported, Harrop also felt 'pressured' to at least start the trial event if she wanted to be eligible for consideration.

From the very beginning interpretations of the Disadvantaged Athlete Clause diverged and shifted. Ainsworth apparently understood it to mean that with demonstrated cause, athletes did not need to enter a selection race in order to trigger the clause. Holmik at first seemed to accept this, but TA altered its position by race day: athletes needed to at least start the race to be eligible for consideration for selection.

Harrop and Stewart were not the only athletes to trigger a version of the Disadvantaged Athlete Clause in the context of the Sydney World Cup. Among the Australian men, neither Chris Hill nor Craig Walton had qualified for the World Championships in Perth. Hill pulled out of the Sydney World Cup due to an incident in which he broke a pedal and landed on the bike stem, bruising his ribs. Walton punctured during the race, but finished, albeit in thirty-fourth place. Originally the TAESC selected Hill for the final spot on the world championship team, as that event's selection policy included a version of the Disadvantaged Athlete Clause and Hill had performed well in recent international races. Walton successfully disputed the decision on advice from his coach, Bill Davoren, by referring to the policy summary published in TA's 1999 Annual Report 'for planning purposes.' The summary specified that selections would be made 'according to finishing order'. As Davoren argued, Walton finished. Hill did not.

Although the detail of the World Championship Policy was different from the Olympic Nomination Criteria, the Hill-Walton case demonstrates the inadequacy of the summaries as a guide to the final selection policies, the general lack of clarity in the final policies, their openness to divergent interpretation, the centrality of discretion in the various versions of the Disadvantaged Athlete Clause included in those policies over time, and the potential for manipulation of the policies during the decision-making process. The Hill-Walton case revolved around application of the clause in the event that an athlete failed to finish. The outcome of the appeal gave precedence to the athlete who did finish. In contrast, the Olympic nominations favoured athletes who did not finish the trial events over those who did.

The Olympic selection process, particularly the task of navigating the many possible applications of Clause 2.2.11, became even more complicated after the Perth World Championships. Following the first Olympic trial, Ainsworth forwarded statements from Harrop's medical advisers in which they argued that the athlete's start at the Sydney race impeded her rehabilitation and compromised her preparation for the World Championships. Di Robinson physically examined Harrop when she arrived in Perth and insisted that she have an MRI scan. The scan revealed that the world champion was suffering from, 'an extensive stress fracture in the upper right tibia,' involving 'at least 75 per cent of the transverse diameter' of the bone. TA accepted, on Robinson's strong recommendation, that Harrop should not even start the race and selected Melissa Ashton to the team in her place. TA also barred four-time ITU World Series champion Brad Beven from starting the Perth race due to injuries from a cycling accident on the eve of the Sydney World Cup. Jackie Gallagher, who had been assessed as suffering from Chronic Overtraining Syndrome, was allowed to start the race. She withdrew during the swim, triggering the Disadvantaged Athlete Clause. Miles Stewart had not recovered fully from tonsillitis and repeated his in-out procedure in Perth as well.

Emma's experience of the Perth World Championships was relatively incident free from a personal perspective. She exited the water in the second main pack, barely a minute behind the swim specialists: Americans Barb Lindquist and Sheila Taormina, and Australian Nicole Hackett. On the bike, Emma worked her way through the strung-out chase pack but the pack itself made little ground on the leaders. Hackett was the fastest runner among the swimmers and held off the chasers in the final leg of the race. At the end of a mistakenly shortened run (7.8 km instead of 10 km), Hacket crossed the finish line first, six seconds ahead of Canadian Carol Montgomery. It was clear that the shorter run presented an advantage to the swimmers and a disadvantage to the running specialists bearing down on them in the closing stages of the race. The result of an error in the production of technical race documents, no athletes planned for the unexpectedly short run. After the race, the ITU quickly determined that the results of the race should stand as all athletes ran the same course. As it was, some believed that Emma's seventh overall, third among the Australians, placed her 'well in Olympic contention'.

The controversial outcome of the world championships did little to simplify the already complex situation facing the TAESC. With Queenbeyan lawyer and Triathlon ACT President Bill Baker now acting as non-voting Chair in place of Holmik, the committee consisted of three former professional triathletes who had subsequently moved into coaching or sports promotion roles within the triathlon community: Marc Dragan, Nick Croft, and Maureen Cummings. On 5 May TA announced the athletes that the TAESC nominated to the AOC for inclusion in the Olympic team. The team consisted of Michellie Jones, Nicole Hackett and Loretta Harrop. TA Executive Director Tim Wilson rang David Carney to inform him that Emma had been named as first reserve.

David Carney immediately proposed that Emma appeal the selection decision.

Emma's older sister Jane was an established solicitor at Freehills, a Melbourne law firm, and helped David to pull together a strong legal team to support the appeal. The team included Queen's Counsel Peter Hayes and Freehills partner Jonathan Forbes.

The appeal process was far from smooth. The Selection Agreement simply stated that an appellant needed to provide TA CEO, that is, Tim Wilson, with written notice within forty-eight hours of the announcement of TA's decision. On the evening of 5 May, David attempted to contact Wilson for further details about the appeals process and sought advice about the grounds for Emma's non-selection. Wilson eventually called back the following evening, but the delay frustrated her already agitated father. Wilson confirmed that in accordance with the Selection Agreement Emma would have the nomination report prior to the TA Appeals Tribunal hearing. Barely placated, David put together a notice of appeal, which he emailed to Wilson. Paranoid about missing out on the chance to challenge Emma's non-selection David rang Wilson the following morning, seeking confirmation that he had received the notice of appeal. Wilson's phone was switched off. David rang TA President Bill Walker and complained that as the chief point of contact for the appeal process, Wilson seemed to be inaccessible, dismissive, and unprepared. David received confirmation of receipt of Emma's notice of appeal from Wilson by fax later that day. It was hardly a promising start for the Carney campaign to secure what they saw as Emma's rightful place on the Olympic Team.

Correspondence and documents produced by Emma and David Carney and their legal team in the first few days after the Olympic Team was announced tested out various arguments in support of Emma's case, many of them inflected with frustration and suspicion. David noted that TA as a sporting body, Loretta Harrop and Miles Stewart as sponsored athletes, and Marc Dragan as Formula 1 Triathlon Series commentator all relied on the financial support of St George Bank one way or another. It is true that in the 1999 Annual Report both the TA National Executive Director (as Tim Wilson's role was now formally known) and TA President alluded to the very difficult financial situation the national sporting body faced at the start of the 1998/1999 financial year and their gratitude to St George Bank for agreeing to support the sport for another two years. In addition, Harrop's manager Di Ainsworth was a former St George Bank sponsorship manager. Reflecting on previous clashes with Ainsworth over Emma's affiliation with National Australia Bank, David strongly believed that it was hardly coincidental that the selection decision favoured St George-sponsored athletes.

David and Emma also expressed with conviction a view that TA favoured a team strategy and wanted multiple swim-cycle specialists to work together. Such a tactic made the combined nomination of Harrop and Hackett desirable. If that was the case, they reasoned, the notion of teamwork should have been specified in the Selection Agreement. The junior elite Perth World Championship Selection Policy included specific clauses relating to teamwork, which the Olympic Selection policy did not.

The TAESC Female Nominations report reached Emma's legal team on Thursday, 11 May, almost a week after announcement of the team's composition. The report presented a seemingly systematic approach to the process, setting most steps of logic against the various clauses of the Nomination Criteria. It laid out the committee's acceptance of Jones' automatic nomination on the basis of her win at Sydney. The committee also determined that the short run course at Perth should not be deemed as the sort of 'circumstance' that might have 'prevented an athlete from competing on equal terms with other athletes', as provided for in Clause 2.2.6 of the Agreement. With the ITU, the TAESC reasoned that the short course 'applied to all athletes' and confirmed the automatic nomination of Nicole Hackett as the recognised winner of the World Championships.

For the one remaining spot on the women's team, the TAESC contrasted the performances of the remaining women who completed the two selection races and concluded that Emma's results were superior. The TAESC then assessed Emma's selection race performances in light of the performances of the two women athletes who had withdrawn from selection races and thus triggered Clause 2.2.11: Gallagher and Harrop. The committee based its preference for Emma over Gallagher on the results of the Sydney World Cup alone. In order to compare performances by Emma and Harrop, the committee determined in accordance with Clause 2.2.8 that they 'should only consider' Emma's selection races, and in accordance with Clause 2.2.11 that they should refer to Harrop's ITU performances since the start of 1999. In light of this comparison the committee decided that the latter's string of World Cup wins and World Championship victory at Montreal the previous year were superior to Emma's selection race performances. In addition, the TAESC pointed out that Harrop won both times that the pair competed in the same race during the 1999 ITU World Cup season (Ishigaki and Montreal). Both comparisons seemed to affirm that Harrop should be nominated for the team.

The logic used to decide between Emma and Loretta Harrop reveals the many problems surrounding the Agreement as a document, including its inadequate guidance for comparison on equal terms and the scope for discretion arising from its contradictory provisions. The report stipulated that the TAESC evaluated Emma's performances at the selection races in accordance with one clause against Harrop's 1999 performances in line with another clause. Yet, comparison of performances on different courses cannot be equal. The two sets of races on which their performances were judged were unequal in terms of distance, terrain, and conditions. The run leg of the second Olympic Trial was shortened significantly; the first Olympic Trial was the standard distance but took place on a technical, hilly course in the rain; the 1999 World Championships was the standard distance on a flat course. In addition, the TAESC report did not comment on a key factor that complicated the direct comparison of performances by Emma and Harrop at the 1999 World Championships and 1999 Ishigaki World Cup. Emma was at a major disadvantage in both instances, breaking her foot during the run leg of the Ishigaki race and returning from the broken foot on limited training for the Montreal World Championships. Again, the terms of the comparison were not equal.

Further, as mentioned earlier, none of the would-be members of the Australian Olympic triathlon team had the opportunity to prepare for such a comparison, as the Selection Agreement was finalised after the races under comparison had taken place. Not knowing the terms of the Disadvantaged Athlete Clause or the basis of the TAESC's decisions, Emma did not have the opportunity to formally lodge and document the fact that she was not competing on equal terms to her uninjured peers at races that might be used to determine her Olympic nomination.

Finally, in supporting their preference for Harrop over Emma the TAESC pointed to the first stated objective of the Selection Agreement, which was to achieve 'the best possible results' at the Olympics. This phrasing may have been a veiled gesture towards the possibility of teamwork, a strategy mentioned in the World Championship junior team selection policy. At the very least the report did not tie the goal of best results to individual athletic potential directly. Not founded on clear, measurable criteria the report's concluding argument demonstrated the extent of discretion and potential for unstated objectives at play in the TAESC's nomination of Harrop.

Only a day after receiving the Nomination Report, Emma's legal team had their 'Grounds of Appeal' ready. The document did not address the possibility raised by Emma and David that TA preferred teamwork over reliance on the ability of individual athletes as a strategy for achieving the 'best possible results.' The Selection Agreement might be read as allowing for teamwork, but the nomination report did not mention it directly and commentary on the possibility would have appeared as speculation. Instead the 'Grounds of Appeal' presented a two-fold response to the argument about achieving the 'best possible results' in the Olympic triathlon, as it related to the respective performances of specific athletes: Harrop, Hackett and Emma. It suggested that Harrop's significant injury made it highly unlikely that she would be in optimum form for the Olympics, and that even at their best Harrop and Hackett were less likely to achieve better results than Emma on the technical and undulating Sydney course. In a supplementary document, Emma supported the arguments around her superior potential as a bike-run specialist to deliver the best results, suggesting that the World Championships did not offer a fair comparison because it was during the crucial final stages of the run that Hackett usually weakened and Emma usually strengthened her attack. By comparing her run times with those of Harrop and Hackett at Ishigaki and Montreal, Emma demonstrated that even when injured she ran faster than both of them. Her over-riding point was that a bike-run specialist with the capacity to run leaders down was more likely to achieve the best results on the challenging Olympic course, than swim-bike specialists with run times that ranked typically in the lower half of the field.

For the most part, the final 'grounds of appeal' document forwarded to TA was shaped in legalistic terms and began with the only premise on which appeals were permitted, 'that the Nomination Criteria have not been properly followed and/or implemented.' The document argued that the Disadvantaged Athlete Clause was meant to 'benefit an athlete' by allowing consideration of injuries, illnesses or incidents that impacted on 'performance during the race'. In Harrop's case, the injury and its inevitable impact on her performance was evident before the race; it did not become apparent after she started. It even appeared that Harrop had been compelled to start the race so that she could trigger the Clause. Recognition of Harrop as a 'disadvantaged athlete', when clearly unable to complete the Sydney World Cup due to her injury, represented an interpretation that was 'contrary to the intention of that clause.' Further, the Grounds of Appeal document suggested that the rationale presented in the Nomination Report, 'denied [Emma] natural justice and procedural fairness,' as it failed to acknowledge Emma's crash during the same race and its impacts on her performance. Not only was Emma's disadvantage not mentioned, it represented a more legitimate application of the Disadvantaged Athlete Clause.

Cautious in its treatment of the suspicions of bias raised by Emma and David, Emma's legal team called for TA to clarify the implications of St George Bank's sponsorship of TA, Harrop, and Hackett and the National Australian Bank's sponsorship of Emma. The team also rejected the Selection Committee's interpretation of Clause 2.2.6 with regard to the short run leg at Perth, a point further supported in Emma's supplement to the document. The 'Grounds for Appeal' concluded by objecting to the appointment of Chris Hewitt as Chair of the TA Appeals Tribunal, owing to his position as solicitor for West Australian Events Corporation, the company responsible for staging the controversial Perth World Championships. Viewed individually some claims made by Emma's legal team might have reflected some of the personal grievances and conspiratorial theories of the Carneys, but embedded in the appeal was a fair and fundamental point: the Nomination Criteria was ambiguous enough for considerable variation in interpretation. To the Carney team the interpretations applied by the TAESC did not seem reasonable, denied Emma her right to consideration on equal terms, and potentially reflected unspoken objectives that at the very least should have been made clear.

Prior to the Appeals Tribunal, Rigby Cooke Lawyers responded to the submissions of all the appellants (Jackie Gallagher, Brad Beven and Greg Bennett all submitted appeals as well) on behalf of TA. In general terms, TA's response reminded the appellants that the Tribunal was only concerned with the question of whether the TAESC followed or implemented the Nomination Criteria properly, not the merits of the committee's decisions.

More specifically, TA's legal team rejected just about every claim and argument contained in Emma's 'grounds for appeal'. In the process, they misrepresented the logic of Emma's appeal repeatedly and avoided addressing her real complaints. They rejected the need to take into account Emma's crash in the Sydney race, reasoning that no written evidence of the incident or its impact had been brought to the TAESC's attention and that the TAESC was not bound to take notice of that evidence even if it had been produced. On the question of the short run leg at the World Championships, the legal team endorsed the committee's conclusion and dismissed Emma's case as unfounded, flippant, and frivolous. One point stuck. Chris Hewitt stepped down as Chair of the TA Appeals Tribunal. He was replaced by talented sportsman (an Olympian who rowed for Australia decades earlier) and Supreme Court Judge, Mervyn Finlay QC.

These responses were not promising, but the Carneys believed in their case and the capacity and strength of their legal team. More than six weeks after the Perth World Championships, Emma, her father, Peter Hayes QC, and Jonathan Forbes, with wishes for a good outcome from ITU President Les McDonald, attended the TA Appeals Tribunal Hearing at Wentworth Hotel, Sydney. Emma was the only athlete present. David was impressed with Hayes' ability to time his contributions and questions so as to catch the representatives of the other athletes off guard, and to nullify their various arguments. He felt confident that there would be a positive outcome. Following the hearing Hayes submitted a final document to the Tribunal concluding that, in the spirit of the principle of 'equal terms', it made sense for 'the TAESC to compare like with like', that is, past performances with past performances.

Released on 22 June, the Appeal Tribunal decision under the direction of Supreme Court Judge Mervyn Finlay QC instructed that the TAESC 'set aside' its female nominations, except for Michellie Jones, and reconsider its selections with a number of key factors in mind. The Tribunal determined that the TAESC erred in not considering Clause 2.2.6 properly, that is, whether the short run leg at Perth 'significantly altered the race outcome'. In the view of the Tribunal the TAESC overlooked the uneven impact of the shortened run on athlete performances when it argued that the error applied 'to all athletes.' It also instructed the TAESC to consider the question of Harrop's intention to race and the allegation of 'bad faith'.

Emma and her legal team were pleased and thought there might be a chance that the TAESC would nominate Emma when taking on board the decisions of the Tribunal. At the same time, they suspected that the Tribunal findings might not change anything. It was likely that the TAESC would rate Hackett's performances in the selection races more highly than Emma's, even if they changed their mind with regard to her automatic selection. Emma's legal team was reliant on a successful case against Harrop's nomination, but the Tribunal seemed less willing to concede Hayes's arguments regarding the improper implementation of the Disadvantaged Athlete Clause.

They were right to suspect that the Disadvantaged Athlete Clause might be the greatest obstacle to a successful outcome. On 7 July, after the TA Appeals Tribunal called for a review of the nominations for the Women's Olympic team and before the TAESC conducted that review, the TAESC chair Bill Baker explained to the selection committee that it was more important to look at statements by Harrop herself than at the media reports surrounding the Sydney

World Cup. He brought to the attention of the members of the TAESC a hand-written note in which he had recorded a statement made by Harrop shortly after she withdrew from the Sydney World Cup. Like Emma's legal team, Baker understood that Harrop's claims to be considered for nomination rested on the Disadvantaged Athlete Clause, and hence on whether her intention to race could be verified. Fearing the worst, Emma's legal team flagged their intention to appeal to the Court of Arbitration for Sport (CAS) even before the TAESC convened to reconsider its nominations.

Initially TA delayed re-convening the Selection Committee while Rigby Cooke attempted to challenge the legitimacy of the appeal to the CAS. Eventually, on 13 July, Baker held a tele-conference with members of the Selection Committee, which had the same members as before. As expected, nothing changed. The TAESC revoked Hackett's automatic nomination but recognized her performances in the selection races as superior to Emma's, without reference to the shortened run leg at Perth or Emma's bike crash at Sydney. The TAESC also decided that Harrop 'intended to race'. Neither the draft nor the final report on the decisions made on 13 July made reference to Baker's handwritten record of Harrop's post-race statement. Instead it alluded to 'statements made by Ms Harrop to doctors and other officials prior to the First Selection Race.' Yet the medical statements do not report directly on Harrop's intention to race. The closest to such a statement was presented in a report produced by TA-approved Team Doctor June Canavan retrospectively, on 7 May. The statement presents Canavan's recollections regarding her inspection of Harrop's injury on the eve of the Sydney World Cup. Canavan simply recalled advising Harrop that, 'if she entered the race the next day she should withdraw if the pain increased.' The extent to which the TAESC engaged with the evidence is unknown, but clearly the committee accepted that Harrop intended to race while the Appeals Tribunal had accepted the TAESC's comparison of Emma's selection races to Harrop's past performances. Harrop was once more nominated for the Olympic team.

Just over a week later, David and the Carney legal team flew to Sydney, this time for Emma's Court of Arbitration for Sport (Oceania Registry) hearing. The Lausanne-based self-regulating arbitral institution was founded in 1983, and initially based its arbitrations in Swiss law for the sake of consistency, though this shifted over time. At the hearing on 21 July, the Panel actually consisted of a sole arbitrator in one of his first cases for the CAS, Henry Jolson, QC. Jolson released his findings and reasons on 31 July. Jolson called for the TAESC to set aside the nominations made at its meeting on 13 July, except for Michellie Jones, and to reconsider the remaining female nominations in light of his findings. He reasoned that the TAESC's comparison of Emma's performances in the selection races with Harrop's past performances seemed contrary to 'notions of fairness and equity'. Acknowledging the potential for divergent interpretations of Clause 2.2.11, Jolson instructed the TAESC on what he viewed as appropriate grounds for comparison. Harrop's past performances were to be used to make a reasonable adjustment to her selection race result, before comparing that adjusted result to Emma's performances in the trial events. Using logic that demonstrated a romantic and arbitrary understanding of athletic performance, Jolson rejected Hayes' point that Harrop's injury was so severe she could not have honestly planned to race competitively. There were many examples, Jolson suggested, of miraculous athletic performances — driven by adrenaline, will power, or desperation — despite injury. The arbitrator instructed the TAESC to consider whether Harrop intended to compete, rather than whether she could, and included a provision for Emma's team to submit further evidence to support their case.

What followed was a frantic scramble on the part of the Carney camp, to assemble, submit, and ensure that the TAESC considered an extensive portfolio of evidence. On 31 July, the day that the CAS decision and reasons were released, Damian Grave from Freehills (temporarily standing in for Jonathan Forbes) faxed Bill Baker requesting the TAESC to hold off its second review of the nominations until the Carney submissions were ready. Grave's fax was met with an error message. He re-sent the fax on 3 August to TA President Bill Walker. Again, he received an error message. The following day David Carney spoke to Bill Walker on the phone, seeking guidance on the process for the TAESC's second review of the women's nominations. Walker responded that TA's legal advisers were preparing guidelines on how the Tribunal and CAS findings should be interpreted.

Bill Baker faxed Grave from the office of his Queenbeyan based law firm Baker, Deane & Nutt on 4 August, requesting that Grave forward his client's further submissions as promptly as possible. From that day, through to 10 August, Grave provided substantial, methodical and detailed statements regarding Harrop's intentions to race, supported by a significant amount of evidence from the print and digital media. But after 4 August, Emma's legal team was unable to elicit a further response from TA personnel. TA's legal representatives faxed Grave once on 7 August. The fax made clear that all further correspondence had to go through the Rigby Cooke office, tersely outlined a minimalist procedure, rejected the idea of calling for oral evidence, and indicated that the TAESC would only, 'have regard to such written information as it considers necessary and appropriate to reach a decision.' Grave responded to Rigby Cooke over the ensuing three days with faxes that were increasingly urgent in tone. Each time, Grave forwarded Emma's itemised arguments as they related to the TAESC decision as well as copies of print articles that seemed to show clearly that Harrop felt pressured to race at the Sydney World Cup.

On 10 August, Grave again faxed the same collection of material to Rigby Cooke along with copies of unanswered faxes to Bill Baker, Bill Walker and Tim Wilson. Once more he received an error message, but this time from the Rigby Cooke fax machine. Yet before the end of the day, 10 August, Grave did receive a fax from Rigby Cooke indicating that the firm had forwarded all received material to TA with the request that it be placed before the TAESC. Oddly, the Rigby Cooke representative asked whether Grave had shared the submissions with anyone else. On the same day, another document was received or sent by the Rigby Cooke fax machine. A copy of the document in the Carney records does not clarify the origins or destination of the fax, but its contents are significant. It contained the first draft of the report of the TAESC's second review of its female nominations, in response to the CAS findings.

Emma's legal team remained unsure as to whether or when a TAESC meeting actually took place, but the final version of the report reached them on 15 August. It advised that the same three women had been nominated and that Emma, as before, had been identified as first reserve. With just one month remaining before the Olympic Triathlon itself, Emma's legal team notified TA immediately that Emma intended to appeal the TAESC's latest decision. TA had already suggested that should Emma's legal team intend to appeal again they should go directly to the CAS rather than the TA Appeals Tribunal. All parties, including the AOC, agreed. Once again Henry Jolson QC was appointed to represent the CAS. It was only in the final days before the second hearing that the CAS presence was enlarged to a panel of three, with Jerrold Cripps QC and Neil Young QC joining Jolson.

For the second CAS Appeal, scheduled for Wednesday, 30 August, Emma's legal team targeted the TAESC's failure to fully reconsider its nominations according to the instructions of both the Tribunal and the CAS. They also alleged that the committee failed to observe natural justice, stating that the reasons provided for its decisions in both cases clearly demonstrated a lack of familiarity with the extensive submissions and accompanying evidence faxed repeatedly to TA's legal representatives. The team requested formally and directly that TA supply all documents referred to in the various TAESC reports and submissions to the Tribunal and CAS, as well as every draft of the TAESC reports and all relevant emails between athletes, managers and TA personnel. The members and Chair of the TAESC, Harrop, Wilson and Walker were also given notice that they may be required to attend the hearing. This process continued throughout the second half of August. On the date of the hearing, 30 August, Emma's legal team called for a deferment to Monday, 4 September (less than two weeks before the women's Olympic triathlon) because of gaps in the records supplied by TA's legal representatives.

Armed with masses of documents and the eloquent talents of Peter Hayes, Emma's team felt confident on the day of the second CAS hearing. In fact, Emma's father recalled that Hayes was so pleased with the morning session he spoke excitedly during the lunch break of having a favourable resolution to Emma's non-nomination by the end of the day. David shared Hayes' conviction. In his eyes, TA's Senior Counsel Alan Sullivan, QC, seemed to struggle in the face of the evidence and Hayes' dominating performance. Their case concerning the lack of natural justice was strong and it seemed clear that the TAESC's second review of the nominations ignored the evidence provided by Emma's legal team regarding Harrop's intention to race.

Yet when the Court reconvened after lunch, Jolson abruptly dismissed the appeal altogether. As David recalled, Jolson justified the sudden decision by saying, 'if we were in a court of law, I would uphold the appeal, but this is not a court of law.' According to David, Hayes was so taken aback and troubled by the outcome he declared that he needed a drink and then volunteered to waive the Carneys' fees.

Released on 8 September, four days later, the CAS panel's decision and reasons provided some insight into the outcome of the appeal, but for Emma's legal team it was hardly satisfying. On the crucial question of Harrop's *bona fides* — her 'intention to race' — the CAS panel cited case law showing that informal forms of evidence were sufficient for the TAESC to make a reasonable decision. On that basis, the arbitrators concluded that the TAESC did not need to view the print media evidence supplied by Emma's legal team; the Committee had ample informal evidence on which to base its decision. The panel referred to two such informal documents identified by TA's legal team: one that presented a short series of typed recollections by the original TAESC Chair, Emery Holmik, and the single page of brief hand-written notes by the replacement TAESC Chair, Bill Baker, which was presented as a record of Harrop's post-race statement. The CAS panel took the time to include the full text of both notes, laboured the rationale regarding the value of informal records of this kind, and concluded that the TAESC had sufficient evidence before it to make a decision on Harrop's intentions.

The first informal piece of evidence on which the TAESC ostensibly based its decision to accept Harrop's *bona fides*, was a page of recollections by Emery Holmik. Vaguely headed 'Record of discussions with Ainsworth and/or Harrop 13 to 29 April', Holmik's page of typed notes documented that he first heard that Harrop, 'was travelling to Sydney to enter the World Cup' from Ainsworth. As recorded in Holmik's note, Ainsworth explained in a phone call that Harrop's, 'injury had improved to the point where she felt capable of competing in the race and didn't want to have everything hinging on just the Perth World Championships.' Holmik recorded in his notes that he was surprised. While clear about his reaction to Ainsworth's announcement and its wording, Holmik's note is less precise about whether he took the phone call from Ainsworth on 13 or 14 April. This vagueness seems odd given that both Holmik and Ainsworth communicated with each other, and others, in carefully worded faxes and emails throughout the pivotal week leading up to Sydney World Cup. Statements submitted by Harrop's legal team suggest that Ainsworth initially believed that medical confirmation of her inability to race would allow Harrop to sit out the race and even remain in New Zealand without damaging her Olympic selection opportunities. It was on 12 April that Ainsworth forwarded the medical statements regarding Harrop's injury to Holmik and 13 April when Holmik responded. Emails supplied to Emma's legal team reveal that Holmik communicated with Harrop during this period as well; in an email dated 12 April, Harrop confirmed that she was booked to fly to Sydney on 14 April. It seems strange that Holmik did not use his emails to clarify the timing of his learning that Harrop intended to race. The 'Record of discussions' appears to contain unexplained silences and offers less clarity about the precise circumstances of Harrop's decision to compete than it could have, given the ample records available to Holmik to document those moments precisely.

The second informal piece of evidence presented to the CAS Panel consisted of the handwritten record by Bill Baker of his conversation with Loretta Harrop shortly after she abandoned the 16 April Sydney World Cup. Unable to gain access to the race compound, Baker dragged the injured athlete and a witness into the rain, in order to obtain and record her account. According to the note, Harrop informed Baker that she tried to use a six-beat kick in the swim, with the result that it intensified the pain in her right leg. In its report, the CAS arbitrators took the time to point out that Baker recorded the conversation as, 'the non-voting Chairman of the Selection Committee.' Yet Baker was not actually the chair of the committee at that time, hence his inability to enter the race area. Reportedly TA produced papers at the second CAS hearing suggesting that the 'necessary formal steps' to appoint Baker as Chair instead of Holmik, 'had been taken' on 14 April, prior to the Sydney World Cup. Yet no papers in the extensive records of the selection decisions and appeals retained by David Carney confirm the specific nature and timing of the 'formal steps' taken to appoint Baker prior to the World Cup. Further, this detail contradicts the list of personnel named in the TAESC's original female nomination report released in mid-May. That report identifies the date of appointment of each member of the Committee and states that Baker formally shouldered the role of non-voting chair on 28 April 2000. Whether Baker was formally recognised as the TAESC chair on 16 April or not, the circumstances surrounding the note highlight the extent of the effort to obtain a statement from Harrop, as well as the self-consciousness with which TA personnel sought to document Harrop's case as a Disadvantaged Athlete. By contrast no effort was made to document, recall, or take into account Emma's own claims to disadvantage.

While the CAS panel presented a strong argument from case law to suggest that informal evidence was acceptable, the rationale paid no attention to the selective content and context of production of the two informal documents on which both the TAESC and the CAS panel based their respective decisions in favour of Harrop. It seems that as far as the TAESC and CAS panel were concerned, the lack of accurate detail regarding the timing and circumstances in which Harrop decided to compete, Holmik's communications with Ainsworth and Harrop about that decision, and Baker's role at the time of the Sydney World Cup, was irrelevant. It was enough that the documents existed and appeared to show that Harrop intended to race.

However, the two documents contradict the reams of evidence found throughout the triathlon and mainstream media. Copies of many such articles were supplied by Emma's legal team prior to both the first and second TAESC review of the nominations, but it appears that the members of the TAESC were instructed on both occasions not to review the material. Prior to the first review, as mentioned earlier, Baker told the TAESC that it was more important to consider statements by Harrop herself, implying that his witnessed record of Harrop's account of the race was sufficient. Around the time of the second review, a Rigby Cooke representative claimed in a fax to Emma's legal team that the evidence was placed before the TAESC and the second CAS panel seemed satisfied that this was the case. To support their conclusion the arbitrators pointed to an email dated 4 August sent by Baker to the members of the TAESC, to which Emma's entire submission was attached. However, it appears that the CAS panellists did not read the email itself. In the email, Baker refers to a conversation between himself and TA's Senior Counsel Alan Sullivan, QC, and informs the members of the TAESC in cautious terms about the outcome of that conversation. He:

> had not had a chance to properly consider the Carney representations, but I have had some general guidance from Alan Sullivan on how we should deal with those representations. We should therefore not form any definite conclusions about them at this stage.

Whether on advice from TA's Senior Counsel, or for some other reason, it appears that the TAESC did not pay close attention to the evidence provided by Emma's legal team.

This possibility is further reinforced when considering the content of the evidence that Emma's legal team amassed. The press reports suggest universally that Harrop felt pressured to start in order to be considered for the Olympic team. In his 7 July email, Baker urged TAESC members not to place emphasis on reports published on the 'back page of the *Telegraph*.' Possibly he was thinking about Amanda Lulham's *Sunday Telegraph* article in which she noted that both Miles Stewart and Loretta Harrop 'believe they must start in the ITU World Cup to strengthen their hopes of being selected.' Lulham quoted Ainsworth as saying about Harrop, 'She has to do what she has to do to be covered.' While Lulham implies a separation between the selection policy and specific interpretations of the Disadvantaged Athlete Clause (Stewart and Harrop 'believe...'), most press reports did not make that distinction. An article authored by one of the members of the TAESC, Nick Croft, reported that Stewart and Harrop both started the race in order to invoke the Disadvantaged Athlete Clause, as advised by their manager, Ainsworth. Assuming that this understanding was outlined in the clause, Croft explained:

The clause basically reads that the athlete must start a selection race even if injured so they can claim a disadvantage.

Likewise equating this interpretation with the clause, an online *SportsToday* journalist reported that Harrop 'complained she had been pressured to start by TA's selection policy.' Another journalist quoted TA Executive Director Tim Wilson, who placed the onus of the 'decision to start the race' on Harrop and Stewart, 'based on wanting to be considered under that clause.'

Reading the press reports carefully a number of things become clear: none suggest that either Harrop or Stewart started with the intention of racing to completion; the dominant interpretation of the Disadvantaged Athlete Clause proposed that athletes had to start in order to be considered for selection; and athletes felt pressure to start the race because of this assumption. While the press reports do not comment overtly on the role of officials in propagating that interpretation, New Zealand medical adviser John Helleman pointed to the pressure they placed on athletes in a statement about Harrop's condition before the Perth World Championships: 'Loretta was advised by Australian officials to start in the Sydney World Cup on April 16th.' By avoiding any reference to the evidence supplied by Emma's legal team, both TA representatives and the CAS panel appear to have not only protected the athlete who felt compelled to line up for the race, but also avoided subjecting to scrutiny the people who pressured her to do so. Emma's evidence presented a plausible motive for ill or injured athletes who decided to start the Sydney World Cup and contradicted the informal pieces of evidence that the CAS panel deemed sufficient to verify that Harrop intended to race.

That the press reports were not included in TAESC deliberations is evident. All specific mention of the press reports disappeared from TA paperwork after Baker's first reference to them in his email of 7 July. Yet the second CAS panel expressed satisfaction that Emma was 'afforded a fair opportunity of being heard,' because Baker had forwarded the submissions to the TAESC members. Peter Hayes, Emma's QC, was reportedly troubled and even dumbfounded at the CAS panel's willingness to advocate strenuously the appropriateness of the informal evidence, and, on those grounds, to accept the TAESC's decision to overlook the

Carney team's submissions in their deliberations. While the panel used case law to justify its stance, to the lay person it seems contradictory to suggest that Emma was accorded natural justice at the same time that emphatic public statements were ignored in favour of vague and tenuous evidence that worked against her case.

Henry Jolson's comment (as recalled by David) that the CAS hearing was not a 'court of law', points to issues raised in literature about the CAS as a body and sports law more broadly. In many cases, CAS panels have not brought satisfaction to non-selected athletes who believe they have been treated unfairly. Only in a small number of instances have panels over-ruled specific nominations relating to 'the legitimate expectations of the athletes'. In a well-known case involving the Australian Judo Federation in the lead up to the Sydney 2000 Olympic Games, a CAS Panel ordered that one athlete be de-selected in favour of another because the nomination criteria was adjusted after the selection events had taken place. In many more instances CAS panels have applied a landmark finding made in the context of the Atlanta 1996 Olympic Games. The ruling placed emphasis on selector adherence to specified criteria and processes as outlined in selection agreements rather than the merits of an appellant's case for selection. Applying the ruling, many CAS panels have tended subsequently to annul prior selection decisions and instruct reconsideration of Olympic nominations against the established criteria, with specific concerns in mind.

The problem with this focus on adherence to policy is that CAS arbitrators often decline to comment on issues of fairness and natural justice or the extent of undisclosed selector discretion that might be embedded in selection documents. Emma's legal team challenged this focus when they requested all relevant documentation from Triathlon Australia prior to the second CAS hearing. Arguing that Olympic nomination has significant financial implications, they re-visioned selection agreements as contractual documents rather than discretionary frameworks beyond the reach of law. TA Senior Counsel Alan Sullivan, QC may have resisted such logic in the context of Emma's second CAS hearing, but he might have been thinking of the case when he published an article a decade later. In it, he suggested that sport was 'regulated by the same contractual rules and principles as any other activity.' Viewed as contracts, he reasoned, the meaning of Selection Agreements should be 'determined by what a reasonable person would have understood them to mean,' where that meaning was framed by the 'surrounding circumstances known to the parties' involved. In the case of the Triathlon Australia 2000 Olympic Selection Agreement, its athlete signatories might have expected reasonably that they would be nominated if they competed in and won either selection race, or performed better in those races than other contenders for the remaining places on the team. Those criteria were objective and measurable. However, the framing of the Disadvantaged Athlete Clause allowed significant scope for discretion. Far from being well understood, multiple contradictory meanings were attributed to the Clause. In particular, Triathlon Australia officials propagated a previously unknown interpretation just days before the first Olympic Trial. The meaning attributed to the Clause in the new interpretation was not framed in accordance with the knowledge and reasonable expectations of its athlete signatories, and it was introduced after hopeful athletes agreed to the terms of the selection policy. The full implications of the new interpretation only became clear when the Olympic nominations were announced. Viewed as a contract, the Selection Agreement was a flawed document, to which new and unexpected meaning was attached retrospectively.

Emma's Olympic ambitions were partly constrained by a serious injury in the year before the Olympic trials, as well as a drop in form over the previous two years due to less than ideal training arrangements and mysterious health issues. But she recovered from her injury and made positive adjustments to her training. Emma may not have delivered the sort of emphatic performances at the Selection Trials that might have deflected the nomination dramas that followed, but she still raced well enough to be ranked third among the Australian women who completed both events. While Emma and David did not trust Triathlon Australia and the TAESC, they believed that the CAS would recognise that she met the requirements for nomination to the Olympic team. A combination of inexperience (or as Emma and David suggest, something worse) on the part of the sport's governing body, a selection policy that rested on discretion, and a system of arbitration that failed to recognise the real, financial consequences and natural injustice embedded in such policies, brought Emma's Olympic dream to an end. Her legal team had no chance of reversing the nomination decision, as, contrary to expectation, Emma's nomination to the Olympic team was not reliant on her performances alone. It was not simply a case of racing faster and placing higher than her peers.

'It wouldn't have passed the pub test' — *David Carney*

As a father, I always stood up for my girls. A simple and clear ideal. The girls knew that if anyone ever treated any of them unfairly, I would support and stand alongside them. If you ask any of my daughters, they would tell you I would never allow my family to endure any wrongdoing.

I have always played a straight bat and fought hard for what is right.

By the year 2000, I had been working in senior positions in the sports industry for over twenty years and seen the ruthlessness of the cutthroat world of sport. In sport, there is only ever one winner in competition and everyone else is a loser. The win or loss is dramatic, extremely emotional, and transcends into everyday life. Emma is a living example of the passion required for this existence. From a very young age I had been holding Emma back, ensuring she was preserved through the destructive junior ranks of sport to develop into a fresh senior athlete, ready to race. I know Emma was often annoyed with my conservative approach because she was born to compete. She only ever raced to win. Emma knew the facts: win and you are a success; lose and you have failed.

There is nothing bigger in sport than the Olympics, and Emma had always spoken about representing Australia in the Olympics. If Emma had remained in her beloved sport of athletics or taken up the sport of cycling, she would have become an Australian Olympian for those sports at the Sydney Olympic Games or most likely even earlier at the Atlanta Games in 1996. Ironically, by being by far the most successful triathlete in the world leading into the Games, Emma 'missed out'.

It was not just Emma who 'lost'. As is generally the case with a toxic culture, the organisation suffers. Triathlon as a sport in Australia has never recovered, and it has never been the same. The Women's Triathlon was the opening event at the Sydney Olympic Games in 2000. Triathlon had a chance to light up every TV in every Australian household with an opening gold medal. The location was breathtaking, and an opening win for Australia would have been even more so. The sport was set to boom with an opening success. But instead, TA manipulated the selection process. The Australian women's triathlon team that raced was not the team that qualified for the Games based upon the published Selection Criteria signed by all competing athletes. Instead it was a team that was quite simply not good enough for the Sydney Olympic course and the results delivered were well below what had been predicted by TA and the AOC. The only medal was won by the only athlete in the Australian women's triathlon team who gained selection according to the published Selection Criteria.

I believe that Emma would have won in Sydney had she started the 2000 Olympic Triathlon. Emma still has the fastest time on the Sydney Olympic Triathlon course by over two minutes. In the case Emma had not won, the dynamics of the race would have changed and Michellie Jones would have won. They were the only two Australians who were proven performers on the course. Everyone knew that when Emma and Michellie raced on a tough course one of them won. Australia would have won gold and silver Olympic medals had Emma been racing. Triathlon as a sport in Australia has never been the same, due to the loss of opportunity TA orchestrated by not winning gold and not attracting more to what should be an outstandingly successful sport for Australia.

Emma's non-selection for the 2000 Olympic Games was at the time the most high-profile athlete omission from the Australian Olympic Team and the details were the most sought after. At the time Emma asked me to refuse all requests from the media to discuss the process she endured. As a result, this is the first time I have spoken publicly or written about the appeal process, which we won on evidence and facts but lost through manipulation. Below is my account of what took place, written with reference to the Appeal documents I retained and conversations I had with various people during the long and difficult process.

The TA selection criteria was incorporated into a document entitled, 'Australian Olympic Committee & TA Selection Agreement. 2000 Australian Olympic Team'. At that stage everything was apparently transparent, known and understood equally by Athletes, TA Board Members, executives and staff, TAESC, Race Directors, Media, Race Officials, and Medical Staff. Athletes, as a condition of racing, signed a document stating that they were:

> *aware of the Australian Olympic Committee / TA Selection Agreement that determines the Nomination of Athletes to the Australian Olympic Committee for Selection to the 2000 Australian Olympic Team.*

But, if the athletes expected they had to race well to be selected, they were wrong. The interpretation of a very significant Clause in the Agreement changed during the selection process, with an enormous impact upon the Team selected. I doubt when the Australian Olympic Committee (AOC) received the Selection Criteria from TA and incorporated it into the Selection Agreement document that the officials at the AOC would have considered the selection farce that would eventuate.

In the official selection process TA selects the team and nominates the athletes to the AOC, who accepts the nominations. At no stage is the AOC a party to or influence on the selection process of any Olympic Sport. Clause 4.4 of the selection document states:

The National Federation [NF, which is TA] must apply the Nomination Criteria so as to ensure that no Athlete is nominated to the AOC where another athlete is, or other athletes are, entitled to be nominated in priority.

In other words, the AOC required TA to apply the Selection Policy correctly. It would be reasonable to assume that it is a simple process to apply a clearly stated and transparent selection policy correctly, as understood by all concerned, particularly the competing athletes.

The TA 2000 Olympic Nomination Criteria appeared to have a very simple objective, 'to achieve the best possible results' in the 2000 Sydney Olympic Games. A noble statement, where nobility was absent. This one statement permitted wriggle room for TA President Bill Walker, Chief Executive Tim Wilson, Olympic Program Manager Emery Holmik, the TAESC, TA Lawyers, TA Board Members and TA appointed Olympic Officials, including the Medical Team, to ignore the published selection criteria and nominate an athlete who did not compete physically and did not have the physical ability to compete in the selection races. As a result of her selection the athlete best suited to the course, who competed in the selection races as if her nomination counted on them, was not selected. The athlete who missed out was Emma. We appealed Emma's non-selection three times.

How can it happen in a Court of Law in Australia that a group of people (the TAESC) can make decisions and not then have to justify them? The reason is, neither the TA Appeal Tribunal nor the Court of Arbitration for Sport (CAS) were conducted under Australian Law. Australian Law has no jurisdiction and athletes were required to sign away their rights (when they signed the Athletes Acknowledgment form) to pursue a legal challenge through the Australian legal system, as a prerequisite to making themselves available for Australian Olympic Team selection. The CAS appears like a court of law, as Australian lawyers can represent Appellants and Defendants, but it is not.

What became clear during Emma's appeal and through our discovery of documents process, was that TA had an agenda when it came to their women's Olympic team selections. Firstly, it was widely known that TA officials strongly supported Brett Sutton when he faced charges of indecent dealings with a minor in court, by declaring that he would be instrumental in coaching athletes to winning Olympic medals at the Sydney 2000 Games. To the amazement of many, the Judge accepted the argument and Sutton only received a two-year suspended sentence. Unfortunately for TA, by the time the Games arrived Sutton's squad was decimated. His entire female squad was either injured or burnt out. TA probably felt obligated to nominate a Brett Sutton athlete for the Olympic team having presented that argument at his trial. Secondly, Brett Sutton was a coach with a swimming background. He convinced TA President Bill Walker and CEO Tim Wilson that a team race strategy made up of predominantly swim specialists needed to be adopted in the Olympic Games. This strategy was not mentioned in the Selection Document and it was clearly flawed. It relied on other countries selecting athletes that favoured the Australian team approach. Also, the Sydney course was designed for strong bike-run specialists and the two fastest times (by far) were both recorded by Emma. The biggest threat to the team strategy was the most prolific winner in ITU racing at the time, the fastest triathlete over the Sydney course, and the triathlete with the fastest run-bike combination in the World, Emma. It was Emma's outstanding brilliance as a triathlete that actually cost her Olympic team selection. Absolutely insanely absurd.

Emma's case was run by Peter Hayes QC, senior Freehills Partners Jonathan Forbes (also an Old Wesley Collegian) and Damian Grave, and me. My oldest daughter Jane and Kelly-Ann McKinnis (they were best friends and had been through Law School together) also contributed much to the appeal process.

Our team relied on arguing the simple fact that the interpretation of the Athlete Disadvantage Clause was contrived. An appalling, new interpretation of the Athlete Disadvantage Clause by TA President Bill Walker and CEO Tim Wilson, together with the TA lawyers, set the recipe for selection of an uncompetitive team for the Sydney Olympics.

Prior to the first selection race in Sydney, Loretta Harrop, the only athlete Brett Sutton had available by that time for his 'team' selection idea, had a serious injury and was incapable of racing at both of the selection races. We argued that Loretta Harrop herself, her manager Di Ainsworth, her disgraced coach Brett Sutton, various doctors and TA officials all knew she was unable to complete the selection races. In the days before the first selection race, interpretation of the

Athlete Disadvantage Clause was altered, requiring athletes not only to start the race, but also to state their intention to finish the race. Accepting the statements, the TAESC could then consider their selection. We argued that Loretta Harrop did not intend to finish the race, because she was physically unable to. She actually had a stress fracture at the time and clearly was in a lot of pain.

From the outset, it was apparent Emma's legal team was far superior to TA's. Emma has always benefited from a strong following and support in Melbourne, her hometown. The way Emma conducted herself as an athlete, the time she took to develop her corporate presentation skills away from racing, the way she developed sponsorship relationships and also donated her time to local causes, combined with her renowned 'race to win' for Australia approach left many lawyers in Melbourne offering their services to represent her. Emma's case was known from the outset to be clearly unfair and many wanted it rectified. As a result, I believe the appeal we ran was the strongest possible appeal, factually and strategically, and led by the best possible legal minds of Peter Hayes, QC and Jonathan Forbes, Senior Partner of Freehills Law Firm.

I had experience in litigation during my corporate career and have skills in the strategic planning and running of a case, even though I am not trained as a lawyer. I have worked with some of the best litigators in the country, and the oldest trick in the book was to try to screw the other side from the outset. As a consequence, the first step in the Appeal process was to decimate the TA Appeal Board. With this approach, before the appeal started, Emma's legal team removed Chris Hewitt as Chair of the Appeals Tribunal. Owing to his position as solicitor for West Australian Events Corporation, the company responsible for staging the controversial Perth World Championships, there was a conflict of interest. With this disruption added, TA was required to reform its appeal board.

Once we had exhausted this avenue of disruption, the appeal proceedings commenced with a new Chairman, Honourable Mervyn Finlay, a retired Judge of the NSW Supreme Court. Finlay was himself a rower, an Australian Olympian and outstanding sportsman, and winner of the Bronze Medal in the 1952 Helsinki Olympics seated at six in the Australian men's eight crew. Justice Finlay was appointed as an interim Chairman and it was just about a certainty that TA did not want him to retain the Chair because he conducted himself with the utmost level of integrity and fairness. Mervyn Finlay took his role seriously, permitted vigorous challenges, and was clearly intent on ensuring the Appeal process was transparent and fair to all parties.

This first Appeal, as heard by Justice Finlay, was by far the most fair and reasonable. It was following this hearing that the selection of Harrop and Hackett was overturned. The only problem was that in overturning the Olympic Team selection, Mervyn Finlay referred the matter back to the very same group on the TAESC, rather than directing that a new and independent committee consider and determine the Olympic Team selection. Had this been done and appointments made with the same high standards of integrity as Mervyn Finlay I am certain Emma would have gained selection, based entirely upon performances in the Selection Races, because the TAESC biases would have been removed. Unfortunately, this was not the case.

Emma attended the first sitting in Sydney and then never attended another sitting. She hated the process and hated the dishonesty, contempt and lack of care anyone associated with TA had towards her. Despite being a tough competitor, the legal process clearly disturbed her. I remained positive and hopeful throughout the appeals as did Emma's lawyers. It was a clear case of misinterpretation of the selection policy and the facts, and in a normal court of law Emma's appeal would have won at every stage.

With the intent of TA in mind, Peter Hayes, Jonathan Forbes and I decided that it was necessary to exit the TA Appeal Tribunal because it was far too close to and could be unduly influenced by the TA lawyers. An application was therefore made to the CAS. This move to the independent CAS was opposed strenuously by TA lawyers, which confirmed in our minds that it was a good step to remove the Appeal from the influence of TA. After all, it is well recognised that all internal Tribunals, whatever the organisation, are inevitably subject to pressures that an independent external Tribunal is not.

TA lost the argument, and the TA Appeal Tribunal was no longer.

Henry Jolson QC was appointed to hear the Appeal by CAS. Henry Jolson had a quite amazing capacity to fail to grasp the issues that were in contention. The first Appeal Hearing he conducted was just a waste of time. He floundered, appeared ill-prepared, and had neither read the submissions nor the findings of the TA Appeal Tribunal heard by Justice Finlay. We were soon back at a second Appeal Hearing at Chifley Tower in Sydney. I can recall asking Peter Hayes how on earth Henry Jolson had been appointed as a QC. Hayes replied along the lines that he had opposed Jolson in court on a couple of occasions and had found him very competent but was surprised at his failure to understand Emma's Appeal, which was really very much a straight-forward case.

Initially Henry Jolson banned me from the hearing. I was stunned and said to Hayes, 'What about Di Ainsworth?' (Loretta Harrop's Manager). Peter Hayes raised the issue and Henry Jolson said that I could stay but had to sit at the back of the room, away from Hayes and Jonathan Forbes. I stayed put whilst Hayes continued to object until finally Jolson stated I could stay where I was next to Hayes at the large, boardroom table. I was still not allowed to speak. I interpreted that as a total climb down by Jolson, as did Hayes, because we spoke on matters as necessary during the Hearing. It was not a good start and certainly not a good omen for the Hearing.

In order to reject Emma's very strong appeal on the grounds of misuse of the Disadvantaged Athlete Clause, TA submitted partial, inconclusive and conflicting evidence. A key inconsistency Peter Hayes argued was about the doctors' evidence. At one point he had everyone tied in knots about Loretta Harrop having a severe stress fracture (and almost a full fracture) before the Sydney race, making it impossible for her to ride a bike let alone run, and as proven by her actions, she was not even capable of swimming. Peter Hayes showed how medical evidence was manipulated to concoct an 'intention to finish' to trigger the 'Athletes Disadvantage Clause'. Through discovery of the various doctors' letters, Emma's lawyers proved that both Loretta Harrop and her manager Di Ainsworth withheld essential information regarding her injury when justifying her withdrawal from the Sydney selection race. It was clear the day before the Sydney event Harrop was instructed to have an MRI, because a stress fracture was suspected. This advice from Dr Kannangara was ignored. When Harrop spoke to Bill Baker, chairman of TAESC, of her injury just after pulling out of the 16 April Sydney event, and stating her claim for Athlete Disadvantage, she failed to disclose the most recent diagnosis from Dr Kannangara. If she had done so, it would have been obvious that the claim that she entered the race 'intending to finish' was spurious. It would have invalidated her claim. Rather than disclose the truth, instead, an absurdly incorrect diagnosis from NZ's Dr John Hellemans was provided to the TAESC which identified bursitis. This diagnosis was clearly wrong, as his letter also mentioned there was no improvement from his treatment. Further diagnosis was attempted by Dr June Canavan, but Harrop was both uncooperative and evasive in her presence and refused to be diagnosed. It was not until the Perth Selection race, some two weeks later, that TA Medical Officer Dr Di Robinson required an MRI of Loretta's leg and a stress fracture was finally diagnosed. Dr Di Robinson advised that the MRI '...

clearly demonstrated an extensive stress fracture in the upper right tibia which involves at least 75 per cent of the transverse diameter of the tibia.' There was no way Loretta could finish a race because the stress fracture was 75 per cent through the bone and simply walking was impossible without a limp. All that Di Robinson offered to the TAESC was, 'I believe without doubt that Loretta should be given special consideration with respect to Olympic selection given the type and severity of the injury sustained.' The selection policy required this statement from two TA doctors, not one.

On behalf of Emma, Peter Hayes pointed out that while Di Robinson reported Athlete Disadvantage for Harrop, she failed in recognising Emma's bike crash which hampered her ability to race the Sydney selection event. Additionally, in an amazing coincidence, TA Olympic Program Manager Emery Holmik also 'lost' my email to him following the Sydney selection event notifying him of Emma's claim for athlete disadvantage. Clearly, 'losing' an email can only result from deleting an email.

Peter Hayes also pointed out the extremely unfair comparison of the race results in 1999, where no consideration was made for the fact that in 1999 Emma missed the season with a serious injury and only raced twice. Both times Emma out-ran Harrop significantly. Everyone knew the Sydney Olympic race would be won on the run. The 1999 serious foot injury Emma sustained in the first ITU race of the season (finishing fourth and outrunning all those who finished ahead of her) that then caused her to miss almost the entire season only to return at the World Championships where she finished third (with the second fastest run), was the window of opportunity that TA President Bill Walker, CEO Tim Wilson and the TAESC used. No regard was given to Emma's injury, her bike crash in the Sydney Selection Race, or the debacle of the shortened run course in the Perth Selection Race. No regard was given to adjust for Emma's injury and the impact it had on Emma's bike and run times.

Further, Peter Hayes QC argued that in the comparison of the 1999 season events, the TAESC also failed to recognise the types of courses Harrop 'beat' Emma on, and the nature of the Sydney Olympic course. The Sydney course was hilly with a wetsuit swim, suited to a bike-runner. The two courses on which Emma was marginally beaten by Harrop in 1999 were predominantly flat with non-wetsuit swims, while Emma was injured and there was no application of Athlete Disadvantage considerations to her performances. The selection policy actually made reference to the importance of the type of course in Clause 2.2.3, which stated that if the Perth selection race were a non-wetsuit swim, then the Sydney race result 'would have a greater bearing on the nomination process', and if both Sydney and Perth races were wetsuit swims, 'then performances in each race had equal bearing on the nomination process.' Emma did not race the other 1999 races considered by the TAESC, because of her injury. Emma had previously raced the events and beaten Harrop in those years, but the TAESC just reviewed 1999. It was another absurd bias against Emma.

In his final argument regarding the 1999 season results, Peter Hayes proved that it was due to Emma's absence from the race circuit in 1999 that Loretta was actually able to even win an event. When both Emma and Loretta raced a full season head to head, Emma was by far the more successful and superior athlete.

In his last point about the comparison of Loretta Harrop's and Emma's track records, Peter Hayes QC identified yet another unjustified claim by the TAESC about where Harrop would have finished had she finished the selection race. The TAESC decided that if she had finished, and not just swum 100 m, she would have placed 'no worse than 3rd'. How this was decided upon was never established and the TAESC was not required to justify the claim. It was also never questioned as to why the TAESC could consider how Loretta would finish with an injury, but when considering Emma racing with an injury in 1999, no consideration was given. The biases against Emma were appalling.

Peter Hayes QC then pointed out that the TAESC had also taken on an interpretation of the Athlete Disadvantage Clause that was unfair. In considering the 'intention to finish' of Harrop, the TAESC only considered whether they 'believed' Harrop, not that she could have possibly finished. When they did discover subsequently that Harrop's injury was a severe stress fracture and that there was no way she could have possibly finished the Sydney race, they refused to take this into consideration in their selection decision. Yet another extraordinary bias towards Harrop and against Emma, who raced to finish with an injured hand.

Peter Hayes also addressed the issue of the automatic selection of Nicole Hackett. Emma's Appeal case had a discrete point that Nicole Hackett should not have received automatic selection, because there was an error which affected the outcome of the race allowing her to win and gain automatic selection by the TAESC.

It has already been noted in the chapters preceding, that the run leg was 2.2 km short or was missing 22 per cent of the race distance. Nicole Hackett crossed the finish line only six seconds ahead of Carol Montgomery.

At the time of the race, Montgomery had achieved the Olympic qualifying time to represent Canada in the 10,000 m Athletics Track event and was a world class runner, capable of running 10 km in 31 minutes. Hackett on the other hand was a swim specialist whose race plan was to get the biggest lead possible going into the run because, as the run progresses, her running style deteriorates terribly. She was noted for being particularly slow in the last quarter of the 10 km run. At the 1999 world Championships she fell through the field so badly she dropped from the first few off the bike at the second transition to finish in twenty-third place at the completion of 10 km. It was clear that as the run progressed in Perth, Carol Montgomery was running herself into first place. Of course, everyone expected the run to be 10 km. Somehow a mistake was made, and the run finished one lap short. Amongst the chaos, the TAESC stated that the race winner, Nicole Hackett, gained automatic selection because all athletes had run the same course. The error, it was decided, did not alter the race outcome. Amazingly the TAESC determined that the run, though truncated by 22 per cent, would not have impacted on the race outcome. This conclusion was based on an absurd assumption that all athletes, despite running at different speeds for the first 7.8 km (and outrunning Hackett), would have all run at exactly the same speed (that is, at Nicole Hackett's slower pace) for the remaining 2.2 km.

In considering the Perth fiasco, Peter Hayes pointed out that the technical error did affect the race outcome. He provided the basic facts that over a distance of 7.8 km or thereabouts, Montgomery was 1 minute 51 seconds faster than Hackett and was just 6 seconds behind at the end of the shortened run. Even if Hackett had not slowed in the final 2.2 km, she would have lost a further 32 seconds to Montgomery. The almost certain outcome would have been Montgomery gaining a further 1 minute to 1 minute 30 seconds on Hackett. Peter Hayes, QC pointed out that a true-to-form Hackett would have slowed as she always did in the last quarter and most likely finished in ninth or tenth place, although it could have been as low as twenty-fourth place, based upon the faster running times of the top competitors. The probability was that Emma would have finished no worse than fourth in the race.

Henry Jolson, I assumed, listened to Peter Hayes, but not only did he ignore the evidence regarding both selections, he also made an absurd statement when he said words to the effect that because the Olympics were such a pinnacle of sporting achievement and adrenalin is so powerful it would not be considered unusual for an athlete to compete with a broken leg and perform as well as they normally would with an uninjured leg (referring to Harrop's severe injury). I am not sure if I refrained from responding because I had been instructed by Jolson not to do so, because I know and understand Court protocol that I should remain silent, or, because for the first time in my life I was physically speechless at hearing the most stupid thing I had ever heard in my life, plus of course the outrageous bias expressed by Henry Jolson in making such a statement. Needless to say, the Appeal Hearing achieved nothing, Henry Jolson revealed his bias and we all returned to Melbourne.

There was one more demonstration by Henry Jolson of his position at the end of the Hearing. Peter Hayes, Jonathan Forbes and I were putting our papers together and preparing to leave when Henry Jolson stood up and went over to TA Senior Counsel Alan Sullivan QC, and started chatting like a long-lost friend about their CAS roles at the Sydney Olympics, quite oblivious to the fact that all participants of the Appeal Hearing were still present. I said to Hayes that I had never experienced such conduct in a Court Room before. Peter Hayes replied that neither had he and further, it was not the sort of behavior in which he would ever engage. He added that it was not a good sign for Emma.

The day before the final CAS Appeal meeting in Sydney, I was walking towards my parked car between 5.00 p.m. and 6.00 p.m. when my mobile phone rang. To my surprise the name Les McDonald was showing on the face of my phone as the caller. Les was in no mood for greetings or small talk and said, 'David, you need to call the whole thing off.'

I told McDonald that I had no idea what he was talking about. He then, beginning with great difficulty (which was unusual for Les), told me that the result of Emma's CAS Appeal would be a loss for Emma. I was both shocked and angry, responding to him that Australia was not a corrupt Third World Country, that the two additional Appeal Judges were QCs of the highest integrity and that a pre-determined Court decision just didn't happen in Australia.

Les told me to shut up and listen. He went on to tell me that he had done everything he could to convince TA President Bill Walker that TA had made a major selection error in excluding Emma because she had rightly qualified. He also told Bill that the whole Triathlon World believed TA was making a huge mistake with their Olympic Team selection. Les then told me that Bill Walker had told him to mind his own business because National Federations select Team Members and not International Federations. Les also told me that the IOC was 'pissed off' that Australia had so many Appeals still undecided so close to the start of the Games and further that Emma losing her Appeal would cause all other Appeals to be resolved within days.

I disagreed with Les and told him so in no uncertain terms. He then floored me by telling me that having worked for so many years in the sports industry I was still so naive, and I had better believe it. More importantly I had better accept it and break the news to Emma as best I could with his apologies. I told Les that I would tell Emma nothing of the sort and that I would be going to the Appeal in Sydney with Emma's legal team to rightfully claim Emma's place in the team to compete in the Olympics.

Les McDonald apologised, told me to take care of Emma because she 'is a wonderful girl' who has done so much for the sport and was sure she would continue to do so. I thanked Les for caring and for his call.

I was stunned of course but said nothing to Emma. I just could not bring myself to believe the outcome of the CAS Appeal had been decided before the Appeal Hearing.

The next day Peter Hayes, Jonathan Forbes and I travelled to Sydney for the second CAS Appeal. I told Hayes of the conversation with Les McDonald, or at least attempted to. Hayes cut me off saying it was nonsense. He just dismissed it as rubbish, which I found very comforting and only reinforced the automatic rejection of the idea I felt when Les McDonald spoke with me.

The second CAS Appeal was the most formal of all the Appeal Hearings. I was surprised there was no transcript of the proceedings and asked Hayes if that was normal. He said he did not know because he had never been to a formal CAS Appeal before but thought it unusual.

Peter Hayes was in fine form. He presented well, forensically taking apart each witness during cross examination with his astonishing attacking, questioning and sharp mind, which demonstrated his total grasp of the subject matter.

By the time we broke for lunch Emma's appeal was clearly ahead on points won and arguments put forward. Peter Hayes, Jonathan Forbes and I were very confident. In our lunch discussions, Hayes said that he could not remember the last time he was so far in front at this stage, but we should hold the elation because TA may introduce a new piece of evidence that could damage Emma's case. He then added that after all the hearings and knowledge of the facts, he did not believe there was anything that could be introduced that was significant. Jonathan Forbes was in full agreement.

The afternoon session continued much like the morning session and my mind drifted from the proceedings to thinking about how pleased Emma would be when we could call her in an hour or so.

Suddenly, Peter Hayes objected to something, I am still not sure what it was because my mind was elsewhere, and in response Henry Jolson QC mumbled along the lines that if this were a Court of Law he would uphold the objection, but as it was a CAS Appeal he would refuse. Judging by the way Peter Hayes fiddled with his papers and shuffled in his seat I could see that he was furious with Jolson.

The next 45 minutes were a disaster. Jolson closed Hayes down on a number of occasions, made a few comments that clearly concerned Peter Hayes, then closed the Appeal, withdrawing with the two QC's that flanked him. Only once did either of the other two Appeal Judges say anything all day and that was to seek clarification of a point that was already very clear to everyone else in the Courtroom.

After a short wait of about 15–20 minutes Jolson led out the other two Judges onto the Bench and declared that Emma had lost.

We walked out in disbelief. In the lift Hayes broke our silence and said, we need to go for a drink. We walked to the same restaurant where we were all so high-spirited at lunchtime. We sat silently for a few moments with our drinks, then Hayes spoke.

Hayes started by saying that we are all fortunate to live in a country like Australia which is one of the least corrupt countries in the world. Based upon the British legal system the Australian system ensures through its various checks and balances that even if the wrong decision is reached very occasionally then there are transparent processes for putting right those very occasional errors. He continued, saying that in all his years working as a lawyer he has never ever witnessed what had happened today, 'what we witnessed was a Corrupt Process'. Hayes apologised to me, and to Emma in particular for being subjected to this, as there 'is nothing that can be done to reverse it.'

He then told me that all he could do was to refuse to bill Emma for his time because he felt he could not accept fees in such circumstances.

Jonathan Forbes was far more circumspect with his comments. He felt he could not make the same forthright comments as Peter Hayes but said with conviction that the 'result reached today, based on the evidence and arguments presented, was wrong, clearly wrong.' He explained that he had partners to answer to at Freehills and could not just write off fees without consulting them and gaining their acceptance, adding that he would ensure the fees charged, 'would be very substantially reduced as a result of the events of today.' He kept to his word.

To this day, I still struggle to accept what Les McDonald told me about the Appeal result. I still struggle to accept that a Barrister (Peter Hayes) could win just about every argument at a hearing and yet lose, and I still struggle, just as Peter Hayes had done, to accept the CAS Appeal Hearing Judgment.

The words of Peter Hayes, 'today we witnessed a corrupt process', still haunt me today and the image of him saying that is still very much with me.

I decided to tell Emma straight away and I had no option other than to tell her by phone rather than tell her face to face. She was completely devastated.

A couple of weeks later, I received a telephone call from TA CEO Tim Wilson. I took the call just because I couldn't believe he would have anything to say. To my amazement he told me that Emma had outstanding legal representation and the TA Barrister and Solicitors had been very concerned because of the strength of Emma's appeal argument. Tim then went on to suggest that now everything was finished perhaps he and I could continue to be friends and he could sit and have a coffee and a chat with Emma at a race next season.

I told Emma that Tim had called, and she vowed she would never speak to him again. True to her word, I am not aware she ever has.

13. Career Carnage

As soon as the appeal was launched, I moved back to Melbourne. I needed to go home. I needed only those who supported me around me, and all I really trusted now was my immediate family. I felt betrayed by everyone, but most of all I felt I was a failure.

A complete and utter failure.

I was defined by what I achieved in sport, and to not make the Olympic Team to me was an absolute and total failure to achieve what I sought in life.

I removed myself from anything that wasn't close to me personally and even geographically. I consolidated everything so much that I sold my apartment in Sydney and my properties in Noosa.

With the proceeds, I bought a historic terrace house in East Melbourne, a prestigious suburb with views of the city. I was aware financial decisions made with emotion are often bad decisions, but I was so broken, I just wanted to re-group in Melbourne away from everything and everyone involved in triathlon. Property in the area was also extremely sought after, so a 'poor' purchase was almost impossible.

Melbourne was somewhere I could be an insignificant person in a city. Someone who just blended in. I felt I could more easily hide from the world.

Above all, Melbourne was home. I needed to be home.

The other benefit of returning to Melbourne was I could return to the training locations and coaches who I knew had my best interests. There were no hidden agendas, no egos, just people I could trust. I enjoyed being back in the familiar surrounds of Eltham where my bike and run work could return to a high quality. I also returned to where it all began and competed in the Victorian state cross country and athletics competition seasons.

Throughout the appeal process, I trained as if I was selected. I had no choice. I wasn't going to fight for my rightful place on the team and not be ready. Dad kept me up to date with some of the appeal process, but I wanted to keep my involvement to a minimum. Through this time, I lost all hope that anyone in

Australian sport cared about me and how I was coping. I began to realise that safeguards for athletes were missing. Perhaps I had been shafted from the team because I dared to go against TA and refused to be involved with a coach who treated athletes badly. It is all very well to encourage athletes to speak up when abused or mistreated, but who was going to then protect the athlete from retaliation by the national federation when they do? To me the system seemed broken. Gaps were there that could ruin lives forever.

The Sydney 2000 Olympic Games came and went. The Australian Women's Triathlon team didn't provide Australia with an Olympic gold medal as had been expected. Michellie Jones was the best performing Australian triathlete and won a hard-fought silver. The women's winning time was slow, over two minutes slower than the times I raced on that course. It didn't really matter now though.

Swiss women won the gold and bronze that day, and the Swiss Head Coach Rene Kissling commented:

I still can't believe the Aussies didn't select her (Emma Carney) for the Sydney Games. Well, thanks to that mis-selection, we grabbed two medals in the Women's Race. Thank you, Aussie Federation.

The TA selection process was seen as a joke worldwide. It was common knowledge that a hilly bike and run course will always be won by a bike-run specialist, not a swim specialist. The results in Sydney that day proved this yet again.

The men's team didn't deliver a medal at all. To this day I have no idea where the other athletes finished, I never had the strength in me to watch the race.

I won the Noosa Triathlon again in November 2000. I flew in last minute and left as soon as I could. I didn't want to see anyone. I didn't feel nice with TA officials around me, but it was still the fastest time over the course since I last won in 1997. This result alone showed I would have been competitive in the Sydney Olympic Triathlon had I rightfully been allowed to start.

I raced the Australian Sprint Triathlon Championships in Wollongong, just south of Sydney, in mid-November and felt ok but I didn't win. I wasn't sure if it was just me lacking confidence. The race was won in a slow time, so again it probably was me. I thought things over on my warm-down ride back to Sydney and put it down to a very bad year and seeing the awfully shallow people from TA for the first time in a while.

December, I raced the long course nationals without any problems. I ended up with another national title comfortably. Nothing seemed at all important anymore. It was like I was just going through the motions.

At the end of the year I raced the Benalla Triathlon. Benalla is a ninety-minute drive from Melbourne north along the Hume Freeway. It was a race I returned to each year, just after Christmas. I won comfortably, but then again at local races I expected to win easily.

To say I struggled through this period following the Sydney Olympic Games is an understatement of massive proportions. I wasn't the only one though. TA was close to financial ruin having burnt so much money on defending their appalling Olympic team selections. In those days there was a lack of empathy for anyone both racing and officiating. No one cared about anyone, and above all if you stopped winning as an athlete you were discarded immediately. There was no athlete care or wellbeing, so everyone involved in triathlon really just struggled along.

I continued to train in Melbourne and race through the domestic summer season of 2000-2001. Despite still being competitive and still managing podium finishes, I knew there was something wrong. Every race now I had a terrible weakness that hit me at the first sign of an increased effort in a race, slowing me considerably as I tried to continue.

Dad started to notice that in races I was almost stopping mid-stroke in the swim and had no power on the bike and was lacking any impact on the run. He started to ask me what was going on. I just told him I felt tired, because I didn't really have an answer. Dad wasn't a fool though. He saw that I would start a race well, then suddenly slow to a crawl as I managed waves and feelings of fatigue. I suggested maybe I was just down physically and mentally. Maybe I was burnt out.

My 2001 ITU season was nondescript to say the least. I didn't dominate, so I saw the entire year-long campaign as a complete and utter failure. I was still finishing consistently top ten in international ITU events, but to me I might as well have come last.

My Achilles injury also worsened through 2001, so much so that all my morning training sessions had to be preceded by close to an hour of Achilles manipulation. I consistently put my heels on ice after training sessions and the constant ache through my heels was very wearing.

Despite my performance drops, help and coaching assistance started to trickle through from national and state sport institutions. The VIS now had a dedicated triathlon program, and I was provided with testing and coaching support. The

AIS also now had a dedicated triathlon program, with retired triathlete Jackie Gallagher as the program lead.

With a better relationship developing with the VIS, I began to do some of my bike training with the road cycling program. I even took up a few opportunities to race. My riding was still strong at times, and must have caught the attention of VIS coaches, because I was invited to ride the five-day Women's UCI tour event in the Snowy Mountains in NSW for the VIS. This tour was notoriously tough, and I was told I was to support a rider nominated by the VIS as the leader.

It was riding this tour that I spent some time supporting Katie Mactier, who then became a very good friend of mine. Katie also attended Wesley College, although I only had vague memories of her because she was younger than me and several years behind me at school.

Katie is an Australian cycling superstar. She won several national road championships on the bike and later won an Olympic silver medal on the track in the 3000 m pursuit at the Athens 2004 Olympic Games. Katie and I got along really well, until we actually rode together. Then I seemed to annoy the crap out of her. I took my 'supporting' role in the VIS cycling team very seriously, and as I had been told, was to work for Katie. I stuck to her like glue. I didn't know what I was doing, so I constantly asked her during the various stages of the race if she wanted me to do anything. I would try to be helpful by offering food or drink or offering my wheel to sit on as a wind buffer or maybe for me to chase down the leaders. Basically anything.

Usually Katie would tell me where to go, so I would take her not so subtle hint, give up 'helping' her, and ride off. As a result, I ended up the VIS team leader on the road, because I managed to out-ride my teammates. Fortunately, Katie never seemed to care, and we spent most evenings laughing about how broken we all were after the day's racing.

With a little success in bike races late in 2002 and my ever-worsening Achilles injury forcing me out of the Noosa Triathlon, I entered a two-day bike event, the Tour of Bright, held in the Victorian alpine country. Day one consisted of a morning 80 km road race, and afternoon 14 km individual time trial. Day two consisted of a morning ascent up Mt Buffalo (approximately 35 km of mostly uphill) and in the afternoon a flat-out criterium race.

I raced only as I know how, basically off the front and hard. I won everything except the last event, the criterium. By the time I rolled to the start line for this last event I was cooked, completely exhausted. I had to just make sure I didn't get lapped, otherwise I was disqualified and would lose the entire tour lead. I held it together and crept around the looped course, just managing to stay on the tail of what seemed to be a very fast-riding field of cyclists.

My little foray into bike riding gave me a bit of a break from the turmoil of the triathlon world. The 2002 and 2003 seasons of triathlon racing were much of the same. I struggled with increasing tiredness which I couldn't pinpoint, regardless of how many doctors and specialists I saw. I managed to win a few national triathlon series races and qualify for World Championship teams, so to most I seemed to still be racing well. I just didn't dominate the way I once did. Some races my vision became blurred as I exited the water, and in 2002 some results had me finishing way down the back of the field.

It is well documented that my performances started to decline in 1998, but no one, not even I, connected my lack of dominance to anything specific. Signs of my heart condition were not at the time seen as interrelated.

With a controlled warm-up in training, I would gradually increase my heart rate. I would continue the workout as all athletes do, work at a higher intensity through the main set or part of the programmed session, and end with a warm-down. As I was giving my heart time to warm into each training session, I was not going into the red-line, high heart rate area from a low heart rate, so my heart had more time to adapt.

What did not make sense to me during this time, was how my seemingly good training sessions didn't correlate to good races. With hindsight this was all very obvious. When I was racing, I planned structured warm-ups as I did in all of my training sessions. But what happened after my warm-up tended to be 10-15 minutes of official requirements such as marshalling, official introductions, official last-minute briefings, and start protocols. The timing of all of this was determined by television broadcast schedules, technical official requirements and race start procedures. In this time, my heart rate generally dropped. Sure, it was elevated through anticipation, race nerves and the general situation, but I think this was too interrupted a preparation for the heart condition I didn't realise I had. As a consequence, the start of most races had terrible consequences for me.

It now seems it was a miracle those dive starts from the pontoon into the water didn't actually kill me. They required a maximum heart-rate effort in the swim sprint to the first marker, with the added hypoxic complication of holding your breath for greater swim efficiency during that critical stage of the race. These starts would suddenly kick my heart rate up, which was detrimental to my heart. What I felt was an overwhelming fatigue, resulting in the loss of power and speed that almost stopped me mid-stroke. Me being me, rather than stop, I taught myself to back off until this initial wave of fatigue passed. I would then continue, albeit at a much slower pace. The fact that I was even able to race from late 1996 onwards with these problems and remain dominant and competitive, does today make me feel a little proud that I was not in any way what I feared I was becoming at the time: soft.

There were some odd nuances attributed to my heart that didn't fit the norms with the sports scientists at the AIS. One particular visit, I was tested for altitude adaptation. This required us to train normally at sea level, and sleep at altitude. The AIS developed sleeping quarters in the sports science rooms adjusted to simulate altitude. We slept wearing heart monitors in this 'altitude house' with sports scientists monitoring us throughout the night and recording our heart rates at thirty-minute intervals. Altitude is supposed to increase the heart rate up to six beats or thereabouts. I recorded a heart rate of 28, providing so much concern for the sport scientists they woke me from sleep to ensure I was ok.

It was obvious my heart was different from the norm, but we didn't realise my heart was actually damaged. From school until I was tested at the AIS in Canberra, I have always known my heart is different from a regular, 'normal' heart. My Vo2 Max test was high, but I was able to race close to my max for most of the two hours of racing. Along with my 'abnormal' heart, I also had a very efficient lactate tolerance threshold, so I could race and train at close to max heart rate with little to no lactic acid build up, remaining faster for longer than my competitors.

I was always proud of my heart. I was told it was very large, didn't beat as often as most, but when it did it was vastly more efficient than a 'normal' human heart. To me that was always good news, to be the best in the world you must have a point of difference. My heart provided this.

With my mindset of racing only to win, the racing and training at close to maximum heart rate had a cost. Unknowingly, I started to 'scar' my heart, as I pushed my body to its absolute limit. Racing the 1996 World Championships was most likely, according to my cardiologists, the start of the scarring. The inability of the heart to repair, coupled with the sheer intensity my training and racing added, bit by bit, to the damage. The accumulated damage increasingly impacted on my racing. This is what my cardiologists thought was happening from late 1996 onwards.

So, with the hindsight of the knowledge of my physiological make up, the impact of my focussed mindset and the developing heart condition, those early feelings of fatigue in 1997 were just the start of a steady decline into poor performances — poor, at least, for me. Yet, in 2003, I was still competitive in world terms and very much part of the TA elite group building to the 2004 Athens Olympic Games.

Around March of 2004 I decided to spend some time at the AIS in Canberra to see if I could make a difference and put together a decent block of training, with support. I always respected the AIS and thought if anything in Australia can get me back on track, the AIS can. TA refused to assist my stay financially, but I wasn't at all surprised by their continued negativity towards me. I trained with the AIS swim squad and ran with the AIS runners who trained under renowned distance coach Dick Telford. I seemed to be making progress and headed overseas in late June of 2004 with the Australian Triathlon Team. I was feeling a little more positive.

The first stop for the Australian team was Edmonton, Canada, for an ITU race. I raced Edmonton the year before and was familiar with the area. TA had opted for a cheap student accommodation option at a local University. Following a long-haul flight, I generally found I was more vulnerable to stirring up my Achilles, calf and lower leg problems. So, my first few days in Edmonton were spent doing some easy rides and an easy swim, all generally on the course. As each session was light, I felt ok, perhaps a little lethargic, but that was understandable following a twenty-plus hour, long-haul flight from home.

Little did I know, everything was about to completely fall apart.

14. An Athlete's Broken Heart

I knew something was wrong a long time before my heart condition was diagnosed.

It is an odd irony that if I had simply damaged a muscle anywhere else on my body it would have been picked up far earlier because every other muscle has a pain sensor. The heart muscle has no sensory feelings, so it wasn't a question of me feeling any pain that comes with normal muscle damage. For a diagnosis I would have had to accept the worsening problems of shortness of breath, dizziness, extreme fatigue, blurred vision, and poor fitness development, recognise that it wasn't just me being soft, and then ask for help. I was never someone who asked for help easily. I also thought that if I said anything to anyone, I would be seen to be looking for excuses. So, the result was that my heart needed to become so damaged it actually failed before I sought help. I was on the verge of sudden death before anyone knew about it.

In Edmonton, the first Australian triathlon team swim session was late morning on 8 July 2004.

I will never forget that date.

The entire squad trained as a group and we booked the local 50 m pool for the purpose. We swam at the 1978 Commonwealth Games venue. The session was typical for two days out from a race. Good warm-up, and a shorter main set peppered with some close-to-max efforts. Short and concise training, designed to get your body moving again, firing up your race speed and then backing off to avoid training fatigue. I felt good. In the last half of the main set we were doing some 100 m repeats as 50 m fast, 50 m easy, mixing up the effort on the fast 50 m. I had done around ten — I think we were doing twelve — when I suddenly felt a weakness wash over me. I backed off on the effort and swam to the wall for a slow time.

'Oh no!' I remember thinking to myself. 'Not now!'

Pushing off the wall, I felt my heart rate suddenly increase. I swam the last two juggling my increasing fatigue and feeling my heart race. I first thought I was now suffering from some sort of panic or anxiety attack, brought on being worried about the whole fatigue thing that was now today affecting me in training. I did not know it at the time, but it was a lot more serious than that. I was having my first major cardiac episode.

I finished the last two reps and was relieved we only had a short warm-down of 400-500 m. I finished the warm-down, with my heart racing, feeling fatigued and terribly out of breath. I got out of the pool as soon as my warm-down was done. I knew I needed to get changed.

Once out of the water on the pool deck, the heavy atmosphere of the indoor pool seemed to make my breathing harder. I changed as quickly as possible but spent a bit of time sitting on the bench in the changeroom trying to get my breath. Some of my teammates started to enter the changeroom and I told them 'I felt off'. There wasn't really much they could do though. We all had a race in a few days time, and that was really everyone's focus. Becoming lightheaded, the last thing I wanted to do was pass out while half dressed. I also wanted to get outside to fresh air, to see if that helped my breathing to improve.

To exit the pool, I had to walk up a flight of about thirty steps. This absolutely took all my effort. I was becoming quite concerned with my heart still pounding in my chest. Once outside I put my bags down and put my hands on my head to see if I could open my lungs. I often did this after a race and found it worked. Today all I could feel was my heart thumping away and shaking my body with its aggressive beat.

I thought I would be able to perhaps breathe a little easier outside, but I could not.

Standing there, waiting for the rest of the team and coaches to get themselves together, the first familiar face I saw was then TA High Performance Manager Bill Davoren. He had only just arrived from Australia that day. He said, 'Hi,' and asked me how I was.

I replied with, 'I don't feel well, and my heart is racing after that swim session.'

Bill obviously asked the question to make conversation rather than actually caring about my response, given he said, 'Oh well, let's get you back to the accommodation for lunch.'

Any elite triathlete under a team manager's care complaining of a racing heart should never be brushed off. The Australian triathlon community had been rocked in 1999 when Australian legend Greg Welch suffered a number of heart episodes during the swim leg of the Hawaiian Ironman Triathlon World

Championship. He never raced again, and had a defibrillator implant a short time later. The triathlon world knew of heart problems, particularly the Australian triathlon world.

For the first time ever, I didn't really want to be left alone. I felt vulnerable.

Despite being the most successful triathlon team on the planet, to get the Australian triathlon team together was like herding cats. Eventually everyone was out of the pool area and gathering at the carpark and ready to board the minibus. I asked if I could ride shotgun, because I needed to keep the window open for air. No one put up an argument, so I climbed in, with my heart still racing.

As the minibus crawled along, stuck in the Edmonton traffic, I found myself increasingly struggling to breathe. Sitting down seemed to make my chest feel tighter. I told the driver, a TA Team Coach, I couldn't breathe. He just looked at me. When he stopped at some traffic lights, I opened the door and stepped out, hoping it would be easier to get air into my lungs outside.

A few people in the bus started yelling at me to get back in. The lights changed and the TA Coach driving the minibus started yelling at me too.

I asked someone to pass my bag.

I tried to explain that I couldn't breathe. I could not say a lot. My breathing hadn't improved. In fact, it seemed even worse.

'Just pass me my bag.'

The bus started to drive off before it came to a sudden halt, and the Team Physio jumped out. I was so thankful that he did.

He started talking, but I interrupted him. I needed to make him panic, because I suddenly realised that I was losing the ability to breathe. My chest was becoming crushingly tight and the fatigue was overwhelming. I told him I needed help; I told him I thought I was in trouble, serious trouble.

His response was to look alarmed, drop his bag and run off. Given he dropped his bag, I assumed he was going to return. I couldn't afford to panic or think he wasn't.

I remember I felt peaceful if I closed my eyes while I lay on the ground. Too peaceful, almost like I was slipping away. I really thought I was going to die.

The Team Physio returned with a cab. Luckily the cab driver realised I needed an ambulance instead. Soon I was surrounded by paramedics who were amazed and concerned at how long my heart had been racing. It had been over an hour.

In the back of the ambulance the paramedics cut my T-Shirt and my one good bra and started sticking defibrillator pads to me. One of them flicked my feet. I couldn't feel anything. Someone explained that my body was shutting down and they had to give me a shock.

Suddenly I realised what was about to happen. Trying to rip the pads off, I yelled at them to stop. I couldn't, and a bolt of electricity smashed through my chest. It hurt like I was hit by a truck, but without the blood and broken bones. Ripping at the pads again, I went beserk.

The paramedics apologised and explained I had been in Ventricular Tachycardia (VT) for so long I was at risk of full cardiac arrest and sudden death. My heart was no longer racing and my whole body felt calmer, but as the ambulance made its way to the University of Alberta Hospital, I kept my arms crossed and remained wary about further attempts at defibrillation.

In Emergency at the hospital I was given a hospital gown. In a cardiac ward you wear these with the seam at the front, I discovered, and rigged up to a cardiac machine. Sticky pads were placed all over my chest to monitor my heart, along with some defibrillator pads just in case there were more episodes. I was adamant that they were not going to zap me again.

Between cardiac nurses keeping an ever-watchful eye on me, various doctors came and went. Initially the main question I was asked was whether I had insurance. 'Yes,' I replied to about four different people. When I responded with a yes, the fourth time, I asked why they kept asking me this. I told them I was travelling with the Australian Team under the Australian Sports Commission Athlete Travel Insurance. That seemed to settle everyone on this subject and presumably the hospital accountants could relax.

The next lot of questions I faced related to drugs. I had several doctors come into my cubicle and ask me quietly, 'Between you and me, what performance enhancing drugs are you using?' The first few doctors left when I said 'what?' Again, after about four visits from different people, I said, 'I have never taken drugs, why do you keep asking that?' I was told it was hospital procedure to ask elite athletes presenting with a heart condition if they took performance enhancing drugs, because diagnosis would be easier. Bloody hell. Could this day get any worse?

I must have been in Emergency for a while before anyone from TA turned up. It seemed to be early evening when the Team Physio returned with Jackie Gallagher and Bill Davoren. Jackie had retired from triathlon shortly after 2000, and was now the AIS U23 Program Head, so was travelling with the team. Jackie and I actually got along pretty well now we weren't racing, so it was good to have her there. The main doctor looking after me came into my cubicle and debriefed them all. They were told I had suffered from Ventricular Tachycardia and would need to spend a few days in the Intensive Care Unit (ICU), as I needed to be monitored. Jackie couldn't resist reverting to our competitive days and asked the doctor if he was sure I had a heart. She explained that when we were racing, she thought I was heartless.

I reacted and said, 'Bloody hell Jackie. This is serious.'

Jackie laughed, and the doctor looked nervous, probably wondering if he was informing my enemy about my medical details, not my friends.

When the doctor finished talking, he left us all alone to chat. Jackie asked me if I wanted anything. I said, 'Yes, please, I need my stuff taken out of my room, including my bike and all my race gear,' and asked if she could pack it all up. I knew the Australian team was leaving on Sunday for a training camp in Aix Les Bains, France. Today was Thursday, and the doctor had just said I needed to spend at least three days in ICU. It was not known how long I would have to remain in hospital.

When I raced in Edmonton the previous year, I had a homestay with a local family, Carmen and Gary Hansen, so I told Jackie to speak to the Edmonton race organiser Sheila O'Kelly about sending my gear to them.

I also insisted that Jackie call my Dad. At first, she said she would call him at a better time in Australia. I said, 'Jackie just call him. Don't delay it. My parents have the right to know asap. Please don't delay this call.' I knew the longer Jackie took to make this call, the more annoyed my Dad would be.

Bill Davoren said nothing up to this point. Jackie turned to him and said, 'Bill? Anything to add?' Bill looked around nervously and said he didn't like hospitals. They made him nervous.

'Not my favourite place either, Bill,' I said.

Bill closed his unhelpful visit with, 'So that's all ok. We call your Dad and move your gear?'

'Yeah Bill, that's all,' I replied.

He then told me he needed to go and have dinner.

I had had enough of Bill that day. His lack of care for my well-being was annoying me. I felt it was completely wrong to be treated like this. A human life is important, regardless of whether you are an elite athlete or not. To take time out to care for others should be at the forefront of the mind of a High Performance Manager. This is basic human compassion and I didn't seem to be receiving any of that from him.

The role of a High Performance Manager is not all about training and planning athletes' lives. A large part is also about making sure the athlete is cared for when their career goes off track or adversity hits. High performance coaching is about looking after the complete athlete, and not just the athlete who is winning at the time.

They all then left. None of them visited me again, although Jackie did call to let me know she moved my gear. Two younger athletes came to see me, just before the team left for their camp in France. They had seen the chaos on the bus and seemed a little spooked from witnessing the entire ordeal.

The doctor returned to my cubicle shortly after everyone left and asked me if I was ok. He said they didn't seem that helpful; was I sure I didn't need anyone else contacted? I said it was ok. I was tired. They would do as I asked eventually.

It seemed to be late at night before it was decided I was stable enough to be moved. I was taken to the ICU in the cardiac ward. In ICU I felt like I was on death row, or at least everyone seemed to be expecting me to die. Maybe I was just oversensitive, but I was a little surprised when I woke up in the morning to find I was still alive. My heart felt strained in my chest, like a tightness. I was rigged up to a heart monitoring machine that had cords long enough for me to go to the toilet, but not get to my door. I was testing out the range of movement when a nurse entered the room.

'We thought you were up. Your heart rate jumped up,' she said.

I realised then I was on a twenty-four-hour monitor and anything I did was going to be picked up by the nurses.

There wasn't really much to do. I didn't particularly like the food, and I really didn't feel hungry yet. Nurses checked on me every hour, which made me nervous. I never had this much attention regarding my health before and I felt like everyone was expecting something bad to happen. I still felt tight in my chest and I was still wearing those frightening defibrillator pads.

Lying there, I just listened to the nurses caring for the other patients. Everyone seemed to be in a pretty bad way and the nurses were on edge all the time. Maybe it was just me in this strange environment.

Just after breakfast a nurse came in with a telephone on a trolley and told me someone was on the phone for me. I took the phone and said, 'Hello.' Dad was on the other end and unleashed.

'Emma is that you? What the hell is going on? Are you alright? Is anyone there from TA looking after you? I'm coming over to get you home.'

'Dad!' I replied. 'If you keep yelling, I'm going to hang up.'

'No!' Dad yelled. 'It has taken me ages to get through to you. No one from TA knows where you are.'

To be honest, I had no idea what was going on, and I had no idea where I was either. I knew I had a heart episode called Ventricular Tachycardia and was in danger of dying. I knew I was now in ICU and all I wanted to do was to go home.

Dad calmed down, and I asked him to organise a few things so I could return to Australia. I told him not to come over to see me, because more than anything I hate sympathy and I hate people sitting and looking at me in hospital. I already had nothing to do and I didn't want to talk to anyone.

Instead I asked Dad to sort out my travel insurance as I was pretty sure there was going to be a hefty claim from my stay here, and to organise for TA to fly me home. It was the least they could do. I didn't want to fly anything but Qantas too, just in case they wanted to find a cheap flight to make this trip any worse.

I also suggested Dad contact the AIS and ask the doctors there to recommend the best cardiologist in Melbourne who could see me when I got home. I didn't think TA would follow anything up and reminded Dad of the time Brad Beven was hit by a car on the actual race site, the day before the Olympic trials in 2000, and no one from TA even bothered to contact him, let alone visit him. That crash ended his career too. Dad agreed TA was not going to help much and agreed to stay in Australia and follow up on all these things.

We then chatted and Dad told me his aunt (Grandma Carney's sister) had lived in Edmonton and suffered a heart attack, only to die in this same hospital. I thanked Dad for the uplifting story. Our conversation wound up, so I hung up, and thought, 'Oh well. At least Mum and Dad now know what happened and where I am.'

I received another call. This time it was Australian triathlete Greg Welch. Greg was always an athlete who took time for others. He was a trail blazer in the sport of triathlon, and always shared his knowledge. Greg, having been through a heart condition diagnosis and now with a defibrillator implant gave me a pep talk and asked me to be careful. It was a very nice call to receive.

Then perhaps mid-morning I had a visitor.

A nurse came to my room and said, 'You have a visitor — his name is Les McDonald.'

Les was of course the ITU President. I decided to give him a hard time, just to amuse myself.

'Nope. Never heard of him.' I replied.

I heard the nurse return to Les and tell him that I told her I didn't know him, and Les reply with an exasperated, 'What?!' He seemed to be negotiating his way in. The nurse came to my door again, with Les behind her. She asked again, 'Are you sure you don't know this man?'

I looked at Les and laughed. 'No, never seen him before!'

Les started to protest and tell the nurse I was being absurd. He was the ITU President. The nurse asked me again if I was sure I didn't know him.

'Maybe he does look familiar,' I muttered.

Les laughed, made his way into my room, grabbed a chair, and said, 'Very funny, Carney.'

I'm not sure why I did that to Les, but it was nice to finally have someone near me who seemed to care. Up to this point everyone I knew had no particular interest in me and didn't even seem to give the slightest second thought for my welfare. I think subconsciously I was testing Les to really, really see if he wanted to check in on me to see if I was ok. He did, and it meant a lot.

Les sat with me for a long time. He was a great storyteller. Initially Les spoke about me. He was never one to shower me, or anyone, with accolades. He had never actually congratulated me on anything that I could remember, but he sat down and reeled off all my wins, called me the greatest triathlete that he had ever seen, and said that my dominance was probably never going to be beaten. I looked at Les and given he was talking so highly of me, I thought maybe the nurses had told him I was going to die.

I asked Les if he was feeling ok, because he had never spoken so highly of me before. 'Just take some praise when it is due, Emma,' he told me.

Sometime later over a beer, he confided to my Dad that he had called the hospital late in the day I was admitted. The doctor told him that he was not certain I would survive and that the first twenty-four hours would be critical for me.

'What are you doing, why are you saying this stuff?' I asked Les. He looked at me and said, 'You almost bloody died.'

'Really?'

We both looked at each other as if the other was nuts.

'No, I was ok. The paramedics almost killed me, but I was in control,' I replied with assurance.

Les then explained to me that given the lack of response from TA Team Management, the severity of my heart episode, and the length of time it took to get medical help, I was bloody lucky to be alive.

He then went into a rant about TA on a whole series of topics and was very critical of certain individuals.

'It doesn't matter Les. I have never liked them anyway,' I said and that seemed to settle him down.

Les was always an individual who put athletes first. He always felt a personal responsibility and connection to all the triathletes on the circuit and cared about every one of them. Not just the elite performers, everyone; those winning races and those that were always toiling at the back end of the field.

He stayed with me for quite a while and asked if I had spoken to Dad. Les told me he had called Dad earlier, and let him know which hospital I was in. He was also trying to find out what the doctors were doing. I filled Les in on what I had asked Dad to organise. He said he would follow up with Dad and my homestay from the year before.

Les visited me every day until he had to fly out of Edmonton and go to the next event on the ITU calendar. Along with Les, Loreen Barnett (ITU Vice President), and Sheila O'Kelly (the Edmonton Race Director) also visited me a number of times. Each of them took time out of their busy schedules to see how I was going, proving that those in charge of the ITU really did put athlete wellbeing first. In comparison, by the time the entire Australian team had left the country, not a single TA staff member checked back in to see how I was going. Not a single visit. TA had never really treated me well, but this lack of support amazed me.

My stay in Edmonton Hospital ended up being twelve days long. I was in ICU for three days then moved to the general cardiac ward. Fortunately, I was in my own room, because I was by far the youngest in the entire ward. I met a number of the patients. Some had been in hospital for months waiting for heart transplants. They seemed to find me a bit of a novelty, all loved the sound of Australia, and the word got out I was an elite athlete so there was always someone who wanted to have a chat. Between meeting patients, I was also able to watch the Tour de France live on TV. For the first time ever, I saw every stage in its entirety without the struggle of the time difference I would normally suffer if I watched from Australia. To further boost my hospital TV habit, I also managed to get a number of the student doctors, who were Indian, to recommend the good Bollywood movies on the movie channel. I found my visits from doctors became a little longer, as we first discussed heart procedure updates then disected the TV guide.

My homestay family also dropped in. Gary and Carmen came to see me every day, and I thanked them for picking all my stuff up and putting it in their house.

269

I had been told by doctors that once I was discharged from hospital, I needed to remain in Canada for two weeks before returning to Australia. Carmen said she hoped I would stay. I again thanked them, unsure how I could ever repay them.

Between the socialising, TV watching, and visits, my heart condition needed to be investigated. I had a number of tests done, but I think I was a complicated patient. I got the impression the doctors wanted to make sure I was stable enough to get home, where Australian cardiologists could diagnose me fully. My extremely low resting heart rate was regularly setting off alarms as I was constantly monitored day and night.

For some reason I copied down the hospital notes from two days after my attack, 10 July. They read:

Patient has had a time of 'being off' for the last few years while competing in triathlon. Problems with weakness while running in the past sound like she may have been symptomatic for a while, but possibly in denial.

I had all the basic tests: blood tests, chest x-rays, an electrocardiogram and an MRI. For the MRI, I was disappointed to learn, I had to go completely into the claustrophobic tunnel. I had had many MRIs before but only for my lower legs (being a runner), so I had avoided this my entire career. I didn't let on that I was worried about going into the machine, and instead just hoped I didn't panic while in there.

Everything managed to go ahead ok.

The final test was conducted on 16 July, it was an electrophysiology (EP) study. This was done to assess my heart's electrical activity and is used to diagnose abnormal heart rhythms (arrhythmias). The test was performed by inserting catheters, and then wire electrodes, through the blood vessels in the groin and up into the heart, to measure electrical activity inside the heart itself. This procedure was the most invasive, and I was sedated throughout. It didn't provide a sound answer to my problem and my recovery from the EP study went a little pear-shaped. I was taken up to my wardroom after the procedure and had to remain lying down for three hours with ice at the groin site to prevent bruising. I was half sedated, so it wasn't really a problem for me to follow those instructions. By the time the three hours passed, there had been a nurse shift change. My new nurse came in and told me I could now get up out of bed. This must be a normal instruction to give a patient, but I don't think this nurse had had me as a patient yet. I felt pretty ordinary, but me being me thought if I am allowed to get up I might as well do it. I decided to go to the toilet, maybe have a shower. Once I was in the toilet, I felt awful, dizzy, suddenly sweaty, and like I was going to pass out. Aborting my toilet trip, I tried to get back to the safety of my bed. Unfortunately, I never made it. I passed out, smashed my heart monitor when I hit the ground and in doing so set off the code blue hospital alarm in the entire cardiac ward.

When I came to, my room was full of doctors and nurses and my face was streaming blood. I managed to split my eyebrow, requiring five stitches, and cracked two teeth. Everything else was fine, except that all the other patients in the ward thought I had had another heart episode.

Due to the black eye and vertigo problems I managed to extend my stay another three days.

Finally, on 19 July, I was released from hospital. I didn't look good — I had a black eye, stitches in my head and a couple of broken teeth — but apparently a stable-enough heart to get back to Australia. I was given a daily dose of beta blocker Metoprolol to hopefully suppress any arrhythmias. The hospital doctors gave me an envelope with test results for my doctors in Australia, told me I couldn't fly for another two weeks, and 'to be careful'. The doctor's notes provided the following for my Australian cardiologists:

Patient admitted to ICU after electrical cardioversion in ER. While in hospital, was stable with no reoccurrences of Vtach. MRI of heart showed no evidence of R ventricular dysplasia. ECHO showed no N function. Electrophysiology did not identify any re-entrant pathway, dx was idiopathic VT episode of syncope after EP study.

The doctor also required me to return on Wednesday, 21 July to have the stitches removed from my head.

Once released from hospital, I felt very vulnerable, because for the first time in twelve days my heart was not monitored. I had no idea what the doctors meant with 'be careful'. I interpreted it to mean you can still exercise, but nothing excessive. I also thought I should carry my phone every time I went anywhere. I wasn't told to specifically stop exercise, so I assumed that was ok in moderation.

During the two weeks at the Hanson's in Edmonton I managed to drag Gary out for a few runs, taking my phone each time. I felt ok, maybe a little weak because I had lost quite a bit of weight while in hospital. I enjoyed my time with Carmel and Gary, but I was looking forward to getting back to Australia.

Finally, two weeks later, I boarded my Qantas flight home. Before I left Canada, I did a little research and was pleased to read every Qantas aircraft carries several defibrillators on board. Nice to know.

Fortunately, I never required the use of the Qantas defibrillator. My trip across the Pacific Ocean to Australia was nice and uneventful. I went straight home to Mum and Dad's place in Eltham.

While I was in hospital in Canada, Dad contacted the then TA President and asked him to contact the AIS doctors requesting a referral to the best Cardiologist in Melbourne. Associate Professor Kieran Fallon, Head of Sports Medicine at the AIS organised a referral for Professor Richard Harper at Monash Medical Centre in Clayton. I had an appointment organised for 9 August. All I had to do between arriving back in Australia and my appointment with Professor Harper was to be sensible. Unfortunately, on 8 August, exactly a month following my heart episode in Edmonton, it appears I was not sensible enough.

It was early morning, and being quite frustrated with not exercising, and also sick of carrying a phone while running, I convinced Dad to come on his mountain bike while I jogged. That way he could carry the phone in his pocket. Dad agreed on the condition that I didn't run too fast. We headed out from Mum and Dad's place in Eltham to my favourite loop of undulating trails, around to Westerfolds Park and back. I felt pretty good and tried to stay ahead of Dad on the bike. We were about halfway when a weak feeling suddenly washed over me. I stopped in my tracks. In fact, I stopped so abruptly Dad almost rode into me. I looked at my heart rate monitor; my heart rate was 220 bpm.

'Dad, I'm in VT.'

Dad looked alarmed.

'We will have to call an ambulance.'

Dad gave me his phone, and I dialled 000.

Once I made the selection for Ambulance, I was talking to someone straight away. I was asked what was wrong.

'I'm in VT, but its ok. Last time I sustained this rhythm for over an hour,' I told them.

'You will not be waiting an hour. What is your location?' was the response.

I suddenly realised I was in the middle of a park, which to run around is 5-7 km, depending on which way you go.

'I'm in Westerfolds Park. Probably the closest entrance is the twenty-four-hour entrance off Fitzsimmons Lane, Templestowe,' I guessed.

I was asked to remain where I was, but I said I would make my way to the entrance, as I had someone with me.

On hanging up Dad said, 'What are we doing?'

I replied, 'We need to head to the edge of the Park, where an ambulance will meet us.'

As we made our way through the park, I could feel my heart racing in my chest. I had to be careful I didn't rush and elevate it further. Very quickly, we could hear the ambulance coming: full siren, full noise.

'How embarrassing,' I said to Dad, 'I hope no one recognises me.'

As Dad and I neared the twenty-four-hour entrance, the Ambulance arrived. I walked over and they insisted I lie on a stretcher.

'Come on. Let me climb in. This is embarrassing. Someone might see me...' I protested, always the compliant patient.

It was useless. I was forced to lie on the stretcher. Once inside the ambulance, I lost another T-shirt and bra as the paramedic fixed defibrillator pads to my chest. One of the paramedics said, 'Hello Emma.' I looked at him. He did look familiar: it was one of my classmates from school.

Awkward.

The ambulance started to make its way to Box Hill Hospital. I asked them if we could go to Monash Medical Centre because I had an appointment to see my cardiologist there tomorrow. Apparently, ambulances can only go to the closest hospital, so Box Hill was my only option. The paramedics asked me to try taking a drug to see if the arrhythmia would stop. I told them the only way I could be fixed is through a shock. They asked me to try anyway, but nothing worked.

We were probably about halfway to Box Hill Hospital when suddenly the ambulance stopped, and I was moved into a MICA ambulance. I was told the MICA ambulance is better equipped for cardiac arrests.

Finally, we made it to Box Hill Emergency. I made sure the paramedics told Dad where I was going before they left as he had to ride home after I left in the ambulance.

It seemed like I was in Emergency for ages. Nothing would slow my VT. An anaesthetist was called so I could be defibrillated. While I was in Emergency, my symptoms became worse. I felt awful. Just terrible. I was also losing patience with waiting for treatment.

At one stage two police officers brought in someone whom they had arrested and needed medical treatment for drug use. He was really violent, and the nurses struggled to contain him. In an attempt to control his fists, he was handcuffed to a hospital bed. His yelling and abuse were unbelievable. I had never witnessed that before and I can't believe ER staff have to put up with that. One of the officers came to my cubicle and apologised for the noise and disruption. I told him I felt awful for them and the nurses, and I offered to use his gun to shoot the arsehole if he liked. The policeman of course declined. Fortunately, my anaesthetist arrived just in time.

By this stage I felt really bad. I had lost all my patience, was struggling to breathe, and felt sick, light-headed, and dizzy. The anaesthetist bound in and said, 'Hi Emma. I was an anaesthetist for your sister Clare when she had a hamstring procedure done.' He then asked, 'How are you going? How is your training going?'

I couldn't believe it. Full of sarcasm I said, 'Oh I'm great. Everything is going to plan. These heart episodes are excellent signs of my progress right now.'

With that comment the anaesthetist said, 'Right, let's put you under then. You are going to now feel a little sleepy.'

As I drifted off, I hoped to God I hadn't offended him too much. After all he was now in control of my life.

When I came to, I had been cardioverted and felt a lot better. I was transferred up to the cardiac ward, which this time was in a public hospital. I was in a room with five others: men and women who were at least forty years older than me. That night I heard noises that put me off growing old. I heard farts that ended badly, snoring that would have woken the dead, and at one stage I saw old balls. I asked the nurses to pull my curtains tightly closed, because there was stuff going on I could never un-see.

The next morning, having made it through a very disturbing night, I was just trying to work out if I could leave when the paramedics who had picked me up the day before came to visit me and see how I had got on. When they came in to see me, I begged with them to tell the nurses they had been asked to transfer me to Monash Medical Centre. I explained to them what had been going on all night and I needed to get out.

The paramedics just laughed at me and said they could get me a coffee. (The paramedics were actually so good to me I called the CEO of Ambulance Victoria and asked him if he wanted to do a publicity shoot, whereby I discussed how good the paramedics are in Victoria. I felt it was the least I could do. Some positive publicity for a change, not the negative stuff you tend to hear. We did the shoot and a story was run in the *Herald Sun* newspaper, and I think also on the free-to-air television news. It's very fortunate I took the time to set this up, because the paramedic I worked with was a guy called Phil Smith. He ended up saving my sister Clare's life some eight years later.)

Finally, I was allowed to leave Box Hill Hospital, and discharged with another envelope of notes. Mum picked me up and we went straight to Monash Hospital to finally have my first appointment with Professor Richard Harper.

Professor Harper's waiting room seemed to be full of elderly people. I sat there thinking I was for sure going to be ok and back racing soon. I didn't look that bad. Margaret, the Professor's Personal Assistant, asked me to fill in some paperwork. She was a little intimidating. Suddenly everything seemed a little serious and I felt nervous. Deep down I still hoped I didn't have a heart problem, and everything had been exaggerated in Canada.

Before long, I was sitting before Professor Harper. The 'Prof', as I now call him, initially intimidated me. I am not sure why, because he is probably the kindest person I have ever met. He looked professorial to me. A bit older, with glasses and quietly spoken. His desk was piled high with patient files, so he also looked damn busy. There were all sorts of plastic models of hearts scattered throughout his room, on his windowsills, and right in front of me. I looked at the model heart and was a little disturbed that it looked quite as complicated as it did. I was still hoping for a cure at this stage and being complicated didn't help things.

I handed him the two envelopes, from each of my hospital stays, feeling a little embarrassed I had spent the previous night in hospital. Obviously, I shouldn't have gone for a run. He asked me how last night was and I said something along the lines of 'disturbing'. I didn't want to say too much, in case he thought I was an idiot for ending up in hospital.

The Prof told me the doctors in Canada had not come up with a diagnosis for my condition. That is, they were not able to explain why I had the episode of VT. I was clearly not a straightforward case and to diagnose me, more tests would need to be done. Even then he wasn't sure that he would be able to diagnose my condition. He gave me the strong impression that even if a diagnosis could be made it was unlikely that my heart could be returned to normal. He was amazed that I had been defibrillated whilst still awake and he was even more amazed that the TA team bus had driven off leaving me on the roadside where I could have easily died.

'Imagine the scandal if that had happened,' he told me.

I had an ECG done in his rooms, and he commented on my low resting heart rate. I think it was about 33 bpm sitting down.

Over the next few weeks I did a number of tests ordered by Professor Harper as my heart diagnosis was made. Following each test, I had to return to see what the next test was. I was getting a little impatient, because I wanted a diagnosis, and a fix, so I could return to racing.

On one particular occasion, he said we are going to have to do a stress test. I asked what that involved, and what the Prof said was music to my ears:

'You will have to run to exhaustion on a treadmill.'

'What?! When can we do that?!' I asked. I couldn't believe I was going to be allowed to run flat out again.

The Prof told me to come back in two weeks.

Two weeks later, I arrived at Monash Heart for my stress test. I had my racing flats on, my running gear and I was really looking forward to 'running to exhaustion'. When it was my turn to be tested, I was told to put a gown on, with the opening forward, and to take everything from my waist up off. I stood in my change cubicle trying to work out if I heard them correctly. Was I supposed to run topless? I decided to leave my running bra top on and exited the cubicle. There was no way I could run with a gown on: I was planning on running flat out. I was promptly told to put the gown on and take my bra top off. I told them to shove it — who did they think I was to run topless? — and stormed off to tell the Prof I couldn't do the test.

The Prof's rooms were only a minute's walk from 'Monash Heart', the dedicated heart specialised procedure area of the hospital. I waited for him to finish with his current patient and told him the test was impossible, given I was required to run topless. He looked at me really blankly and told me to follow him. We went back to the testing room, and a discussion ensued as to how I could be tested while running in a bra top. I couldn't believe this was such a problem for everyone. I couldn't believe people did this test topless.

The Prof organised everyone, and pads were stuck on my chest, under my bra, allowing my heart readings to take place. I thanked him, and I got myself ready to run.

'How long does this test take?' I asked.

'We don't normally get past 6-8 minutes,' I was told.

'What?' I thought. 'Eight minutes??'

'It will have to be going fast if you want exhaustion in eight minutes. How fast does this thing go?' I asked.

'We start at 5km/hr,' I was told.

'That's a walk?' I said.

I suddenly realised my expectation for the test was completely different from the test that was 'normal' in a heart hospital.

'If you want me to get to exhaustion, this is going to take over an hour. I need to be running at 20 km per hour or sub-3-minute kilometres to trigger VT,' I informed everyone.

Everyone in the room looked at me.

'This is a thirty-minute booking,' I was told.

I gave up trying to get everyone to understand what I needed. The test started and I began walking. The treadmill increased in speed and incline every 2-3 minutes. The incline increases completely annoyed me, because it badly affected my Achilles. I decided to ignore that particular pain today. As the test progressed, I was still walking. It was about fifteen minutes before I even considered breaking into a jog. Finally, I started running. As the treadmill approached 13 km per hour, I began to stretch out and enjoy myself, but at 23 minutes, the machine cut out and I almost ran off the front of the treadmill as it shut down.

I looked at everyone in the room.

'What's happened?' I asked.

'I think we have got to the end of the test,' someone said.

'That's it?'

I was really disappointed. I had been looking forward to a good solid workout, and all I really got was about 2, maybe 3, kilometres of jogging and a hell of a lot of walking. I got myself changed and went to see the Prof again. I told the Prof what had happened, and I said if they really wanted to test me, the treadmill test needed start at 12 km per hour and increase every 3 minutes by 1 km per hour. By the time the treadmill hits 20 km per hour I should be in VT. I also asked that the treadmill remain flat for the entirety of the test, because my Achilles couldn't handle the incline and the incline affected speed, which was ultimately what I needed to trigger my heart.

The Prof just looked at me. I think I had said enough. He explained that my tests to date suggested that the right ventricle was not working as well as it should and that this was probably the source of my VT. He also told me that he wanted my case to be jointly handled by a close colleague, Dr Jeffrey (Jeff)

Alison, who is a leading Cardiologist and Heart Electrophysiologist. The Prof had already discussed my case with Jeff and they both agreed that the next step should be to repeat the electrophysiology (EP) study I had done in Canada. This time Jeff hoped to induce my arrhythmia, map it and ablate it, with the intention of a complete cure of the VT. The Prof then told me it is very hard to estimate the chance of achieving this, but it is probably less than a fifty per cent chance.

My mind, always looking for a cure for my heart, processed the fifty per cent to mean one hundred per cent cure.

'Ok. When will we do this?' I asked eagerly.

A few weeks later, I was admitted to Jessie McPherson Private Hospital at Monash Medical Centre. I met Jeff Alison for the first time, not realising he would remain very important to me for the rest of my life. When you have a life-long medical condition, you actually require this person forever. Not quite being the model patient, I have always wondered what Jeff actually thought of me.

At our first meeting, Jeff took time to explain the procedure while I sat in my hospital bed. I was sure he was going to fix my VT and listened carefully. He asked me if I had any questions, but I didn't. I completely trusted and agreed with him. Jeff seemed very calm and in control, and I immediately felt comfortable with him as my specialist. I noticed he was also left-handed like me, so I thought he had to be talented.

A couple of hours later, I was wheeled down to the Catheterisation Laboratory (Cath Lab) for my EP study at Monash Heart. EP studies are really odd: you need to remain awake, but sedated. Once sedated I was moved to the procedure room and was surprised at how many people were in the room. For the second time in just a few months, I lay on an operating table while wires were threaded through my groin to my heart. One side of my groin had a wire which stimulates an arrhythmia by using electrical impulses. The other side of my groin had another wire for delivering radio-frequency current, which Jeff used to ablate (to kill off) any rogue cells. The aim was to try to recorrect the abnormal pathway responsible for my arrhythmia. This process of chasing the arrhythmia is called mapping.

Jeff told me he was going to start. Apart from the initial groin incision, there was no pain or feeling at all. Regardless of the lack of pain, I just didn't feel comfortable lying on an operating table. I think I was pretty annoying throughout the entire procedure, because lying still is not one of my strengths. I complained a lot, and I know I also fidgeted. I kept hearing Jeff respond and ask his assistant to increase my sedation every time I made a comment, moved or indicated I was uncomfortable. I have no idea how long I was lying there, but a few times I remember my groin felt stirred up, so I complained, and Jeff asked to increase my sedation again. Once the arrhythmia had been recreated, I felt short of breath. I was given an oxygen mask, which covered my face, giving Jeff a bit of a break from me whinging. I must have also been flicking my feet with nervousness, because someone was called in to just hold my feet still. I'm not sure if I slowed the procedure down, but I am pretty sure I wasn't the model patient.

Throughout this part of the procedure, I could vaguely hear talking, and see Jeff looking very intently at the screen showing my heart above me. He told me he was going to start ablations. Things seemed to be going ok. From the conversation, I could tell Jeff was ablating things, or actually getting somewhere, and relaxed a little.

At one point I saw the Prof walk past the room. I asked Jeff why the Prof wasn't doing this procedure, 'Was he too old?' I asked. Jeff laughed, as did a few others. Jeff stopped what he was doing, told me the Prof specialises in another area of cardiology, and asked if I could stop talking, because I was moving. He asked his assistant to sedate me a little more.

I remember complaining about my back being sore and asking why there wasn't more padding on the bed I was lying on. Jeff had me sedated again.

At one point, I heard Jeff say, 'Oh dear!'

Normally that simple comment wouldn't really mean much, but when your cardiologist says, 'Oh dear', it doesn't fill you with a lot of confidence.

Jeff turned to look at me and said, 'You are going to feel lightheaded Emma.'

I thought I already was, but that was the last thing I remember. I must have passed out. When I came to, everyone in the room was standing a little away from the operating table looking at me. I realised I had been cardioverted (defibrillated).

Jeff came and spoke to me and said, 'Emma we are going to stop there.'

I got the impression suddenly that my less than fifty per cent chance of a cure had dropped to zero per cent. I was wheeled up to my room to recover.

That evening, Jeff came to see me. He told me he had successfully reproduced my VT and mapped it to my right ventricle. He had ablated twice, the first being successful, and the second resulting in ventricular fibrillation (VF). I then required external defibrillation. He believed the VF was quite significant and easily inducible in the setting of my right ventricular cardiomyopathy, so he recommended I have a defibrillator implanted.

I just listened, but honestly, I knew what he was going to say. I knew the news wasn't going to be good.

Jeff said I needed to think about it.

I asked, 'what do I need to think about?'

Jeff told me that some patients don't want a defibrillator. I knew I didn't, but I also didn't have a choice.

The quickness of the VF in the EP study frightened me, given it was about twenty seconds between Jeff saying, 'Oh dear' and telling me I would feel light-headed, and me passing out. I really didn't think I would ever feel safe again without back up, knowing my heart could do that.

'Jeff — I agree with you.' I wasn't going to go doctor shopping.

I saw the Prof a little later, and he told me he was sorry they couldn't fix my VT but even if my VT had been ablated successfully this wouldn't have made any difference to my damaged right ventricle. I looked at the Prof thinking, 'You are a professor, one step down from a wizard. You are supposed to be able to fix everything.'

The Prof also told me I needed to stop exercising until I had an automatic Internal Cardioverter Defibrillator (ICD) fitted. He said I needed to 'decondition' to see if the right ventricular strength would improve after a prolonged period of rest.

'What the hell is that?' I asked. 'Is "deconditioning" even a thing?'

Apparently deconditioning is the 'losing of fitness'. I was disgusted at the mere suggestion of this process.

Professor Harper provided the following explanation of his diagnosis of my heart condition, and the decision that I required a defibrillator implant:

The most accurate diagnosis of Emma's heart condition is 'Exercise-induced right ventricular cardiomyopathy'. This condition is confined basically to elite endurance athletes and has only recently been accepted as a diagnosis. The condition had not been described when I first saw Emma in 2004. The condition explains some but not all of the sudden deaths and heart attacks that have occurred in elite endurance athletes in recent times.

The word cardiomyopathy implies weakness of heart muscle which in Emma's case is the muscle of the right ventricle. Her left ventricular muscle is fine. The right ventricle, via the pulmonary artery, pumps blood into the lungs to be oxygenated. It has recently been discovered by researchers that at the time of the peak of extreme exercise the pressure in the pulmonary artery rises thus imposing strain on the right ventricle which in turn can result in damage to the right ventricular muscle, some of which becomes replaced by scar tissue. With repeated episodes of scarring the overall strength of the right ventricle starts to diminish thus reducing the overall performance of the heart.

This is what has happened to Emma. Emma's right ventricle has been significantly damaged as seen on the MRI study of her heart and on the echocardiogram. Currently her right ventricle is sufficiently strong to allow her to do what most would consider high level exercise but certainly not strong enough to allow her to do the extreme exercise she did in the past.

Scar tissue in the heart not only weakens the heart muscle it also provides a substrate for cardiac arrhythmias such as ventricular tachycardia (VT). Arrhythmias only occur when there is a relatively large amount of scar tissue. That is, they only occur late in the process. I am sure the deterioration that Emma noted in her performances after 1998 were related to the gradual and progressive deterioration in the strength of her right ventricle rather than any arrhythmia. If Emma had been getting VT before the episode in Canada, she would have known about it and the VT wouldn't have self-corrected.

*Currently the most dangerous part of Emma's heart condition is the tendency she has to developing VT. Fortunately this seems to only occur when her natural heart rate gets beyond approximately 150 bpm which of course will occur if she exercises sufficiently hard enough. That is why I am always warning Emma not to push herself too hard. When VT occurs the heart suddenly becomes fast as per the episode in Canada when her heart rate was 250 bpm. Most importantly in VT the heart muscle pump function is very inefficient. The cardiac output and blood pressure drop dramatically, and you feel terrible, but the sort of VT Emma has is **not** cardiac arrest. Cardiac arrest means the heart is not pumping any blood at all. That is, there is no cardiac output at all. The usual cause is ventricular fibrillation (VF). If you go into cardiac arrest you rapidly lose consciousness and unless the cardiac arrest is corrected within 3 to 4 minutes you will either die or if it is corrected towards the end of this time frame you are likely to suffer brain damage. You cannot have a cardiac arrest and still be conscious apart from the first 20 seconds or so.*

The main danger of VT is that at any time it can degenerate into VF and cardiac arrest. The longer the VT lasts the more likely this is to occur. When Emma had her episode in Canada, she was not in cardiac arrest technically, but it was very much a medical emergency and she was in imminent danger of having a cardiac arrest. This is the reason she was given a shock to correct the VT and restore normal heart rhythm thus preventing cardiac arrest.

The management of Emma's condition has several aspects. Unfortunately, at this point in time we cannot replace the scar tissue in her right ventricle with new normal muscle. This is the hope of stem cell therapy. Nevertheless, by avoiding extreme exercise (which she can no longer do) we are hopefully preventing further scarring of her right ventricle and the follow up echoes we have done suggest that this is the case.

With respect to the VT this can be avoided by preventing the heart rate from getting to 150 bpm and of course there is the backup ICD (cardioverter / defibrillator). This clever device constantly monitors Emma's heart rhythm and if it recognises VT it immediately delivers some pacing impulses which will usually restore the heart rhythm back to normal without Emma even knowing. If this fails or if VF occurs Emma will get a shock which is unpleasant but life-saving.

I had a couple of weeks between the decision to have a defibrillator, and the time the defibrillator was actually implanted. I managed to put myself into VT again in this short period. On this particular occasion, I was out for a morning run. It was a Saturday and I was running my favourite loop from home in Eltham, around Westerfolds Park and back. My regular '10 miler' or 16 km. I didn't run particularly hard, but on the way back I felt a bit ordinary. I didn't feel like I was getting enough air to my lungs, and I could feel my heart rate was elevated. It wasn't like my previous episodes, so I was undecided as to whether I was in VT or becoming 'detrained' as the Prof hoped.

When I got home, I lay on the floor and tried to decide if I was in VT. I found that if I lay there quietly, I could feel my body shake. I realised it was the aggressiveness of VT shaking my body slightly. Just as I decided I was in trouble, Dad walked into the living room where I was lying.

'What are you doing?' he asked.

'I think I'm in VT,' I said as I got up, 'I need to ring Monash Medical Centre.' I called a number the Prof had given me, it was ER.

I explained to whoever answered that I was a patient of Professor Harper, that I suffer from VT and I thought I was in VT now. They asked my name and was told to call an ambulance. I explained that if I did that I would end up in the wrong hospital (I wasn't keen on going to Box Hill again) and asked whether I could drive there. I was told that I couldn't drive, but someone could drive me.

Dad took me to Monash ER. On arrival, the waiting room was packed full. I went to the window and said, 'I just called, I'm Emma Carney.'

With that the doors to ER flew open, someone threw me into a wheelchair, and I was taken to a bed. Dad followed.

I was told the Prof had been called, but they expected I needed an external defibrillation. I asked if we really needed to bother The Prof, as he had told me not to exercise. I didn't really think he needed his weekend ruined by me. Were they sure he needed to come in?

'He insisted,' I was told.

'Oh...' I remember saying. 'Do you think he is annoyed with me?'

Everyone ignored that question.

Lying there the symptoms worsened and my VT became increasingly unbearable. I needed an anaesthetist again. At one point a nurse told me they were going to try a drug to stop the VT.

'Drugs don't work,' I told them.

'Yes, we know, but Professor Harper has told us it is worth a try.'

I was already rigged up intravenously. A nurse came over and said, 'I am about to give you a drug that may give you a feeling of "impending doom",' and stepped forward to administer the drug.

'Woah, what?' I said pulling my arm away. 'What the hell is impending doom? Am I going to feel dead, or am I going to see stuff, or am I going to feel like aliens are in me? What does that mean?' I asked, shocked.

The nurse looked at me and said, 'I don't know, no one has ever asked, but we are required to tell patients that.'

'Really! Every patient is ok with impending doom?'

The nurses around me nodded.

I couldn't believe it, 'Ok. Inject it slowly, and I will let you know how I feel,' I said begrudgingly.

The drug was administered, with a few nurses now interested to know what 'impending doom' actually felt like. I felt nothing, and still my VT continued.

For some reason I thought I would frighten everyone and yelled out 'Boo!' Everyone jumped.

'Nothing. The drugs don't work. I need to be defibrillated,' I announced.

The nurses dispersed, some amused.

Finally, the doctor arrived. In an absolute coincidence of life, the doctor to arrive at my bedside was the daughter of the babysitter Mum and Dad used way back in the late 70s. Last time I saw her, we were both about five-years old. Dad started chatting and I asked them to hurry up.

I was all ok by the time the Prof arrived. He seemed more concerned than annoyed with me. I apologised for ruining his Saturday. He wanted me admitted to hospital. I told him it was all ok, I had done my run for the day, so could I go home.

Begrudgingly, after much consideration of my heart readings and intense monitoring I was allowed to leave ER.

The Prof again asked me to be careful.

On 7 October 2004, I was admitted once again to Jessie McPherson Private Hospital, part of the Monash Medical Centre, to have my ICD fitted. Prior to the device implant, Dr Jeff Alison explained the procedure with me. He showed me a pacemaker implant, then showed me a defibrillator implant. The ICD was twice the size of the pacemaker, being about 6 cm long and 4 cm wide. I thought he was joking, as I was expecting something the size of a phone SIM card.

'Where the hell are you going to put that?" I asked him.

Jeff is a leading electrophysiologist in the way he has developed implanting ICDs. He told me he would fit the device under my left breast so that it was not visible and would produce a 'good cosmetic result'.

I was a little apprehensive, because I thought the device was maybe bigger than both my breasts together. After all my training I wasn't exactly well endowed in that area.

'How much does it weigh?' I asked. It looked heavy.

'About 200 grams,' Jeff replied.

I remember thinking, 'Bloody hell, that is more than an empty bidon (bottle) on my bike.' I used to throw them off while racing, because I thought they weighed too much.

Jeff then asked me to slip my arm out of my gown so he could mark on the skin where my bra strap sits. He would place the wires there so they would not show. I was impressed he had actually thought of this.

I asked, 'What if a wear a halter neck?' Jeff looked at me. 'What's that?' he asked.

'Don't worry, I don't get out much,' I replied.

He asked if I wanted a local or general anaesthetic. I didn't want to see or hear anything, so I told Jeff to completely knock me out. I expect Jeff was relieved to hear that.

My ICD implant was scheduled for early afternoon. I was wheeled down and seemed to be in a similar operating theatre to the EP study. I hadn't been put under yet, so had a good look around the room. I shouldn't have done that, because I didn't really like what I saw. It all looked a bit too much like an operating theatre to me. Jeff was over at what seemed like his laptop. Maybe sending emails? Probably not, but everyone seemed ok with the room except for me. I was quietly beginning to panic. Jeff came over and asked how I was. I told him I wasn't really enjoying sitting there. I think because I was a renowned 'tough athlete' people assume I can handle most situations. In reality, I am absolutely pathetic in medical scenarios, where I am the patient. Fortunately, the anaesthetist arrived.

I came to in the recovery area. My heart monitor alarm was sounding, probably because my HR was so low. I didn't really care. I felt really sore. Someone wheeled me up to my ward, and I lay there I don't know how long.

Prior to the procedure Jeff told me there would be 'moderate pain'. Now I realise that when a doctor tells you 'moderate pain', it is similar to when a race organiser describes a course as 'picturesque'. Both are massive understatements. A 'picturesque' course means there are hills that are going to rip your legs off, and a 'moderate pain' description from a doctor means you will be in agony.

Either that or I am just plain soft.

As I lay in my bed, the pain became nothing like I had ever experienced before. I couldn't move, and God help me if I needed to sneeze. Nurses came in and asked me how I was feeling, and I told them everything hurt. I was given pain killers, but they didn't seem to last long. I was told I couldn't leave the bed to go to the toilet, so I stopped drinking. There was no way I was going to pee in a pan. I didn't see how I possibly could anyway because I couldn't sit up.

That evening I think I actually gave up on everything. I refused to drink, and I constantly asked for pain relief. I couldn't turn my TV on, I couldn't move, and I was just generally really, really pissed off with everything.

The next morning a 'tech' (technician) came into my room wheeling a trolley. She told me she was going to test my device.

'WTF!?' I thought.

'No, you aren't, leave me alone,' I said. 'I am in maximum pain, and I don't want anyone fiddling with my defibrillator right now.'

I was told it wouldn't hurt, but I no longer trusted or believed anyone who told me things weren't going to hurt. I noticed that all these people telling me things weren't going to hurt weren't walking around with defibrillators in their chests.

'I'm not doing a test,' I repeated and asked her to leave.

Jeff must have been told I was being a difficult patient, because he came to see me shortly after. He asked me how I was, and I told him I was in pain. He told me the nurses had said I hadn't taken on any fluids and I needed to. I told Jeff I wasn't drinking because that would make me need to pee and he wouldn't let me out of bed. Jeff asked if he let me go to the toilet would I drink?

I said yes.

Jeff also asked me why I wouldn't let them test the ICD. I told Jeff I was sick of being prodded around. I asked him if he tested the device when he implanted it and he said he had.

'That's good enough for me then, its tested,' I informed him.

Jeff assured me the test wouldn't hurt.

'How can a shock from this device not hurt me right now Jeff?' I asked.

Jeff told me testing the device just meant checking the connection, there was no need to actually administer a shock.

'Are you sure, do you promise?' I asked, still sceptical. 'I can't do any more pain.'

With his assurance, I agreed to allow a test of the device.

In all my pain, I had assumed a test of the device meant testing the device shock. In reality, all I had to do was lie there while a mouse or similar device was placed over my defib and readings were taken on a screen. Jeff left me with the instruction to drink fluids and stay on top of my pain medication.

I lay in bed, getting more and more pissed off.

The Prof came and visited me. I think I was maximum 'grumpy Emma' at this stage, so his visit was poorly timed. He asked me how I was.

'Prof,' I asked, 'what side is your heart on?'

'Your left,' he replied.

'So,' I said, 'why the hell does every nurse keep putting everything on the table to the left side of me in bed. I can't reach a bloody thing, that side of me is totally un-usable. Is everyone trying to kill me with pain?'

The Prof looked at me, turned, and walked out, without saying a word.

Within a minute, someone came into my room and moved all the furniture to the other side of my bed and then left. The Prof returned and asked me how I was.

'I'm in pain,' was all I said.

He checked my charts, looked at whatever cardiologists look at, and asked me if the pain had subsided.

'No. I actually think it's getting worse.'

Once the Prof had gone, I decided to attempt going to the toilet. I was a little worried I would pass out again, like I did in Canada, but had a go anyway. I didn't think I could be more uncomfortable than I already was. It took me ages to sit up; it amazed me just how much sitting up requires your chest muscles. I safely made it to the toilet and back to bed but stirred up my pain again. I remember wondering if it would be easier if I just gave up. This was all a bit too hard.

I remained in hospital for two more days. Jeff came to see how I was both days, and again before I left. On one visit Jeff told me I would be able to do some exercise in a few weeks when the pain had subsided.

'Really?' I said. In my present state I couldn't see how I would ever lead a normal life let own exercise: I was so uncomfortable.

'Yes, you should be able to swim, ride and run again,' Jeff told me. He looked pretty pleased to tell me this.

I was very sceptical. Given how my left side was hurting, I didn't think I would be capable of lifting my left arm again, so swimming to me seemed impossible. How I would ever run with my left side so swollen and sore baffled me.

'What do you consider to be a run Jeff?' I asked.

'I don't know, twenty minutes,' Jeff replied.

'Jeff, I run a minimum of one hour if I really want to have a good run,' I informed him.

'What about swimming?' I asked.

Jeff looked a little bit uncomfortable. 'Fifteen minutes?' he suggested.

'Jeff, I wouldn't bother to get wet for that,' I replied.

Jeff and I then realised we were on completely different pages when it came to swimming, biking and running. Jeff's idea of a bike ride was also something I wouldn't bother to count as exercise. I felt even more discouraged. Jeff must have thought I was mad.

'We can work it out when you are feeling better,' Jeff told me before he left.

'I'm absolutely screwed,' I thought.

I wasn't pain free when I was discharged, but I was able to walk slowly and just wanted to leave so I could mope around at home in peace. My mental state must have been a concern for both the Prof and Jeff, because both made recommendations in their medical notes for me to have psychological support as I adjusted to both my defib implant and also the loss of my career. Both spoke to me about this, but I just couldn't see how anyone could fix, or help me get through, the useless, terrible scenario I now found myself in.

Mum picked me up from hospital. Jeff was in my room when Mum arrived, and he brought up the issue of psychological support with Mum present.

'No one can fix this,' I told Jeff.

On leaving the hospital, I asked Mum to drive really slowly, because every bump on the road hurt like hell. As we made our way out of the Monash Medical Centre, we had to negotiate speed humps.

'What moron puts speed humps in a hospital exit?' I muttered as we lurched over them.

Once home, I had an adverse reaction to something. I suddenly needed to go to the toilet every time I managed to get into bed. I hadn't eaten for a few days, was still in pain, and now I couldn't lie down for more than a few minutes without needing the toilet.

I was a mess. I asked Mum to call Jeff. He had told me if anything gets worse once home, I needed to let him know. I asked Mum to tell Jeff, 'Thanks for all your help, but I think I am going to die.'

I'm not sure what Mum said to Jeff, but he asked to speak to me. Jeff asked me to come back to hospital.

'Jeff, I can't be bothered,' I told him.

He told me if things didn't improve in four hours I needed to return.

'Ok,' I replied and hung up.

Mum asked me what Jeff had said and I told her Jeff said I was right — I was probably going to die. Mum looked startled and I told her I didn't want to talk about it. I have no idea if Mum called Jeff again, but I really was over everything.

It took two weeks for me to become pain free. I think I am the most pathetic patient Dr Jeff Alison has ever had. Once the pain subsided, I started to adjust to having a defibrillator implant. I was scared to exercise as I didn't want to set the device off. According to the Prof, the shock from this device would never be like the external shock I received from the paramedics in Canada, but I didn't want to see if he was correct or not. Simple things were also a little frightening. I became aware of the security systems in storefronts, the ones that beep when people shoplift. These are all magnetised systems. I was told by Jeff that a strong magnet will clear or turn off my defib, so shopping frightened me at first. Music that was so loud you could feel it in your body (not that I was ever really a party goer) frightened me, as it felt like an arrhythmia in my chest. I was also a little grossed out that I now relied on a device under my skin. I used to be one of the fittest athletes on the planet; now I couldn't live without some chunk of metal inside me monitoring things.

Having been through the process of my heart diagnosis, I also, for the first time in my life, realised that sport is not the most important thing. Here was Professor Harper and Dr Jeff Alison performing life-saving surgery every single day. Jeff had actually devised a way of performing the implant of an ICD so people like me didn't have a very noticeable box sticking out under their skin on their chests. I wasn't privy to the specialist work Prof Harper had done, but you don't become a Professor in cardiology by being average. Sure, I raced and won world titles for Australia, but suddenly everything in my life seemed really, really pointless.

In May 2005 I returned to Monash Heart for an echocardiogram and another stress test. The echocardiogram (ultrasound of my heart) showed no improvement in my condition which was disappointing. It confirmed that the damage to my right ventricle was permanent.

'Is there any way this can be fixed?' I asked.

'Unfortunately, no,' the Prof told me.

He also explained that at this stage there is no known way to turn scar tissue back into healthy heart muscle. There are hopes that eventually this may be achieved by stem cell technology but so far progress has been disappointing. The Prof said I needed to avoid further damage to the right ventricle by not putting it under the stress of extreme exercise.

'It is good enough to still allow you to still exercise to levels that a normal person would consider quite high, as long as you can avoid further damage to the right ventricle.'

The Prof told me he had organised for me to have a stress test so he could see how my heart responded to exercise, because we needed to work out what level was safe for me. This time, the test was a little more interesting. Given the lack of result on my first stress test and my comments, Monash Heart set up a treadmill test designed just for me. The Prof organised for me to have the test on 2 May 2005. Much to my surprise, he had taken on board my suggestions, and I was extremely excited to be able to test myself physically again. The testing room was full of cardiologists and technicians, so I decided to take a calculated risk. With all the electrodes strapped to my chest, I could see my heart was carefully monitored by several cardiologists. I also had a defibrillator implanted this time, should anything go wrong. I decided, without telling anyone, that I was going to 'run to exhaustion' regardless of what went on during the test. In other words, I was going to run until someone, or something, actually stopped me.

That is exactly what I did.

The test was going fine, until I hit about sixteen minutes. Suddenly I felt awful. Something must have shown up on the screen, because a cardiologist in the room asked me, 'How are you feeling Emma?'

'Fine,' I said, feeling awful, weak and dizzy.

There were now three Cardiology Technicians (techs) and several Cardiologists looking at the screen. I kept running.

Suddenly I felt really bad, very weak and out of breath.

I was shoved off the treadmill onto the waiting bed by two cardiologists. As I went down, I had a look at the treadmill timings. I was disappointed I only made eighteen minutes. I lay on the bed and could feel my defib pace my heart. This was the first time I actually felt it doing something. I could feel I was in VT because my heart was racing. At first the device responded to this rhythm by attempting to pace my heart to correct it, rather than immediately delivering a shock. The pacing felt similar to the sensation of holding opposing magnets. My heart was trying to race, and there was a slight pulling sensation of the device trying to override and correct it. Fortunately, the pacing option worked, and I avoided a shock.

Everyone in the room was silent, watching how my heart was behaving on the various screens and monitors.

The test ended there.

A few days later in Prof's room, I sat opposite him while he looked at me.

'What were you thinking?' he asked.

'I was thinking I was safe,' I answered, shrugging.

'You frightened everyone. They aren't used to that.' The Prof could not help smiling though.

'I can see you need special attention with your treatment Emma.'

He did say that they learnt a lot from the stress test. The VT that occurred during the test kicked in when my natural heart rate reached 160 bpm. Therefore, if I could keep my heart rate below 150, I probably wouldn't get VT.

Following this exercise test, the Prof made the following notes, dated 6 May 2005, to AIS Head of Sports Medicine Professor Kieran Fallon:

Putting all things together, I think Emma has a form of exercise induced arrhyth-mogenic right ventricular cardiomyopathy. Emma can date the decline in her performances in triathlons to 1996 and it is probable that she developed her cardiomyopathy then. Considering the extent of her right ventricular dysfunction, it is really quite amazing that she was able to compete so well up until recently.

Exercise induced arrhythmogenic right ventricular cardiomyopathy is a new diagnosis that is only now starting to be recognised in elite endurance athletes. The Prof thought it important that sports doctors and physiologists be aware of this condition and he asked my permission to write up my case in the medical literature. I readily gave permission.

And that was that. My professional racing career was over.

I am not sure whether TA ever made an announcement regarding my retirement.

I received a letter from the AIS thanking me for my contribution to Australian Sport. That was nice to receive. Nice to know the AIS had noticed me.

Everyone seemed to have accepted the fact I would never race again, except of course for me.

As it turns out, you can take me out of triathlon, but you can't take triathlon out of me.

15. Losing Jane

In the new year of 2005, my older sister Jane and her husband Justin announced they were expecting their first child in July, around the time of my birthday. It was some really good news for everyone, with Mum and Dad to be first time grandparents and Clare and me to become aunties.

Following my disastrous stress test in May 2005, I seemed to be managing my heart condition well. I did avoid setting of my defibrillator for a few months. To be honest though, I still felt vulnerable. I mostly took the dog for a walk, rather than run. I was too scared.

It was about July 2005 when I first set my defib off. I was in a gym with a mate, and we got into a discussion as to which cardio machine burns the calories the quickest. I said the elliptical, he said the treadmill. An argument developed, a bet was made as to who could burn 100 calories the quickest and off we went to test our theories. I jumped on the elliptical machine and got stuck into the challenge. In just under three minutes I burned 80 calories. Suddenly I felt an awful wave of fatigue wash over me. I looked at my mate's screen: he was on 65 calories, so I was ahead. I decided to push on. I reached 100 calories first, yelled out, 'I win', and decided to get out of the room because I was feeling awful.

As I exited, my defibrillator gave me a shock. I didn't want to attract attention, and forced myself to keep walking, just stopping momentarily. I found a chair and sat for about a minute until I felt ok again.

The Prof was right: the ICD shock was nothing like the external defibrillation I experienced in Canada. It really felt similar to touching an electric fence, like a quick moment-stopping zap. Still unpleasant, nonetheless.

The Prof had told me I needed to call him if I set my defib off and given me his mobile number. As instructed, I called and told him. He asked what I had been doing, and a little embarrassed I said, 'Umm. I was in a competitive situation.'

The Prof didn't ask anything else but instructed me to see him.

When I saw the Prof, I think it must have been quite obvious to him I was struggling with 'normal' life. I remember him asking what I was doing, and I struggled to come up with anything productive or sensible to offer him. I was lost, and he knew it and he cared. We then discussed exercise. I questioned his advice on my heart and exercise. In all my time as an athlete, if you want full recovery from a muscle tear or strain such as a calf or hamstring problem, the advice is that you continue to strengthen, mobilise, then exercise that muscle rather than just give it complete rest. If the heart is a muscle, then shouldn't it receive the same treatment and continue to be exercised to maintain function? The Prof agreed my theory was sound, but he said, 'We do know the heart muscle does not behave like other muscles,' and added, 'The device is also there to save your life, not allow you to continue to exercise at a high level.'

Feeling dejected, I asked, 'Can I just try my theory? What if I remain active, but keep my heart rate capped below 150 bpm?'

The Prof told me it was all good in theory, but the heart muscle was not like other muscles and I needed to be careful, it hadn't really been done before. That wasn't really a deterrent to me though, because that is what I had been doing all my life. Trying to do stuff that had not been done before.

We kind of agreed to disagree, but also that I could have a go within reason. I was still scared at this point though, so I dabbled with a few runs, but nothing serious in my eyes.

My parents were never really the type to push me to be motivated, they seemed to have faith in me and my ability to achieve things. Nothing was really said about my lack of commitment to anything since my defibrillator implant the previous year. Maybe it was too early to worry about that yet in their eyes, but I took on some of the Prof's advice, and thought perhaps I should do something productive with my life. I enrolled in what I considered a lame Personal Training course. Apparently, I needed to be qualified to train people. The course was about six weeks long, and it almost killed me with boredom. In one lesson we were learning about aerobic and anaerobic training and I stepped in to point out that the teacher had her rest and training periods back to front for each training method. She offered for me to take the class when I corrected her, so I did. It was common sense to me and something I had worked out when I was probably about ten. That was about the most interesting part of the course, teaching it. I never worked as a personal trainer. I felt disheartened at the inaccurate coaching that the course tried to drum into people.

Jane was heavily pregnant by the time I completed the course. I was still doing nothing productive and did not really have any plans to be productive anytime soon. To be honest, everything bored me and seemed lame in comparison to training and racing for Australia.

I was in a bad place. Everything annoyed me.

I had been brought up to 'just get on with things' so again I didn't tell anyone that I was struggling. It was my heart condition all over again, but this time it was me dealing with my heart condition and end of career. In his correspondence about my heart diagnosis with the AIS Head of Sports Medicine, Keiran Fallon, the Prof wrote that he thought I should be supported in coaching triathlon, because I was having trouble adjusting to my retirement. Probably as a consequence, TA did invite me to some high-performance coaching courses, which Bill Davoren encouraged me to attend. I took up the opportunity and attained my Triathlon High Performance accreditation. The ITU, through Les McDonald, invited me to attend a development coaching course in Singapore for the IOC sport development program. Les also wanted me to become involved with the Japanese High Performance Triathlon Coaching program, but I pulled out last minute citing my heart condition and saying it wasn't stable. But really, my heart wasn't in it. The problem was that basically everything to me was not what I wanted, regardless of what everyone offered me. I could not do what I had always wanted to do.

Unknown to me at the time, things were about to get a whole lot worse.

Jane became a mum on 2 August 2005. It was early morning, about 5 a.m., when little Zoe was born. I went in to visit Jane as soon as I could. Jane, Justin and Zoe were a complete little family in the hospital room. I had a hold of Zoe, but honestly just tried not to break her. I didn't have a lot of experience with babies, and now I was an aunty I didn't want to mess things up.

I asked Jane how she felt, and she said tired. Jane then looked really worried and said she had a lump on her head and her breast. I was startled at this confession and tried desperately to find a reason as to why.

'Maybe you bumped your head in the panic to get to hospital?' I offered.

Jane was definite in her response and said, 'No. I didn't.' Something else must have happened in the room, because our conversation ended there.

Nothing further was said until little Zoe was ten days old, when I received a call from Jane. Jane was on a tram, going to see her family doctor. She sounded a little worried and told me she had some abnormal blood tests when she was pregnant. They were put down to her pregnancy at the time, but Jane's doctor followed up on them after Zoe had arrived and there were still some abnormalities. Now her doctor wanted to do some scans.

Jane finished up with, 'I might have bloody cancer.'

'No. No one in our family has ever had cancer,' I replied trying to sound convincing. But Jane was worried, and rightly so.

She had the scan. She was riddled with it. Secondary melanoma cancer.

Pre-empting this horrific diagnosis, Jane had a melanoma removed from her neck in 1996, which was cleared five years later. In 2003 she had another melanoma removed from the back of her neck — the size of a pin head, but a nodular aggressive type. When she had this second melanoma removed in 2003, I helped her dress the scar, and I was shocked at the size of the incision and stitches she had across her shoulders. Despite this excessively large clearance area cut out by the specialists at the time, it failed to remove every single cell. With hindsight, the doctors explained that the cancerous cells had spread into Jane's bloodstream, affixed themselves on vital organs and then lay dormant. While Jane was pregnant, her body's defences were down, as the baby was the priority. The cancer went wild and established itself on almost every vital organ in her body. The lumps Jane felt on her head and breast were tumours that were beginning to protrude.

Suddenly some things made sense. Jane had suffered from a very, very sore back towards the end of her pregnancy. Everyone just put it down to her pregnancy. Once she had been scanned, we knew that Zoe had been adding pressure from the womb on a tumour on Jane's liver.

Jane never had a chance, but I didn't seriously consider that at the time. Dying wasn't something our family did. Especially Jane. She was by far the most sensible family member and she had also worked hard all her life. Jane did not deserve this at all.

Once diagnosed with cancer, Jane went through hell. It absolutely breaks my heart every time I think about it. Her treatment required aggressive rounds of chemo. Jane was breastfeeding but forced to stop immediately. For Zoe to adapt to formula, she had to be taken from Jane until her breastmilk dried out. So, Jane, a new mum, was told she could not touch or hold her little baby girl. Zoe spent a lot of time with my Mum and fortunately adapted well. It was almost as if she knew her Mum needed her to do so.

Jane took on her treatment in the same way we were all brought up to face adversity in the Carney household. Don't buckle, don't give in and fight to the end.

I still cannot believe the way cancer is treated. Jane was hit with round after round of chemotherapy, with different medical treatments designed to prevent her cancer cells from growing and spreading by destroying the cells or stopping them from. The problem is, while chemo drugs can stop cancer cells growing and from dividing, they also affect normal, healthy cells in the process. For Jane the result was devastatingly aggressive cancer aided by failing chemo rounds speeding up the process of destroying her body. The advancements in melanoma treatment were not available in the early 2000s and Jane became a victim. I wasn't privy to the treatment Jane undertook; she and Justin were referred to an oncologist. I do know though that Jane did not receive one single piece of good news. It was DefCon 1 from the outset. Every single scan, every single round of chemo saw the progression of the cancer. It was completely hopeless.

I am not entirely sure, but I think Jane was given a year to live. Jane never really discussed this with me, and I was never able to ask or even consider entering that type of conversation. I never had that conversation with anyone in the family. We were not brought up to consider death. We just battled on.

Early on, Jane asked me to come along to an appointment she had with a specialist. Justin always took her, but he must have had to go to work that morning. I completely screwed up and got caught in traffic and was late. Jane told me to 'get out of her life, if I couldn't make her a priority when she was so ill.' Rightly so. I felt awful and would have done the same, maybe gone harder on the 'get out' bit. Jane banned me from her house and told me she never wanted to see me again.

I was devastated, but not exactly going to take my banishment from Jane's life without a fight back. I tried to think of what would help Jane and decided as she was inside all day recovering from rounds of chemo, I could wash her house windows, so at least she was looking out of clean windows. I got all Mum's window washing gear together and drove over to Jane and Justin's house.

I started at the front of the house. Jane's bedroom was at the front. I decided to start on her window. As always, I thought I might as well tackle the argument from the outset. Jane must have heard me and pulled her curtains back. She looked tired and was starting to lose weight from the chemo, and obviously didn't have much energy. Being a Carney though, she was able to yell out a nice loud, 'I told you to get lost!'

I ignored her instruction — as a younger sister should — and yelled back, 'I will go when I have cleaned your windows.'

She gave me a glare and went back to bed.

The house was a single storey old terrace. Jane had plans to renovate, but surviving cancer was now her priority. I washed the back windows by jumping the back fence. Jane ignored me. I then decided I would wash the inside of the windows. That way the job was done properly. I still had a key, so I let myself in.

Jane yelled, 'Get out!'

I walked into Jane's bedroom and told her I was going to wash the insides of the windows then I would go. Jane told me she hated me. I ignored her; it wasn't exactly the first time my big sister had told me that anyway.

I managed to clean the inside of all the windows. When I was done, Jane was lying in her bed looking at her ceiling. I think she was crying quietly. It broke my heart to see. I told Jane I was going to make myself a cup of tea, because I had done so much work for her and her house now looked so good. Did she want one?

Jane said, 'No.'

I made Jane a cup of tea and took it to her. I sat beside her bed and drank mine while she ignored me.

Jane suddenly said, 'Emma if I ask you to do something, you need to make it a priority. I'm dying here.'

I told Jane I would never let her down again.

Fortunately, Jane forgave me, and I spent as much time as I could caring for her. It was almost as if life had done a complete circle. Jane had spent so much time looking after me when we were young, and now I could finally help her out when she needed help.

It was mid-August when Jane was diagnosed, so September, October and November were spent with rounds of chemo. Jane asked me to look at trying to find a diet that could help build the immune system. I came across a guy called Steve Acuff, who had some very strong views on cancer treatment. His ideas focused on slow cooking and fermentation; organically sourced food, including plant-based protein and fish; and short-chain fats such as coconut oils over other oils. It all made sense to my family. Jane obviously needed her immune system boosted. Mum was always interested in diet and organic eating and took to preparing all Jane's food. Still to this day, Mum follows this diet — we all do really — because what you put into your body really is important.

Among the hopelessness of the situation, with the cancer progressing despite rounds of chemo, Jane also endured radiotherapy. This seemed to contain some of the tumours, but the problem was almost every vital organ was affected. Laser guided pinpoint radiotherapy was only in its trial stages, and every time Justin and I tried to have Jane involved in a treatment trial, we were told she was too far advanced to be included. Everything was negative, and every day Jane became increasingly ill. It was absolutely depressing and very, very sad.

I think Jane accepted her fate well before any of us did. She went to a cancer retreat in NSW with Justin and returned telling us all she needed to stop 'fighting' and try to meditate, remain calm and relax more. This was quite the opposite approach we were all brought up with. They do say the immune system is boosted when you remain more relaxed and release the stresses of life. I just helped Jane with whatever she needed and whatever she believed in. There was no judgement, just desperation to try to find something that worked.

As Jane became more and more ill, she could not care for Zoe. Zoe spent some time at Mum and Dad's and some time with Justin's parents. Noise would irritate Jane as she dealt day and night with the pain of the cancer, so we were all on eggshells. She became adamant that she didn't want everyone caring for her and asked Dad and Clare not to visit anymore. She then became irritated, impatient and demanding with those close to her: Justin, Mum and me.

I spent as much time with Jane as she needed and started to stay over so I could help through the night. Some days Jane told me to have a break, get out of the house. When I did leave the house, I found everything so depressing. People wasting their lives at shopping malls and buying crap. On one particular occasion I was wandering through some shops when I was stopped by someone selling daffodils on behalf of the Cancer Council to raise money to help cure cancer. I said, 'No thanks,' when they approached me, and the volunteer said to me, 'Don't you want to cure cancer?' I snapped, turned around to face them, and said, 'Can you tell me what a useless $2 daffodil is going to do for my sister right now?'

They apologised.

I realised I needed to do something I enjoyed. That is when I started exercising again.

I was still scared to exercise, but I was also seeing first-hand how short life is. I saw how important it is to spend time doing things you enjoy. Maybe I was just looking for an 'out', but I needed to do something for me. I thought running may increase my heart rate too much and set off the defibrillator, so I decided to start riding my bike. The first few rides I only headed out for a couple of hours, but on days when Jane told me to go out for the entire morning, I decided to go further.

October 2005, I had my first annual check-up on my defib with Dr Jeff Allison. Jeff asked me how I was. He was the first person who had asked how I was in ages. As a result, I burst into tears. He must have thought I was really struggling with my defib implant, but I explained to him my sister had been diagnosed with cancer. Jeff looked shocked, and I then told him I thought she was going to die. I hadn't said that to anyone yet. I am not sure why Jeff copped everything. He told me not everyone dies of cancer.

We discussed my heart. I only set the defib off once, earlier that year while testing gym equipment. It seemed so long ago. Jeff then interrogated the device. There were some alerts showing from my device downloads and I told Jeff I had started exercising regularly. I said mainly riding.

Jeff asked how long I would ride, and I said, 'Oh about 200.'

'200 what?' he enquired.

'200 kilometres.'

Jeff looked at me very blankly. He asked me where I rode, and I said Albert Park to Portsea and return. This was a ride in Melbourne following the Port Phillip Bay coastline. I told him my theory was that if I ride for longer at a steady pace my heart rate would not increase excessively. He probably guessed I was also trying to escape reality and waste an entire day doing something I enjoyed.

Jeff didn't tell me off, but it was clear he wasn't overly impressed. We completed the check up, and I continued riding.

Over the next few weeks, the problem was that — now I was getting a bit fitter — I was starting to head out with some training groups and of course the rides became a little quicker and a lot more intense. My bike riding was my 'out', my escape from reality, so I just tried to be careful.

Christmas of 2005 was just plain depressing. Awful. We all went to Mum and Dad's in Eltham. It was a hard slog. Jane was really quite ill. She was still able to walk but deteriorating badly. We all tried to celebrate Christmas, but I don't remember smiling much. Later in the day, Jane asked me if I would do something for her, and I of course said 'Yes.'

Jane asked me to move in with her and Justin permanently, to look after her. She said there were times when Justin had to go to work, and it was too much for one person to look after her. Jane said I had to look solely after her; if Zoe was in the house and cried, I had to ignore Zoe. Someone else would look after her. Jane told me Mum would also be at her house, and she was going to make sure the food in the house was all done according to Steve Acuff's diet.

I moved in the next week. Jane didn't want to go to hospital, she wanted to be at home. Her doctor lived nearby and visited often. She gave me her mobile number and told me to call her anytime I needed her.

Jane only lived another four weeks. I spent all my time with her. We spent the days watching really lame TV, juggling appointments and trying to keep her comfortable.

Jane insisted I took Wednesday and Saturday mornings off, so I would just ride my bike in that time, usually 200 km because it took all morning.

One particular ride, I was rolling back towards Jane and Justin's house, along the beach front in Albert Park. In the distance I saw someone who looked like Justin pushing a wheelchair with a frail silhouette of what looked like an old lady. I stopped and watched from afar. Something made me keep staring. Suddenly I realised it actually was Justin and he was pushing Jane along the footpath in a wheelchair. I couldn't believe that was my big sister. She was so old and frail looking. I watched full of an overwhelming sadness.

New Year's Eve 2005, I was with Jane and Justin at their house. We were all indoors but could hear the celebrations from the city of Melbourne. We were close enough to hear the main fireworks too.

When midnight arrived, and 2006 was here, Jane said, 'Happy New Year! Can someone carry me to bed?'

That was the worst New Year's Eve on record.

As Jane became increasingly frail, she became increasingly bitter about her situation. Jane told me many, many times she hated me and wished I wasn't her sister. She told me she only got skin cancer because she always tried to be like me: fit, tanned and always outdoors. Jane told me if she had her childhood again, she would have done things she enjoyed, not do the stuff I enjoyed. She said she wished she had done ballet, not athletics and running and not been influenced by me. She also told me she hated the way we had been brought up, to always be strong and stand up for what you believe in. She said it always causes problems and makes life hard.

I wasn't really in the position to argue, so I just let Jane berate me. It was hard to take all this criticism. Often, I wanted to remind Jane that when we were growing up, I had been forced to play musical instruments, learn languages and take up gymnastics briefly. All things I hated, and she loved. There was no point though. It was awful to hear someone tell you how much you ruined their life, but at the same time I wanted her to get everything 'off her chest' and maybe, maybe somehow feel better.

Some days, everything I did was wrong. Jane told me I didn't cry enough in front of her. She said she knew I had been crying, and she knew I was hiding it from her.

'It's not weak to cry you know Emma!' she would say to me angrily.

I just didn't want to be crying all the time, because I thought she would see what a hopeless situation I felt we were in.

The most common thing Jane said to me was she just wanted to grow old with Justin and see her little girl grow up. It was heartbreaking. This I couldn't offer to fix.

Our discussions were not always negative. Jane told me she was really lucky I had retired from triathlon, because I would have never had the time to help her if I was still racing. This shook me up a lot. I hadn't really thought how self-involved my racing career had been. Jane also told me she felt safe with me around, because she could rely on me to get through terrible scenarios. She liked me to recount how I stayed alive in Canada when my heart went mad and I didn't panic, and she also liked that if she asked me to do something I would do it no matter what.

One day, Jane was looking out her bedroom window when the neighbour across the street parked in front of her house. Justin had gone out in their car and the park was free.

Jane commented and said, 'I wish that neighbour cared and wouldn't always take my park.'

All the neighbours knew Jane was ill. I told Jane I would go and fix it. I opened her window so she could hear me, went outside and yelled, 'Hey mate, can you please move your car? This is my sister's car spot, and she needs one close to her house.'

'I can park anywhere,' was his reply.

'If you don't move your car, I will have it towed, along with that piece of junk and that one,' I yelled, pointing to his other two cars.

He turned and asked me, 'On what grounds will you tow them?'

'On the grounds of being a complete arsehole. Move it.' I replied.

I went back into the house to Jane. She looked at me and asked if I had to be quite as aggressive, yet she laughed. To the neighbour's credit, he moved the car and never took the park again.

Jane was right. I would have done anything for her, I would even yell at anyone for her. Every day I tried to do as much as I could, but every day it was obvious we were losing the battle to keep her alive.

In all the time we spent together, Jane only spoke to me on one occasion about dying. She told me very matter-of-factly that she had the easy job of dying. I would have to live with the pain of it forever. She also told me that she believed she would still be around in spirit. She said she knew I would never believe this.

I wasn't convinced, I always thought you just die. Just in case she was right, I asked, 'If you are around in spirit can you make sure you are really obvious, because I don't do subtle very well.'

Jane also made me promise to never ever butt in with how Justin raised Zoe when she was gone. She said Justin will probably do it differently, but we weren't to get involved. She also told me she thought Justin would remarry quite quickly, and I wasn't to be annoyed with him. She asked me to buy a new pair of running shoes as a present for Justin: his birthday was on 28 January, and she didn't think she would live that long. I sat and listened to Jane, promised, organised what she wanted, and kept my word. Jane was right in all her predictions.

As the cancer ravaged Jane's body, she became skeletal from the waist up. The only recognisable feature on Jane's face were her blue eyes. I never understood the saying, 'your eyes are the gateway to your soul', until Jane was at this stage. Jane's eyes were the only connection left to my big sister. When I spoke to her and only focussed on her eyes, I could half-pretend things were ok.

With regard to the rest of her body, from the waist down, as her lymph glands shut down, Jane's body retained fluid and bloated. This meant Jane needed two people to help her move. Simple things like eating and going to the toilet became major missions. Day and night became one long period of time. I felt guilty eating and drinking when Jane couldn't, and hardly slept, preferring to stay up and help her. I didn't know what day it was, and was with Jane always, trying to relieve her pain. The tumour on her liver was so large now, she almost looked pregnant again.

Towards mid-January, Dad and Clare had a business trip overseas. Jane asked me to call Dad and tell him that if he went on this trip, she didn't think she would be alive when he returned. I called Dad. Dad was really upset. He said Jane didn't want him over and he didn't want to upset her. The business trip was important. Basically, he didn't know what the hell to do. Neither did I. Following my call, Jane asked me what Dad was going to do. I said I didn't know. I felt like I was in the middle of a family feud. Jane said, 'I don't think I will ever see Dad again.' I left the room in tears. Jane was right, she never did see Dad again.

One evening, in a similar instance to me in Canada, Jane managed to fall and split her head, requiring stitches. She was really upset by this. She thought she would no longer be able to move around. I tried to reassure Jane and told her I did the same in hospital. Jane was right though, soon after she was bedridden.

Once bedridden, bedsores became a problem. Justin organised a hospital bed and nurses started to visit, as Jane was really in a bad way. Pain management was the priority, and I would sit for hours trying to massage areas on her body where the pain wouldn't let her rest. Justin would go to work for about four hours most days. One particular day I went into Jane's room and she was asleep. To me she looked dead: I couldn't see if she was breathing from the doorway. I didn't want to wake her, because sleep was so hard for her to get now, with all her pain. Jane was ok but it was so frightening. I didn't want to be the one who lost Jane when in my care.

During this time, while her cancer was advancing, some tumours began to protrude. The tumour on her breast looked like it was going to burst the skin. Justin then had to decide whether to treat the tumour with another round of radiotherapy, or just allow it to become an open wound and something else we would have to treat. I am not sure how he decided, but Jane had another round of radiotherapy, and the tumour stopped growing. The only problem was the extra round of radiotherapy weakened her even further.

On the evening of 20 January, Justin and Jane must have decided her pain was not manageable. I think a call was made to her Jane's doctor to organise a home nurse visit. When the nurse arrived, Jane was put onto a driver. This administers pain relief every few seconds. She was hooked up intravenously to morphine, so the pain subsided artificially.

For the first time in a long while, Jane was able to get some sleep. She woke early and called out to Justin and me the next morning. It was Saturday, 21 January 2006. Jane said she wanted to go to the living room and sit on the couch. Justin and I carried her to her wheelchair, rolled her to the living room and transferred her to the couch.

Being late January, it was hot. Melbourne was in for a scorcher that day, with a predicted temperatures around 40°C. Jane and Justin's house didn't have air conditioning, so the house was beginning to heat up. We positioned a pedestal fan near Jane to keep her cool, and I gave her some water. The driver was keeping Jane's pain under control by maintaining a constant drip of morphine, so she was able to chat.

I am not sure how long we all sat there. Mum was also there with Justin and me. Perhaps around mid-morning, there were periods where Jane could not breathe properly. She would look frightened; her eyes would open wide and she would grab at breaths of air. No one knew what to do, so I jumped in and took over.

I would look straight into her eyes and say, 'Jane, this is exactly what I had in Canada. Don't panic, just concentrate on breathing in and out.' I would sit Jane up, put her forehead on mine to support her neck and hold both her hands. I could feel how terrified she was, and I didn't know what I was doing. I was basically guiding her through the early stages of death. These periods of difficult breathing started to become more frequent and more aggressive. Justin said he was going to call the doctor.

Along with breathing difficulties, Jane's voice started to disappear. She lost the ability to speak clearly, then lost the ability to speak at all. I also noticed how little black dots started to appear in her eyes. I assumed she was now going blind. It was quite a horrific, aggressive decline right in front of us.

Her doctor arrived just as Jane was going through another difficult breathing episode. She looked horrified and said, 'Emma you can't cope with this.'

'I have no choice,' I replied.

I was beginning to worry that Jane was going to suffocate, as each breathing episode was getting slightly worse. We must have been managing this for over an hour, and it was just getting out of control.

Her doctor called an ambulance.

When the paramedics arrived, they took one look at the situation and it was decided Jane needed to go to a palliative care hospital. Jane could not speak or move and had to rely on us to make sure the paramedics knew what had been going on. I spoke to Jane and told her we were going to move her. Her eyes looked frightened, but I could also see she wasn't focussing properly.

Jane was taken out to the ambulance and transferred to Cabrini Palliative Care Hospital, probably a fifteen-minute drive away. Mum and I followed in the car, while Justin was in the ambulance with Jane.

In the hospital, Jane fought the inevitability of her death for three hours. She must have now been blind. Her eyes were dark. I held her hand and told her I was really proud of her. To this day I still can't believe I didn't tell her I loved her. We just didn't say that stuff to each other.

Mum, Jane's doctor and I left Justin to spend some time with her. At one point, Justin decided he would stay the night and Mum and I returned to their place to get him a change of clothes. We had picked up some stuff for Justin and were about halfway back to the hospital when he called.

'We have lost Jane,' he told Mum.

Jane died around 5.30 p.m. She was only thirty-five years old.

My world stopped. I remember Mum asking Justin, 'Are you sure?'

Mum and I were stunned.

Poor Mum, I don't know how she got through that day. She witnessed her eldest daughter die in the most horrific way.

I always thought Dad was the tough one.

Back at the hospital, the door to Jane's room was shut. I assumed this meant the patient had died. Mum and I opened the door. Justin was sitting crying beside Jane. Her body already seemed stiff. Mum gave her a kiss on her forehead. I just stood there, frozen at the end of her bed. Justin had called his best mate to ask what to do. He couldn't think. His mate told him he would call a funeral service group to come and pick up Jane's body. Within what seemed like thirty minutes they had arrived.

Two guys dressed in what I thought looked like cheap suits walked in and asked us if we wanted to leave the room. I immediately didn't like them, but it was more that I wished they weren't required. I declined the offer to leave the room, as I wanted to watch and make sure Jane was removed with dignity. Justin and Mum stayed also. A board was slid under her body, and sheets were rolled out beneath it. Jane was wrapped with one sheet over her head and down to her feet, then another sheet was wrapped along her body, so she became completely covered and wrapped, similar to a mummy. She was then carried out and put into a van.

That was the last time I ever saw my sister.

Mum and I drove Justin home. Back at their place, everything looked a mess. There must have been a massive panic to get Jane out, because tables and furniture was all over the place.

The house felt empty.

I had never before felt such overwhelming sadness; a sadness that doesn't abate no matter how much crying you do. I felt really sorry for Justin, and all that he had lost. Zoe was only five-months old and she had just lost her Mum.

Everything, everywhere, was so damn unfair.

I said to Mum we needed to call Dad and Clare. We called their hotel, but the time difference messed things up. I sent Dad an email. I sent Dad the worst email you can ever send your Dad. It read:

Dad. Jane died today just after 5.30 p.m. Please call Mum.

I didn't know what to say, so I didn't say much. In China, Clare told me Dad opened his emails that day and sat and cried at his laptop. Clare said he was inconsolable. She had to leave him while she attended the business meetings alone. Clare held everything together because Dad was broken.

The next morning, we realised it hadn't been a bad dream, and Jane was gone.

Forever. Justin said he was going to tell some close friends. He asked me to contact Jane's close friends. Jane had not seen most of her friends throughout her illness. She didn't want them to remember her ill, so most of them didn't know and were shocked because it seemed she died so quickly.

As others gradually learnt of Jane's death, their grief had to be dealt with. Every person that heard the terrible news made you re-live and re-tell the fact that Jane was gone. It was hard emotionally and really tiring mentally. I took on a lot of the questions from Jane's friends, because I could see Justin was struggling. He didn't need to rehash everything, and I knew Jane would want me to speak to her friends for her.

I will never forget when Jane's best friend from school, Leah, came over to see Mum and me at Jane and Justin's house. The front door was pinned back, trying to get some breeze into the house in the early morning, as the day was going to be another scorcher.

Leah knocked on the flywire and as I walked up the hall to see her, she said between sobs, 'I want my Jane back.'

Probably the same day, Mum and I went for a walk down Vic Ave in Albert Park, near Jane and Justin's house. We just wanted to get out. I bumped into a lady who I worked with throughout my NAB sponsorship. She was sitting outside a café discussing something with her friends and saw me. We said our hello's and then she said she was just telling her friends of a really sad story. She told me she lived behind Reed Street (which was Jane's street), and a young couple lived in the house behind her there. This couple just had their first child, and now the mother had just died of cancer, leaving a five-month-old little girl and the husband. I listened and didn't say a word. For the first time, someone was telling me the story I had been living.

I let her finish and I said, 'That was my sister.'

Everyone looked at me, stunned.

Those early days, after Jane died, I cried until I could cry no more. We all did.

Amongst all this, I had a call from a TA staff member regarding a coaching clinic I was to attend in the next fortnight, or thereabouts. He was calling to discuss some clinic details. I told him I would not be attending, because my sister just died. He told me that was disappointing, because they had planned for me to be there. In all my grief, I didn't know what I was supposed to say to that, so I didn't say anything. He then asked me if he could have a copy of Jane's death certificate so he could get a refund for TA on the plane ticket (MEL-BNE) they had bought for me. I couldn't believe what I was hearing. I hung up. I never sent the death certificate and I never spoke to him again.

I never had anyone in the family die like this before — none of us had — so we didn't really know what to do. It may have been two days after Jane died that someone from the funeral parlour came to the house to start to organise the details. They produced a booklet where we could select a coffin.

I couldn't believe it as Justin started to flick through the pages looking at coffins. At one point, Justin said, 'I definitely can't get a pine coffin, Jane hated pine furniture.'

I don't know what Justin selected. I couldn't get through the entire booklet.

Justin must have been told he needed to select a cemetery. Apparently the 'nicest' or most picturesque setting is the Eltham cemetery, just over one kilometre from home. Justin looked at a few places with a close friend and he decided on Eltham. He called me to come and have a look at the plot and said it has a nice view, just in case she can see.

Organising the funeral was the next thing. I had no idea. Justin called me one day and asked me if I could call Wesley College. We all loved school, maybe they would be able to organise Jane's funeral. I agreed. I hadn't been back at school for ages. I had been asked back in the 1990s when I was racing well to attend an assembly, but I missed most of my school reunions so far. I looked up who the current Principal was, and was surprised Wesley had a female Principal in Dr Helen Drennen.

Helen was new to Wesley in my final year at school in 1989. I remembered her but didn't know her well. I didn't take any of her subjects, so she hadn't taught me as such. I wasn't sure if I could remember her filling in a lesson or two at one stage. I hoped not, because my policy at school was basically a 'stop work' with fill-in teachers and I usually became very disruptive. I called Wesley and hoped for the best.

When I called the main campus in St Kilda Road, Melbourne, I asked the receptionist if I could speak to Helen Drennen. Asked who was speaking, I said, 'Emma Carney'. My call was immediately taken by Helen, and she said:

Emma, we have heard, and we are very sorry to hear of your family's loss. This morning I announced to staff that one of the Carney girls has died. We have the flags flying at half-mast at every single campus. If your family would allow us, Wesley would like to run Jane's funeral.

I couldn't believe what I was hearing. I think I cried a lot. I realised Wesley College is not just a world class school, it is also a community that will support you and care for you for life. You don't just go to Wesley to be educated; you go to Wesley to be a part of a community you have for life. I will never forget what Wesley did for my family. Helen could tell I was a mess, so told me to bring Jane's husband when we were ready, and she would organise a meeting with the appropriate college staff.

Justin met with Wesley staff, and Jane's funeral was organised. It was decided the College Chapel was too small, so it was moved to the Uniting Church in Malvern. Wesley organised everything, right down to the finest detail. Even Mr Webber the school chaplain at the time we all attended Wesley was called in to run the service.

The day of Jane's funeral arrived. I wore a dress Jane had lent me two years ago and I had never returned. She had asked me so many times, 'Emma, where is my bloody black dress?' but I had kept it and kept wearing it — as an annoying little sister does.

I never thought I would wear it to her funeral.

Justin asked me if I could speak at Jane's funeral, so I prepared something. I was the only member of the family involved in the service. As the family of the deceased, we entered the church from a different door. We were met by Mr Webber. I was surprised he remembered me. I wasn't a particularly good student when it came to chapel service at school. Dad lost it at the door. Jane and Dad had been really quite similar people. Jane was the only daughter to have a professional career as a lawyer, and there were other things growing up that Jane would discuss with Dad. She studied subjects like politics and legal studies. I hadn't really shown any interest in much other than sport, so I knew there was a difference in what Dad discussed with Jane growing up.

It was heartbreaking to see Dad so sad. I had never seen him cry like that. Dad was very old school and just didn't cry, didn't flinch really. He was always our protector. His reaction was just the start of a very, very sad and emotional day. Mum was visibly shaking, but she held herself together. She strategically wore her sunglasses, so no one could really see what was going on.

Once inside the church, I couldn't believe the number of people there. Wesley had predicted a large number, but the place was packed. I noticed a lot of Wesley teachers including the Principal Helen, school friends and Jane's personal and professional friends. A lot of my friends also turned up. It was a large group of people who represented Jane's life in different ways. It surprised me how many people were there and how it spanned and covered all the people and times of Jane's life.

At the front of the church sat Jane's coffin. I couldn't stop looking at it. I declined to view Jane at the funeral parlour, because I knew her body didn't look like my sister should anymore. I sat and stared and stared at her coffin, wishing it wasn't there but also in what was like a stunned disbelief that my sister was inside.

As the immediate family, Mum, Dad, Clare and I took the front row seats. Behind us, Justin was seated with Zoe on his lap. We all acknowledged each other but nothing was said. None of us could speak. I think Mum gave Justin a hug, but I was now concentrating on holding myself together. After all, I needed to speak soon.

The service took place, and I honestly have no idea what was said. When Mr Webber spoke, his voice took me back to my days at Wesley. It was nice to have him run the service. He knew us all as a family and would have remembered Jane well. There was a eulogy from Field Rickards, another Wesley College connection and then I spoke.

I stood at the pulpit of the church with two of Jane's friends. Her good school friend Leah and a more recent friend Mindy. Justin wanted us all to speak, because I represented family, Leah school and long-term friendships, while Mindy represented recent great friends to Jane and Justin. I can't remember what I spoke about, but it was all about my life with Jane and how I will always keep Jane alive in my life. I can't remember what Leah and Mindy spoke about either. I do remember a lot of crying up there. I also remember looking at two things: Jane's coffin and little Zoe in the crowd sitting in her Dad's lap.

Both were heartbreaking.

At the completion of the service, Jane's coffin was taken out, and we all followed behind. I couldn't stop watching it and saw it being placed in the back of a hearse. I wanted to go and sit with it. It seemed odd, we were all there for Jane, and she was on her own.

Everyone gathered in the church grounds. People came up to us constantly, but I can't really remember who. A lot of familiar faces, and a lot of people I hadn't seen in ages. I didn't feel like chatting. Mum, Dad, Clare and I really just stood there, waiting to be told what to do next. As I stood there, I wondered how they all knew Jane had died, and I wondered how many would come to my funeral.

Perhaps fifteen minutes later close family members were asked to follow the hearse. Jane's burial was open to all, so there must have been a long line of cars following. We drove to Eltham. As we had grown up in Eltham, it seemed odd driving to the cemetery on Mount Pleasant Road. Our family house was up the same road, and we drove past the cemetery every day. Not once did I ever think I would be burying a family member there.

We arrived at Eltham Cemetery and were allowed to drive in. Jane's grave was in a new section to the south-west of the cemetery. Her coffin was carried from the hearse and placed beside the grave. We all gathered and suddenly the coffin was lifted over the grave and lowered down. I wanted to yell out to tell them to stop. I wanted everything to stop. It was all going too fast, and it was all too final. I wanted Jane to remain up with us, not buried. I just watched sadly as her coffin was lowered, without saying a word. It was so sombre. We were asked to step forward and throw some dirt onto her coffin. I stood there and looked down. It was way too far into the ground for my liking. She was too far away now. I threw in some dirt and stepped back.

That was the last I saw of Jane's coffin.

Jane was really gone.

That was pretty much it. I have never understood why people call a funeral a 'celebration of someone's life'. It isn't. It is sealing off someone's life and trying to accept they are gone. Like an official farewell; 'we told you they died' message. There was a wake at Jane and Justin's place, but I didn't stay for long. Do people really need to eat and celebrate after that horrendous day?

On the way home, we stopped to visit Jane. We all sat and cried at a pile of newly turned earth where Jane was now freshly buried. Dad was inconsolable.

And that was that.

In eighteen short, horrific months I had lost my racing career, had a life-saving implant for my heart, and now I had lost my big sister to cancer.

I had another check up with Jeff Alison. It was the regular, six-monthly check-up. Jeff asked me how I was going, and again I cried. He probably wished he never asked …

'My sister died,' I told him.

Jeff was a little lost for words. 'I'm sorry,' he said.

Poor Jeff, he will probably endure all that goes on in my life. Not in a day-to-day sense, but he will end up knowing all my major life events and major life stuff ups, which seemed endless, just because he is unfortunate enough to be my heart specialist. In my cloud of negativity, I wondered later that day if Jeff would think

I was too hard a patient. I didn't think any other patients would have as much baggage as me. I expected he didn't need all this negativity.

I had my check-up. There were some abnormalities, but that was due to my regular rides. I left with Jeff telling me to look after myself.

At that stage in time, I was constantly heavy-hearted and gloomy. I hardly smiled. I actually spent some time feeling guilty that I had used up all the family's good luck in Canada by managing to stay alive and avoid cardiac arrest. Maybe there had been no luck left for Jane.

I pretty much did nothing except ride my bike and said little to anyone outside the family, apart from my bike group. Everything was pointless. My heart was now both damaged and heavy.

Perhaps a month following Jane's funeral, Helen Drennen's PA called me and asked me to see Helen at Wesley. I thought maybe Helen was going to tell me I had been a bad student and she hadn't forgotten.

I made a time, and once in Helen's office, she asked me what I was doing now.

I was a little sick of pretending to everyone that I was fine, and said something along the lines of, 'I don't know. Nothing. I'm struggling.'

Helen must have already guessed this. She invited me to come back to school.

In my negative mindset, I told Helen, 'I'm not a teacher.'

She suggested I could return, not as a teacher, but as a coach, and contribute to the College sport program.

'I'm not qualified,' I told her, still negative.

'Emma, you are a Wesley Collegian, and a valuable member of the College Community. You are also a World Champion. You are well qualified,' Helen told me.

I took Helen up on her offer.

16. Nothing to go Home To

The year 2006 had started in the worst way possible.

Jane was gone.

In April 2006, Melbourne hosted the Commonwealth Games. Jane and Justin had bought some tickets to the athletics. Justin didn't want to use them. It was too sad. I didn't want to use them either. I was asked to do some commentary for the Commonwealth Games Triathlon to be held in St Kilda, but I didn't want to.

I didn't want to do anything. I had lost hope in life.

I wanted time to stop. Every day, every minute, every second that passed, I felt like I was leaving Jane behind.

Sometimes I felt like I was forgetting what she looked like. I hated myself when I had these thoughts.

I didn't want to forget her.

I wasn't the only one struggling. Mum and Dad visited Jane's grave every day. Every night they lit a candle at her grave. It was a wonder Dad didn't start a bushfire in Eltham that summer.

Mum spent time looking after Zoe while Justin was at work. Mum loved every minute with Zoe and this time was really important for my family. The connection with Zoe now was disjointed. While she was a direct family line, we as a family lost our connection with Justin. Jane was no longer there, so there was no one keeping us involved. Justin understandably needed space, and within three months, he put Zoe into day care and told Mum she was no longer looking after her granddaughter. Mum was incredibly heartbroken. Dad was speechless, and we all were really sad again. It was awful.

I assumed Justin was just as broken but couldn't talk to any of us about it. Nothing was going to bring Jane back, so everyone coped in different ways.

Justin also removed all Jane's things. We assume he put them into storage, but we were never told. Jane had a lot of things that had been passed on through our family because she was the first born. Many had been for generations, so my family lost them too.

I promised Jane that I would not interfere with Justin's decisions, and told Mum, Dad and Clare we could do nothing.

It was an awful time. My family had lost Jane, and now it seems we were being cut from Zoe's life as regular and consistent family members.

Zoe gradually grew up, and we saw her for birthdays, Christmas (never Christmas day) and other odd special occasions we could grab. To this day, Zoe has never been allowed a sleepover or long visit with any of us. I have never understood why. I hoped that Zoe would have enough Carney in her to grow older and want to spend time with us when she could decide to do so.

Justin remarried within eighteen months, and the gap from my family grew wider still.

I spent all of 2006 house-sitting a friend's place in Albert Park, quite near to Jane and Justin's house. I lived alone and looking back that probably wasn't a good thing to do. I didn't talk much, didn't socialise much, I didn't really do anything.

What I did do was throw a lot of stuff out. It was hard going back to Mum and Dad's and seeing Jane's things. I decided I didn't want to leave things behind that everyone had to sift through if anything happened to me. I had a large 'cull' of anything I hadn't used in the last few years. I was going to throw out all my trophies and medals too. They seemed so pointless to me now, but Mum and Dad wouldn't let me.

To fill in this time in my life, I helped out with a few bike charities. I would ride and help corporates who were raising money for charities to get through their required days' ride. As a result, over the next few years I rode my bike from Adelaide to Melbourne, Sydney to Melbourne (three times), Canberra to Melbourne, Port Macquarie to Noosa, Bundaberg to Brisbane, and around Tasmania. All very slowly I might add.

Each time, on the final day, as we approached our destination and the week of slow riding was ending, the entire group would be pleased to be going home. For me, the terrible sadness always returned. I felt I had nothing to go home to anymore. The previous few days while distracted with the group, I could pretend everything was ok. Now, going home, the terrible heaviness of losing Jane, losing my career, losing everything, always returned to leave me feeling helplessly heartbroken all over again.

Through this year I constantly carried a heaviness in my heart. It was a very sad time. I wondered if I would always feel this sad, or whether I would develop an ability to live with the loss of Jane better.

I commenced coaching at Wesley College, thanks to Principal Dr Helen Drennen's suggestion, and Mr Mark Hibbins (Hibbo) was the lucky (?) man to be my first ever boss. I was back wearing the purple and gold I had worn throughout my childhood, this time the staff version.

While I enjoyed my time there, I did not think I was productive enough to warrant a salary. I'm not sure what it was. Perhaps I doubted everything I did, because everything in my life was such a disaster to me at that time. I felt I was letting Wesley down, and by the end of the year I spoke to Hibbo to suggest I just coach athletics and cross country part-time. I thought I couldn't possibly mess that up, after all I practically pioneered that for girls at Wesley. Hibbo had been very patient with me, and he told me I needed to look after myself.

As I continued riding and still managing big kilometres throughout the year, I was really quite fit. So fit in fact, I decided to enter a bike race. The Melbourne to Warrnambool bike race is a 300 km event run at the end of October each year. I called the race organiser and was surprised I got a start — it seemed not everyone had written me off.

With an event of this distance, you always hoped for great weather. On the morning of the race the weather was outstanding. Sunny with light winds. Perfect conditions. At the start there were a few people who looked a bit too serious. I was still trying to convince myself I was 'just going easy' when we rolled out for the start. When racing began, the pace seemed a little too furious for a 300 km event. I decided I would have to ride towards the middle to last third of the pack to ensure I was warmed up properly. I basically drafted and wheel-sucked (sat in the slip-stream of the rider in front) as many people as I could so I was conserving energy.

This tactic was fine, but the obvious problem was that the less experienced riders were also towards the back with me. Watching the peloton ahead as we negotiated various traffic islands, I decided someone was going to crash soon, because there were too many 'near misses' for my liking. I started to weave my way through the peloton towards the front, taking particular care to remain to one side to avoid crashes. Within a minute of me predicting a crash, one occurred. About five blokes all took themselves out through a roundabout, splitting the peloton.

I must be hard wired, or maybe I am just plain stupid, but as soon as the crash happened, I reacted and pushed to catch up with the riders who were ahead. Once I had got back onto the peloton, I suddenly realised that I had just done an all-out sprint.

I knew for sure my heart rate was over 160 bpm and aware that the defibrillator corrects any heart rate recorded above that, regardless of whether it is an arrhythmia or not. This was the main problem with pushing myself too hard. I looked at my speedo and I was rolling at 55 kph. I decided my only option was to brace myself — there was no way I could stop in time — so I held onto my drops and hoped for the best.

Sure enough, a shock was delivered by my defibrillator. I managed to keep my bike upright but could feel my heart rate was still high. I pulled over and got off my bike, trying to calm my heart. I knew I only had thirty seconds to the next shock. By this time the following motorbikes and some media had pulled up. I couldn't talk, because I was trying to calm my heart rate.

Suddenly my defibrillator delivered another shock. Some of the people around me worked out what was going on. I told everyone I had stopped because I didn't feel well.

Fortunately, I managed to assure everyone gathered around me that I was ok, so I was left alone. The race continued, while I turned my bike in the opposite direction and rolled home.

Following the disaster of that attempted 'non-race' I was really quite dejected with myself. Nothing made me happy. I also decided I missed my running. I was running a bit, but not as often as I liked because my Achilles were so sore all the time. I couldn't remember the last time I had got up in the morning without suffering unbearable Achilles soreness for the first thirty minutes of the day. I decided to do something about it. I knew I needed surgery, and I figured while I was being so unproductive, perhaps I should get my injuries addressed finally.

I ended up in the rooms of renowned foot and ankle surgeon Dr Mark Blackney. Mark took one look at my heels and Achilles and said 'Yes, they need surgery.' He diagnosed me with 'Hagland Syndrome' on both heels. This is a condition where the heel bone protrudes and irritates the Achilles from the inside of the tendon. The solution is to remove the Achilles, slice off the protruding heel bone and then re-attach the Achilles with screws. Mark said I needed both done, but perhaps we should do one at a time. The recovery was slightly horrendous, with a non-weight-bearing period for ten days after surgery. I then had a surgical CAM walker for ten weeks. We decided my left foot was slightly worse, so I was booked in for 27 November 2006. Exactly twelve years to the day after winning my first world title I was having my first Achilles operation.

As usual with me, things were slightly more complicated. Dr Jeff Alison was consulted regarding my defibrillator and an ICD tech was called in for my Achilles operation to turn it off, and then turn it back on following the surgery.

Mark Blackneys' procedure did not result in quite as much pain as my defibrillator implant, but the operating theatre was far more frightening. Mark had what looked like a saw, a hammer and a screwdriver at the ready when I was wheeled in. I couldn't stop thinking about the sight of them as the anaesthetist put me to sleep.

The recovery for my Achilles surgery wasn't as bad as I thought it was going to be, and before long I was able to jog lightly on my 'new' pain free Achilles.

During this time, Dad and Clare were building a clothing brand and were travelling more as the business grew. On one particular business trip, Clare met her husband to be. She was on a Qantas flight with Dad and Alex just appeared, like a long-lost friend.

You could always strike up a conversation with Alex. He was a man of supreme style and class.

In contrast to Clare's classy meeting of her husband to be, in 2007 I also met my husband to be.

Not quite the same 'lost in love' fairytale developed from my meeting though.

17. My son Jack

In 2007, still very, very sad from losing my sister Jane, I met a guy who would, for a few short years, help me to forget I was broken. He introduced me to a world where training was not the focus, where my personal failures and life's tragedies didn't matter.

Despite a slow start, during which we got to know each other, I really felt like I had met my perfect match. Looking back, I now think the underlying attraction for me was probably the contrast of his lifestyle to my own. In just under ten years, my sport had dumped on me in a very public way, I had lost my triathlon career through a forced retirement, I was faced with a life-threatening health condition, and I had watched my sister die tragically from cancer. I had been sad for a very, very long time. If I had been honest with myself, deep down I was annoyed and disappointed with how things turned out. I had always looked after myself, always eaten healthy, but I ended up with a heart condition. My sister had always worked hard, but now she was dead. I had been brought up to work hard, and I felt that had let me down too. I could no longer do what I had always wanted: my lifelong goal was to be a professional athlete, to race and compete at the highest level for Australia. Heartbroken with being unable to do that, I was trying to ignore triathlon. But I missed it so much. Suddenly I had someone who provided a way to escape what I had been through. I wasn't the type to talk about my problems, I just tried to move on. He wasn't a part of my past and didn't ask about it, so it was 'safely' ignored.

Meeting someone meant that, for the first time in a while, I didn't feel sad. I seemed to have got through my awful times and felt that perhaps 'normal' life without triathlon wasn't so bad.

Early on in our relationship, I decided to renovate my house in East Melbourne. I had put the money aside, so I thought it was about time I had a place I could call home. I had not lived in the one place and actually unpacked in a home since I left school almost twenty years earlier.

The house needed an awful lot of work. It was an 1890s terrace house and behind the heritage-listed façade, I needed to knock everything down and open the entire place up with an open-plan design. I decided on wooden floors in the front two-storey terrace section and polished concrete floors in the main open-living area added to the back. White walls and an exposed wooden staircase were also a feature, but City of Melbourne Council regulations slowed the project, and did my head in. Finally, after around eight full house designs and six applications to council, my plans were approved in mid-2009.

While the building application was in progress, I project-managed the rest of the renovation. I sourced everything required internally and externally myself, and drove myself crazy with the finer details of taps, ovens, water tanks, cabinet designs, kitchen benches, benchtops, heating, window designs, doors, toilets, tiles, solar panels ... It was endless. Soon I had spent the money I had set aside for the renovation. I took on a loan. Very importantly, as would soon be revealed, all financial contribution to my East Melbourne property was borne by me alone.

Things were going well, and before long I was engaged to be married. The wedding took place in November 2009, in the beachside town of Lorne, along the Great Ocean Road in Victoria. My sister Clare and best friend Katie Mactier were my bridesmaids, with Jane's little Zoe was my flower girl. My other lifelong friend Tiffany Cherry was MC for the day. I missed Jane all day.

I found myself worrying on my wedding day, as to whether I was doing the right thing. It was hard to pinpoint. I felt like once I was married, I would no longer be me. I decided I was just feeling apprehensive, and this was normal.

From all reports, it was a 'great wedding' to attend. Not long afterwards, I found myself feeling tired. I also felt a bit queasy in the mornings. It dawned on me that maybe I was pregnant. Of course, I was. Everything happens quickly with me. We were now newlyweds, had a major house renovation to finish, and a baby on the way.

Given my heart condition, mine was considered a 'high risk' pregnancy. The Prof required me to have the baby at Monash, where both he and Dr Jeff Alison were based, but my pregnancy was actually very simple. Apart from the initial slight morning sickness, I had no real problems. I had my regular six-monthly defibrillator check-up with Dr Jeff Alison in my first trimester, and he said I would need my defibrillator changed early in my second trimester because the battery was low. Jeff didn't seem to think this was a problem, so May 2010, I was admitted to Jesse Macpherson Private Hospital at Monash Medical Centre for the heart procedure.

Otherwise, my pregnancy proceeded as normal. Exercise-wise, I swam a little to keep myself sane, but didn't ride or run. Doctors told me to 'use discomfort' as a guide to exercise intensity. I figured that I had no sane measurement of exercise discomfort, so I just steered clear of exercise. I just wanted a healthy baby.

I hardly looked pregnant. I was actually so small that with four weeks to go I still hadn't bought any maternity clothes. I decided maybe I was going to blow out in the last month, so I took myself shopping. While shopping, I asked the shop assistant if I had the right size and she asked how many weeks I had to go. I said, 'Four'. The look of shock and surprise on her face made me call my obstetrician and ask if she thought I needed a further scan, because I was still hardly showing.

Soon afterwards, a scan revealed that everything was 'perfect'. What they didn't tell me was my baby was the right length, but very, very thin.

My baby was due on 7 July 2010, but at around 4.20 a.m. on 22 June, my waters broke. I called Monash Maternity Hospital. They must have a lot of false alarms, because I was grilled over the phone on what I interpreted as my waters breaking. I arrived at Monash about 5.30 a.m.

On arrival, I was asked by the maternity staff for my papers and my birthing plan. I forgot to bring anything with me, apparently you are supposed to also pack a bag. I had nothing. I was informed that my obstetrician was overseas, but a replacement had been organised. The Prof was also called in. I felt a bit sorry for him, this was really outside his cardiology duties.

Once admitted, I told the staff that as there was no post-event drug testing (every race I ever did there was post-event drug testing according to international sporting anti-doping laws), I would like full drugs used.

Everyone thought I was joking. I had never been more serious in my life. I wasn't going to take on any more pain and discomfort. I had done enough of that in my life. For the first time, I was taking the easiest option available. I couldn't see the point in making what already seemed to me to be a very difficult life experience any harder. I also had my heart to worry about. No one really knew what reaction it would have. For the first time in my life I was going full drugs.

With an epidural administered, and no pain, I can honestly say having a baby was much simpler than I imagined. I do feel like I cheated a little though.

My baby was born at 11.35 a.m. He was immediately noisy but calmed when held. As my baby was lifted to me, I saw he was a little boy. Very, very little. Very thin and old looking. Wrinkled and worried. There was obviously something a little different about him, because a paediatric doctor was called in and he told me to, 'Hold him quickly, because he has to go upstairs to be kept warm.'

He was weighed and was 1.9 kg or just under 4.2 lb, about half the weight of a 'normal' baby. He was a normal length though, which showed just how thin he was.

After a very brief hold of my little baby, he was taken away and I told everyone to make sure he was tagged and named as my child on both feet and both wrists. I asked my doctor if he could do this in front of me, but as he was underweight, they insisted on removing him because he needed to be incubated to remain warm.

As everyone left, my tiny baby, his dad pushing, and two midwives along with the doctor, I panicked. During Jane's funeral, I sat in the church and thought to myself that I hoped I was the next person to die in my family, because I didn't think I could get through another funeral for someone I loved and cared for that much. Now I had only just met my little boy and suddenly, if anything happened to him, I would be back to how I was feeling at Jane's funeral. I sensed there was an urgency to him being taken for medical attention and I was immediately worried for him.

I was told I wasn't able to see my baby for another twenty-four hours, because I had to go to cardiology, while he was to go to the special care nursery in the maternity ward. It was two floors away in the Jesse McPherson Private Hospital. This was an awful time for me and just broke my heart.

Once in my hospital room, I waited to hear news of where my little baby was, and what the panic was to get him into an incubator. I asked his dad when he returned down to my room. He said he didn't know, but all looked ok. I asked him to find out what was wrong, and I was promptly told to stop being emotional.

At this point we discussed names. I liked Garth but was told there was no way we were naming him Garth because everyone would know it was after Garth Prowd. I couldn't really see the problem in that. The name 'Jack' was brought up. We both liked Jack and my Dad's name was added.

With that, Jack David was named.

As time ticked by, my parents arrived and visited Jack. They came down with photos of them holding him, and I became upset again. Jealous really. Why couldn't I see my son? One of the cardiology nurses was checking my vitals, and I asked if I could visit Jack. She said the Prof had said I was to remain rested until the morning.

'But I won't tell the Prof,' I begged.

The nurses must have all been mums, and back at their nurse's station they decided to sneak me out in a wheelchair. I had to agree I would not walk, because if anything happened to me, they were in trouble. I was told they would wheel me up to visit Jack. Of course, they didn't wheel me fast enough, so I complained the whole way. My complaining aside, those nurses in cardiology that afternoon were absolute life savers. I have no idea if the Prof knew his cardiology nurses did this for me.

Upstairs I saw Jack for the first time. I asked to hold him, and the midwives said Jack had already been out of the incubator today and needed to remain in there. I wore them down and was able to hold my baby properly for the first time. He was tiny. So tiny it frightened me. Jack's little arms lay outstretched on my lap as the light shone onto his tightly closed, scrunched, little eyes. He momentarily opened them, to reveal dark eyes that were obviously trying to focus but couldn't. This little human being completely won me over, and I was immediately protective of him. The midwife came to me and said he needed to go back into the incubator. He also needed to be fed. I asked what she was going to feed him, and she said formula.

The word 'formula' grated my soul.

When Jane had been ill, she was forced to feed Zoe formula, as the chemo treatment prevented her from breastfeeding. All Jane ever wanted to do throughout her sickness was be a mum to Zoe. The smell of formula and the entire process of distancing me from my baby just irked me and reminded me of that horrible time. I asked the midwife if Jack could be completely breast fed.

It was agreed I would express milk and Jack would be fed my breastmilk. I had a discussion with the doctor also, and as Jack needed to gain weight, there would be some formula in between feeds to boost calories. Once this was organised, I was wheeled out leaving Jack alone in his incubator. It broke my heart to leave him.

Fortunately, the next day I was released from Cardiology. I almost pushed the Prof out of the way when he said I could go up to the maternity ward. I went straight to visit Jack.

While I held Jack properly for the first time, I wanted to feed him and care for him instead of the midwives. But I understood he needed to rest. I sat with him the entire day in the nursery. The Prof came in to see us. He asked me how I was, and I told the Prof I was worried something was wrong with Jack.

'Why is he in here Prof?' I asked him

No one had actually told me why Jack was in the special care nursery. The Prof left, must have spoken to the doctors, and returned to tell me that Jack was just underweight and needed more intense care and twenty-four-hour watch. The doctor said Jack needed to weigh 2.5 kg to leave and go home. I thanked the Prof for caring. He was beginning to become more like a second Dad rather than 'just' my cardiologist.

While it was really special to finally be with Jack, I felt really sorry and sad for what Jane must have gone through with her new little baby, becoming ill and then realising she was never going to see her little girl grow up. I really struggled with these constant sad thoughts of Jane and what she went through as a new Mum. Almost a guilt that I was able to be a mother and knowing that all this was taken away from Jane.

I was discharged from hospital before Jack made his departure weight. I was told to go home and just come back for regular visits. I was not going to walk out on my son's care.

The feeding routine at that time was on a 2-hour cycle, with night feeds at 3-4 hours. I told the midwives I would make every feed except for the one at 3 a.m. Everyone told me that was ridiculous, including my husband. I was told that had never been done before.

Being the first to do something never put me off trying and nothing was going to stop me from looking after Jack. Absolutely nothing. I had always been an early riser, so early starts didn't faze me, and I was also so looking forward to seeing Jack I had no trouble getting up in the morning. My husband and I argued about my feeding plan. Things were becoming tense all the time between us.

I really felt being there for Jack was the right thing to do for him, regardless of what anyone thought of me. I could tell my husband was not impressed with my plans to care for Jack as we left the hospital because he hardly spoke to me. I felt uneasy in the silence of the car ride home. There had been a lot of looming differences in our approach to parenting over the past five days, and on reflection a lot of signs that it would be like this before Jack arrived.

Fortunately, Jack made weight ten days after being born. He left hospital at 2.4 kg, slightly under the target weight, but I think the doctor knew I would have been distraught if Jack failed his weigh-in. Jack was tiny in his car capsule, he hardly reached either end.

It was wonderful to have him leave the hospital with us finally.

Finally, Jack was with us.

Finally, our little family was together.

But I still had mixed emotions driving Jack home. Jane's little girl Zoe had been ten days old when Jane was diagnosed with cancer. She had only been able to be a mum for ten days. It was such a short time.

So very sad.

A few months after Jack was born, we were ready to move into East Melbourne. Those early days were difficult. I really think it would be helpful if babies came with instructions. I was muddling along, and considering we were all surviving, I thought I was doing a good job. My Mum dropped in a lot and was a life saver, as everyone's mum is with a new baby. Getting out of the house was becoming a daily achievement. Jack wasn't a baby that slept well, didn't like prams, hated the car, and just loved being held.

What was becoming glaringly and increasingly obvious during this time was the difference in opinion my husband and I had towards parenting. Whatever I did seemed wrong in the eyes of my husband. We argued more and more, and I used my own coping mechanism again. The same way I had coped with adversity all my life: block it out, carry on. Ignore it. I just managed on my own and I stopped asking for help.

As 2010 closed out, from the outside we looked like the perfect family. But I felt very alone and isolated from my husband. What had started as a loving and caring relationship, had disappeared. It felt like every time something happened between my husband and I, it was like picking a scab off a sore. Everything became slightly worse with every little argument. There was no healing, just a decline in our relationship. It was through this period, under the stress of everything, that my husband started to become violent. Initially it was doors and walls punched in, toys thrown and kicked: then I started getting hurt. We never ever spoke of the 'incidents', but they were always lurking in the back of my mind. We were moving further and further away from ever being close again.

It is a well-known fact that if you suspect you are in an abusive relationship, try the 'no' test. That is, start saying no to things. If your partner blows up, they have been controlling and manipulating you. I decided to test this theory on my domestic situation and noticed increasingly aggressive behaviour from my husband as a result. It had developed subtly, with quiet sulking that developed into rants. Outbursts becoming more and more common. I also noticed my financial independence was slipping away from me as my husband's controlling behaviour took over all areas of my life. This too started subtly, with his requesting all my bank login details, passwords and pin numbers and small comments about my spending. I found myself increasingly reliant on my husband for money for the household. At the same time, his resentment of my way of work, training people and coaching, grew. He constantly removed my independence and undermined my control over my own living. I began to also notice all the household debt was being placed in my name, which didn't make any sense to me, given he was the one earning a salary.

As I began to realise the control my husband had gained over me, Jack's welfare became my major concern. I prioritised my time with him, started to cancel things, and change my mind. I even dared to do what I wanted. My husband responded to my effort to be slightly more independent, and especially my focus on Jack, in a 'how dare you' fashion; in a silent, passive aggressive manner.

In this way, Jack saved me. If I hadn't started doing things for Jack, I probably would have always put up with my situation, because I loved my husband. I had been turning a blind eye to the control, the constant questioning. The difference was now I had Jack, and I didn't want Jack growing up in that strained, negative environment.

Looking back at our relationship, I think this tendency had always existed in him. I would justify his behaviour towards me as just him being tired from work, or maybe me being difficult to live with. I considered that perhaps Jack had just changed the dynamics of our relationship and his father couldn't adjust to not being the centre of my attention anymore.

Whatever was going on was no longer enjoyable.

After an argument in early 2011, where both Jack and I were pushed over, I started to worry about the impact of the stress on my heart. My finger was broken so badly a few months later it required surgery. Things were getting out of control.

I don't know why but I remember I called Les McDonald during this time, for a chat with someone I missed. Les had now stepped down from the Presidency of the ITU and in his very direct fashion seemed amazed at the situation I was in.

'Why do strong women marry such fools?' he asked me.

He told me to look after myself and that I should get involved in the ITU, after all I knew triathlon so well. Triathlon seemed very distant from my life at the time.

My husband's financial control reached a new low point when I was locked out of the 'family' bank account. It was the breaking point for me. Up to this point, every argument, every little push or shove, I could look at and justify that perhaps I had caused or contributed to the conflict. After all it takes two to argue. But locking me out of a bank account was calculated, a planned deceit. This time I could not find an excuse for his behaviour, and suddenly trust was gone from our relationship.

I decided I would say nothing, I had a little bit of hope that maybe he would tell me. He never did. Everything was futile though, because within a few weeks, after storming out of the house, he requested I remove all his property. I did as he asked.

Despite all that had happened, and all my husband had put both Jack and me through, I missed him terribly once this had happened. With hindsight though, I think when I missed him, I was actually just mourning what I thought I had in my marriage but in reality, never had at all. I struggled with the concept of simply giving up on something. It took two to fix this, I could not do it alone. I had never given up on anything before, and it seemed the first thing I chose to give up on was my marriage to Jack's dad.

But there was one good thing to come out of my marriage: my son is and always will be the highlight of my life. They do say there is a special bond between sons and their mum, and although I do not have a daughter to compare, there is something very special between my son and me. I think all parents can attest that your love for your own child surpasses any love you have for anyone else. It is absolutely true for me, and my love for Jack.

18. My 'Shit Cup' Theory

I have developed a theory over my life, and I call it the 'shit cup' theory. I believe everyone can manage a particular level of stuff (problems, or 'shit') in their lives. An individual can manage others problems to an extent, but everyone at some stage needs to also help themselves. You cannot help people if they will not help themselves or recognise that they need help. Sometimes there are exceptions to the level of stuff you can take on for a person, and Jack was my exception. I would always have time in my shit cup for whatever Jack needs to put in it.

When the equilibrium of your cup is exceeded (that is, it is overflowing, and you can no longer manage it), you have no option other than to remove the source of the excessive shit because it has no positive value in your life. Life is too short for too much negativity.

I have always been a very independent person, and my 'shit cup' has predominantly been filled with my close family issues and life issues. Since being married, I also had my husband's shit. His had got way out of hand.

As my husband's behaviour, deceit, lying, and manipulation of the facts all piled up, my shit cup overflowed, and I wanted out. There was nothing I could do other than to stop the overflowing and protect Jack and me.

We briefly tried to work things out, but everything seemed broken now. Nothing was the same and within a few weeks we separated for the last time.

Once I realised finally that my shit cup was too full, I could start to accept that my marriage was over.

I believe my husband had been planning a separation for a while, because he commenced Family Law Court proceedings within a few weeks of storming out of the house.

Family Court is a place everyone should avoid if possible. In the family court, no one 'wins.' At best you can attempt to minimise the damage to your life, your children, and your assets, but this can only be achieved at a very high financial cost in legal bills. Nothing to do with the family court is pleasant. The entire process is toxic. It is also depressing. The system basically requires each party to put together self-serving affidavits regarding the items to be allocated. In our case and this type of system, even little Jack became an item.

The lack of compassion and empathy in that courtroom chilled me to the bone. The court provides that 'the child's best interests' are the focus, but I found the procedural way the process carved up my son's future time between his mother and father to be clinical, repulsive and poignant.

To top it all off, it was glaringly obvious I was in a dire financial state. Prior to my marriage, I had been debt free. I now had legal bills, a mortgage and I was earning next to nothing. To put more of a financial strain on things, Wesley College notified me that Jack had been accepted into their Early Childhood Learning Centre class for three-year-olds, commencing in 2014, at a cost of $4000 to secure his place, and another $16,000 throughout the upcoming school year. Despite also enrolling Jack at Wesley, his father refused to contribute financially, so Jack's education costs were going to be borne by me alone.

I somehow had to keep Jack and me going financially.

The trial was set for 28 March 2014. My husband was the applicant and sought the even distribution of assets and allocation of the care of Jack. I was the respondent and wanted my house retained, leaving him the money he had hidden from me while married (siphoned off while I was locked out of the 'family' bank account), and Jack to be cared for as guided by a Court-ordered family assessment.

The result was three days in the Federal Circuit Family Court. I relied heavily on my lawyers to do the right thing by my responding application, but it was really all about minimising losses. I felt vulnerable and broken. It was awful and I hated every moment in that place. Fortunately, our judge, while intimidating, was fair in his judgement.

The trial ironically concluded on April Fools' day 2014.

With the sealed court orders agreed upon, I left the courtroom that day brokenhearted and in financial ruin. I might have saved my house from my husband, but my lawyers almost took it from me anyway as I struggled to pay their exorbitant fees.

My husband walked out the courtroom that same day, bought himself a BMW car, limited his financial contribution towards Jack's upbringing to just equal to the minimum amount required by law, and has refused to contribute a cent towards Jack's private education into which we both enrolled him.

The financial and emotional games continue today, and they will continue until Jack is old enough to make his own decision on his own time allocation with his parents. I'm surprised at how hard it is to remove the excess shit from your life.

19. Saving Clare

In November 2012, we almost lost Clare (technically we did for 45 minutes). Suddenly, I was not the only member of my family with a heart condition. Once again, the fragility of life struck me as another sister of mine fought for her life.

It was a Sunday evening and Mum and Dad had dropped in to have dinner with Jack and me. They were doing this a little more often, dropping in on me and seeing how I was going. They knew I was struggling with the fallout from my disastrous marriage. Our conversation was interrupted when Dad received a call from Clare's phone. On answering his phone, he was surprised that Clare was not speaking on the other end.

Dad asked, 'Who is this?'

Mum and I could tell Dad was concerned, given his question and tone.

Dad was told that Clare was receiving CPR at Melbourne Sports and Aquatic Centre (MSAC) pool deck in Melbourne and asked if he could get down there immediately. With that Mum and Dad rushed out. On arriving at MSAC pool, Albert Park (only a fifteen-minute drive away from my place in East Melbourne), Mum and Dad saw Clare lifeless on an ambulance stretcher, being defibrillated and receiving CPR from several paramedics with no response.

I was about five minutes behind them, slowed a little by getting two-year-old Jack into my car. As I drove, I received a call from Dad.

'We have lost Clare,' he told me, his voice cracking.

'No way. Do not let anyone stop CPR!' I yelled down the phone to him.

At that point, Clare was clinically dead, and I was Mum and Dad's only remaining daughter. A frightening moment in time.

When I arrived at the pool, it had been cleared of all members of the public and was eerily quiet. There were three fire trucks and two ambulances jamming the access road. Jack was confused and thought we were going swimming.

I tried to explain to him that his Aunty Clare was in trouble. I could see paramedics working on Clare and I remember wondering what was wrong with my life: 'Why do I keep losing my sisters?' Fortunately, this time luck was on our side. I have never really believed in luck before, as I think you really control your own destiny, but somehow everything worked in our favour that day.

As I approached the pool an MSAC attendant tried to stop me.

'The pool is shut,' she told me.

'I know, I am Clare's sister,' I replied.

I was then told they had done everything they could, and they were sorry.

I stopped in my tracks and said, 'I don't want to hear that anyone here has given up, I have already lost one sister and I'm not losing another tonight.'

I must have raised my voice, because the paramedics working on Clare looked over at me.

By complete coincidence, luck, or whatever you want to call it, the main paramedic working on Clare was Phil Smith, the same paramedic who I had spent some time with when involved in a publicity shoot for Ambulance Victoria way back in 2006 because I was so impressed and grateful for their help with me.

Phil recognised me when he looked up, looked at Clare, must have realised she was my sister, and decided to break protocol and just get Clare to hospital asap. He decided on the spot that Clare must have an underlying heart condition.

Normally a patient needs a compelling reason to be moved, Phil decided to move Clare regardless.

In another stroke of luck, Phil also had a prototype board that the paramedics were trialling (there were only three in the country) that provided compressions and defibrillations continuously. They were thought to be more efficient than a human administering CPR combined with a defibrillator machine. He put Clare onto this life saving board. While on the board, Clare was taken to The Alfred Hospital, Melbourne. As it was a Sunday evening, the traffic was light, and it was under a two-minute drive. While in the ambulance, a faint reading of Clare's heart rate was made. Clare was still with us.

I rang the Prof to see if he could speak to the staff in ER and let them know what my heart condition was. Once again, the Prof's weekend was interrupted by me.

When admitted to ER, Clare was put into an induced coma for one-and-a-half days. When a patient in Clare's situation is put into an induced coma, their body temperature is reduced to reduce possible swelling of the brain which could cause potential brain damage. In this state, the patient is reliant on machines to keep all vitals going, as the body is kept at a low temperature. Once stable, the patient is brought back to normal body temperature. The body should take over and start functioning on its own.

Once Clare got through this lowered temperature stage ok, we were told the doctors were going to increase her body temperature gradually and her normal body vitals should take over. This happened, which was a good sign.

Doctors now had Clare to the stage of complete sedation, at normal temperature and with her lungs, heart and vitals working themselves. Clare was then monitored to ensure she remained stable. Once stable for around twelve hours the sedation was slowly reduced with the hope Clare would wake. We were told Clare should wake at 11.30 a.m. on the Tuesday (she had been dragged from the pool on the Sunday night).

We all got ourselves bedside at 11.30 a.m. on the Tuesday. We asked doctors what a good sign would be, and they said Clare needed to wake and then try to pull the tubes out of her mouth to speak. They warned us she would have bad short-term memory loss when she woke.

Clare woke at exactly 11.30 a.m. and grabbed at her tubes. We were all relieved. The doctors stepped in and told Clare to remain still. You could tell by looking at Clare she had no idea what she was doing or where she was.

As Clare gradually adapted to being awake, the tubes were removed and slowly she was able to speak. Her memory loss was almost comical. She would speak to her boyfriend Alex on one side of the bed, have a conversation with someone on the other side of the bed, and then look surprised when she saw Alex again.

Being a Carney, Clare decided she was fine and attempted to get up and walk out. We all tried to explain to Clare what had happened, but she really thought everyone was making a fuss over nothing.

Amazingly, Clare got through all this and made a complete recovery.

Throughout this time, Mum, Dad, and I coped as best we could, but we were all outshone by Clare's Alex. He remained positive and at Clare's bedside every minute. Alex remained adamant Clare would be fine.

Once Clare was stable, she was put through several heart tests and procedures, but specialists could not find any connection between her heart diagnosis and mine. We had either uncovered a genetic problem that hadn't been discovered yet, or we had completely different heart conditions by chance.

Regardless of the diagnosis differences, the treatment was the same. Clare received her defibrillator implant a few weeks later.

We were all very thankful Clare made it out alive.

20. Reconnecting with the Mothership

In the years following my divorce, I really struggled. It wasn't just a financial struggle; it was also a day-to-day struggle with life.

Financially, I had no substantial income stream and I had to make sure I could pay all of Jack's Wesley College school fees. I also had to keep our little household going.

My priority was and always is Jack. I could go without, but Jack never would go without under my watch.

That is all very well, prioritising your child's life, but it was hard work moving forward. What I didn't expect to struggle with was getting a job and moving on. I simply didn't fit in. Apparently elite athletes are an asset to the corporate world. I didn't see this benefit. I found most had preconceived ideas as to how I was as a person, because of what they saw on TV. The ruthless athlete, not the constructive work colleague.

As I worked through things, I discovered early that sport was still my passion. I developed an online training website (emmacarney.com) which a very good friend and successful businessman John Gowdie helped me to launch. In fact, without John's help it would have remained a dream. I started selling my training plans, and to this date, everyone who I have coached through my programs has improved.

I did some intermittent coaching in the Sport department at Wesley College. With my knowledge of sport and the program, I began to see areas where the school could vastly improve the structure and delivery of their coaching practices. I shared my ideas with the then Head of Sport (Hibbo was no longer in the role). My ideas were not received well, and before long, I was in the College Principal's office being reprimanded, similar to my experience as a student almost thirty years earlier.

Incredible sadness also hit my family again.

In 2017 Clare's husband Alex was diagnosed with kidney cancer. His battle to survive lasted a little longer than Jane's at just over two years, but we lost him in January of 2019; a week from the date we lost Jane thirteen years earlier.

Alex left behind a devastated Clare and their little boy Harry, who was only three.

The triathlon world also lost Garth Prowd at this time. Triathlon would never be the same in Australia, but above all my heart broke for his family. It really was a sad time.

Over a period of four years, at the time I was probably at my lowest, I oddly enough received some very high recognition from the sports world. In 2012, I was inducted into the TA Hall of Fame. I really didn't want to attend, still scarred from how they treated me. Nevertheless, I turned up, accepted my award and left. In 2014 I was inducted into the ITU Hall of Fame. The awards were held in Edmonton, Canada. I took Jack over to accept the award with me. I hadn't returned there since my cardiac 'incident' in 2004. This was the inaugural ITU Hall of Fame induction and Les McDonald was also inducted for lifetime service. It was nice to see Les again and fantastic he was able to meet my little Jack.

Dear old Les McDonald passed away shortly after meeting Jack, and I was annoyed I never finished this book in time for him to read. I hope he knew what a wonderful leader he was for Triathlon.

In 2016 I was honoured to be inducted into the Sport Australia Hall of Fame. With that final induction, I had received the greatest honour possible in Australian sport. I actually still can't believe I am a part of that esteemed group of Australian sporting legends. As a part of my induction, I told Jack, I would meet him along with Grandma and Grandad (my parents) at the National Sports Museum for the unveiling of my plaque.

Jack said 'Wow, a museum. Will I see dinosaurs?!'

Needless to say, despite my excitement and honour regarding induction, my four-year-old son was not only disappointed with the lack of dinosaurs in the museum he was also dead bored.

At the Awards Dinner though, he did for the first time watch a highlights reel of my career when I was announced as an inductee. Jack seemed very surprised, because I had never told him of my career. Up to this point, all Jack had ever seen me do is mess around and run the legends event at the Noosa Triathlon. Each year, much to the amusement of those in the VIP tent he would scream at the top of his lungs, 'That's lame Mum!' as I trundled around the course, trying not to send my defibrillator off. Suddenly even Jack gave me kudos and to be honest, my son's kudos was the best of all.

With my sporting career recognised, I gained some self-confidence back.

Maybe with this type of recognition, I could get a break in sport and coach. I knew that with high standards and specific quality training under my guidance, success was possible for anyone I coached.

The sporting landscape in Australia started to shift in 2018-2019, as the lack of female recognition in sport became a focal point for improvement. Along with female sports stars, women in high performance sport as coaches and administrators were also regarded as lacking. I started to realise that maybe I was missing out on roles, just because I was a woman. I had never considered that before.

Late in 2018 I saw an advertisement for an AIS-led high performance coaching leadership program designed for women coaches. I decided to apply and was accepted. TA never publicly acknowledged my involvement in the program, which was odd, but I didn't expect or need their support. I wasn't going to wait around until I was accepted into the narrow coaching network within TA. I wasn't going to conform or lower my standards to simply 'fit in'. If I was to become a coach, I needed to start now. The triathlon results for Australia had dropped off internationally and it broke my heart. Something needed to change, and it seemed it was up to me to start this process. I decided that if I started to put together a group of athletes, I could coach them to become the world's best triathletes and in doing so, prove my theories correct; and most importantly, develop Australian Triathletes to be the best in the world again.

Remembering Les McDonald's advice, I also returned to the mothership of triathlon and am now heavily involved with the ITU (now World Triathlon, WT) Coaching Development program. I really enjoy spending time working with athletes and coaches in developing the sport of triathlon worldwide. It is really nice to be involved in the other side of an organisation that has done so much for the sport I love.

Commentating WT World Series events on the live feed broadcast has also been added to my workload, consolidating my involvement with World Triathlon.

I have also started to dream big again.

As is always the case with me, I have aspirations of more. I would like Australia to dominate the sport of triathlon again. I would like to coach Australian triathletes to Olympic, Commonwealth and World Triathlon Grand Final gold medals, after all I owe Australia the Olympic gold medal that I never had the chance to contest.

How I plan to do that is a whole other story.

Appendix A
Emma Carney race results, Athletics

YEAR	CHAMPIONSHIPS	CATEGORY	EVENT	RESULT	TIME
1984	Victorian Championships	U15 Girls	3000m Track Championships	Gold	10.29.2
1985	Victorian Championships	U14 Women	3000m Track Championships	Gold	
1985	Victorian Schools Championships	U15 Girls	3000m Track Championships	Bronze	
1985	Victorian Championships	Open Women	4x1500m Relay Championships	Bronze	
1985	City of Melbourne Athletic Championships	U15 Girls	1500m Track Championships	Silver	4.52.5
1985	Ringwood Junior Athletics Championships	U15 Girls	1500m Track Championships	Silver	
1985	Victoria 150 Celebration	Open Women	Melbourne, Victoria	Gold	
1985	New Years Eve Run	Junior Women	Melbourne	Silver	
1986	Victorian Championships	U16 Women	Cross Country Relay Championships	Bronze	
1986	5km Road Race	U15 Women	Eltham, Victoria	Gold	
1986	5km Road Race	Junior	Boroondara, Victoria	Gold	
1986	Victorian All Schools Championships	U17 Girls	Road Relay	Gold	
1986	Victorian All Schools Championships	U17 Girls	4x800m	Silver	
1987	Victorian Championships	U16 Women	3km Cross Country Championships	Bronze	
1987	Victorian Championships	U16 Women	3km Cross Country Team Championships	Gold	
1987	Victorian Championships	U16 Women	5km Road Championships	Bronze	

335

YEAR	CHAMPIONSHIPS	CATEGORY	EVENT	RESULT	TIME
1987	Victorian Championships	U16 Women	Road Relay Championships	Bronze	
1987	Australian Schools Championships	U17 Girls	4000m Cross Country Team Championships	Silver	
1987	Victorian Championships	U18 Women	5km Road Championships	Silver	
1987	Victorian Championships	U18 Women	5km Road Team Championships	Gold	
1987	Victorian Championships	U18 Women	4km Cross Country Championships	Gold	
1987	Victorian Championships	U18 Women	6km Cross Country Championships	Silver	
1987	Victorian Championships	U18 Women	Cross Country Relay Championships	Gold	
1987	Victorian Schools Championships	U17 Girls	4km Cross Country Championships	Bronze	
1987	Victorian Schools Championships	U19 Girls	Road Relay Championships	Gold	
1988	Australian Schools Championships	U17 Girls	4000m Cross Country Championships	Silver	
1988	Victorian Championships	U18 Women	4km Cross Country Team Championships	Gold	
1988	Victorian Championships	U18 Women	6km Cross Country Championships	Gold	
1988	Victorian Championships	U18 Women	4km Cross Country Championships	Gold	
1988	Victorian Championships	U18 Women	Cross Country Relay Championships	Gold	
1988	Victorian Championships	U18 Women	5km Road Championships	Silver	
1988	Victorian Championships	U18 Women	5km Road Team Championships	Gold	
1988	Victorian Championships	U18 Women	4x800m Track Relay Championships	Gold	
1988	Victorian Championships	U18 Women	Road Relay Championships	Bronze	
1988	Victorian Championships	U18 Women	3000m Championships	Gold	
1988	Victorian Championships	U18 Women	6km Cross Country Team Championships	Gold	
1988	Australian Schools Championships	U19 Girls	1500m Championships	Gold	

YEAR	CHAMPIONSHIPS	CATEGORY	EVENT	RESULT	TIME
1988	Australian Schools Championships	U19 Girls	3000m Championships	Gold	
1988	Victorian Championships	U20 Women	4km Cross Country Championships	Silver	
1988	Victorian Championships	U20 Women	10km Road Championships	Silver	
1988	Victorian Championships	Open Women	4x1500m Track. Relay Championships	Gold	
1988	Victorian Schools Championships	U 20 Women	4x800m Track Relay Championships	Gold	
1988	Victorian Schools Championships	U19 Girls	3000m Championships	Silver	
1988	Victorian Schools Championships	U19 Girls	Road Relay Championships	Silver	
1988	Victorian Schools Championships	U19 Girls	1500m Championships	Silver	
1989	Victorian Schools Championships	U17 Girls	4km Cross Country Championships	Gold	14.2
1989	Victorian Championships	U18 Women	4km Cross Country Championships	Gold	
1989	Victorian Championships	U18 Women	4km Cross Country Team Championships	Gold	
1989	Victorian Championships	U18 Women	1500m Track Championships	Gold	
1989	Victorian Championships	U18 Women	Road Reay Championships	Gold	
1989	Australian Championships	U18 Women	1500m Track Championships	Bronze	
1989	Australian Championships	U18 Women	3000m Track Championships	Silver	
1989	Victorian Championships	U20 Women	4km Cross Country Championships	Silver	
1989	Victorian Championships	U20 Women	4km Cross Country Team Championships	Gold	
1989	Victorian Championships	U20 Women	Cross Country Relay Championships	Gold	
1989	Victorian Schools Championships	U19 Girls	4km Cross Country Championships	Gold	
1990	10km Road Race	Year 18-19	Melbourne	Gold	36.12
1990	Olympic Dream 1500m	U20 Women	Olympic Park, Melbourne	Silver	4.32

337

YEAR	CHAMPIONSHIPS	CATEGORY	EVENT	RESULT	TIME
1990	Victorian Championships	U20 Women	4km Cross Country Championships	Silver	
1990	Victorian Championships	U20 Women	10km Road Championships	Gold	
1990	Victorian Championships	U20 Women	6km Cross Country Championships	Gold	
1990	Victorian Championships	U20 Women	3km Cross Country Relay Championships	Gold	
1990	Victorian Championships	U20 Women	Road Relay Championships	Silver	
1990	Victorian Championships	U20 Women	4x400 Track Relay Championships	Silver	
1990	Victorian Championships	Open Women	4x800m Track Relay	Silver	
1990	Victorian Championships	Open Women	4x1500m Track Relay	Silver	
1991	Victorian Championships	U20 Women	4km Cross Country Championships	Gold	
1991	Victorian Championships	U20 Women	4km Cross Country Team Championships	Gold	
1991	Victorian Championships	U20 Women	Road Relay Championships	Gold	
1991	Victorian Championships	U20 Women	3000m Track Championships	Gold	
1991	Victorian Championships	U20 Women	1500m Track Championships	Silver	
1991	Australian Championships	U20 Women	3000m Track Championships	Bronze	
1991	Victorian Championships	U20 Women	10km Road Championships	Gold	
1991	Victorian Championships	U20 Women	10km Road Team Championships	Gold	
1991	Australian Championships	U20 Women	3000m Track Championships	Bronze	9.47.01
1992	Victorian Championships	Open Women	8km Cross Country Championships	Bronze	
1992	Victorian Championships	Open Women	6km Cross Country Championships	Bronze	21.10.
1992	Australian Championships	Open Women	6km Cross Country Team Championships	Bronze	
1992	Victorian Championships	Open Women	4x1500m Relay Championships	Silver	

YEAR	CHAMPIONSHIPS	CATEGORY	EVENT	RESULT	TIME
1993 (25 Feb)	NEC Meet - Top 10 Australian All Time	Open Women	3000m	3rd	9.07
1993 (26 April)	5km Road				16.05
1993 (15 May)	Victorian Championships	Open Women	10km Road Championships	Gold	34.14
1993 (19 June)	Victorian Championships	Open Women	4km Cross Country Championships	Silver	
1993 (3 July)	Victorian Championships	Open Women	8km Cross Country Championships	Gold	29.00.
1993 (31 July)	Victorian Championships	Open Women	6km Cross Country Championships	Silver	
1993 (14 Aug)	NZ Championships	Open Women	6km Cross Country Championships	4th	20.42.
1993 (25 Aug)	Australian Championships	Open Women	6km Cross Country Championships	7th	
1993	Australian Championships	Open Women	6km Cross Country Team Championships	Gold	
1993	Burnie 10km	Open Women	Burnie, Tasmania		34.40.
1993	Athletics Australia Representation	Open Women	Chiba, Japan Ekiden relay, Fastest time	Team bronze	16.30.
1993	Year Best		3000m 9.07		
1994 (30 Jan)	Athletics Grand Prix - Personal best Run	Open Women	1500m		4.23.11
1994 (11 Jun)	Victorian Championships	Open Women	4km Cross Country Championships	Gold	13.23.
1994	Australian Championships	Open Women	3000m Track Championships	Silver	9.13.87
1994 (15 Dec)	Zatopek Classic 10,000m	Open Women	Olympic Park, Melbourne		33.18.
1994	3km Road Race	Open Women	Surf n Sun' 3km	Gold	
1995 (25 Feb)	NEC Meet 5000m	Open Women	Olympic Park, Melbourne		16.11.
1995 (25 Mar)	World Cross Country Championships	Open Women	Durham, UK	52nd	21.45.
1995 (14 May)	5km Road Race	Open Women	Melbourne, Victoria	4th	15.46.
1998 (29 Mar)	10km Road Race	Open Women	Melbourne	Bronze	33.37.
1998 (2 May)	10km Road Race	Open Women	Sydney		34.41.
1999 (7 Mar)	5km Road Race	Open Women		Silver	
1999 (28 Mar)	10km Road Race	Open Women	Melbourne	Bronze	34.07.

YEAR	CHAMPIONSHIPS	CATEGORY	EVENT	RESULT	TIME
1999 (25 Jul)	Road Race	Open Women	Sutherland, NSW	Bronze	
1999 (15 Aug)	City to Surf Fun Run	Women 25-29	Sydney, Australia		50.06.
1999 (10 Oct)	10km Road Race	Open Women	Burnie, Tasmania	6th	34.43.
2000	Victorian Championships	Open Women	Road Relay Championships	Silver	
2001	Road Race, Half Marathon	Open Women	Sydney, Australia	Silver	
2001	10km Road Race	Open Women	Melbourne	Silver	
2003	Victorian 15km Road Championships	Open Women	Melbourne	Bronze	
2003	Victorian 10km Road Championships	Open Women	Melbourne	Bronze	
Athletics Australia Representations AA #700					
1993	Ekiden Relay — 6km	Open Women	Soul, Korea	19.49	
1994	Ekiden Relay	Open Women	Chiba, Japan	Bronze	Fastest leg
1994	World Cross Country Championships	Open Women	Budapest, Hungary	68/148	21.59
1995	World Cross Country Championships	Open Women	Durham, UK	52/133	21.45
Personal Best Times					
1994	Zatopek Classic, Olympic Park Melbourne *Emma only ran one 10000m track event		10,000m	33.18	
1998	Road Race, Melbourne		10km	33.37	
1995	NEC Track Classic, Olympic Park Melbourne		5000m	16.11	
1995	Road Race		5km	15.46	
1993	NEC Meet, Olympic Park, Melbourne		3000m	9.07.11	
1992	Sydney Grand Prix		1500m	4.23	
1991	Interclub Olympic Park, Melbourne		800m	2.11	
1987	Interclub Doncaster Track, Melbourne		400m	59.7	
Athletic Club Awards					
1984-85	Box Hill Womens Athletics Club		Junior Distance Award		
1985-86	Box Hill Womens Athletics Club		Distance Runner Award		

YEAR	CHAMPIONSHIPS	CATEGORY	EVENT	RESULT	TIME
1987	Box Hill Womens Athletics Club		Best Winter Athlete Award		
1988	Box Hill Womens Athletics Club		Best Winter Athlete Award		
1998	Box Hill Womens Athletics Club		Best Winter Athlete Award		
1989	Box Hill Womens Athletics Club		Best Winter Athlete Award		
1988-89	Box Hill Womens Athletics Club		Distance Runner Award		
1990	Doncaster Athletics Club		Junior Distance Athlete		
1990-91	Doncaster Athletics Club		Best A Grade Track Athlete		
1991	Doncaster Athletics Club		Senior Distance Athlete		
1992	Doncaster Athletics Club		Senior Distance Athlete		
1993	Doncaster Athletics Club		Senior Distance Athlete		

Appendix B
Emma Carney Race Results,
Triathlon and Cycling

DATE	YEAR	CHAMPIONSHIPS	CATEGORY	EVENT	RESULT	TIME
20-Dec	1992	Nike Triathlon Series	Elite Women	Elwood, Melbourne	Gold	1.04.54
17-Jan	1993	Victorian Sprint Triathlon Championships	Elite Women	Ballarat, Victoria	Silver	1.05.53
24-Jan	1993	Country Triathlon Series	Elite Women	Cobram, Victoria	Gold	
31-Jan	1993	Australian Sprint Triathlon Championships	Elite Women	St Kilda, Melbourne	4th	1.04.03
7-Feb	1993	Australian Triathlon Championships	Elite Women	Geelong, Victoria	5th	
14-Feb	1993	Country Triathlon Series	Elite Women	Hastings, Victoria	Gold	2.09.16
20-Feb	1993	Country Triathlon Series	Elite Women	Benalla, Victoria	Gold	2.02.21
7-Mar	1993	Melbourne Triathlon Classic	Elite Women	Patterson Lakes, Melbourne	DSQ	2.02.51
21-Mar	1993	Country Triathlon Series	Elite Women	Deniliquin, Victoria	Gold	
	1993	Victorian Duathlon Series	Elite Women	Winner all 5 races 9 May, 30 May, 27 June, 1 August, 10 October	Gold	
17-Oct	1993	Noosa Triathlon	Elite Women	Noosa, Queensland	Silver	
24-Oct	1993	Australian Duathlon Championships	Elite Women	Kew, Melbourne	Gold	
14-Nov	1993	Pepsi Duathlon Cup	Elite Women	NSW, Australia	Gold	
5-Dec	1993	Nepean Triathlon	Elite Women	NSW, Australia	Gold	

DATE	YEAR	CHAMPIONSHIPS	CATEGORY	EVENT	RESULT	TIME
12-Dec	1993	Australian Triathlon Series Event	Elite Women	Port Stephens, NSW	Silver	
	1994	Australian Duathlon Championships	Elite Women		Gold	
9-Jan	1994	Australian Triathlon Series Event	Elite Women	Geelong, Victoria		
16-Jan	1994	Australian National Series Event	Elite Women	Adelaide, Australia	Gold	2.01.36
20-Feb	1994	New Zealand National Triathlon Championships	Elite Women	Wellington, New Zealand	Silver	
13-Mar	1994	Australian Triathlon Series Event	Elite Women	Devonport, Tasmania	DNF	ill
24-Apr	1994	Australian National Series Event	Elite Women	Mooloolaba, Queensland	Silver	
30-Oct	1994	Noosa Triathlon	Elite Women	Noosa, Queensland	Silver	2.00.43
	1994	Victorian Triathlon Series	Elite Women	Brighton, Melbourne	Gold	
27-Nov	1994	World Triathlon Championships	Elite Women	Wellington, New Zealand	Gold	2.03.18
	1994	World Triathlon Championships	Elite Women Team	Wellington, New Zealand	Gold	
11-Dec	1994	Victorian Triathlon Series	Elite Women	Queenscliff Victoria	Gold	
8-Jan	1995	Australian Sprint Triathlon Championships	Elite Women	Blacktown, NSW	Gold	
15-Jan	1995	Australian National Series Event	Elite Women	Canberra, ACT	Gold	
19-Feb	1995	Australian Triathlon Championships	Elite Women	Geelong, Victoria — Course Record	Gold	1.55.
19-Mar	1995	Australian National Series Event	Elite Women	Devonport, Tasmania	Gold	
23-Apr	1995	Australian National Series Event	Elite Women	Mooloolaba, QLD	Gold	
20-May	1995	Fiji International Triathlon	Elite Women	Fiji	Gold	
17-Jun	1995	World Triathlon Series Event	Elite Women	Derry, Northern Ireland	Gold	2.01.21
25-Jun	1995	World Triathlon Series Event	Elite Women	San Sebastian, Spain	Gold	2.02.37
6-Aug	1995	World Triathlon Series Event	Elite Women	Drummondville, Canada	Gold	1.53.12

DATE	YEAR	CHAMPIONSHIPS	CATEGORY	EVENT	RESULT	TIME
13-Aug	1995	World Triathlon Series Event	Elite Women	Cleveland, USA	Gold	1.58.49
27-Aug	1995	Chicago triathlon	Elite Women	Chicago, USA	3rd	
15-Oct	1995	World Triathlon Series Event	Elite Women	Sydney, Australia	Gold	2.00.51
12-Nov	1995	World Triathlon Championships	Elite Women	Cancun, Mexico	7th	ill
	1995	Triathlon World Cup Series Champion	Elite Women			
	1995	World Number 1 Triathlete	Elite Women			
	1995	Australian Duathlon Championships	Elite Women		Gold	
4- Feb	1996	Australian Sprint Triathlon Championships	Elite Women	Melbourne	Gold	
25-Feb	1996	Triathlon Grand Prix Series	Elite Women	Race 2 St Kilda, Melbourne	Gold	
3-Mar	1996	Triathlon Grand Prix Series	Elite Women	Race 3 Canberra, ACT	Gold	
21-Apr	1997	Womens Triathlon	Elite Women	Gold Coast, Queensland	Gold	
12-May	1996	Triathlon World Series event	Elite Women	Ishigaki, Japan	Gold	2.01.00
19-May	1996	Triathlon World Series event	Elite Women	Gamagori, Japan	Gold	1.57.54
10-Jun	1996	Triathlon World Series event	Elite Women	Paris, France	Gold	1.06.23
23-Jun	1996	Triathlon World Series event	Elite Women	Drummondville, Quebec Canada	Gold	1.57.45
30-Jun	1996	Triathlon World Series event	Elite Women	Hamilton, Bermuda	Gold	1.49.34
25-Aug	1996	Triathlon World Championships	Elite Women	Cleveland, Ohio USA	Silver	1.51.43 ill
13-Oct	1996	Triathlon World Series event	Elite Women	Auckland, New Zealand	Gold	2.03.19
20-Oct	1996	Triathlon World Series event	Elite Women	Sydney, Australia	Gold	1.58.15
10-Nov	1996	Womens Invitation Triathlon	Elite Women	Amami Island, Japan	Gold	
	1996	Triathlon World Cup Series Champion	Elite Women			
	1996	World Number 1 Triathlete	Elite Women			

DATE	YEAR	CHAMPIONSHIPS	CATEGORY	EVENT	RESULT	TIME
	1997	Victorian Triathlon Series	Elite Women	St Kilda, Melbourne	Gold	
	1997	Victorian Triathlon Series	Elite Women	St Kilda, Melbourne	Gold	
	1997	Australian Sprint Triathlon Championships	Elite Women		Gold	
23-Mar	1997	Australian National Series Event	Elite Women	Devonport, Tasmania	Gold	
6-Apr	1997	Victorian Triathlon Series	Elite Women	Sandringham, Melbourne	Gold	1.01.00
13-Apr	1997	Triathlon World Series event	Elite Women	Ishigaki, Japan	Gold	2.02.05
20-Apr	1997	Australian Triathlon Championships	Elite Women	Mooloolaba, QLD	Gold	
27-Apr	1997	Triathlon World Series event	Elite Women	Auckland, New Zealand	Gold	2.02.15
15-Jun	1997	Australian Duathlon Championships	Elite Women		Gold	
30-Jun	1997	Triathlon World Series event	Elite Women	Monte Carlo, Monaco	Silver	2.09.47
6-Jul	1997	Triathlon World Series event	Elite Women	Gamagori, Japan	Gold	2.03.44
9-Aug	1997	Triathlon World Series event	Elite Women	Tiszaujvaros, Hungary	Gold	2.00.22
24-Aug	1997	European triathlon Series event	Elite Women	Geneve, Switzerland	Gold	
21-Sep	1997	Triathlon World Series event	Elite Women	Hamilton, Bermuda	Gold	2.03.54
26-Oct	1997	Triathlon World Series event	Elite Women	Sydney, Australia	Gold	2.00.32
2-Nov	1997	Noosa Triathlon	Elite Women	Noosa, QLD - Course Record	Gold	1.54.22
16-Nov	1997	World Triathlon Championships	Elite Women	Perth, Australia	Gold	1.59.22
20-Dec	1997	Benalla Tri Club	Elite Women	Benalla, Victoria	Gold	
	1997	Triathlon World Cup Series Champion	Elite Women			
	1997	World Number 1 Triathlete	Elite Women			
11-Jan	1998	Australian National Series Event	Elite Women	Devonport, Tasmania	Gold	
1-Feb	1998	Sunsmart Series Race	Elite Women	Portarlington, Victoria	Gold	

DATE	YEAR	CHAMPIONSHIPS	CATEGORY	EVENT	RESULT	TIME
8-Feb	1998	Victorian Triathlon Series Event	Elite Women	Sandringham, Victoria	Gold	
1-Mar	1998	Victorian Triathlon Series Event	Elite Women	Portarlington, Victoria	Gold	
5-Apr	1998	Victorian Triathlon Series Event	Elite Women	St Kilda, Melbourne	Gold	
	1998	Victorian Triathlon Series Event	Elite Women	Brighton, Victoria	Gold	
	1998	Australian Triathlon Series	Elite Women	Series winner		
12-Apr	1998	Triathlon World Series event	Elite Women	Ishigaki, Japan	Gold	2.03.24
26-Apr	1998	Triathlon World Series event	Elite Women	Sydney, Australia	DNF	Hypotherima
10-May	1998	Australian Triathlon Championships	Elite Women	Mooloolaba, QLD	Gold	
12-Jul	1998	Triathlon World Series event	Elite Women	Gamagori, Japan	15th	2.04.23
2-Aug	1998	Triathlon World Series event	Elite Women	Corner Brook, Canada	9th	2.11.26
30-Aug	1998	World Triathlon Championships	Elite Women	Lausanne, Switzerland	DNF	Mechanical
6-Sep	1998	European triathlon Series event	Elite Women	Neuchatel, Switzerland	Gold	
20-Sep	1998	London triathlon	Elite Women	London, UK	Gold	
1-Nov	1998	Triathlon World Series event	Elite Women	Auckland, New Zealand	4th	2.01.26
	1999	Victorian Triathlon Series Event	Elite Women	Portarlington, Victoria	Gold	
7-Feb	1999	Nowra Triathlon	Elite Women	Nowra, NSW	Gold	
14-Feb	1999	Kurnell Triathlon	Elite Women	Kurnell, NSW - Course Record	Gold	51.46.
28-Feb	1999	Victorian Triathlon Series Event	Elite Women	Portarlington, Victoria	Gold	
20-Mar	1999	Dubai invitational Triathlon	Elite Women	Abu Dhabi, UAE	Gold	
11-Apr	1999	Triathlon World Series event	Elite Women	Ishigaki, Japan - Broken Foot	4th	2.00.48
29-Aug	1999	Chicago Triathlon	Elite Women	Chicago, USA	4th	
12-Sep	1999	World Triathlon Championships	Elite Women	Montreal, Canada	Bronze	
19-Sep	1999	London Triathlon	Elite Women	London, UK	Gold	
17-Oct	1999	World Duathlon Championships	Elite Women	Huntersville, USA	Silver	

DATE	YEAR	CHAMPIONSHIPS	CATEGORY	EVENT	RESULT	TIME
7-Nov	1999	Triathlon World Series event	Elite Women	Noosa, Queensland	Silver	1.55.49
19-Dec	1999	Australian Long Course Triathlon Championships	Elite Women	Callala, NSW	Gold	
3-Jan	2000	World Triathlon Oceania Championships	Elite Women	Gisborne, New Zealand	Silver	
30-Jan	2000	Australian National Series Event	Elite Women	Geelong, Victoria	Gold	
13-Feb	2000	Australian Sprint Triathlon Championships	Elite Women	Woolongong, NSW	Gold	
16-Apr	2000	Triathlon World Series event	Elite Women	Sydney, Australia	13th	2.05.55
30-Apr	2000	World Triathlon Championships	Elite Women	Perth, Australia - Course error	7th	1.55.55
8-Jul	2000	Triathlon World Series event	Elite Women	Toronto, Canada	7th	1.59.05
	2000	Edmonton Triathlon	Elite Women	Edmonton, Canada	Gold	
	2000	Noosa Triathlon	Elite Women	Noosa, Queensland	Gold	2.01.09
11-Mar	2001	Australian National Series Event/Oceania Cup	Elite Women	Devonport, Tasmania	Bronze	2.02.35
	2001	Australian Duathlon Champion	Elite Women		Gold	
	2001	Victorian Triathlon Series Event	Elite Women	Mordialloc, Melbourne	Gold	
	2001	Victorian Triathlon Series Event	Elite Women	Brighton, Melbourne	Gold	
	2001	Victorian Sprint Triathlon Championships	Elite Women	Ballarat, Victoria	Gold	
	2001	Australian Long Course Triathlon Championships	Elite Women		Gold	
15-Apr	2001	Triathlon World Series event	Elite Women	Gamagori, Japan	9th	2.00.05
22-Apr	2001	Triathlon World Series event	Elite Women	Ishigaki, Japan	12th	2.02.14
	2002	Victorian Triathlon Series Event	Elite Women	Portarlington, Victoria	Gold	

DATE	YEAR	CHAMPIONSHIPS	CATEGORY	EVENT	RESULT	TIME
	2002	Victorian Triathlon Series Event	Elite Women	St Kilda, Victoria	Gold	
	2002	Victorian Triathlon Series Event	Elite Women	Elwood, Victoria	Gold	
17-Feb	2002	Australian National Series Event/Oceania Cup	Elite Women	Canberra, ACT	6th	1.59.40
17-Mar	2002	Australian National Series Event/Oceania Cup	Elite Women	Devonport, Tasmania	Bronze	2.04.01
21-Apr	2002	Australian National Series Event/Oceania Cup	Elite Women	Mooloolaba, Queensland	DNF	Heart Problems
8-Mar	2003	Australian National Series Event	Elite Women	Devonport, Tasmania	DNF	Heart Problems
	2003	Australian National Series Event	Elite Women	St Kilda, Melbourne	Gold	
15-Mar	2003	Triathlon World Series- Oceania Championships	Elite Women	Queenstown, New Zealand	5th	2.09.09
7-Jun	2003	Triathlon World Series event	Elite Women	Tongyeong, Korea - Heart Problems	23rd	2.03.46
15-Jun	2003	Triathlon World Series event	Elite Women	Gamagori, Japan	6th	1.59.29
13-Jul	2003	Triathlon World Series event	Elite Women	Edmonton, Canada	17th	2.03.00
20-Jul	2003	Triathlon World Series event	Elite Women	Corner Brook, Canada	9th	2.10.02
27-Jul	2003	Triathlon World Series event	Elite Women	Salford, UK	16th	2.06.55
10-Aug	2003	Triathlon World Series event	Elite Women	New York, USA	11th	2.02.10
6-Sep	2003	Triathlon World Series event	Elite Women	Hamburg, Germany	7th	1.56.07
12-Sep	2003	Triathlon World Series event	Elite Women	Nice, France — Heart Problems	31st	2.06.23
21-Sep	2003	Triathlon World Series event	Elite Women	Madrid, Spain	DNF	Mechanical
7-Dec	2003	World Triathlon Championships	Elite Women	Queenstown, New Zealand	DNF	Heart Problems

DATE	YEAR	CHAMPIONSHIPS	CATEGORY	EVENT	RESULT	TIME
				Cycling		
23-Jul	1994	Victorian Championships	Elite Women	Individual Road Time Trial 30km		47.53.
16-Feb	1997	National Mountain Bike Series Race	Elite Women	Doncaster, Melbourne	3rd	
	2001	Victorian Championships	Elite Women	Individual Road Time Trial	Bronze	
	2001	Victorian Championships	Elite Women	Individual Road Time Trial	Silver	
	2002	Tour of Bright	Elite Women	Bright, Victoria	Winner	
				Awards		
	1994	Victorian Sport Star of the Year Award				
	1995	Leader Associated Sports Star of the Year awards				
	1995	Australian Triathlete of the Year				
	1997	Outstanding Achievement Award Presented by PM John Howard				
	1997	Triathlete Magazine Triathlete of the Year				
	2000	Australian Triathlete of the Year				
	2012	World Triathlon Hall of Fame - inaugural induction				
	2014	Triathlon Australia Hall of Fame				
	2016	Sport Australia Hall of Fame - Athlete Member				

349

Acknowledgements

For my entire life I have been fiercely independent, believing I could achieve things alone. In reality I always achieve my greatest feats with the support of those around me. This autobiography is the same — without the support of others, this would still be a pile of training diaries, newspaper cuttings, letters, files and journal entries gathering dust at Mum and Dad's mudbrick house in Eltham.

So, in no particular order, because there is no logical place to begin, I will start with the youngest …

To my wonderful son Jack, who constantly had to put up with me leaning over my laptop as I wrote this manuscript, when we should have been enjoying a camping holiday, weekend away, an evening together or just some mother and son time. Thank you for your patience.

To Mum, thank you for remaining the calming influence in the Carney household and for also providing the creative mindset to think outside the box. Thank you to Dad, you backed every little dream I had in sport and you taught me to always see the positives. To both of you, thank you for your unwavering support, through everything; thank you for allowing me to be me and understanding sometimes I just needed to let off a bit of steam! Dad, thank you for your contribution to my autobiography. Your meticulous care to ensure the details were retained pained you as much as it did me, but you were always the one to make sure the truth prevailed.

To my big sister Jane, I miss you every day and I wish you were here to grow old with. To your little Zoe, my autobiography should make it very clear to you that your mother was the most wonderful, caring and considerate mother any little girl could ever dream of.

To my little sister Clare, we achieved a feat in Sport for which I cannot find an equal example. I am so proud to have shared that with you. I hope your little Harry reads about this one day to understand what his Mum achieved. I wish Alex was here for both of you.

To Assistant Professor Dr Jane E. Hunt thank you for sifting the facts from the opinions and myths and in doing so, providing my story with the factual account of events it requires. Thank you for all your time spent perfecting my manuscript and for helping me through the process of publishing a book.

To Professor Geoffrey Blainey AC, through my discussions with you about this project I have gained a wonderful insight into your brilliance as an author and academic. I appreciate the time and patience taken to show me how to edit a very rough draft.

Thank you to my cardiologists Professor Richard Harper and Dr Jeffrey Alison, not only for putting up with me as a patient but also providing the correct medical terms and the correct chronological order of all my procedures undertaken throughout the diagnosis and treatment of my heart condition. I truly can also add, thank you for keeping me alive.

Thank you to my coaches, particularly the original three Matt Paterson, Alwyn Barrett and Harry Shaw who all set me in the right direction and believed in me from the start.

To those who kept my body working, thank you. Thank you to Garry Miritis the best sports therapist and masseur in the world, you always managed to keep everything moving forward, when the body really was broken. My Chiropractor Nick Kiss von Soly I never kept my appointment times or days, but you always fit me in. Thank you. To Kay Macpherson for your treatment, generosity, hospitality support and endless laughs. On top of all this, thank you also for not kicking Clare and I out of your house when a six week stay turned into six months. From this time, we are also still truly sorry we ate your pantry bare.

At Wesley College, thank you to former Principal Dr Helen Drennen AM and College President Marianne Stillwell for reading manuscript drafts and to Mr Ian Thomas Head of the Old Wesley Collegians Association (OWCA) for providing the ever so important facts, dates and titles of various teachers and college staff at 'The best school of All'. Thank you also to my teachers who had the foresight to back a student who had a passion for something big in sport, and not so much passion for paying attention in class.

To dear Les McDonald, thank you for taking a sport that myth suggests was dreamt up in a bar as a bet between mates, and preparing it for the Olympic Games. I wish you were still here to read my autobiography and know how much I thought of your work in pioneering Triathlon to the sport it is today. Thank you also Loreen Barnett for keeping everything in place. To World Triathlon, thank you for always supporting me and providing a sport which brings so much to the wonderful triathletes that compete on your racing circuit. I will forever be involved.

To the Prowd Family, thank you. Garth contributed so much to my career but the support from you all as a family is so very special. Thank you, Robyn, for feeding and housing me for so many meals and nights. Sally and Megan I am so sorry you were dragged out for too many training sessions and Katie, lucky you were always too young to have to run and swim! I miss Garth so much, but most of all I miss him with you all.

To all those who contributed to this book by sitting for interviews, providing written statements and to Jero Honda who permitted to use his photograph for the cover, Jane and I would like to say Thank You. You have helped to make this book what it is.

To all my fans, sponsors and friends who cheered, supported and backed me, you made it all worthwhile and gave the journey the drama it deserved. You all still make me smile.

Endnotes

1. 1   Adding the Swim and the Bike ' Nic Bideau, 'Carney to show her doubters,' cutting, no citation details in Emma Carney private collection (ECpc).
2. Wesley College Chronicle, various, Wesley College Archives, https://www. wesleycollege.edu.au/about-wesley/our-history/archives-art-and-collections.
3. Both comments were widely quoted in Australian newspapers. For example, 'A year of Titanic bravado, porridge, power and inflatable dolls,' *The Canberra Times*, 29 December 1993: 32; 'Wang's record run saps the joy for Jennings,' *The Canberra Times*, 10 September 1993: 29.
4. Dave Scott, Interview with Jane Hunt, 20 June 2012, Jane Hunt private collection (JHpc).
5. Caroline Overington, 'Triathletes Set To Start Long Haul For Sydney Olympics,' *The Age*, 31 December 1996: np.
6. Emma Carney to Emery Holmik, correspondence, 13 October 1998 in David Carney private collection (DCpc).
7. Emery Holmik, 'Selection Policies for 1999 and 2000,' correspondence to OAP Athletes/coaches [and] TA Elite Selection Panel, 25 September 1998, p4, in DCpc.
8. David Carney to Emery Holmik, correspondence, 25 Feb 1999, in DCpc.
9. '2000 Olympic Games Selection Criteria,' TA AGM, Nov 1999, np; Claire Deutsher, 'Master of the Game,' *Triathlon Multisport*, 5, no. 8 (Nov 2000): 61-2.
10. Annexure C, Australian Olympic Committee & TA, Selection Agreement — 2000 Australian Olympic Team (AOC & TA Agreement), 23 December 1999, in DCpc.
11. Annexure 1, AOC & TA Agreement, in DCpc.
12. David Thorpe, 'Contract and athlete selection,' *Australian and New Zealand Sports Law Journal* 3, no. 1 (2008).
13. Louise Evans, 'Foreign Legion On The Road To Nowhere, Say Elite Locals,' *Sydney Morning Herald*, 25 March 2000.

14. Michellie Jones, Interview with Jane Hunt, 31 July 2012, in JHpc; and Timothy Carlson, 'Drama Down Under,' *Inside Triathlon* 15, no. 7 (July 2000): 18.
15. Louise Evans, 'Walking wounded forced into battle; Triathlon,' *Sydney Morning Herald*, 17 April 2000: 34.
16. Deborah Robinson to 'Whom It May Concern,' correspondence, 12 April 2000; and John Hellemans to TA, correspondence, 12 April 2000, both in Freehills, 'Court of Arbitration for Sport Oceania Registry,' Appeal Book (CAS Appeal Book), in DCpc.
17. Emery Holmik to Diane Ainsworth, correspondence, 13 April 2000, CAS Appeal Book, in DCpc.
18. Miles Stewart cited in Jane E. Hunt, *Multisport Dreaming: The Foundations of Triathlon in Australia* (Varsity Lakes, QLD: Write Press, 2014), 203; and Evans, 'Walking Wounded.'
19. Evans, 'Walking Wounded'; AAP, 'Race marred by controversy,' *Sports Today*, sportstoday.com.au, 17 April 2000, copy in DCpc.
20. Noel McMahon, 'Where's Walto?' *Australian Triathlete*, [2001]: 26.
21. McMahon, 'Where's Walto?'
22. John Helleman to 'Whom it may concern,' correspondence, 25 April 2000; Guy Kemp to 'Whom it may concern,' correspondence, 24 April 2000; Diane Ainsworth to Bill Baker, correspondence, not dated, all in CAS Appeal Book, in DCpc.
23. Diana Robinson to Bill Baker, correspondence, 29 April 2000, CAS Appeal Book, in DCpc.
24. Darren Smith, Correspondence to Triathlon Appeals Committee, undated, cited in Hunt, *Multisport Dreaming*, 210.
25. Rod Cedaro, 'Dawn of an Era: ITU Championships, Perth, Australia,' *Triathlon & Multisport Magazine* 3, no. 5 (June 2000): 36.
26. Louise Evans, 'Hackett's victory jig cut short; Triathlon,' *The Sydney Morning Herald*, 1 May 2000: 29.
27. Cedaro, 'Dawn of an Era,' 36.
28. Annexure 1, 7.1.3 (a), AOC & TA Agreement, in DCpc.
29. Bill Walker, 'President's Report,' and Tim Wilson, 'National Executive Director's Report,' both in Triathlon Australia Ltd., Annual General Meeting, Noosa, QLD, 6 November 1999, unpaginated Appendix.
30. TA, 'TA Selection Policy — Junior Elite Team, 2000 ITU Triathlon World Championships,' *The Ultimate Challenge*, Feb 2000, pp.10-11, in DCpc.

31. TA Elite Selection Committee (TAESC), '2000 Olympic Games Team Nomination — Female Nominations', in TA Appeal Tribunal Hearing — Female Athlete Appeal Documents (TA Appeal), in DCpc.

32. TAESC, 'Female Nominations', TA Appeal, in DCpc.

33. TAESC, 'Female Nominations', TA Appeal, in DCpc.

34. TAESC, 'Female Nominations', TA Appeal, in DCpc.

35. Jonathan Forbes, Freehill Hollingdale & Page, 'Grounds of Appeal', copy, 12 May 2016 in DCpc.

36. Forbes, 'Grounds of Appeal', in DCpc.

37. Forbes, 'Grounds of Appeal', in DCpc.

38. 'Response to Athlete Appeal Submissions', TA Appeal, in DCpc.

39. Tim Wilson, 'New Chair Appointed — TA Appeal Tribunal', TA media release, 19 May 2000, loose notes in Dcpc.

40. Les McDonald to David Carney, correspondence (Fax), 11 June 2000, correspondence in DCpc.

41. Peter Hayes, 'Appeals to Triathalon [sic] Appeal Tribunal — Supplementary Reply Submissions', 15 June 2000, in DCpc.

42. Triathlon Australia Appeals Tribunal, Olympic Selection Appeals, Awards and Reasons 35-6, 38-40, in DCpc.

43. Bill Baker, 'Report to the TAESC', 7 July 2000, loose bundle of notes in DCpc.

44. Chip Le Grand, no title, *The Australian*, 8 Aug 2000: 18, cutting in DCpc.

45. Bill Baker, Meeting of TAESC, 13 July 2000, CAS Appeal Book, in DCpc.

46. June Canavan to Tim Wilson, correspondence, 7 May 2000, CAS Appeal Book, in DCpc.

47. Bill Baker, Meeting of TAESC, 13 July 2000, CAS Appeal Book, in DCpc.

48. *Arbitral and Disciplinary Rules of International Sports Organisations*, edited by Robert C.R. Sickmann & Janwillem Sock (The Hague: T.M.C. Asser Press, 2001).

49. Henry Jolson QC, CAS Awards and Reasons, 31 July 2000, 29, 30, 44 in CAS Appeal Book, in DCpc.

50. Jolson, Reasons, 59, CAS Appeal Book, in DCpc.

51. Damian Grave to Bill Baker, 31 July 2000; and Damian Grave to Bill Walker, 3 August 2000, both in CAS Appeal Book, DCpc.

52. Damian Grave to Bill Baker, 5 August 2000, CAS Appeal Book, in DCpc.

53. Bill Baker to Damian Grave, 4 August 2000, CAS Appeal book, in DCpc.

54. Ian Fullagar to Damian Grave, 7 August 2000, CAS Appeal book, in DCpc.

55. Fullagar to Grave, 10 August, CAS Appeal book, DCpc.
56. Damian Grave to Bill Baker 4 August, 5 August, 10 August 2000, and Grave to Rigby Cook, 7 August, 8 August and 10 August 2000, CAS Appeal Book, in DCpc.
57. Jolson, Reasons, 39-46, CAS Appeal Book, in DCpc.
58. [Emery Holmik], 'Sydney World Cup/ Perth World Championships'; and Bill Baker, hand-written note, 16 April 2000, CAS Appeal, in DCpc.
59. 'Outline Statement of Diane Ainsworth,' CAS Appeal Book, in DCpc.
60. Henry Jolson, CAS Awards and Reasons 8 September 2000, 69, CAS Appeal Book, in DCpc.
61. TAESC, 'Female Nominations,' TA Appeal; TA press release, 28 April 2000, both in DCpc.
62. Bill Baker, 'Report to the TAESC,' 7 July 2000, loose bundle of notes, in DCpc.
63. Fullagar to Grave, 10 August 2000, CAS Appeal Book, in DCpc.
64. Bill Baker to Marc Dragan, Maureen Cummings, Nick Croft, 4 August 2000, loose bundle of notes, in DCpc.
65. Amanda Lulham, 'AUSTRALIA: Selection fever/sick pair ready to race,' *Sunday Telegraph* 16 April 2000, in Reuters business briefing, 1 August 2000; and Amanda Lulham, 'Courting Danger: Triathletes prepare for a different battle,' *The Daily Telegraph*, 17 April 2000, CAS Appeal Book, in DCpc.
66. AAP, 'Race marred by controversy,' *sportstoday.com.au*, 17 April 2000, p.2; Nick Croft, 'Energy Australia 2000 Sydney ITU World Cup Triathlon,' *Triathlon Sports* July/August 2000, 26-29, CAS Appeal Book, in DCpc.
67. AAP, 'Race marred by controversy,' CAS Appeal Book, in DCpc.
68. John Helleman to 'Whom it may concern', correspondence, 25 April 2000, CAS Appeal Book, in DCpc.
69. CAS Awards and Reasons 8 Sept, par 74, p37, folder with CAS Appeal Book, in DCpc.
70. CAS Awards and Reasons 8 Sept, par 75, p.37, folder with CAS Appeal Book, in DCpc.
71. Rachele Downie, 'Improving the performance of Sport's Ultimate Umpire: Reforming the Governance of the Court of Arbitration for Sport,' *Melbourne Journal of International Law* 12, no.2 (2011): np.
72. Antoine Duval, 'Getting to the games: the Olympic selection drama(s) at the court of arbitration for sport,' *The International Sports Law Journal* 16, no.1 (2016): np; Gabrielle Kaufmann-Kohler & Raghunandan S. Pathak, 'Foreword',

in Court of Arbitration for Sport (CAS), *CAS Awards — Sydney 2000: the decisions delivered by the ad hoc Division of the Court of Arbitration for Sport during the 2000 Olympic Games in Sydney* (CAS: Lausanne, 2000), 7.

73. Duval, 'Getting to the games'; Kaufmann-Kohler & Pathak, 'Foreword'.

74. Thorpe, 'Contract and athlete selection', pp.48-9.

75. Freehills, 'Further Submissions', 31 August 2000, CAS Appeal Book, in DCpc.

76. Alan Sullivan, 'The role of contract in sports law', *Australian and New Zealand Sports Law Journal* 5, no.1 (2010): 12, 23; Thorpe (2008), 61.

Lightning Source UK Ltd.
Milton Keynes UK
UKHW020633021121
393250UK00014B/777